STREET LEVEL JAPAN

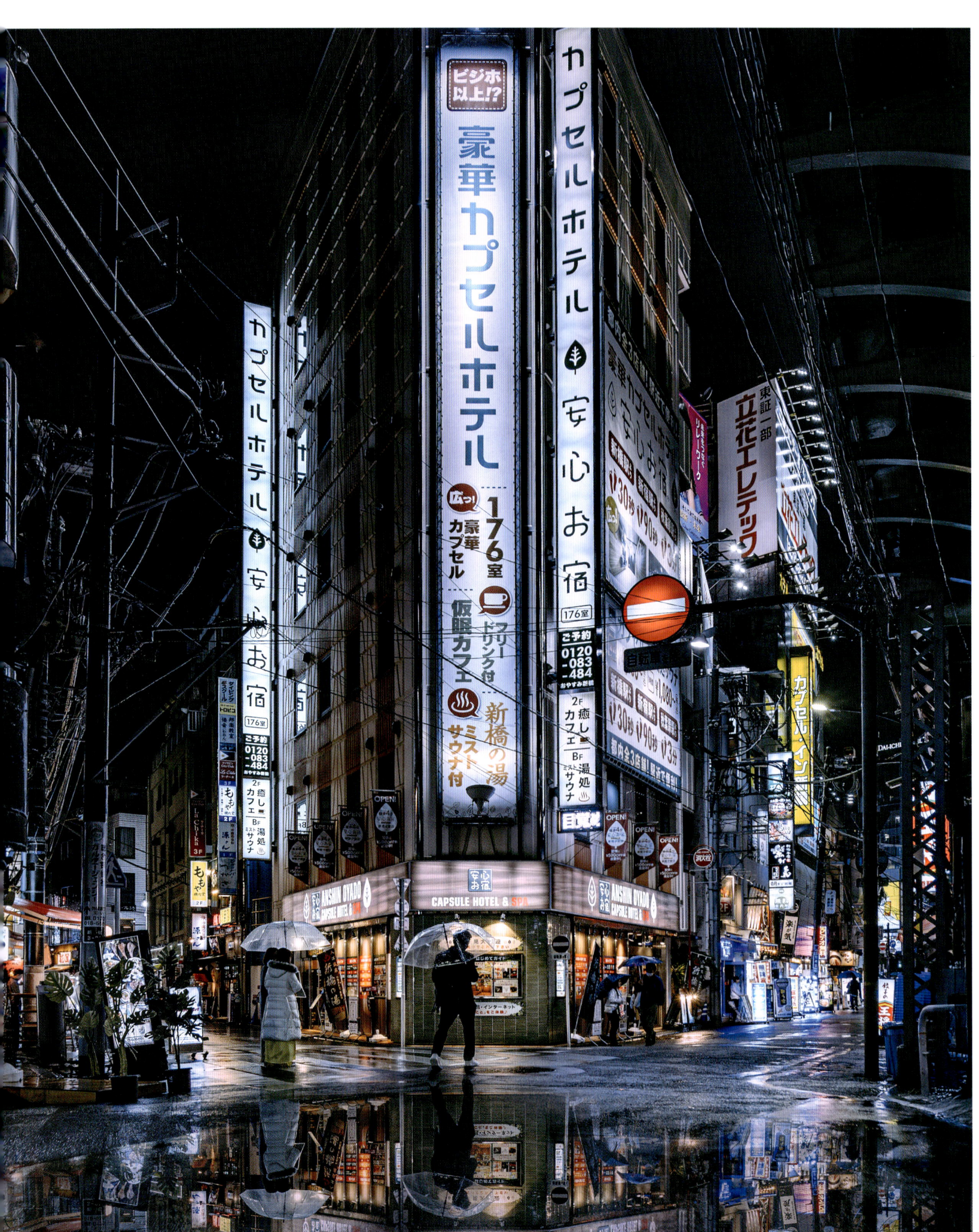

STREET LEVEL JAPAN

JAPAN

EXPERIENCE
THE BUSTLING
STREETS OF
JAPANESE CITIES

Hiroki Harada

EPIC INK

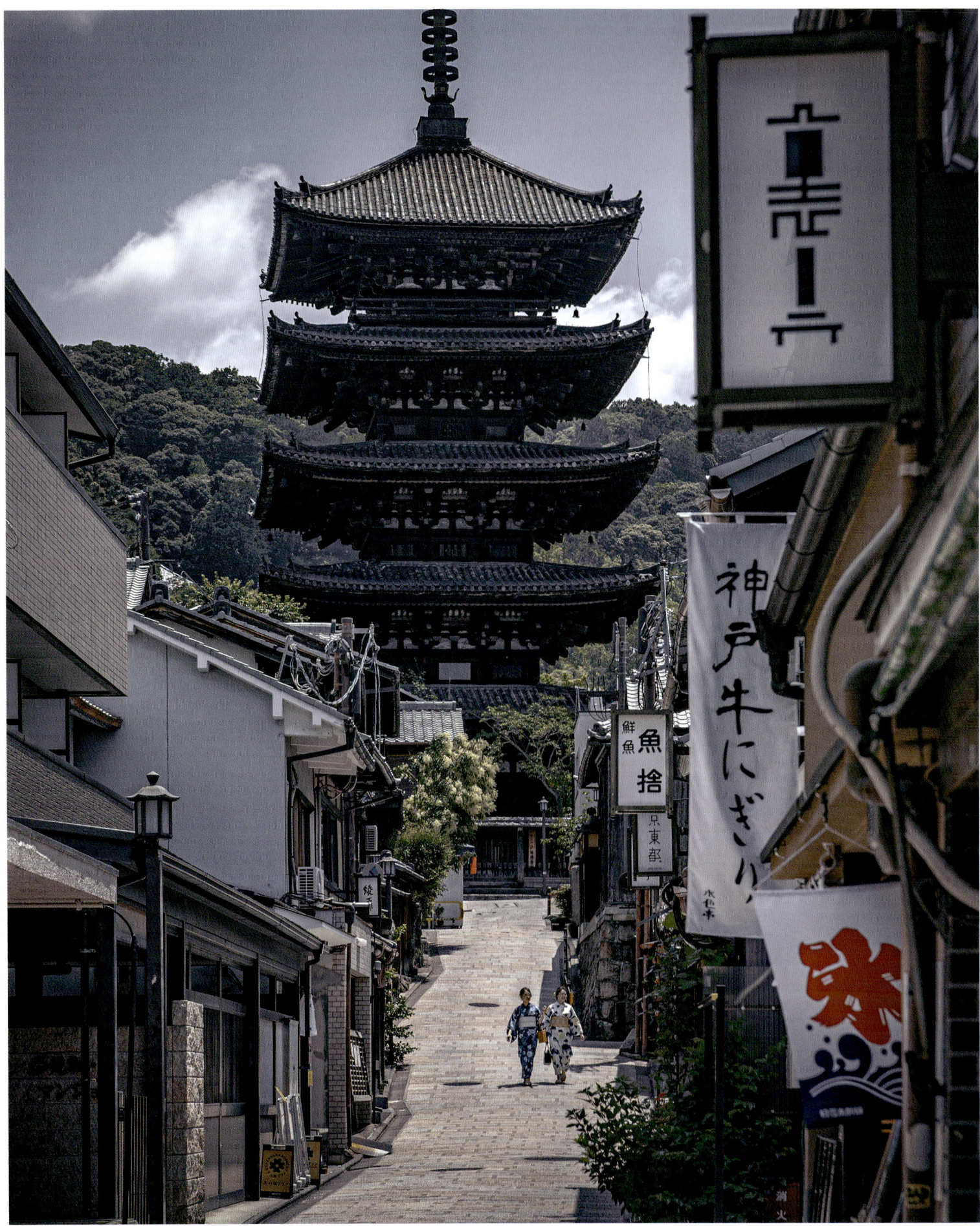

CONTENTS

previous spread Shinbashi Capsule Hotel. Shinbashi, Tokyo. Capsule hotels are unique Japanese lodging facilities. They offer small, box-shaped, private rooms with only a bed.

Hokanji Temple. Kyoto. If it is not crowded, you can take a photo like a postcard, featuring Yasaka Pagoda and women wearing kimonos. The red logo on the right indicates a shaved ice store.

Although not widely known, Japan is considered one of the oldest countries in the world, founded in 660 BCE, 2,700 years after its foundation. The entire country is surrounded by the sea and has developed its own unique culture.

Its capital, Tokyo, is ranked third in the world, according to the Global Power City Index (GPCI), in terms of overall city strength, following London (No. 1) and New York (No. 2), because of its special coexistence of modern and classical cultures, along with its livability and accessibility. It is also one of the top travel destinations in the world.

In this book, I'm happy to share over two hundred of my favorite street photos I've taken of Tokyo—as a Tokyo native—and other Japanese cities, including Kyoto, Yokohama, Osaka, and more. I grew up in a bustling shopping district in Tokyo, where numerous small stores stand side by side and many people live. These childhood memories have influenced my work in which I focus on the "beauty" created by the light of the place, such as the time of day, the weather, and the neon lights of the city.

Now, let's explore the Tokyo (and Japan) you won't find in travel guides.

Sanbangai Street at Night. Nakano, Tokyo. At night, Third Avenue looks very beautiful with its distinctive triangular streetlights. It is one of my favorite places.

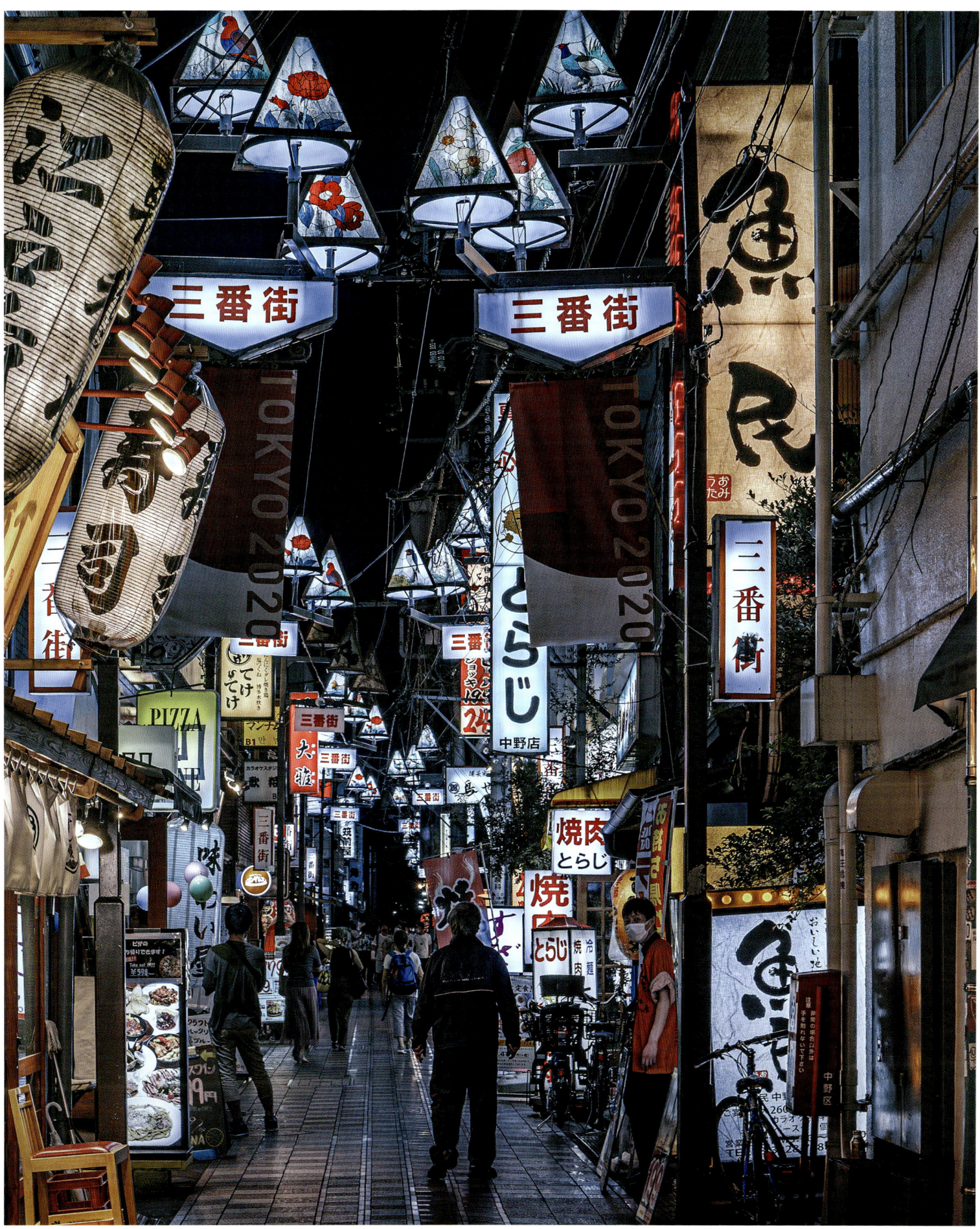

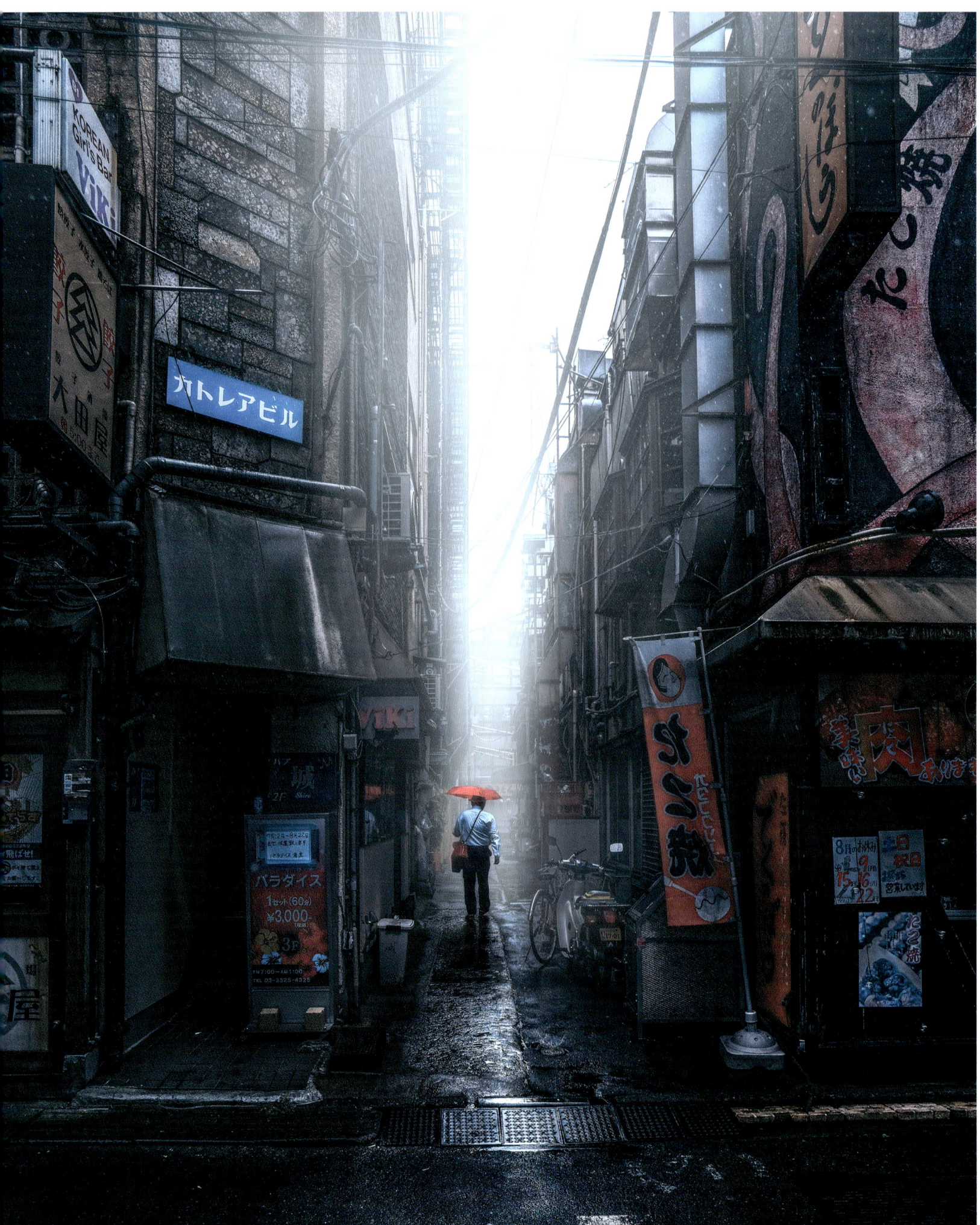

路地

The black market (*yami-ichi*) in Japan does not mean the sale of illegal drugs or dangerous goods. After Japan's defeat in World War II, people were living on government rations, so there was a shortage of goods in the city center. The black market was a natural outgrowth of that situation.

Even today in Japan, if you go down a side street in the heart of the city, you will find *yokocho*, a narrow alleyway with small stores clustered together that originated from the black market. The nostalgic atmosphere of these streets lined with lanterns reminds me of my own childhood memories of growing up in shopping arcades, which I feel an affection for.

Narrow Alley in Drizzle. Kanda, Tokyo. The area around Kanda Station is filled with people at night but has a completely different feel during the day.

Nostalgic Streets. Sangenjaya, Tokyo. Sangenjaya began as a black market after World War II, becoming very prosperous with many stores, restaurants, and movie theaters. It is a nostalgic area where time seems to have stopped, even though it is located next to Shibuya.

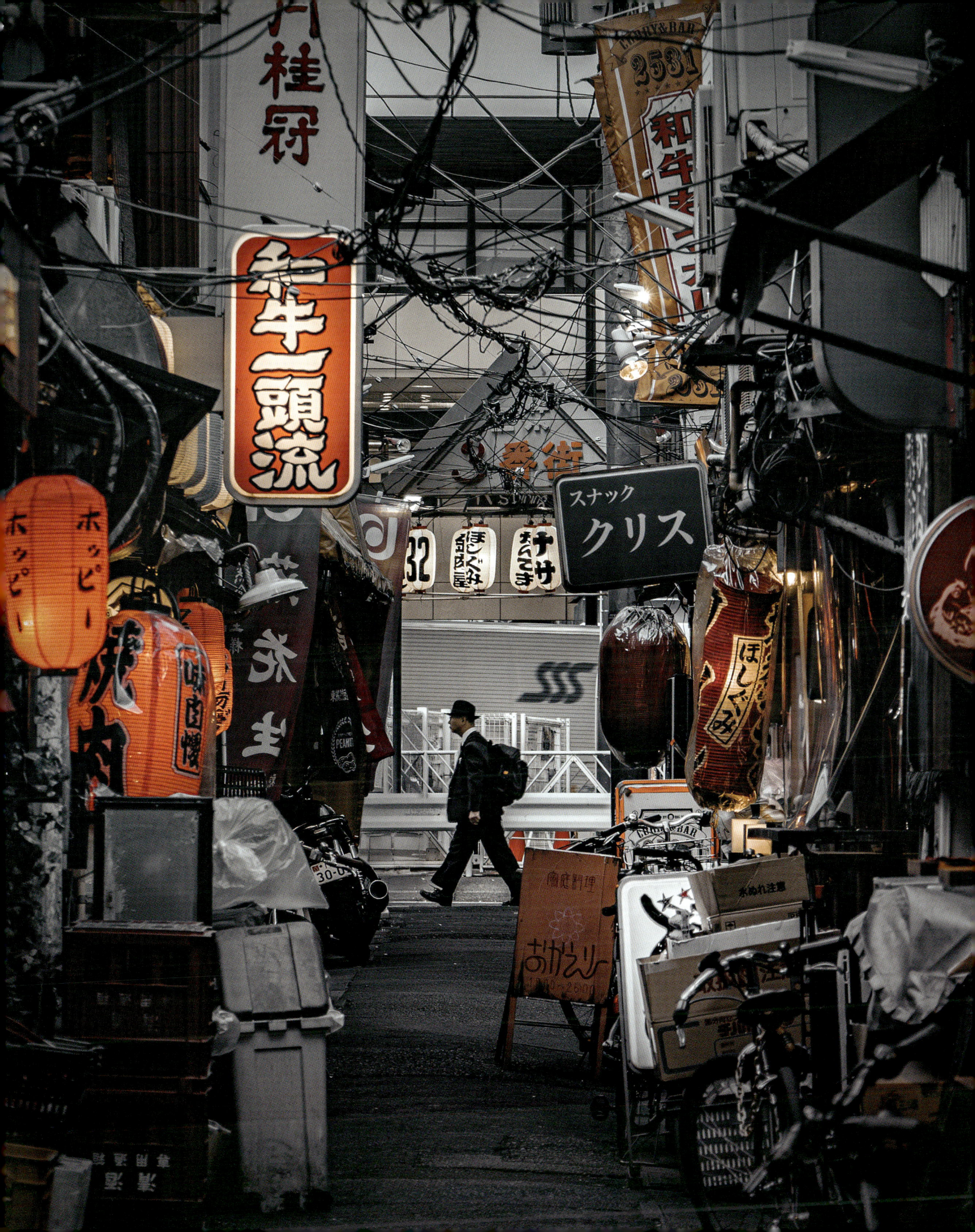

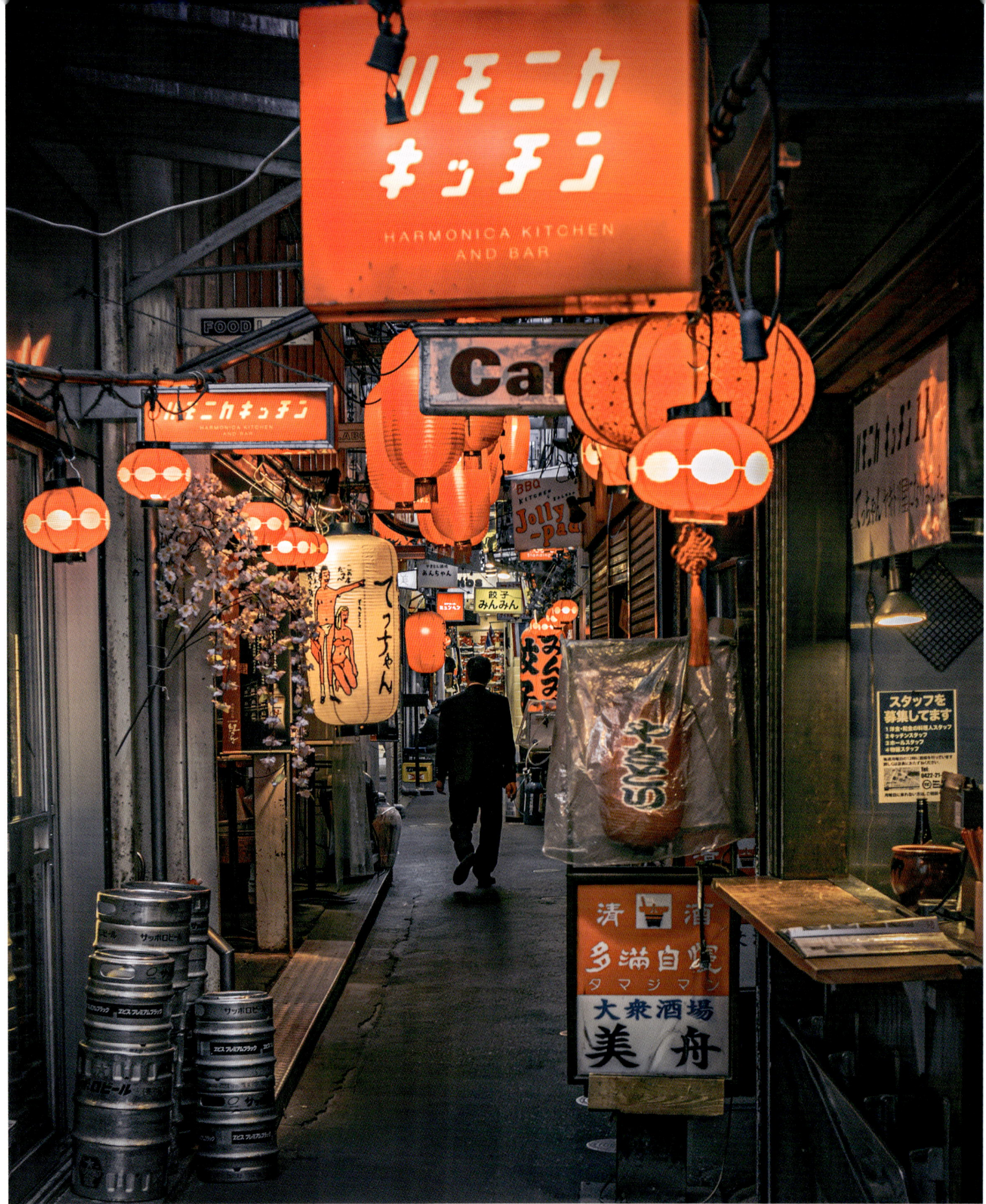

Harmonica Alley. Kichijoji, Tokyo After the war, this area was established as a black market in front of the devastated Kichijoji Station. Today, it is a charming place where small, cozy stores chaotically stand side by side in narrow alleys.

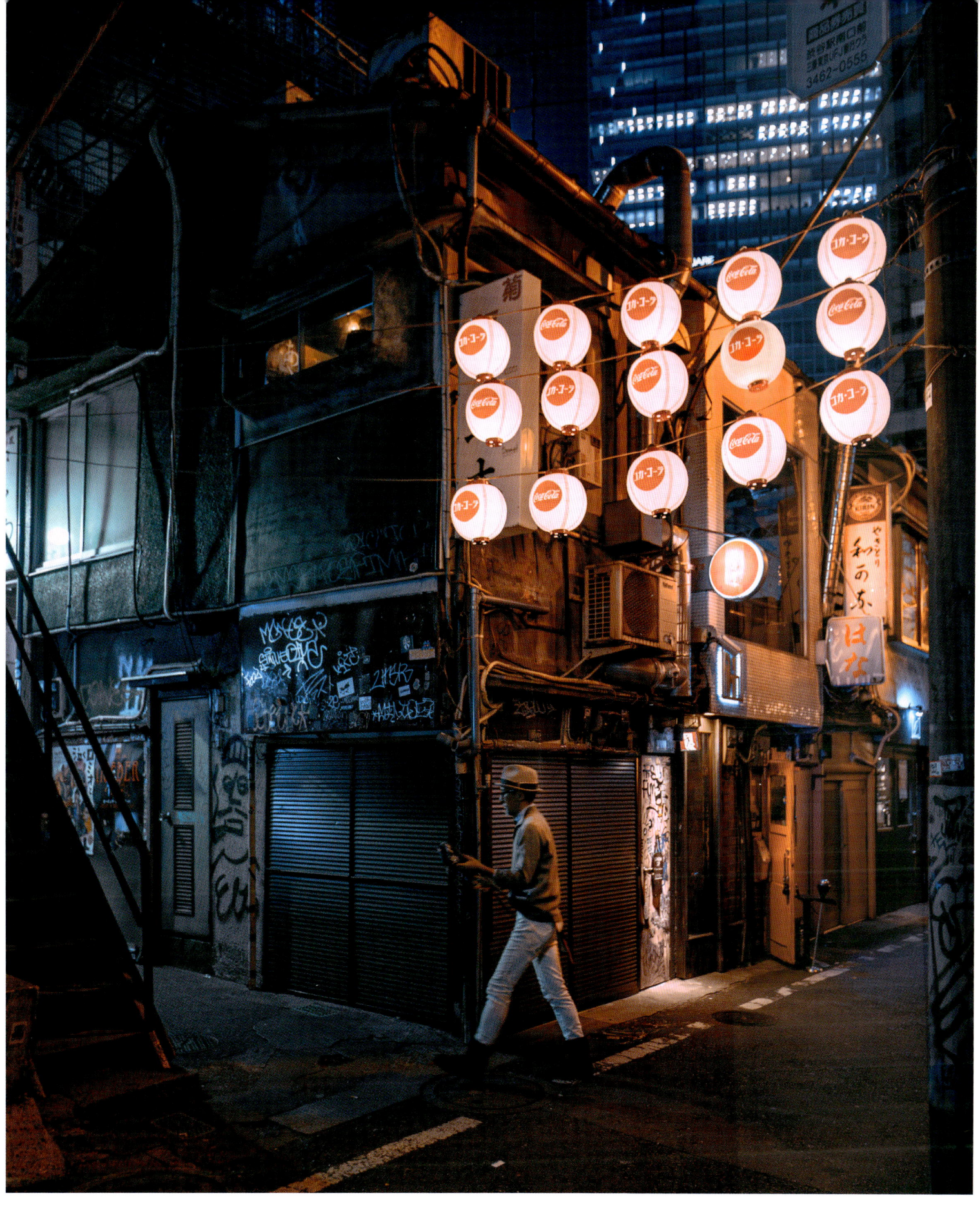

A Corner of Nonbei Yokocho. Shibuya,
Tokyo. Shibuya is an area for young people,
and Nonbei Yokocho is located in its
center. In this Showa-era side street, you
will find many unique izakaya that look
like they haven't changed since then.

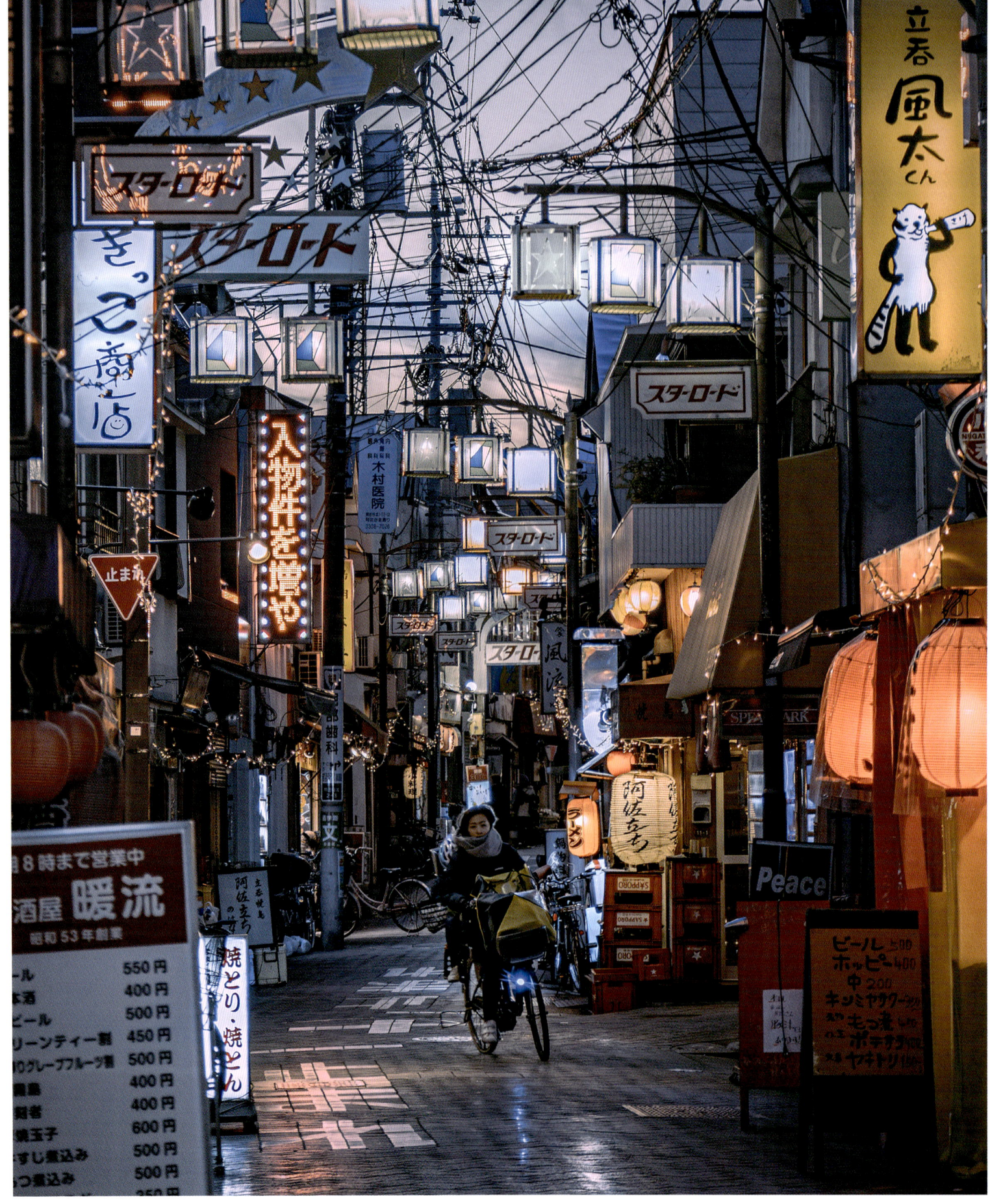

Evening Star Road. Asagaya, Tokyo. When this shopping street is lit up, it transforms into a very beautiful street. Each little store here has its own unique view of the world and welcomes visitors.

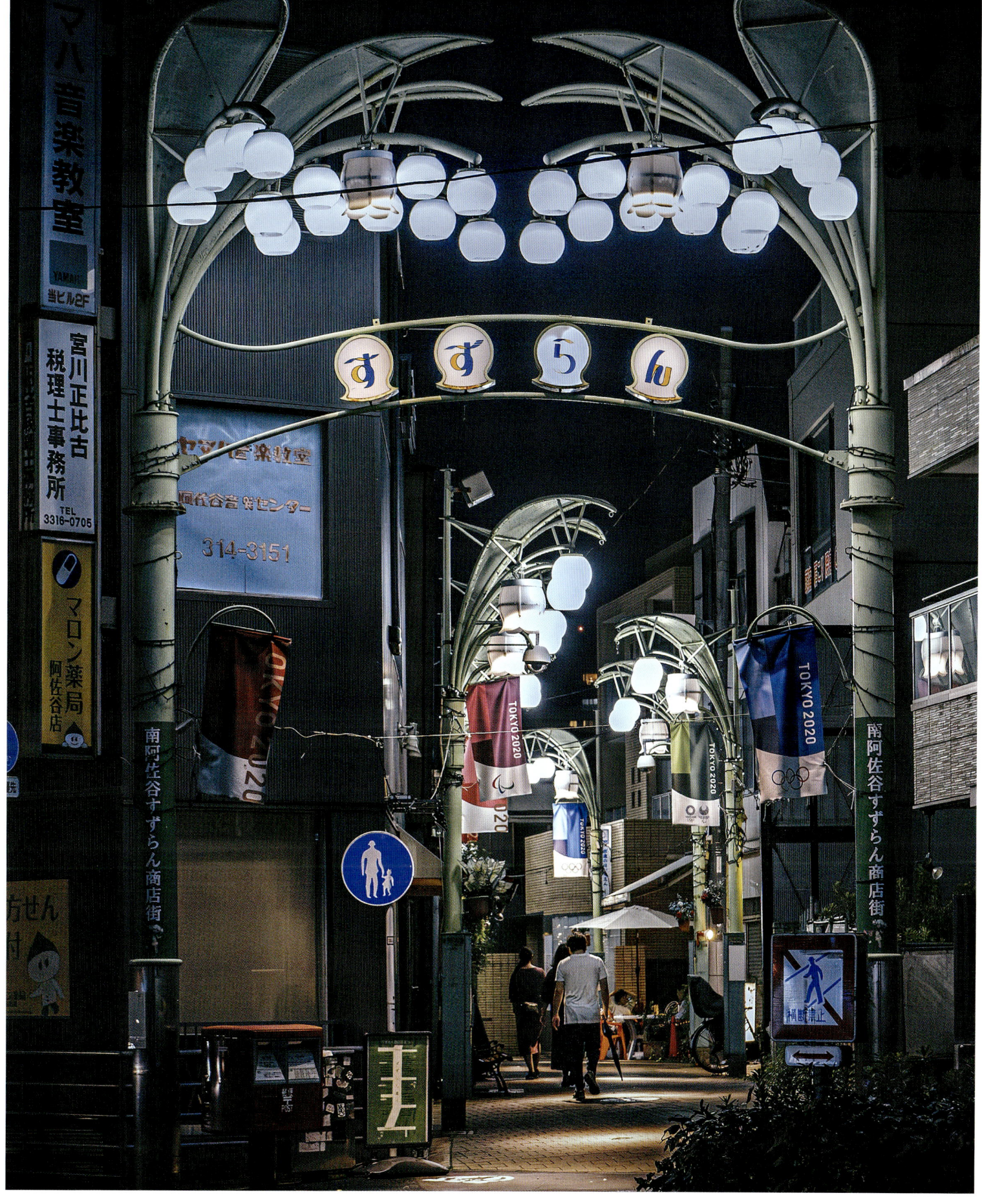

Suzuran Shopping Street. Asagaya, Tokyo.
The name of this shopping street is Suzuran, which means "lily of the valley." The beautiful streetlights are also in the shape of lilies of the valley.

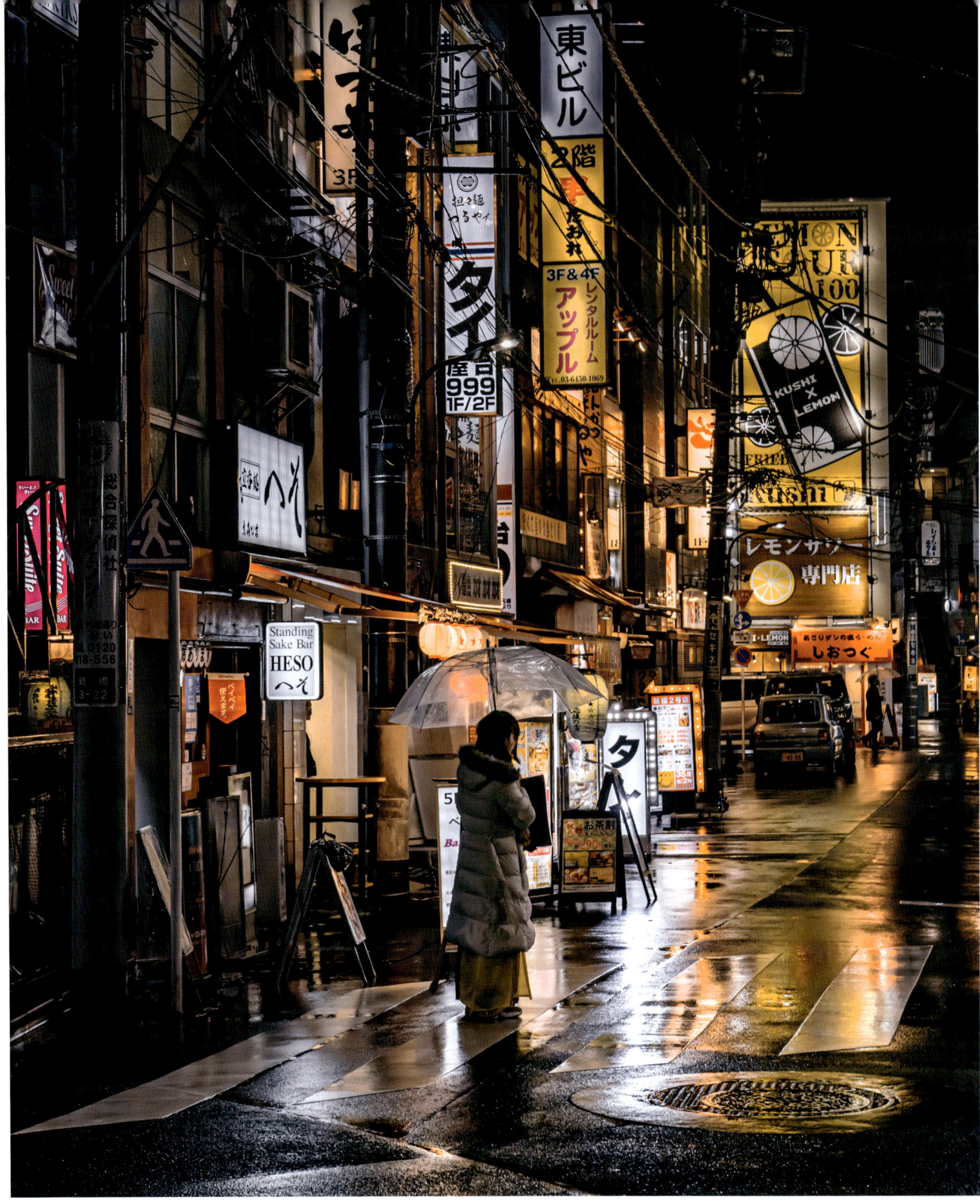

Reflections 1. Shinbashi, Tokyo. This street by the railroad tracks has beautiful reflections on its wet surface. The name of the store where the woman is standing is called Navel, which is a standing bar. Behind it is a Thai-style food stall.

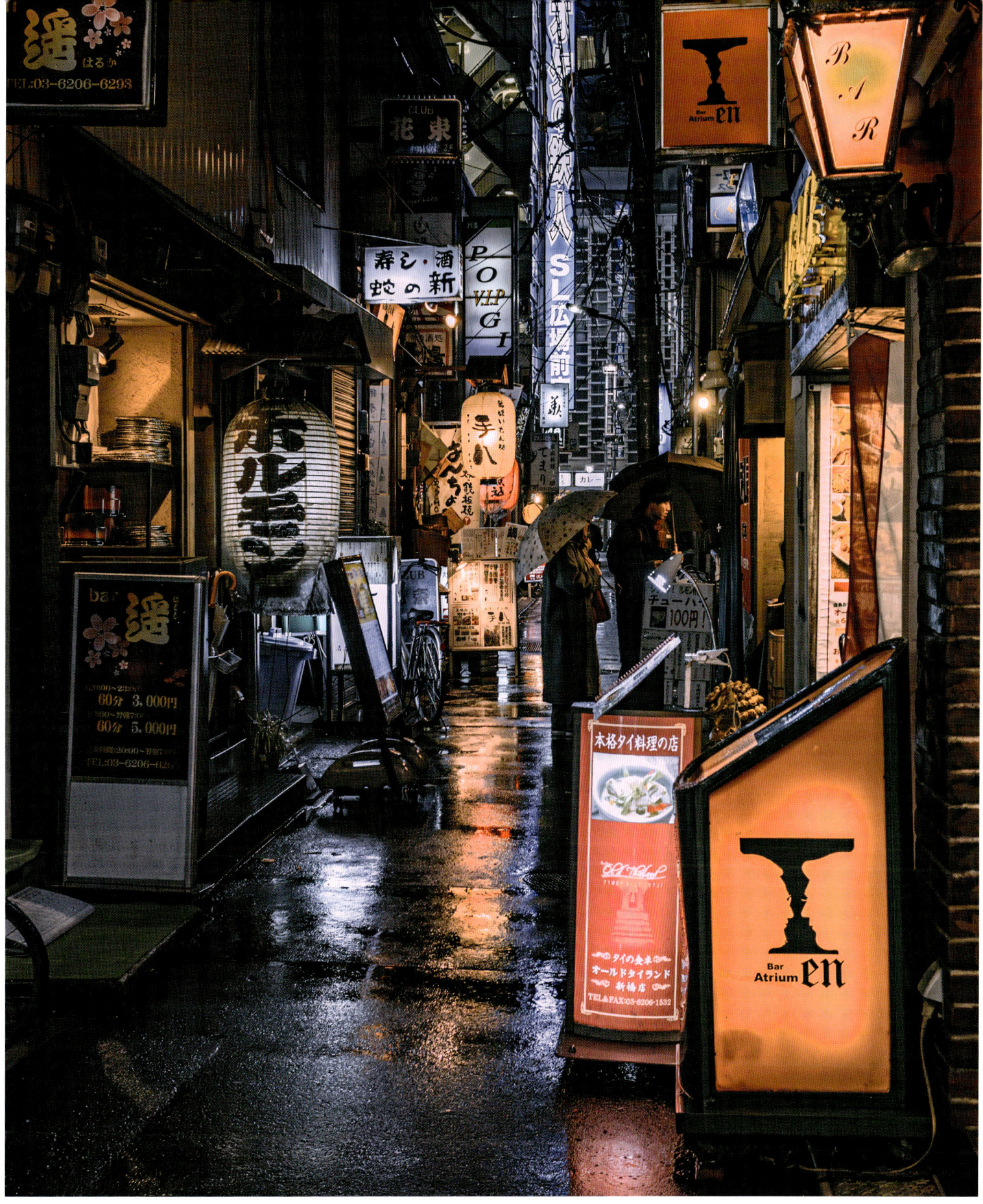

Reflections 2. Shinbashi, Tokyo. Here is another narrow alley with beautiful reflections on the wet road. There are many of these alleys in Shinbashi.

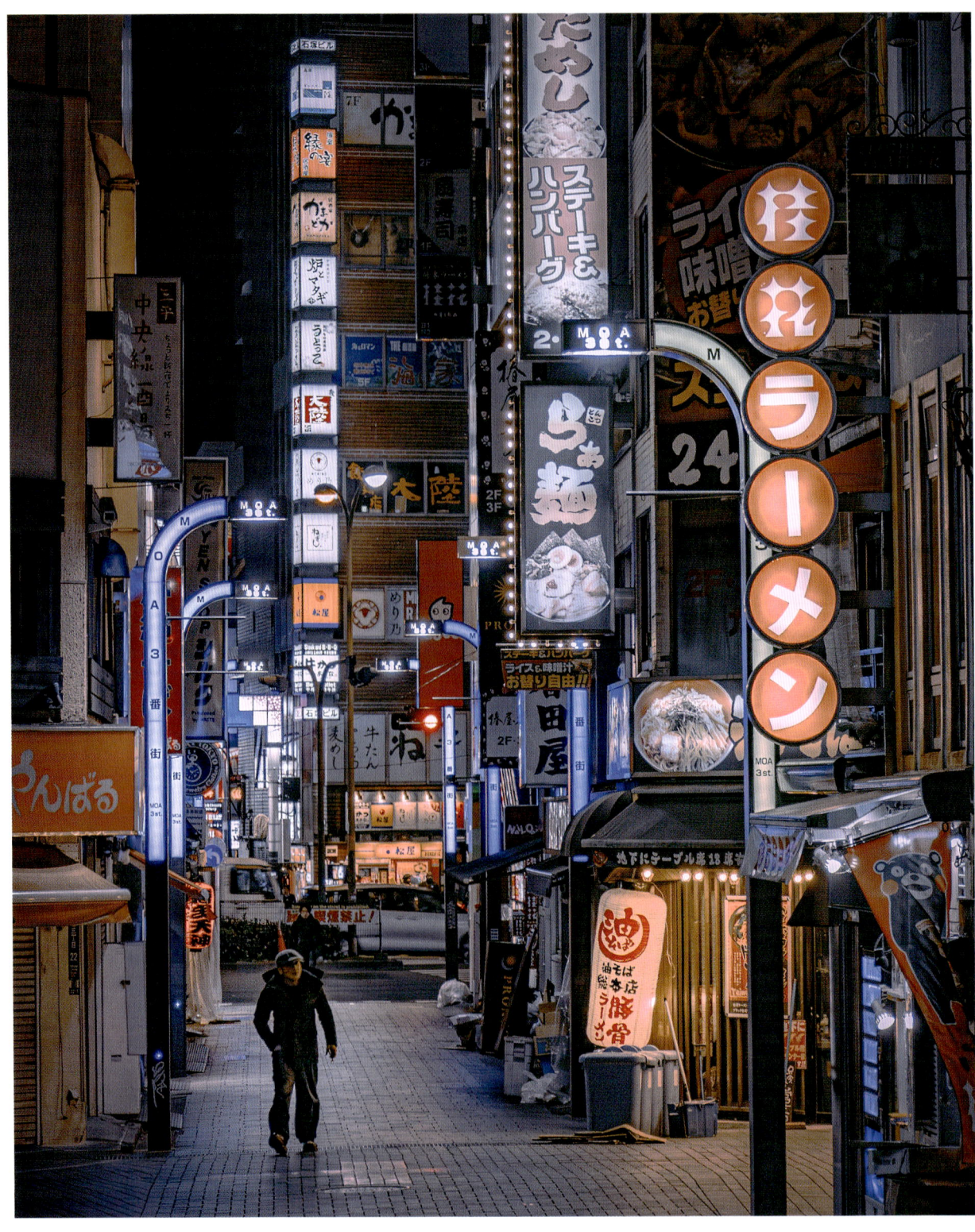

MOA Sanbangai. Shinjuku, Tokyo. MOA Third Avenue is an iconic shopping street in Shinjuku, located at the east exit of the train station.

Shrimp Street. Shinjuku, Tokyo. Ebi-dori, known as Shrimp Street, runs from Kabukicho Ichibangai Arch to Seibu Shinjuku Station.

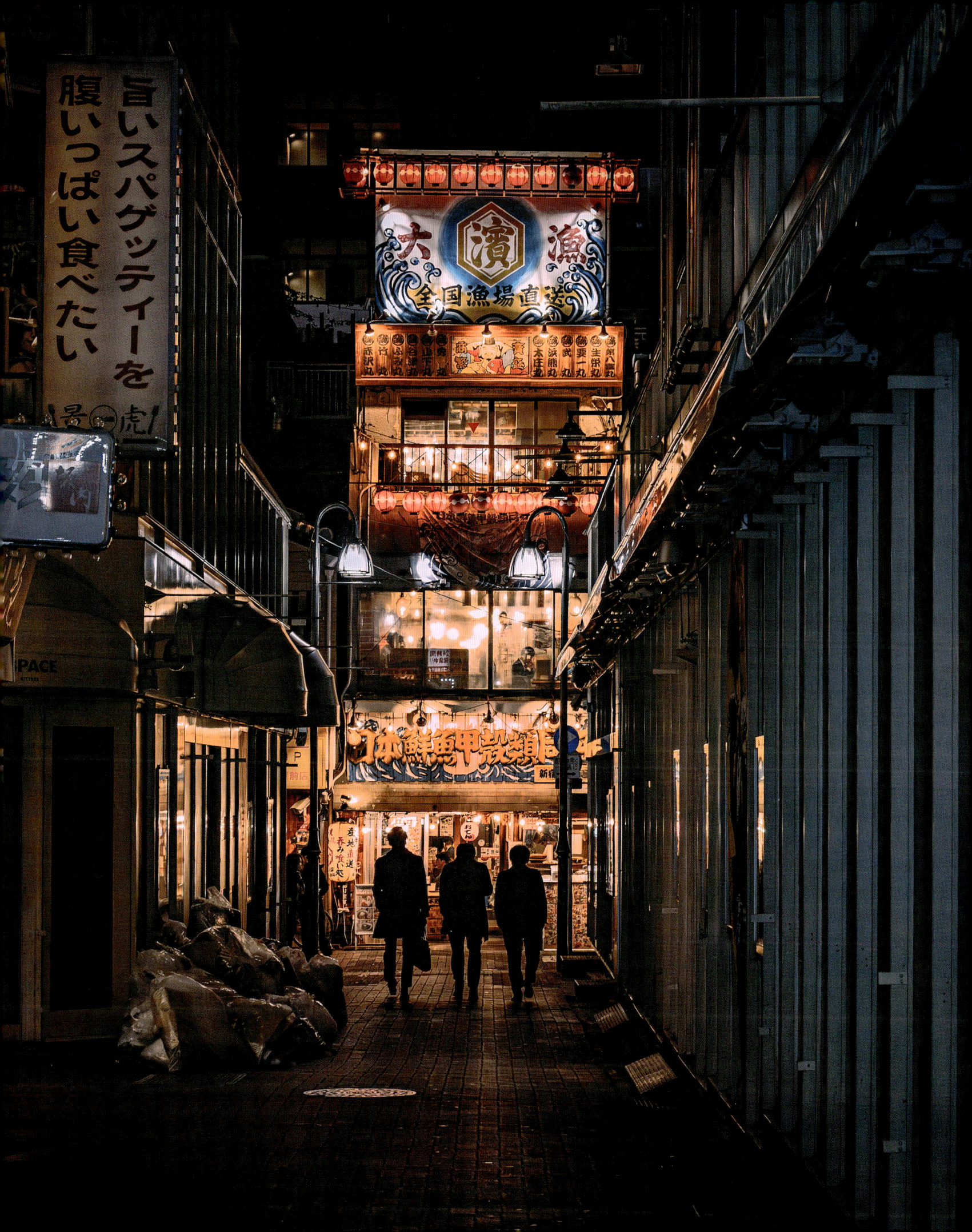

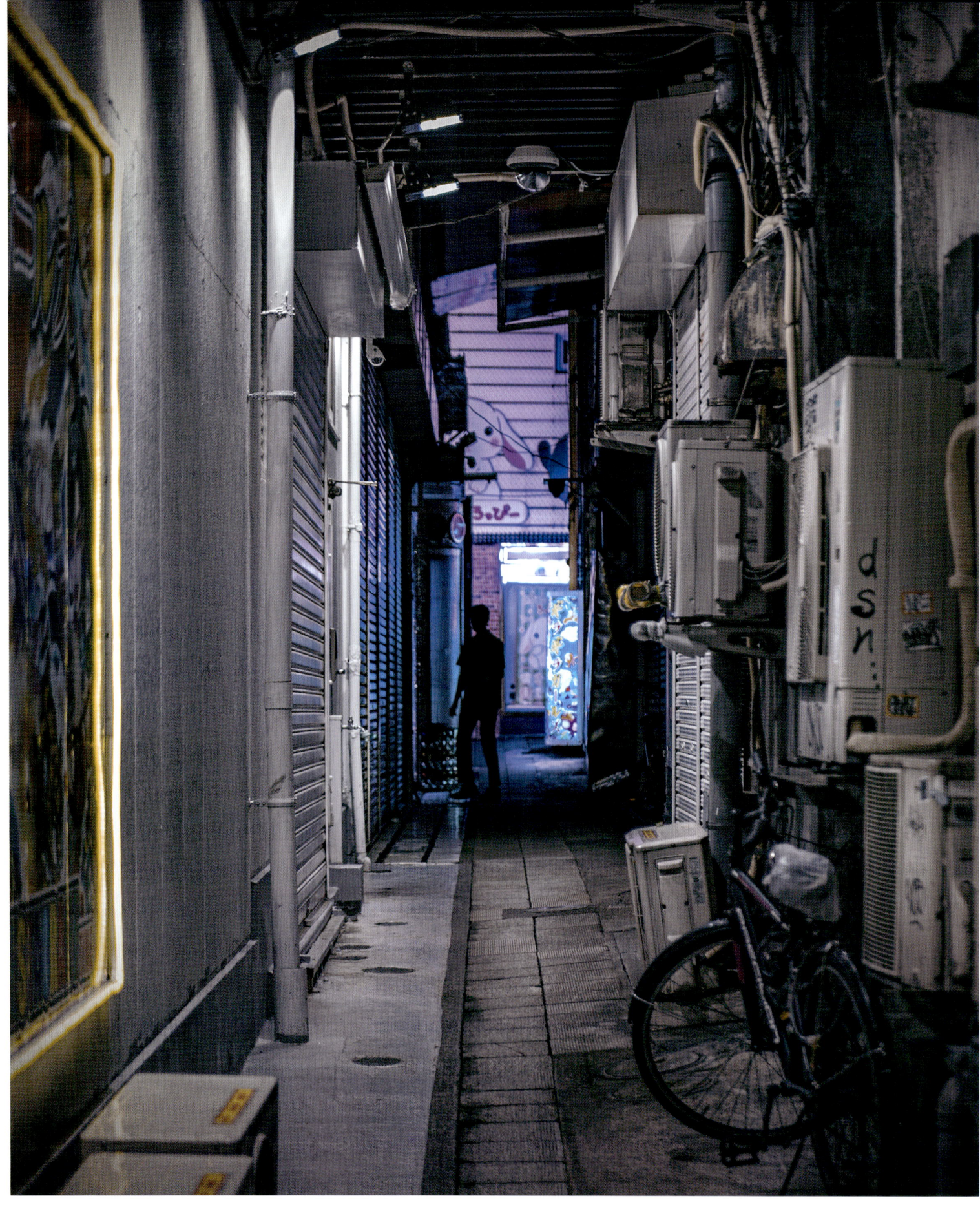

White Alley. Shinjuku, Tokyo. This unique, narrow alley has a nice contrast of blue light and shadows, with a person in silhouette.

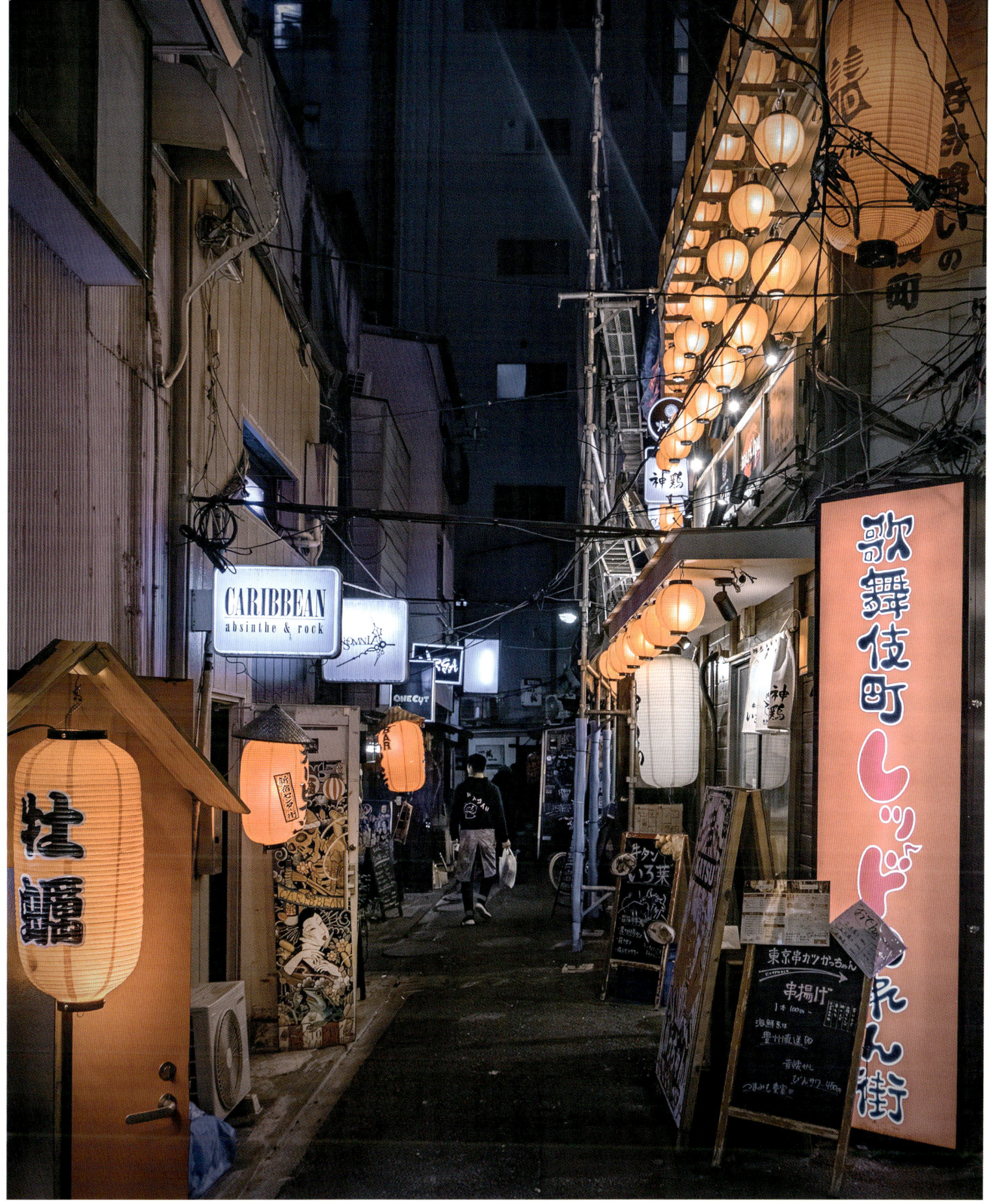

Memory Loophole. Shinjuku, Tokyo. The Showa era–style building on the right is Kabukicho Red Norengai, where seven restaurants coexist.

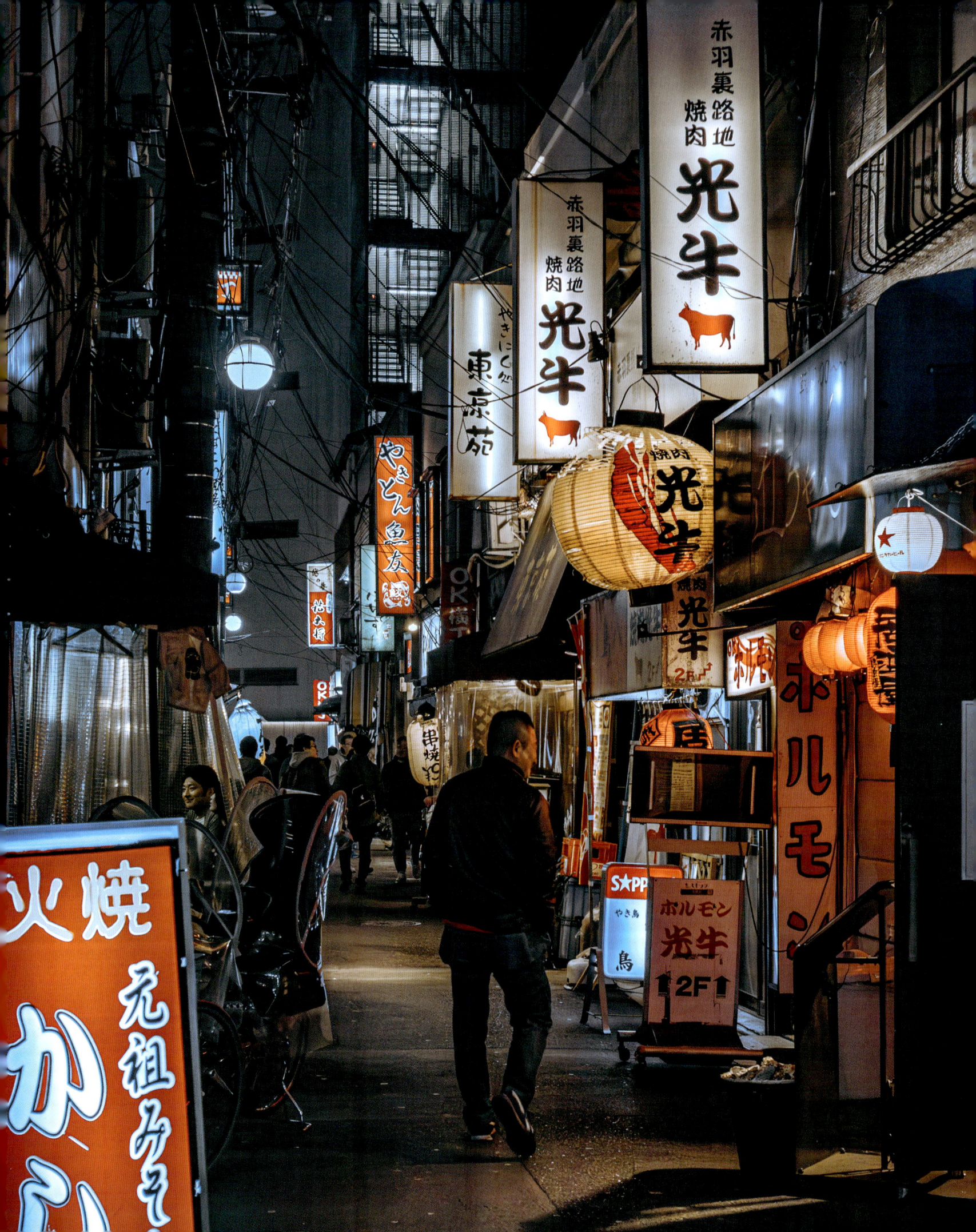

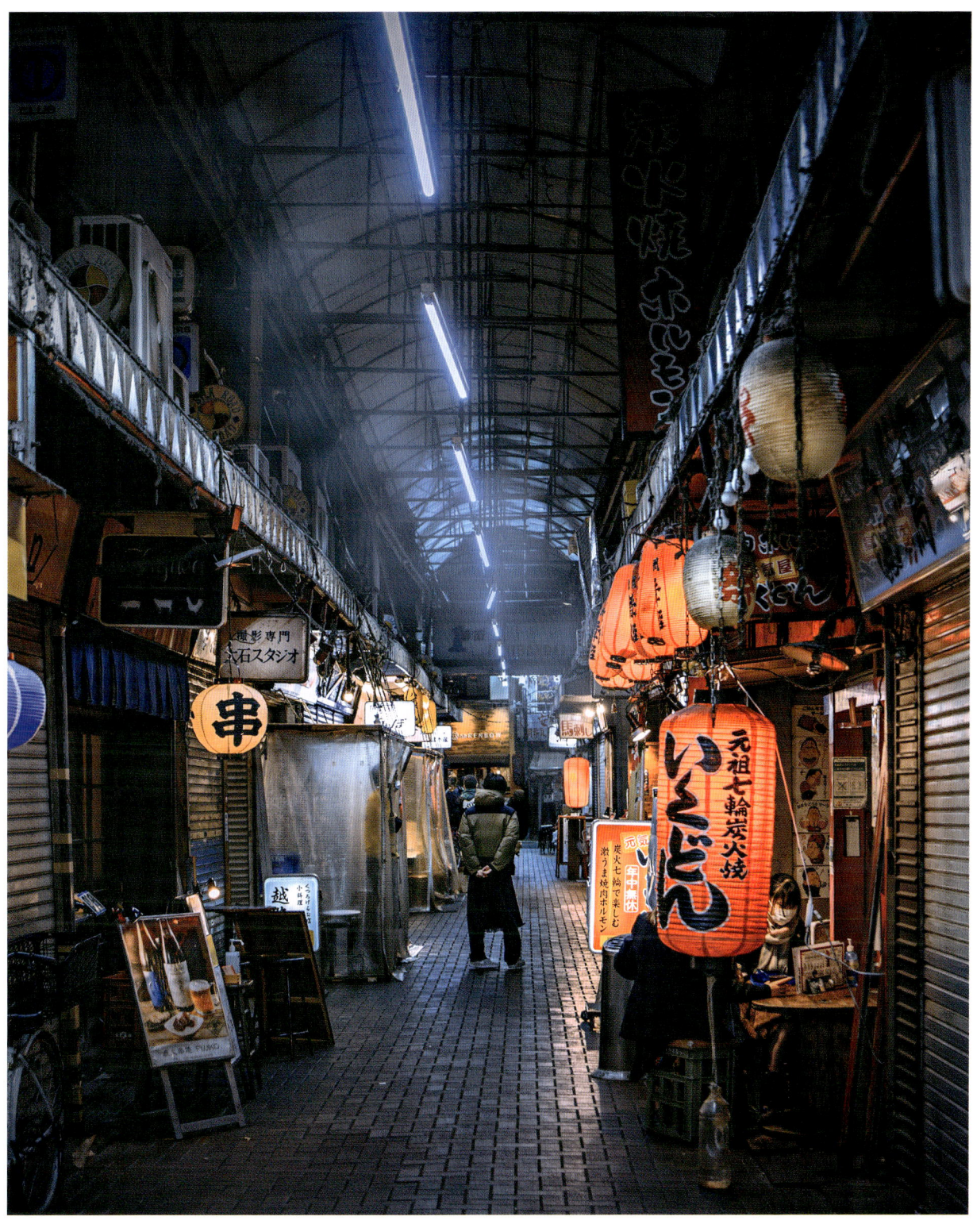

Happy Hour. Akabane, Tokyo. This popular drinking alley, called OK Yokocho (because "any order is OK"), is a fun place where everyone has a smile on their face.

Smoke-Filled Arcade. Akabane, Tokyo. The izakaya section in Akabane is quite extensive and was once located in the center of the area. It's made up of small arcades like this one with smoke in the air.

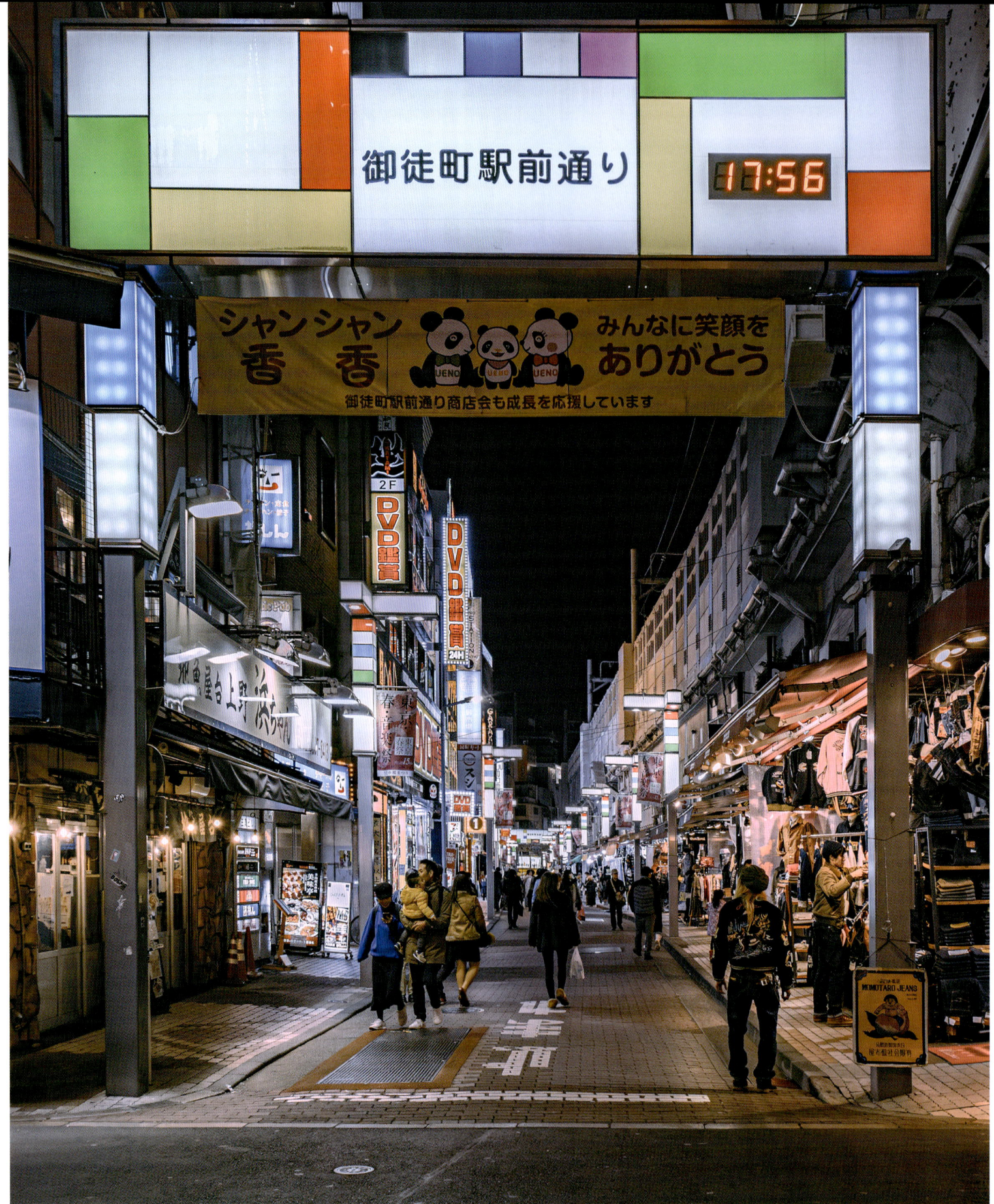

Ekimae Street. Okachimachi, Tokyo. This shopping street runs alongside the railroad tracks, so people are always coming and going, making it a lively area.

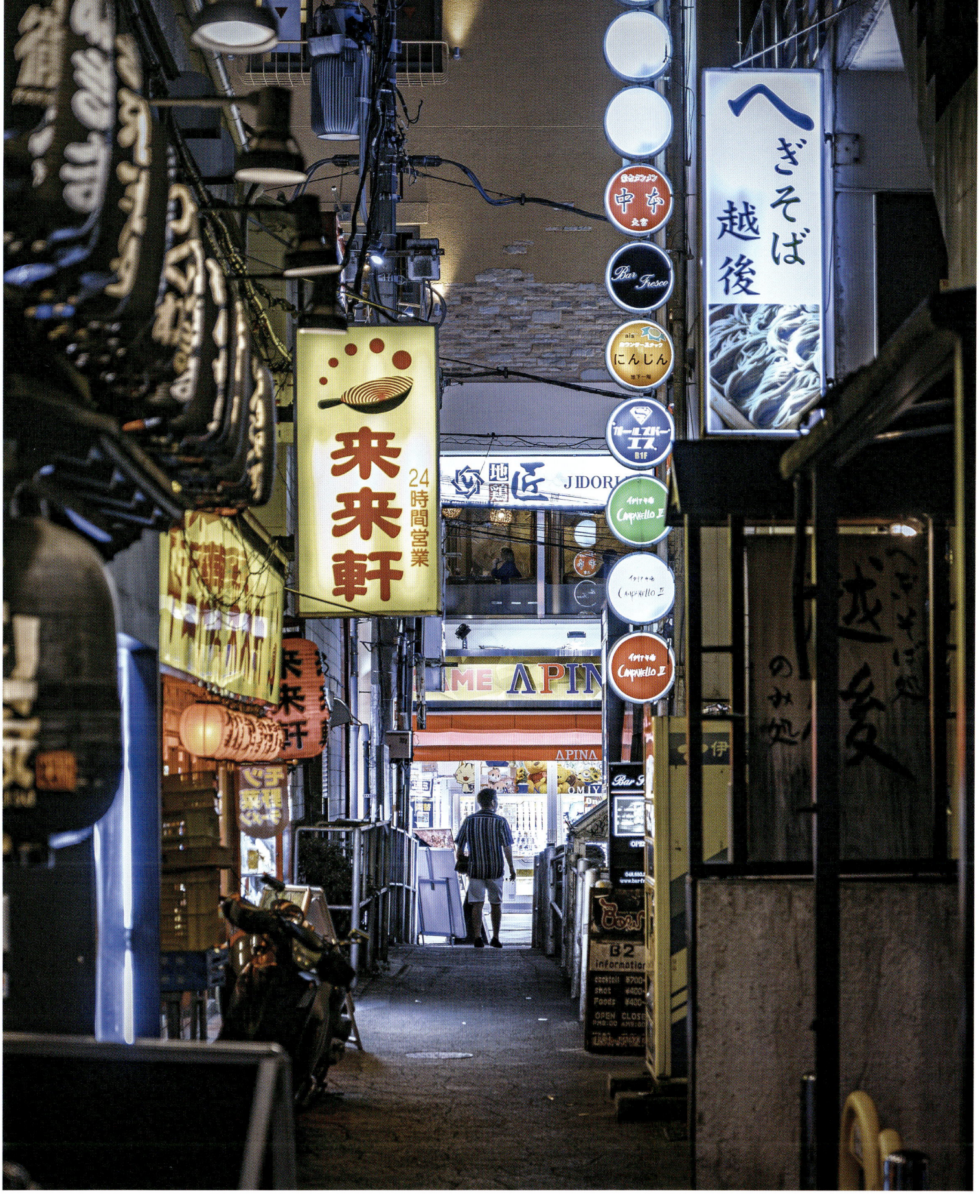

Alley in Nakamachi. Omiya, Saitama. A little south of the east exit of Omiya Station is this nice alleyway that intersects with the station. It is a place that has retained a tasteful, old-fashioned ambiance.

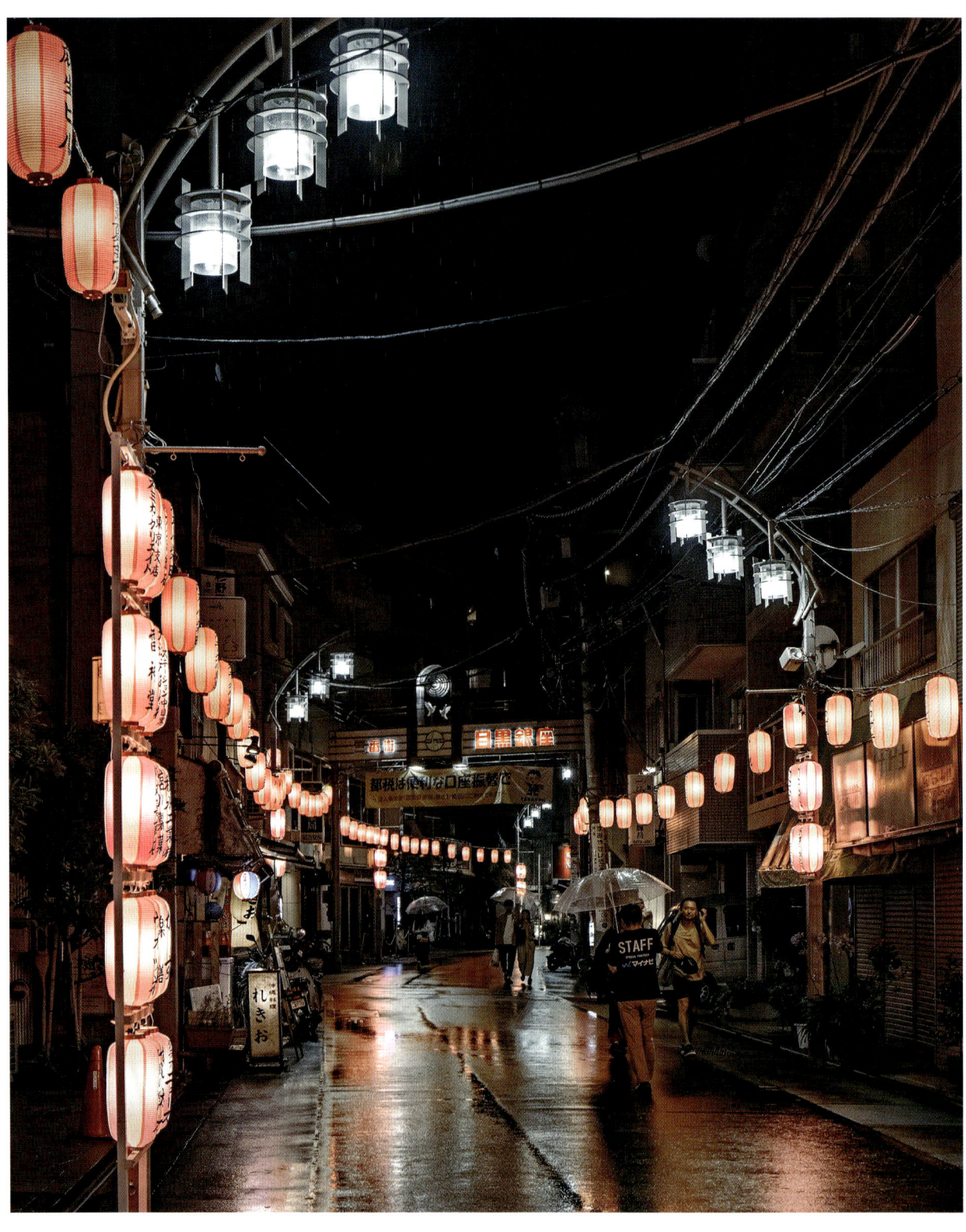

Meguro Ginza Shopping Street.
Nakameguro, Tokyo. The Nakameguro
Summer Festival features performances of
two types of traditional dance: Awa Odori
and Yosakoi. During the daytime, the festival
parades through these lantern decorations.

Nakameguro Summer Festival.
Nakameguro, Tokyo. These lanterns are
part of the Nakameguro Summer Festival,
which has a history of more than half
a century and has become a summer
tradition in Meguro Ward.

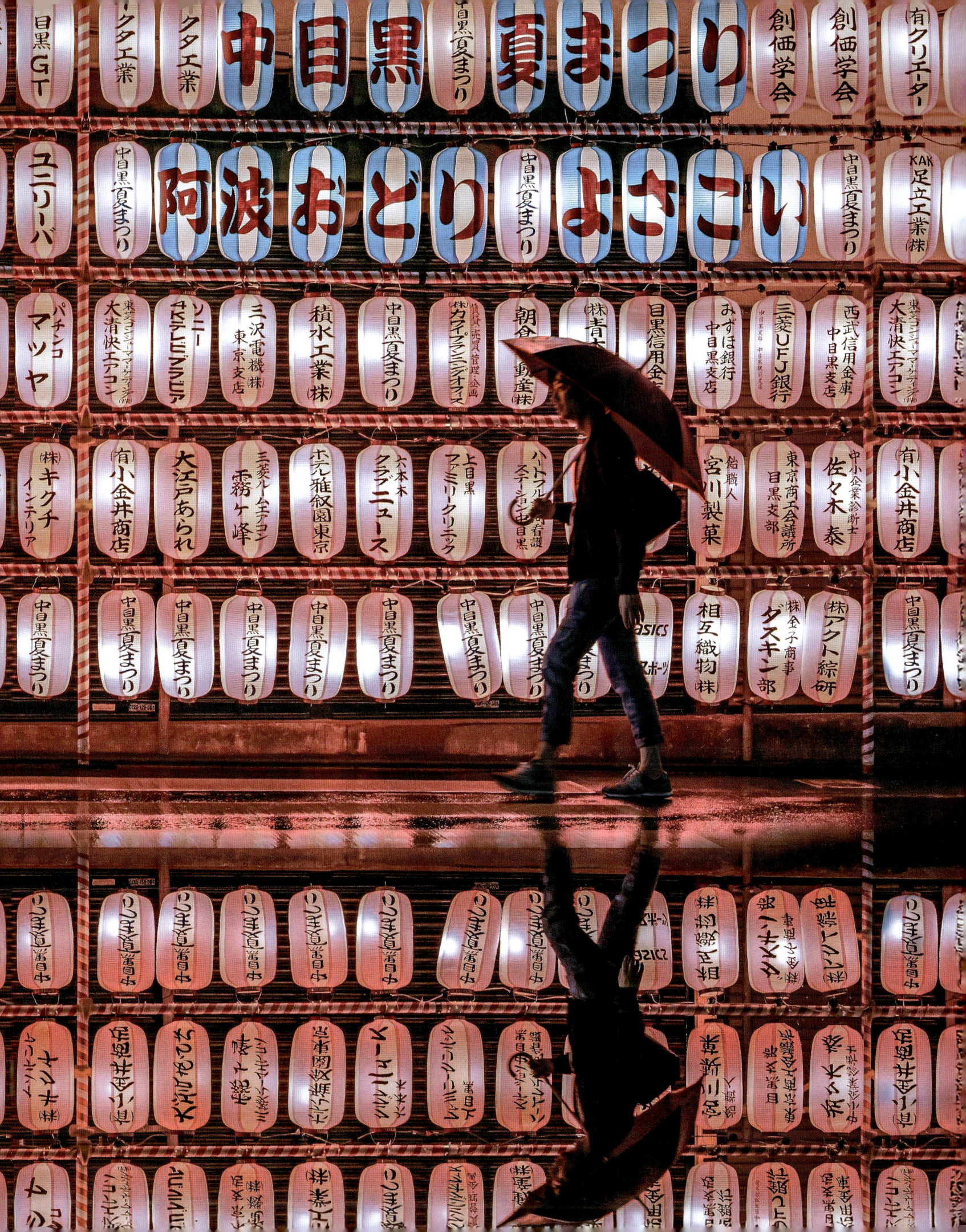

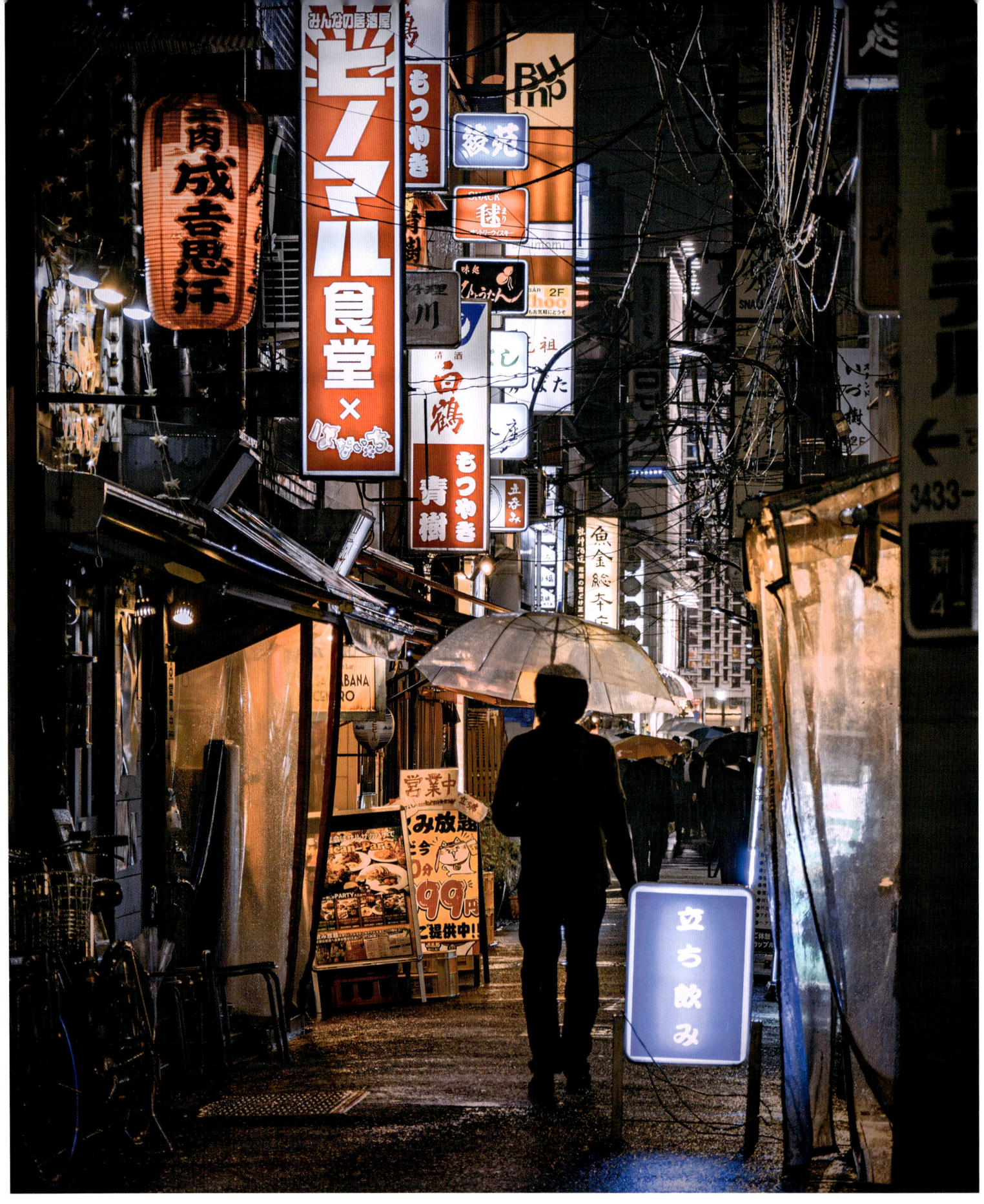

Hinomaru Restaurant at Night. Shinbashi, Tokyo. Clear vinyl umbrellas and tarps diffuse the neon light.

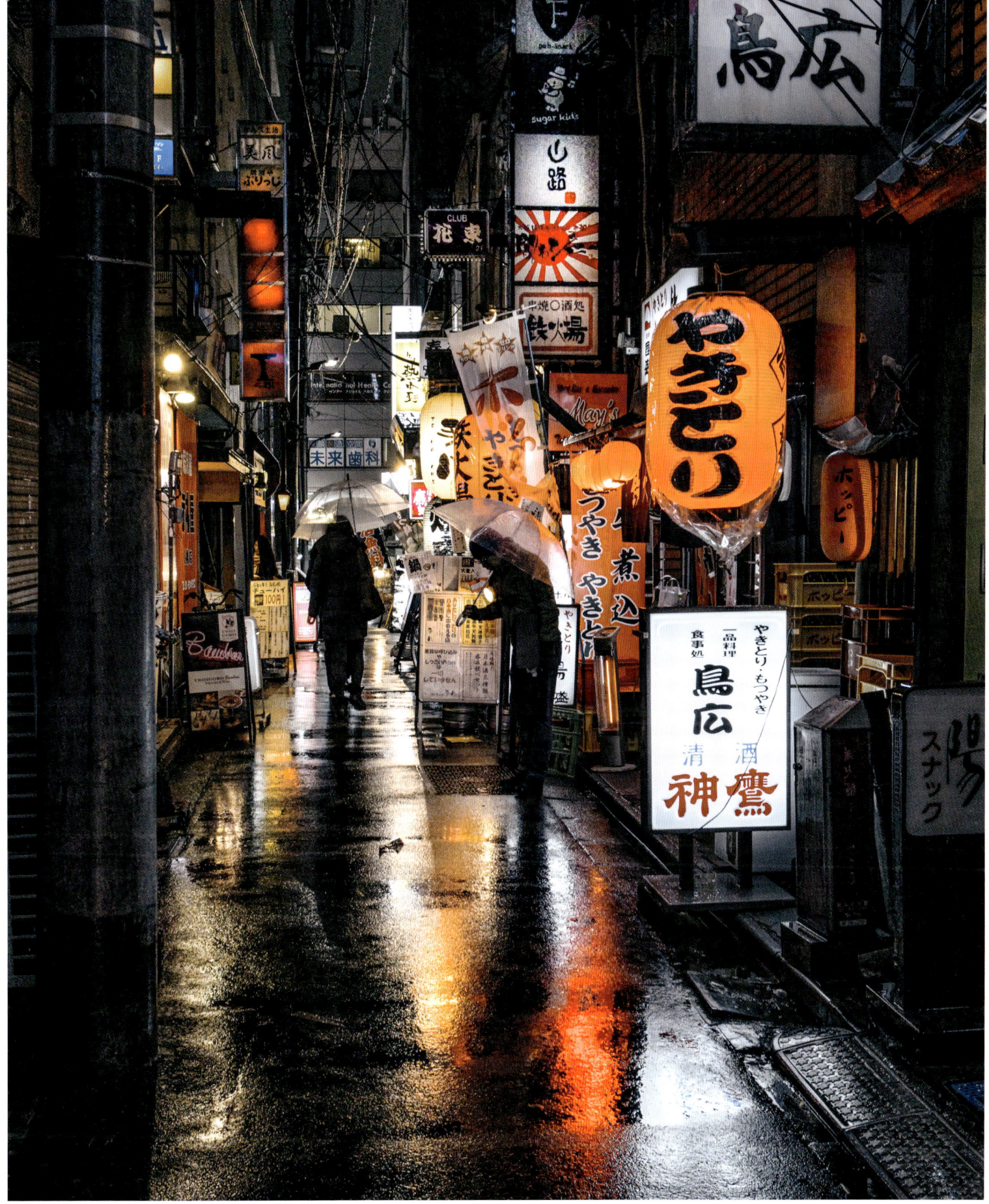

A Rainy Night in Shinbashi. Shinbashi, Tokyo. This is my favorite place among the many izakaya streets in Shinbashi. On rainy days, there is always a shopkeeper standing here with an umbrella.

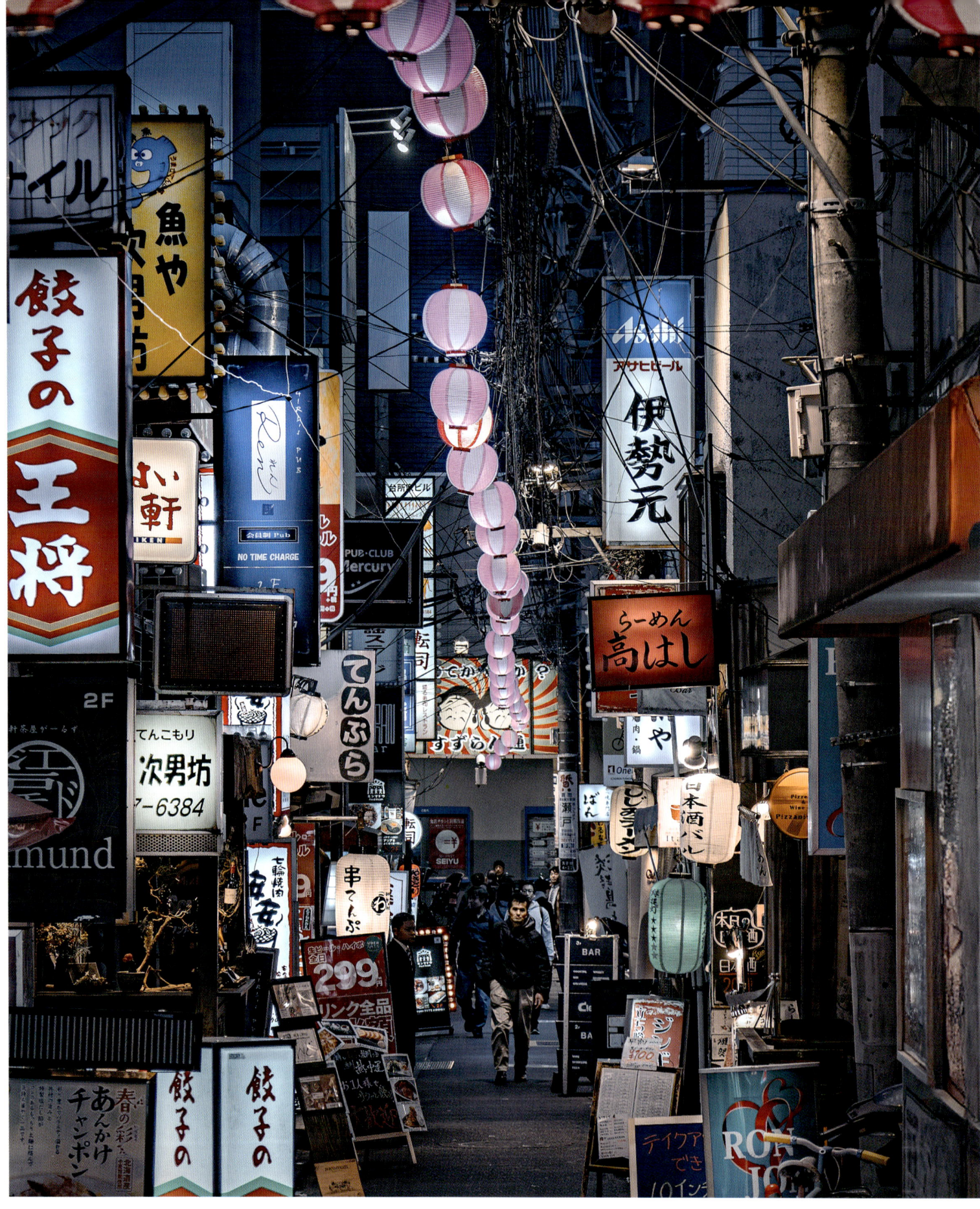

Suzuran Street. Sangenjaya, Tokyo. This small side street stretches between Sangenjaya Station on the Tokyu Den-en-toshi Line and Setagaya Line.

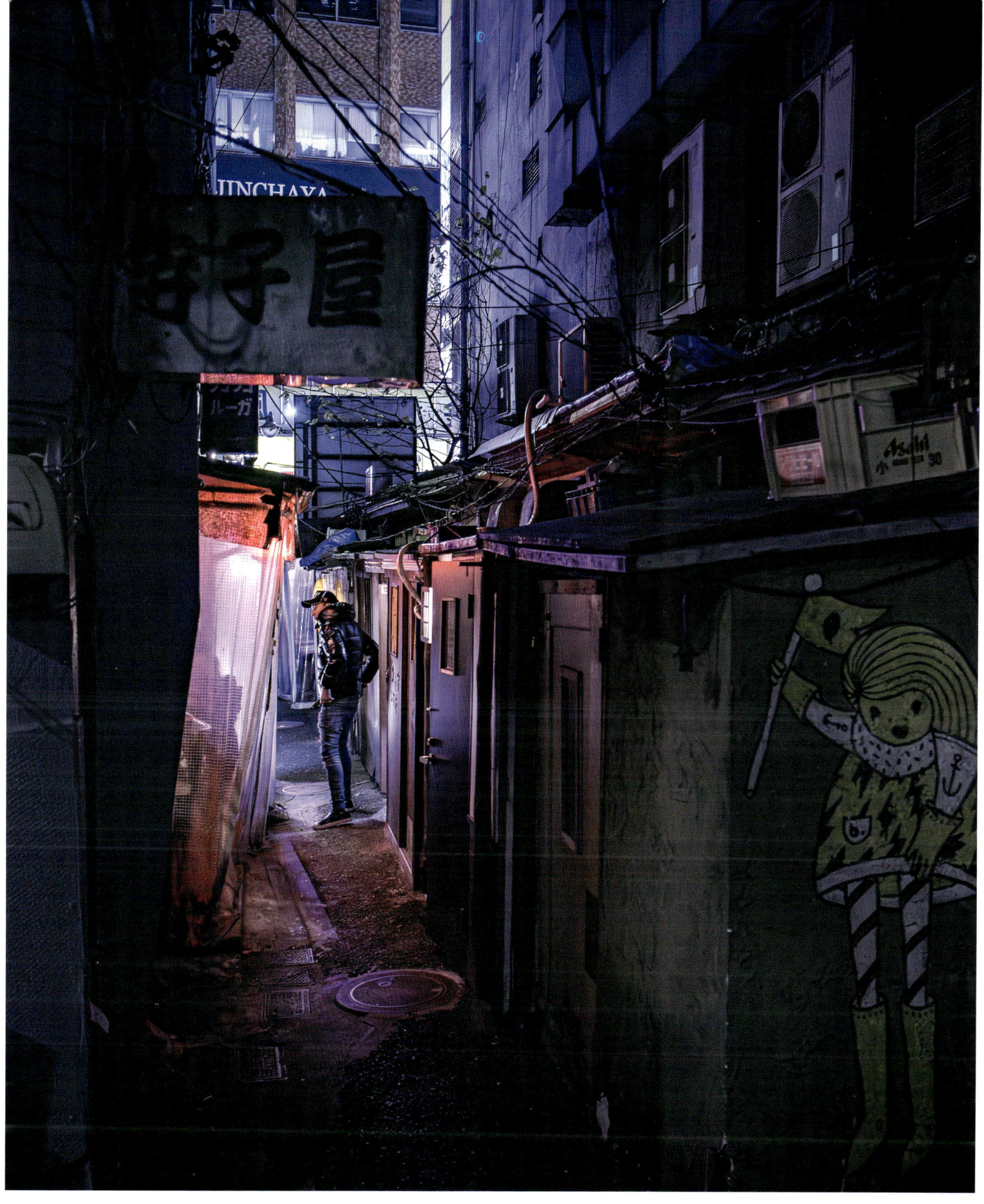

Terakoya Alley. Shinjuku, Tokyo. Terakoya is located in the Memory Loophole. In addition to its standard izakaya menu, there is a menu of grilled dishes of crow, pigeon, and rat.

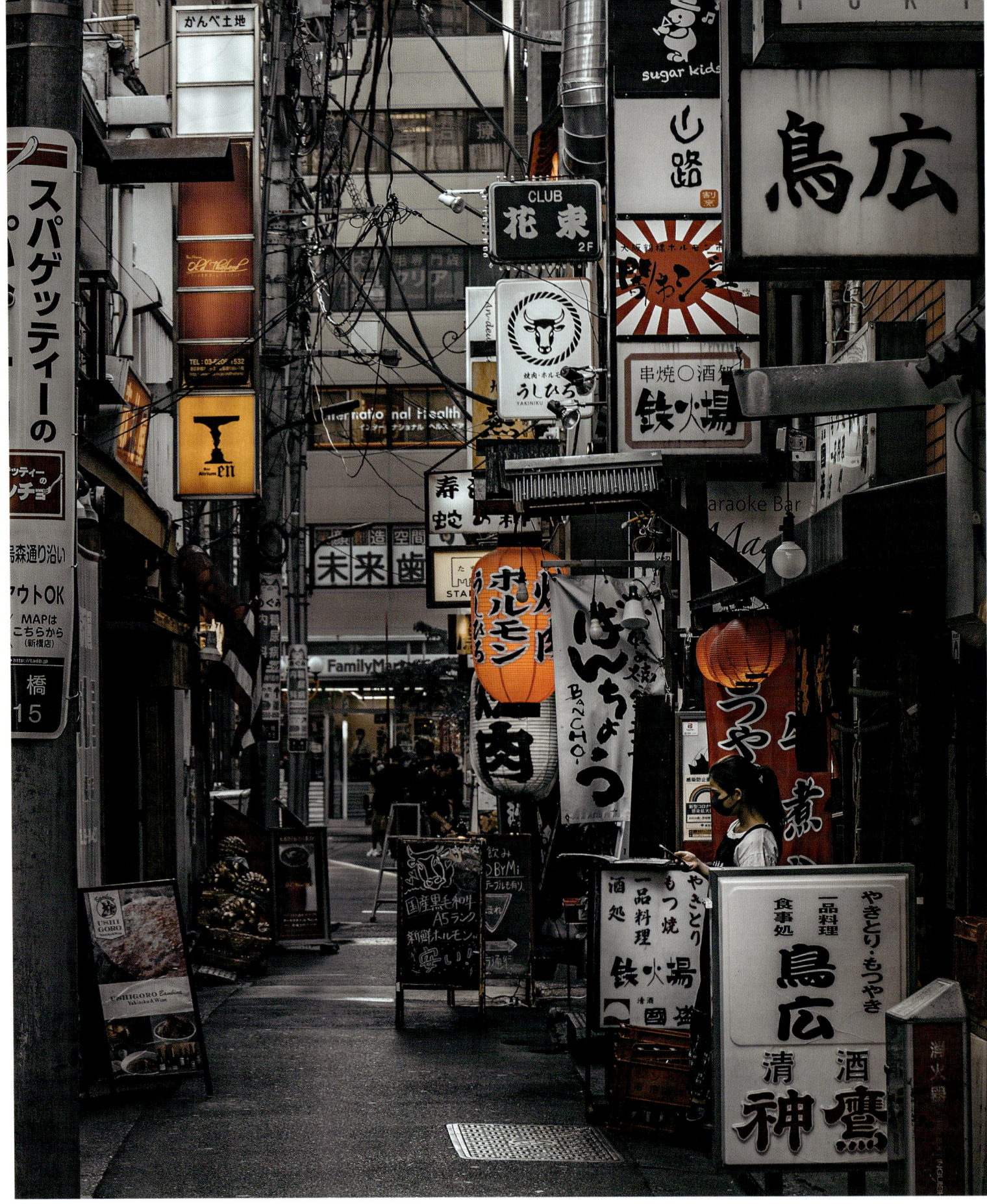

Daytime Alley in Shinbashi. Shinbashi,
Tokyo. This is a daytime shot of one of my
favorite places. It is a charming scene even
when there are no neon lights lit up.

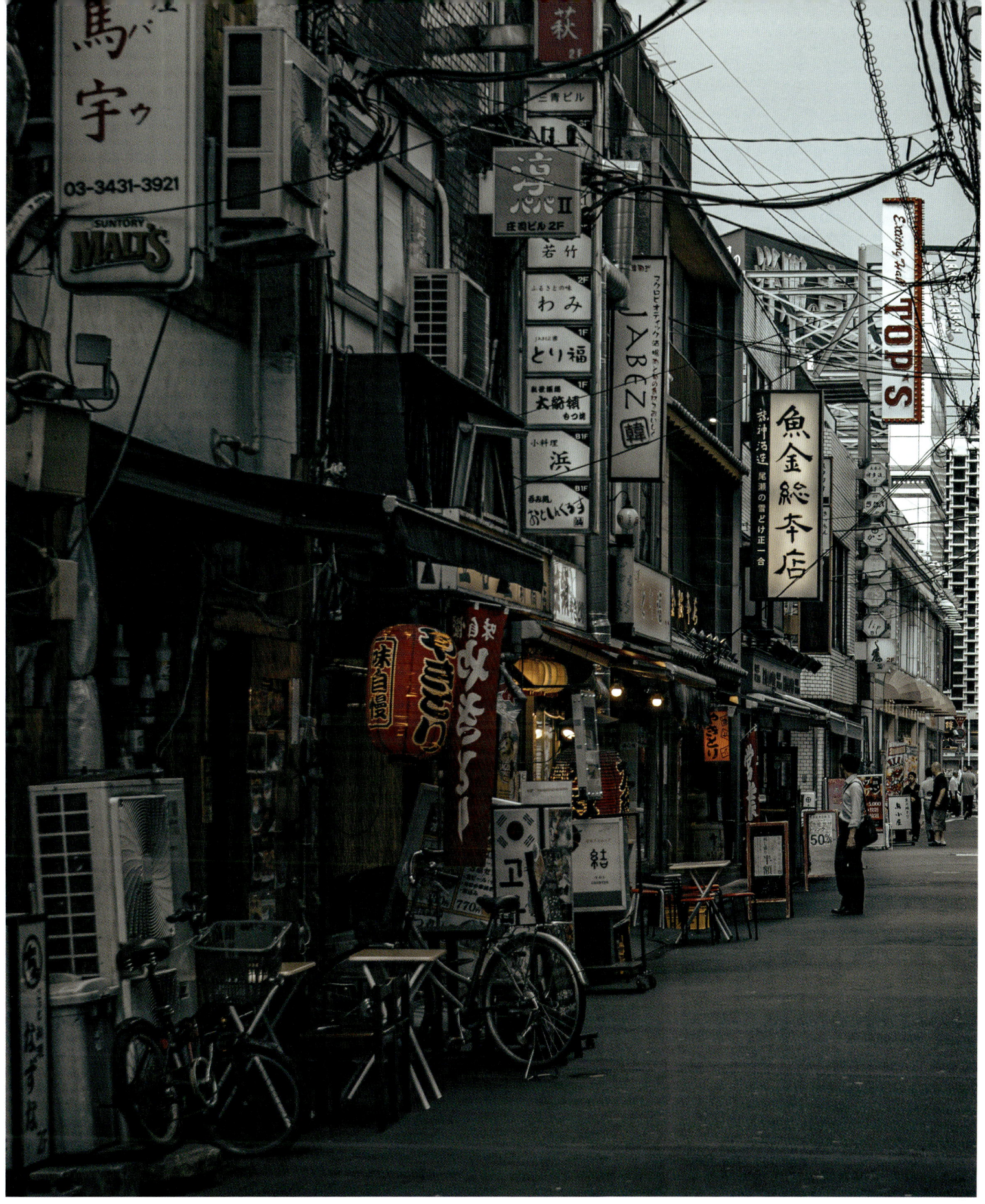

Uokin So Honten. Shinbashi, Tokyo. The restaurant in the center with the large sign written in kanji has been in business for thirty years. It is a well-known restaurant that has long supported those who enjoy drinking.

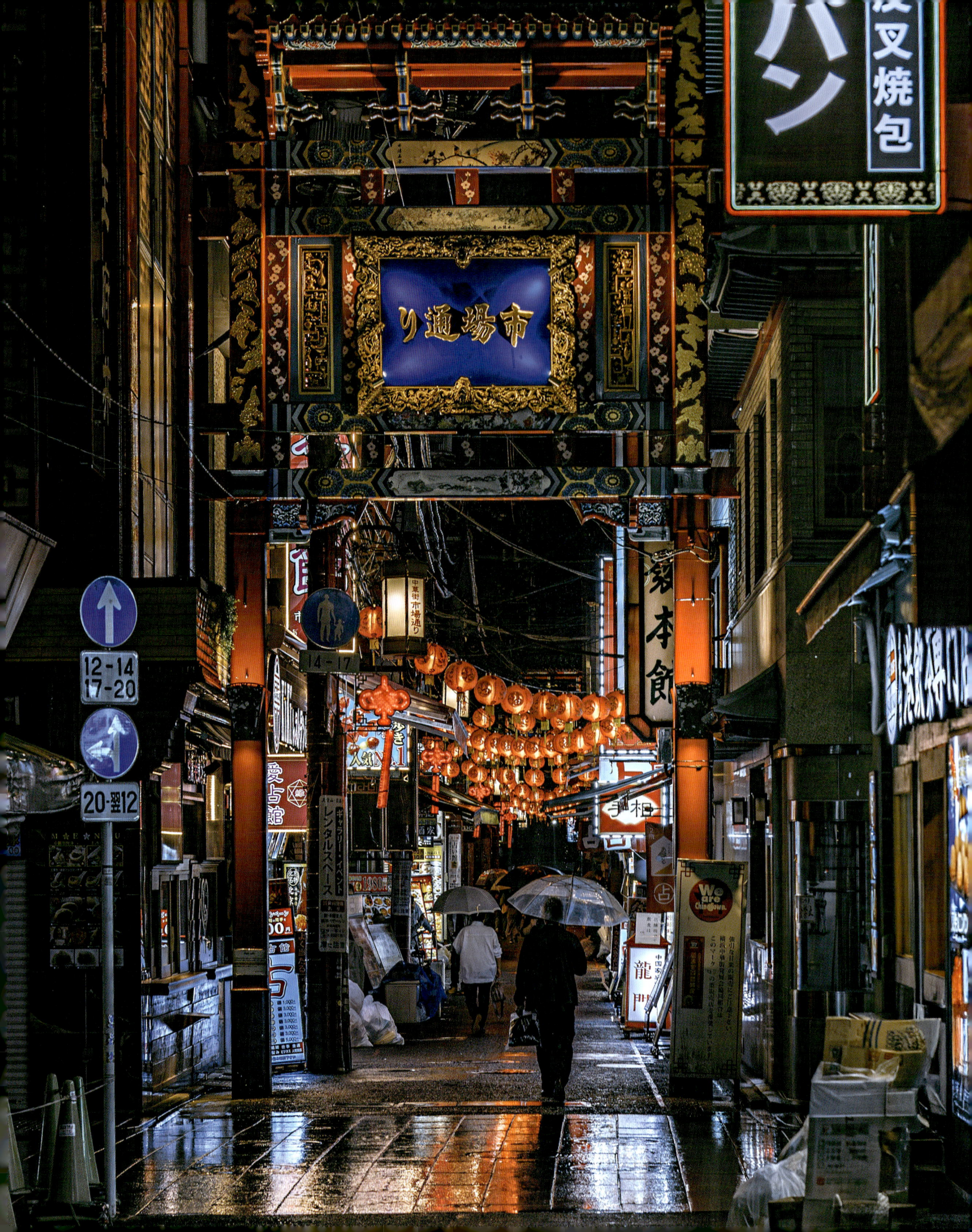

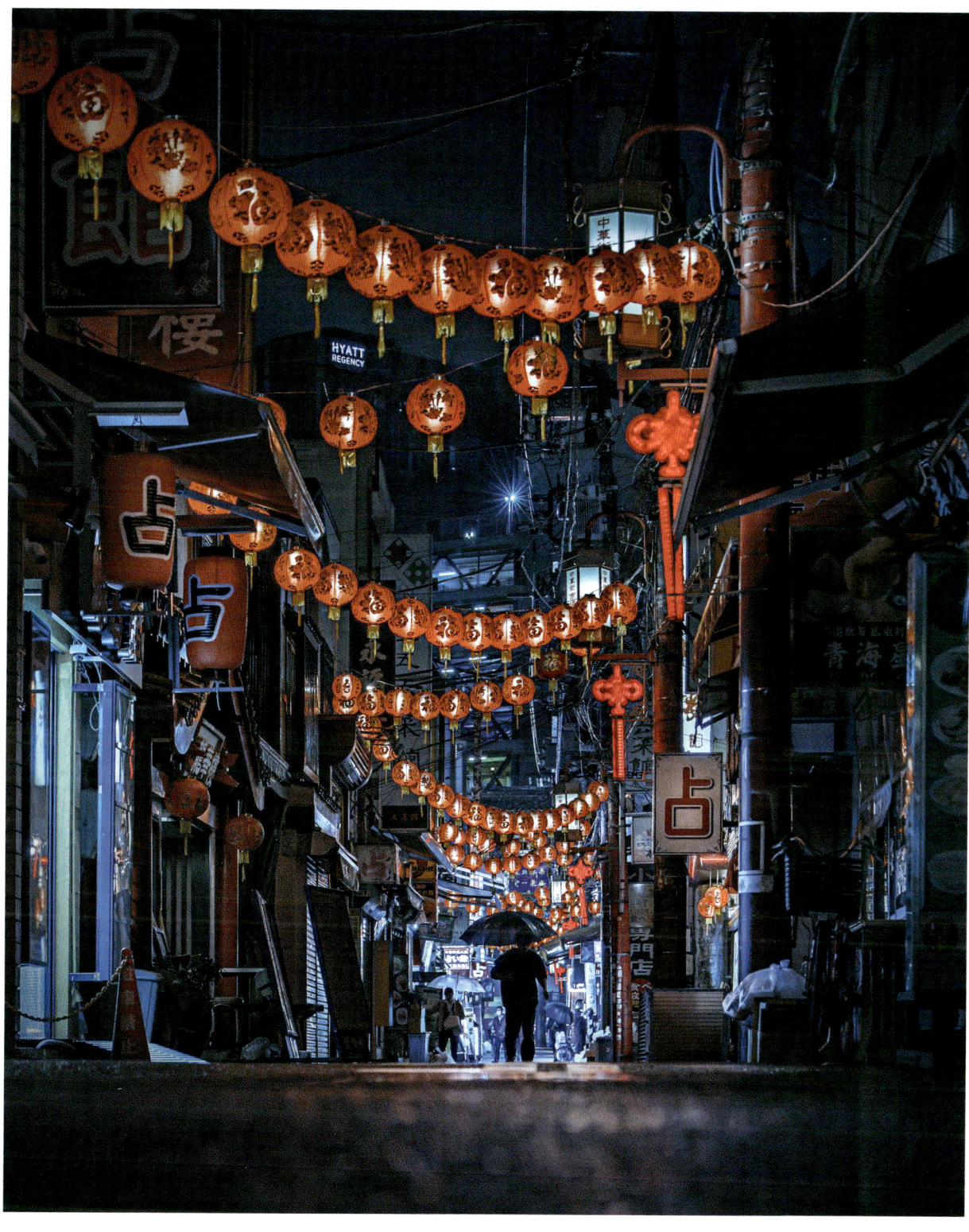

Market Street South Gate. Chinatown, Yokohama. Market Street is the symbol of bustling Chinatown. There are two gates on Market Street, at the south and north ends.

Ichiba Street. Chinatown, Yokohama. This area is lined with many fortune tellers, and while it is crowded during the day, it has a completely different look when the crowds are gone.

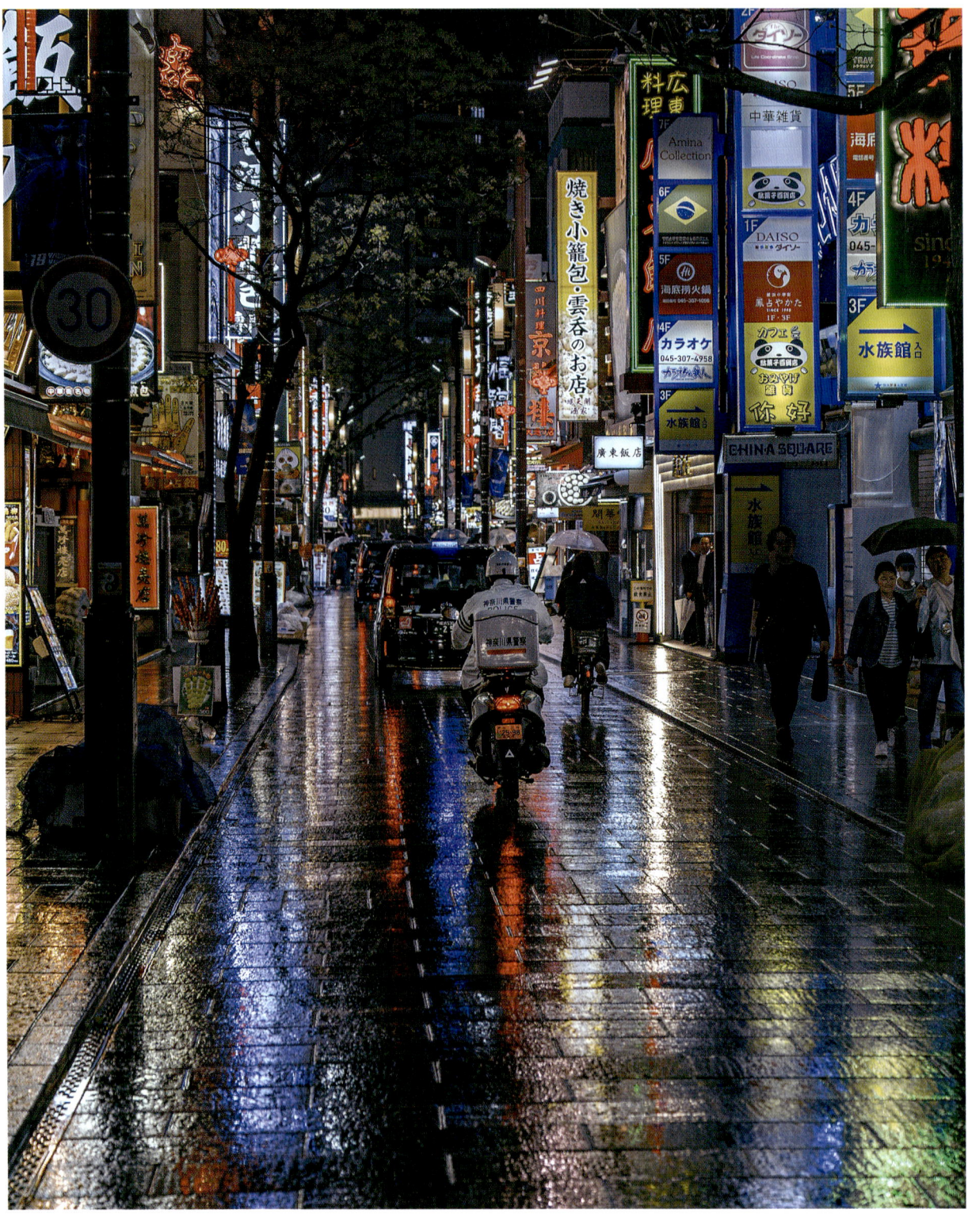

Rainy Chinatown Main Street. Chinatown, Yokohama. The colorful lights reflect beautifully on the wet road.

Dragon Lanterns. Chinatown, Yokohama. In Chinatown, dragon lanterns are displayed during the Chinese New Year. The dragon soaring in the sky is believed to bring happiness.

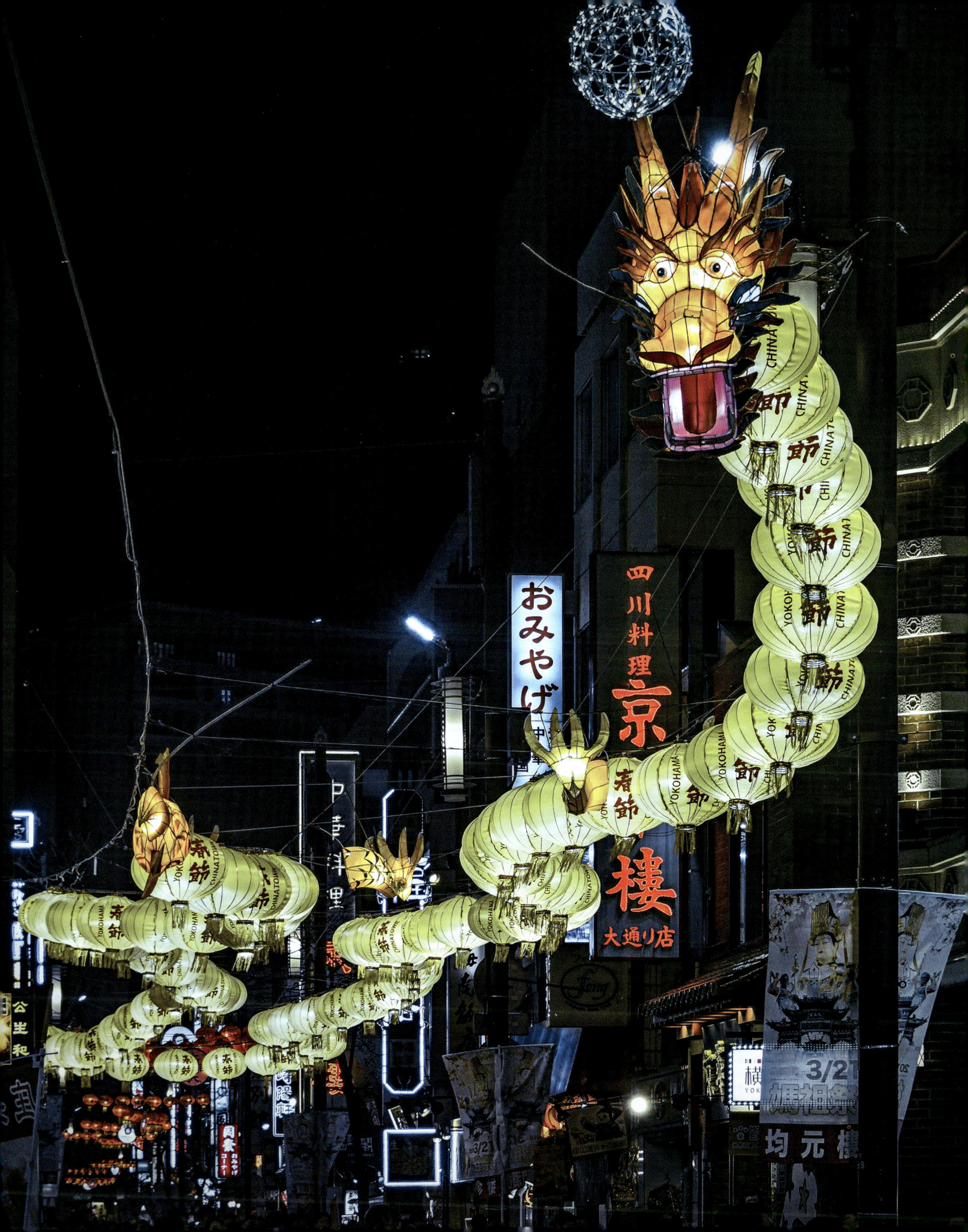

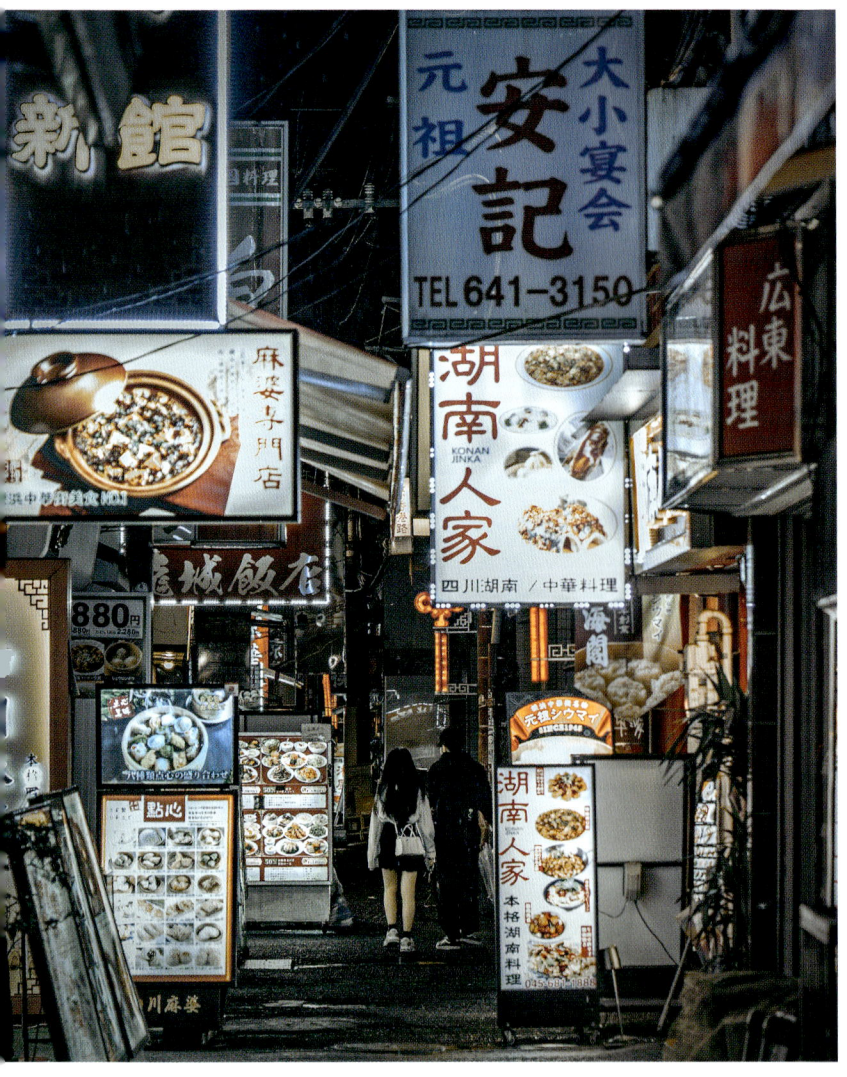

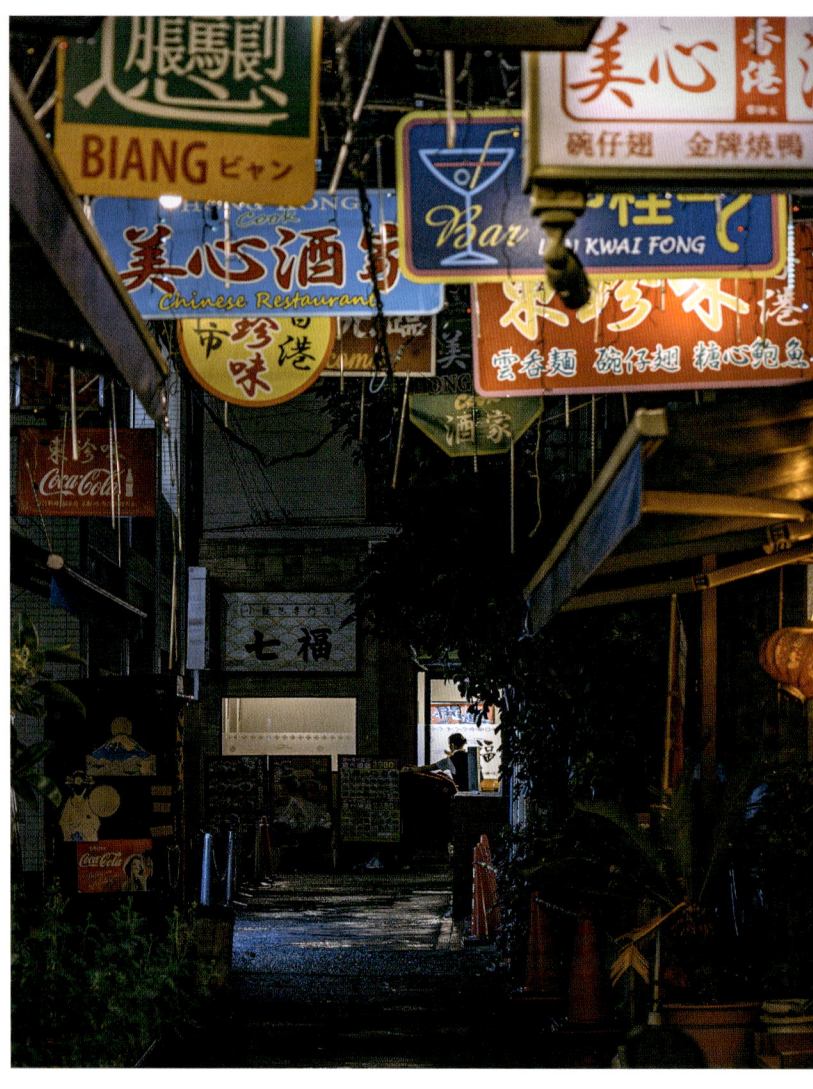

Alley Full of Signs. Chinatown, Yokohama. This is my favorite place to photograph whenever I visit Chinatown. One of its charms is that the atmosphere is completely different during the day than at night.

Alley of Bishinshuka. Chinatown, Yokohama. This is the back of the alley near the Kuan Ti Miao (Kanteibyo) Temple. It is a bit daring to walk there at night, when it is dark, but the bright lights illuminating the signs attract a lot of people coming and going.

Parent and Child in Chinatown Alley. Chinatown, Yokohama. Chinese cuisine varies by eight regions, so only Szechuan restaurants are concentrated in this part of Chinatown.

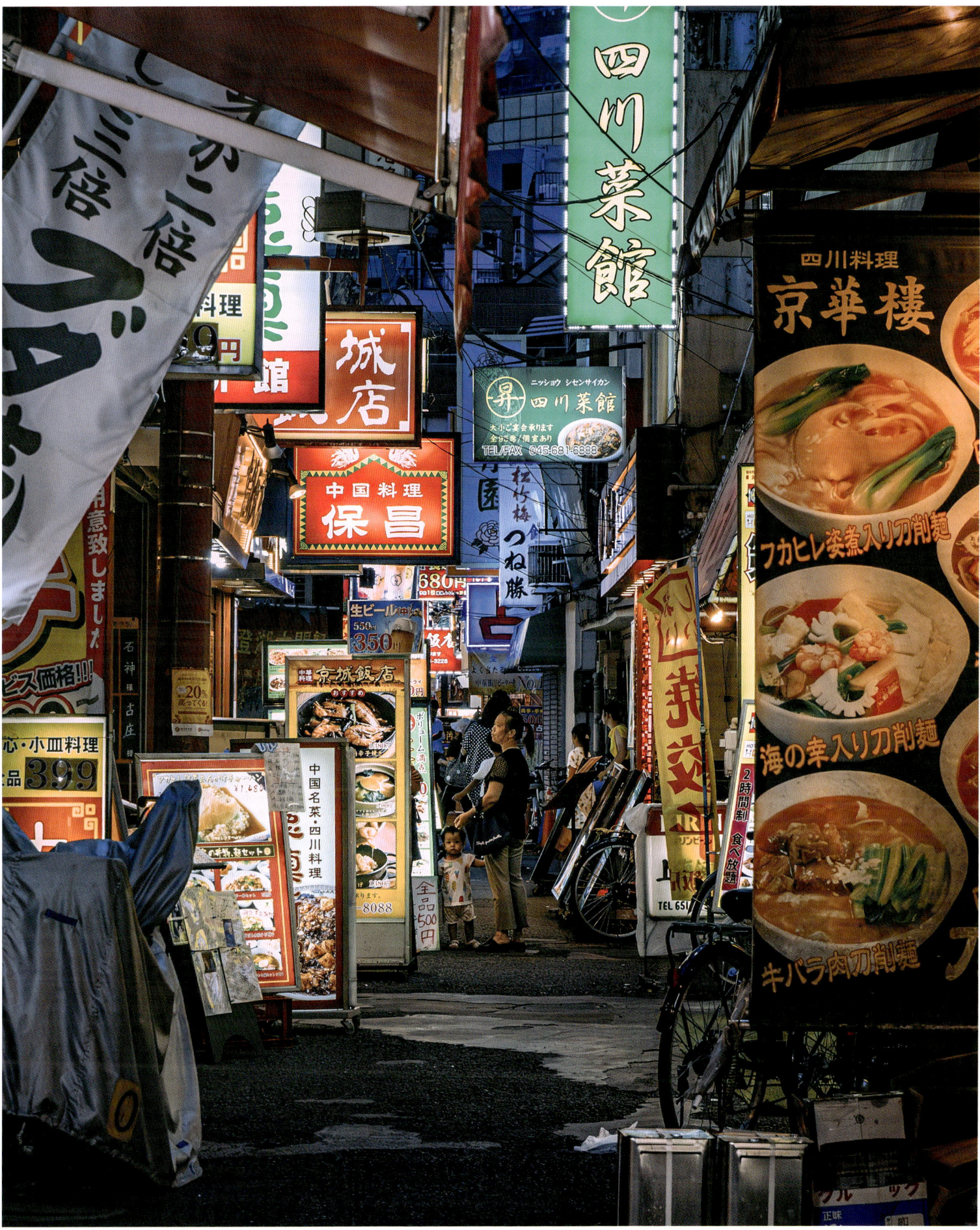

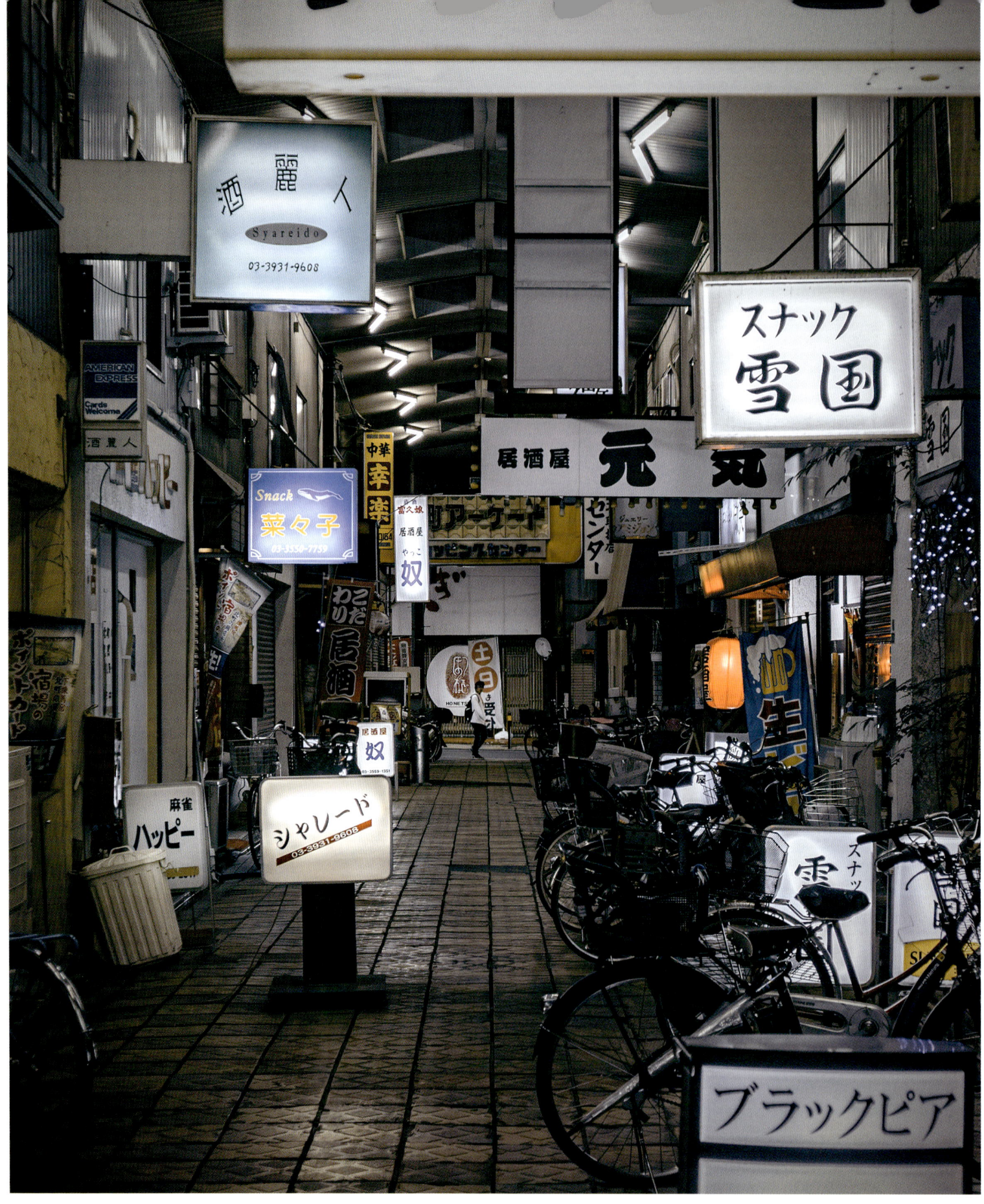

Kitamachi Arcade. Tobu-Nerima, Tokyo.
This arcade was built around 1975 and
appears as if time has stopped.

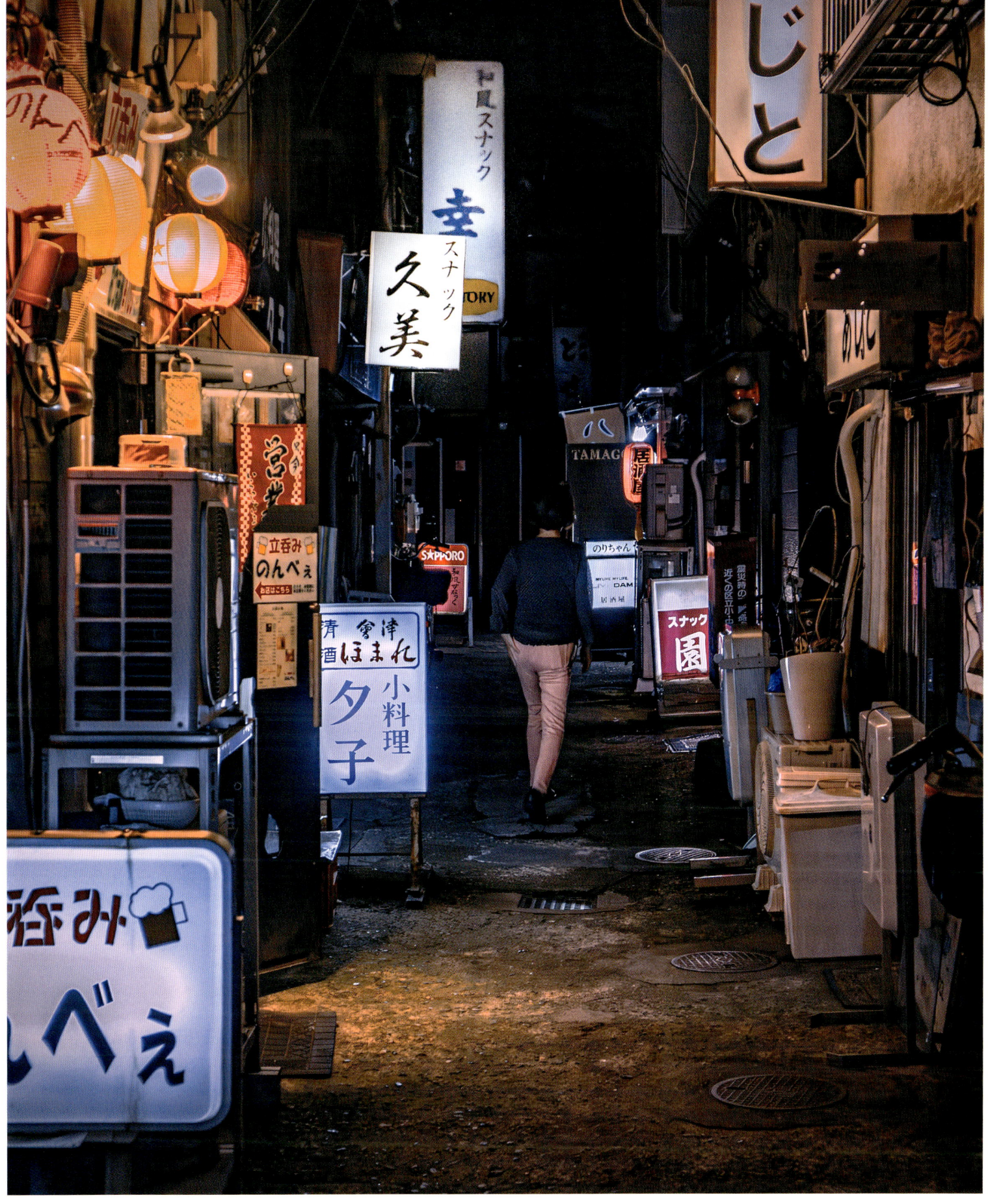

Kitamachi Rakutenchi. Tobu–Nerima, Tokyo. This area has remained unchanged for fifty years.

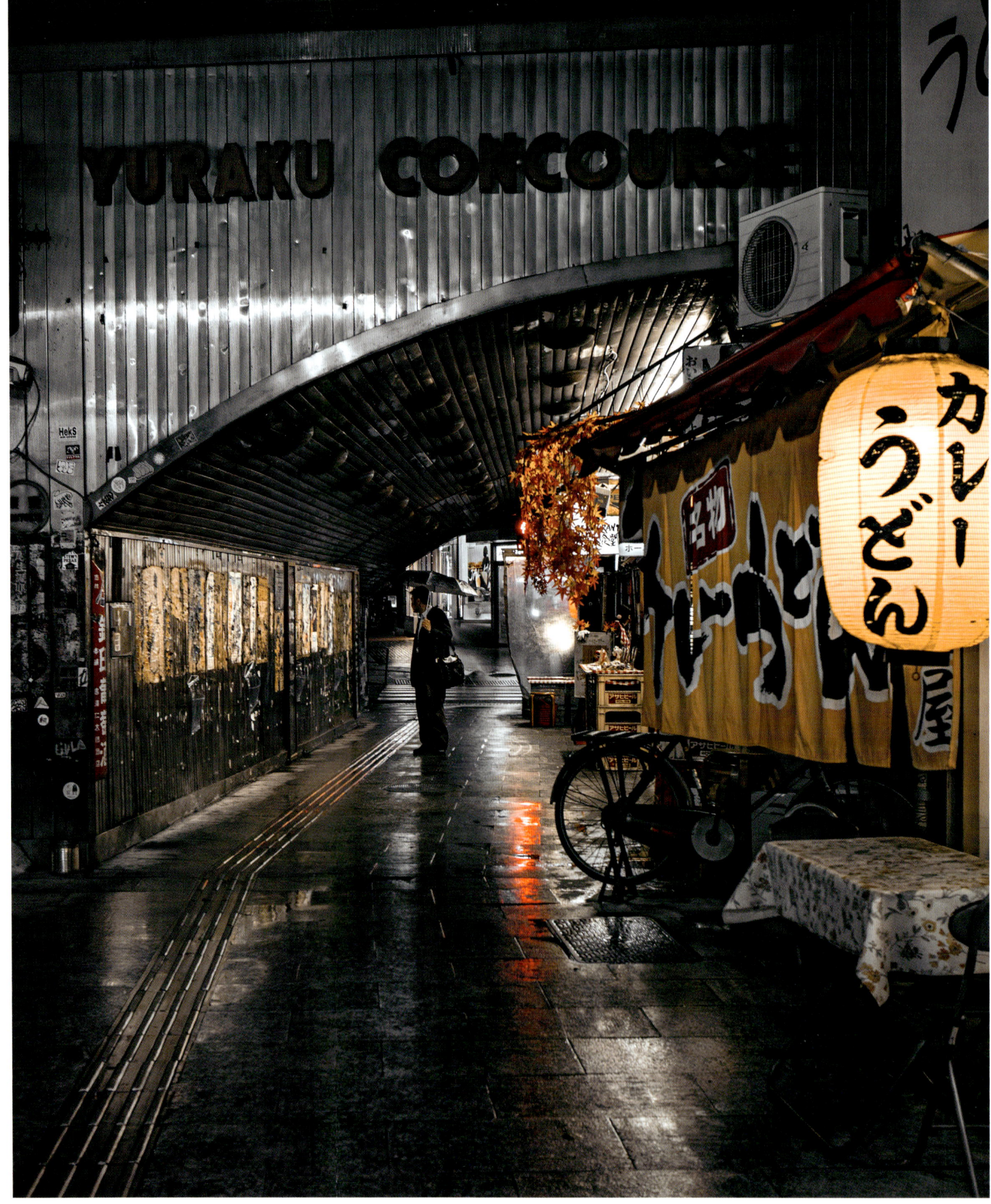

Yuraku Concourse. Yurakucho, Tokyo. This concourse is located under the elevated train tracks, connecting the Ginza and Hibiya sides of the JR Yurakucho Station. Construction was completed in 1966, and the walls are covered with old Japanese movie posters.

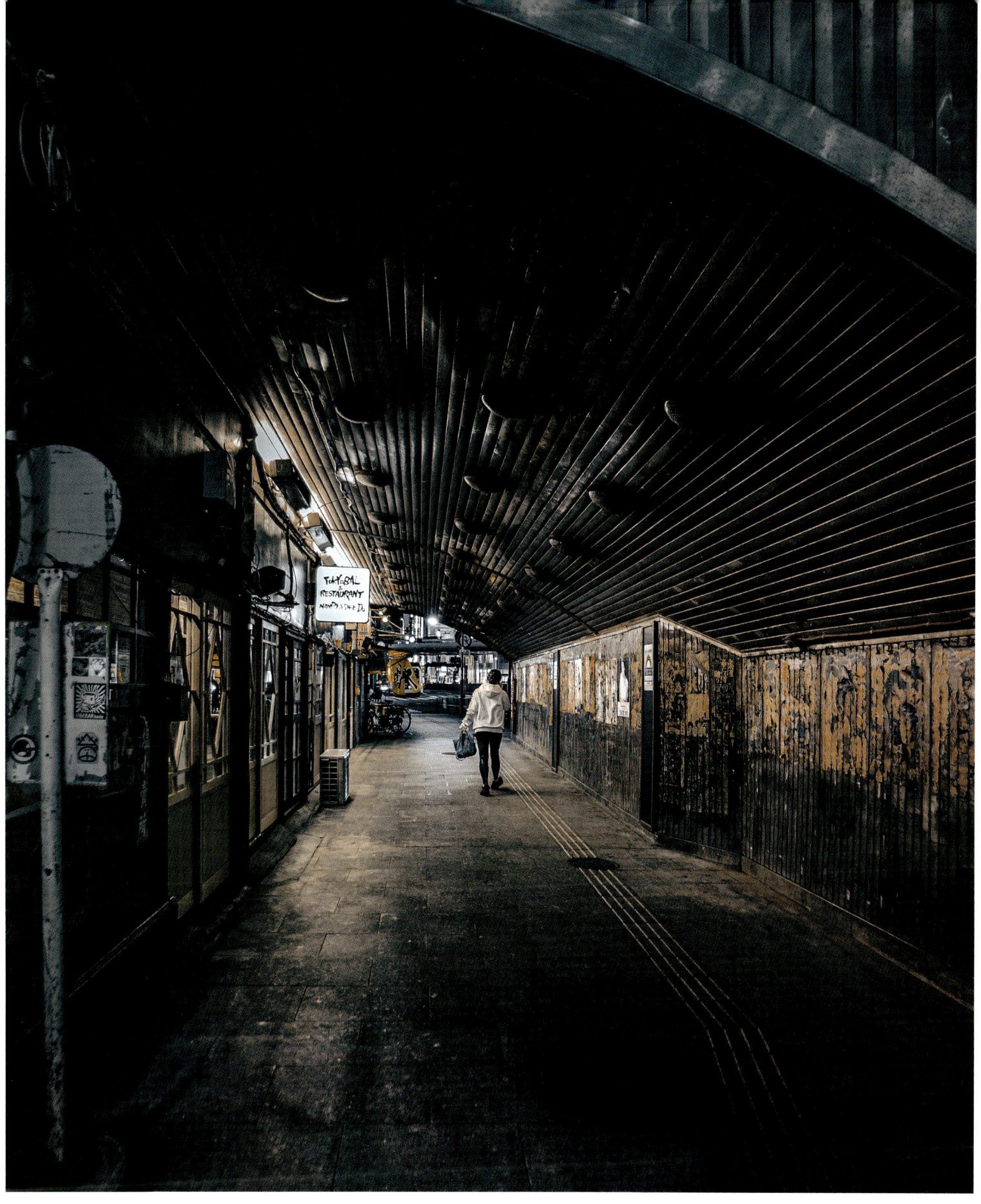

The Other Side of Yuraku Concourse. Yurakucho, Tokyo. This photo was taken from the opposite side of the Yuraku Concourse (see photo opposite). The futuristic ceiling, which looks like the inside of a spaceship, in contrast with the old movie posters on the walls is interesting.

Smoke Tunnel. Yurakucho, Tokyo.
Motsuyaki Fuji is a year-round restaurant
located under the elevated railway tracks
in Yurakucho. It offers a wide variety of
dishes and makes for a unique dining
experience, despite its smoky atmosphere.

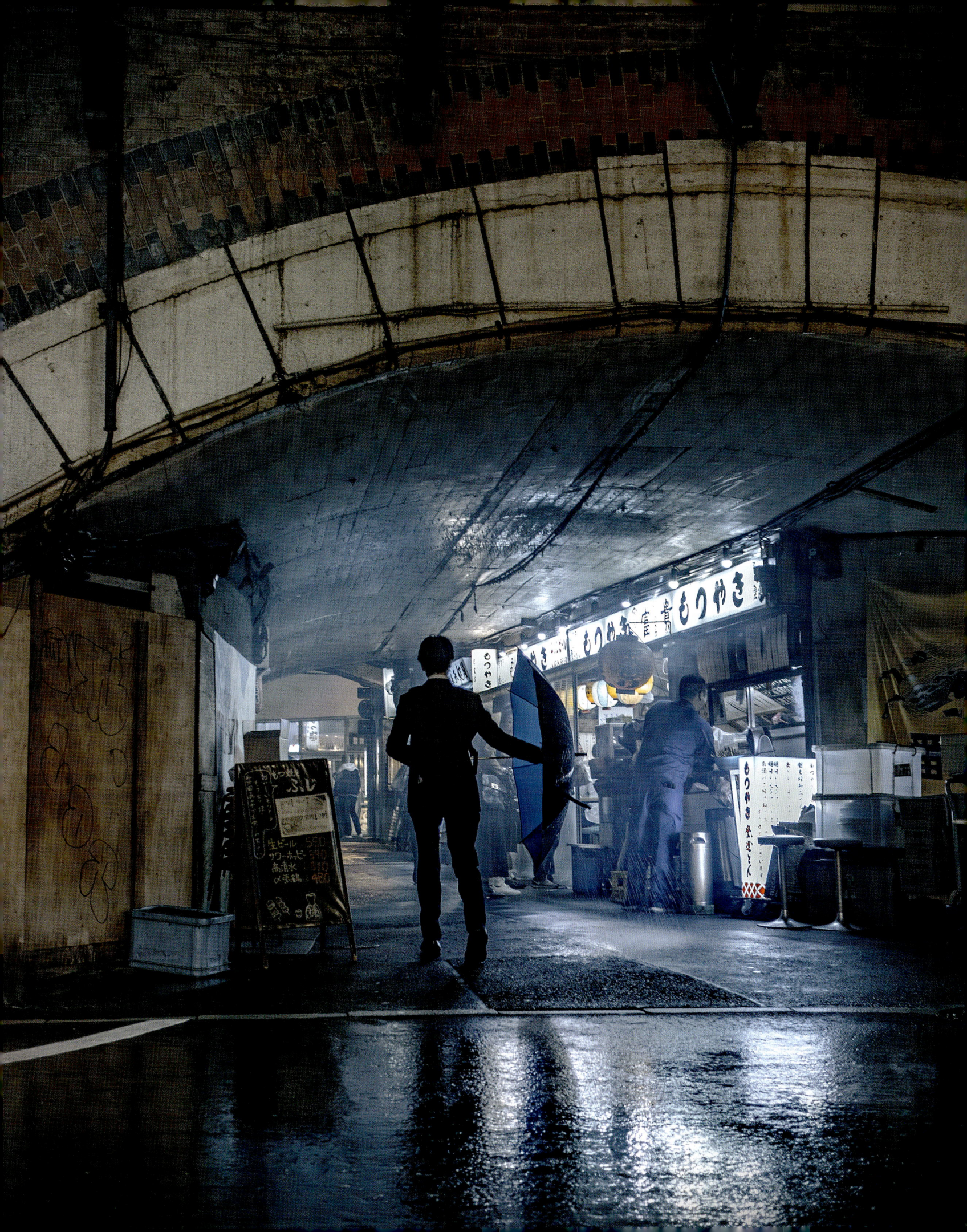

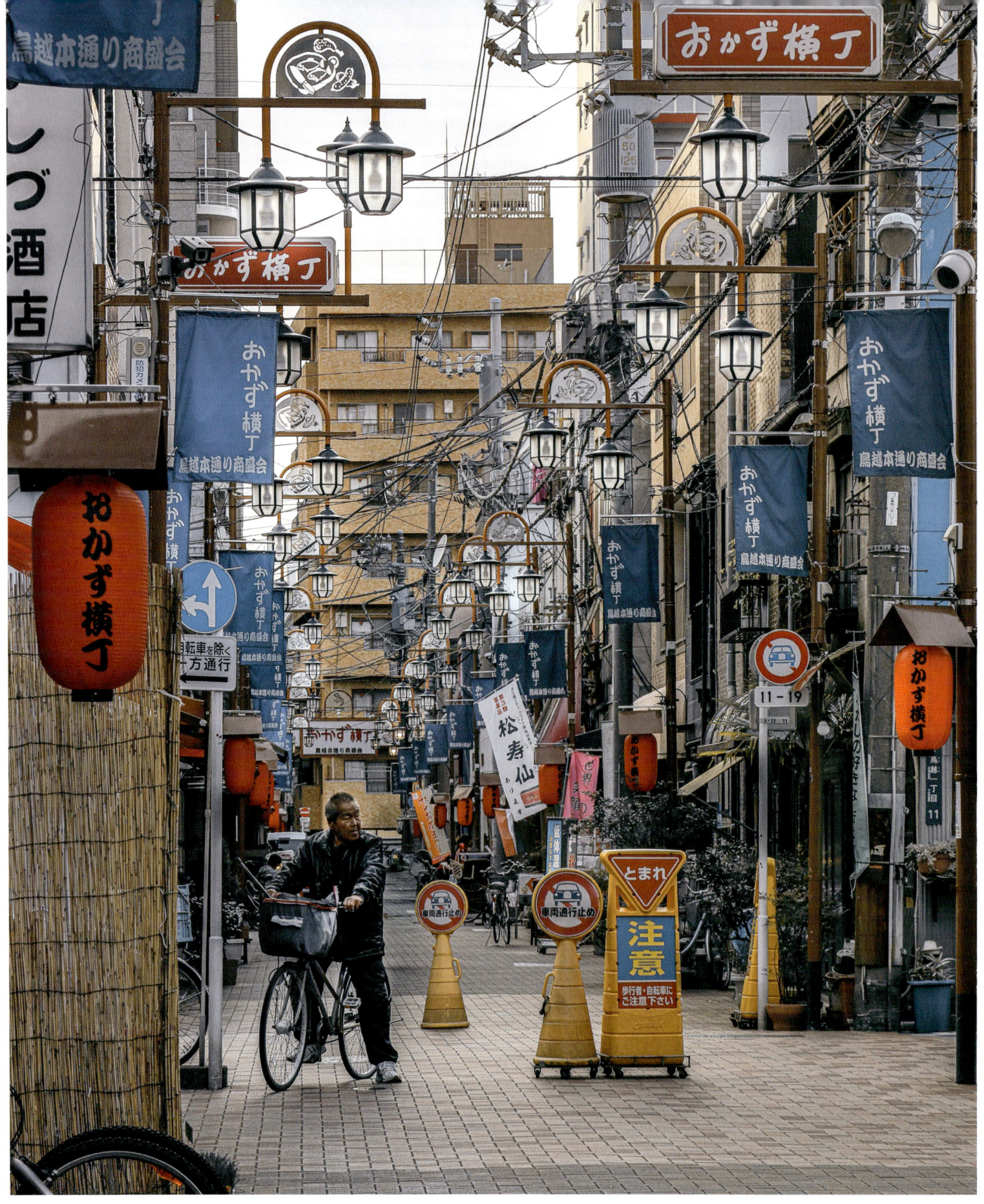

Side Dish Alley. Asakusabashi, Tokyo. This shopping street is commonly known as Okazu Yokocho. With its long history and nostalgic scenery, it often appears as a location in television dramas. *Okazu* means "side dish."

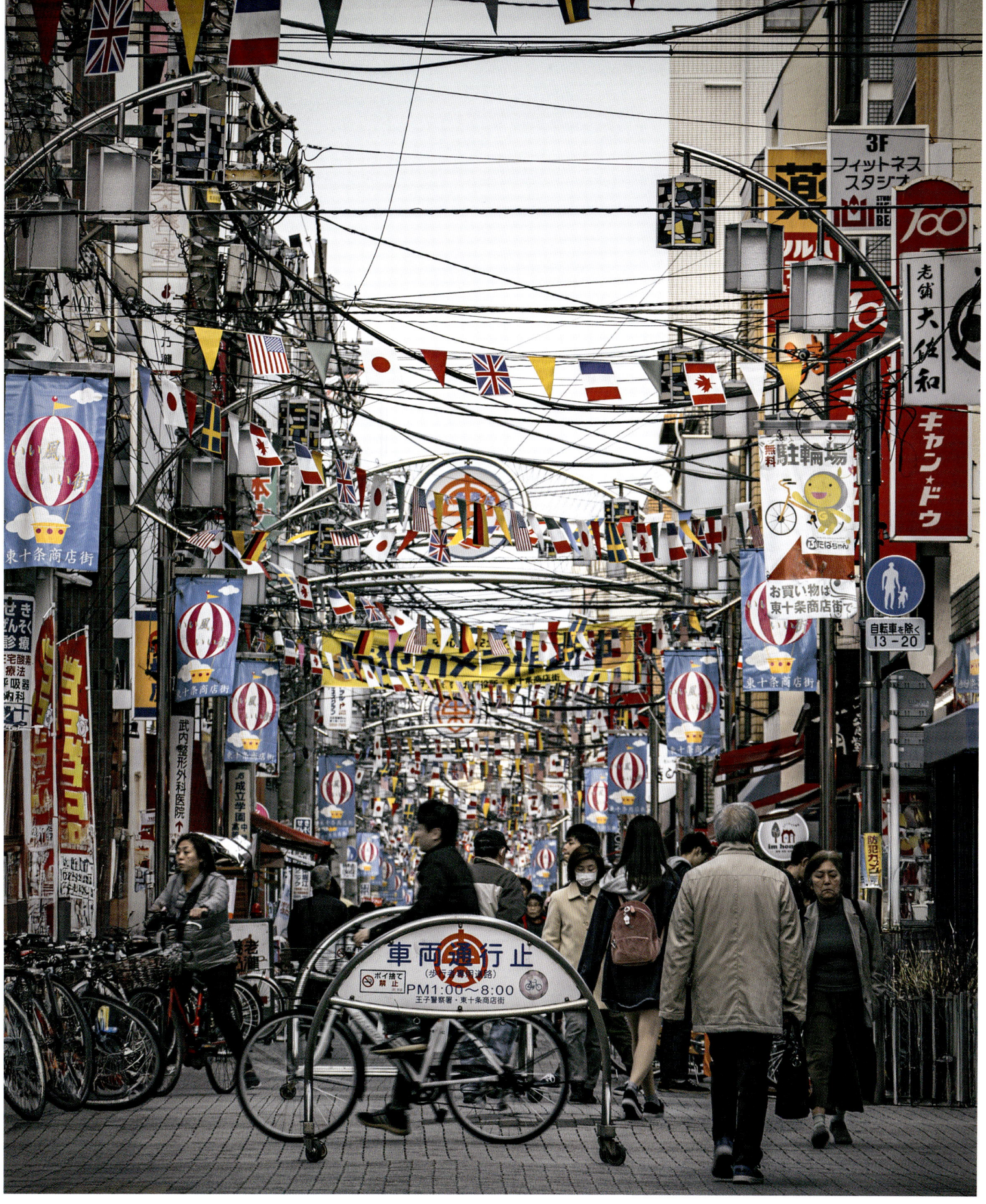

Higashi-Jujo Shopping Street. Higashi-Jujo, Tokyo. This lively shopping street has numerous flags of all nations fluttering above. During the daytime, the street is closed to cars, making it pedestrian only.

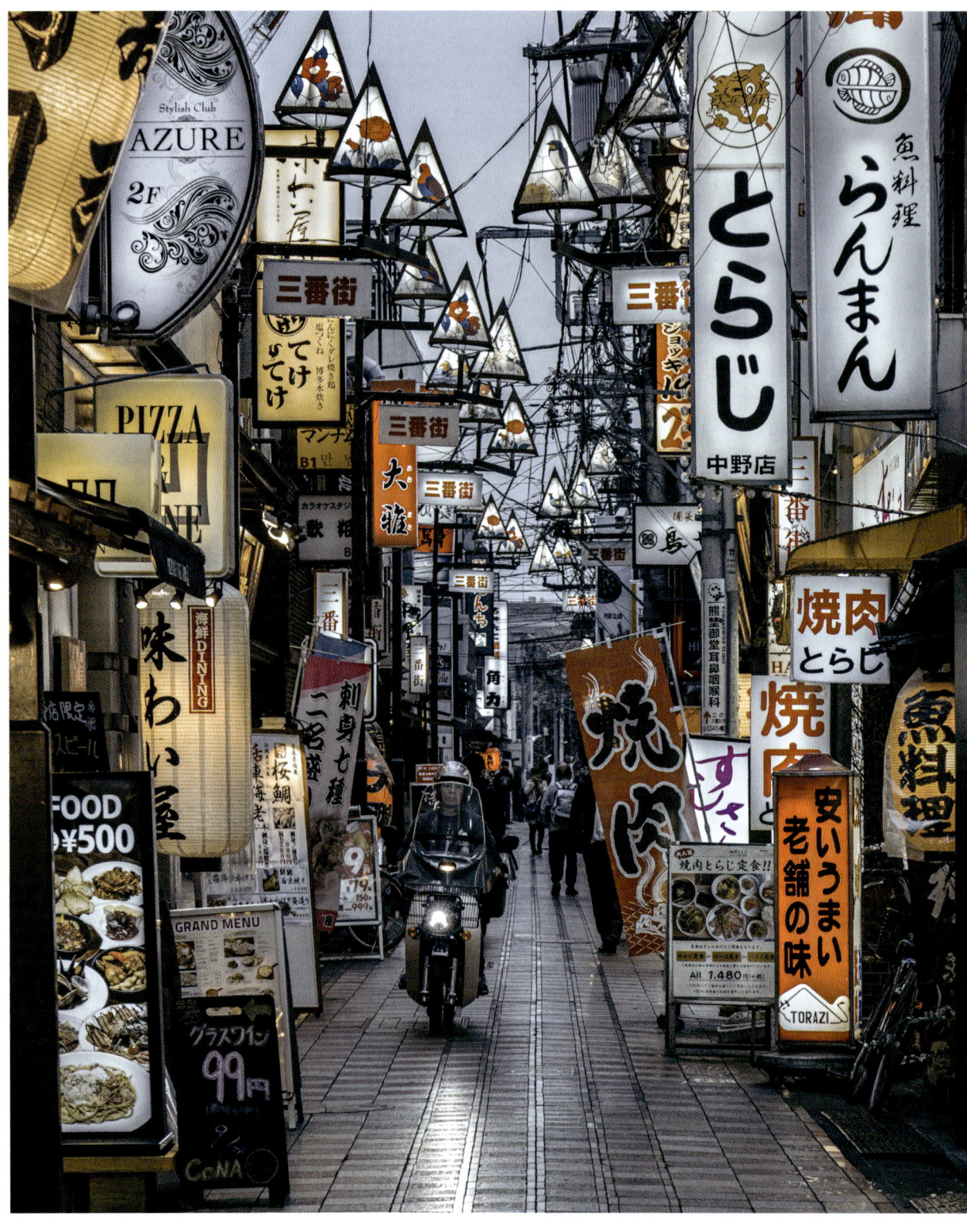

Sanbangai Street. Nakano, Tokyo. Nakano is known as the second sacred land of otaku, but once you enter the backstreets, you will find a maze of narrow alleys and izakaya.

Looming Signs. Nakano, Tokyo. This shot was taken with a zoom lens, creating the effect of streetlights and billboards looming over the scene.

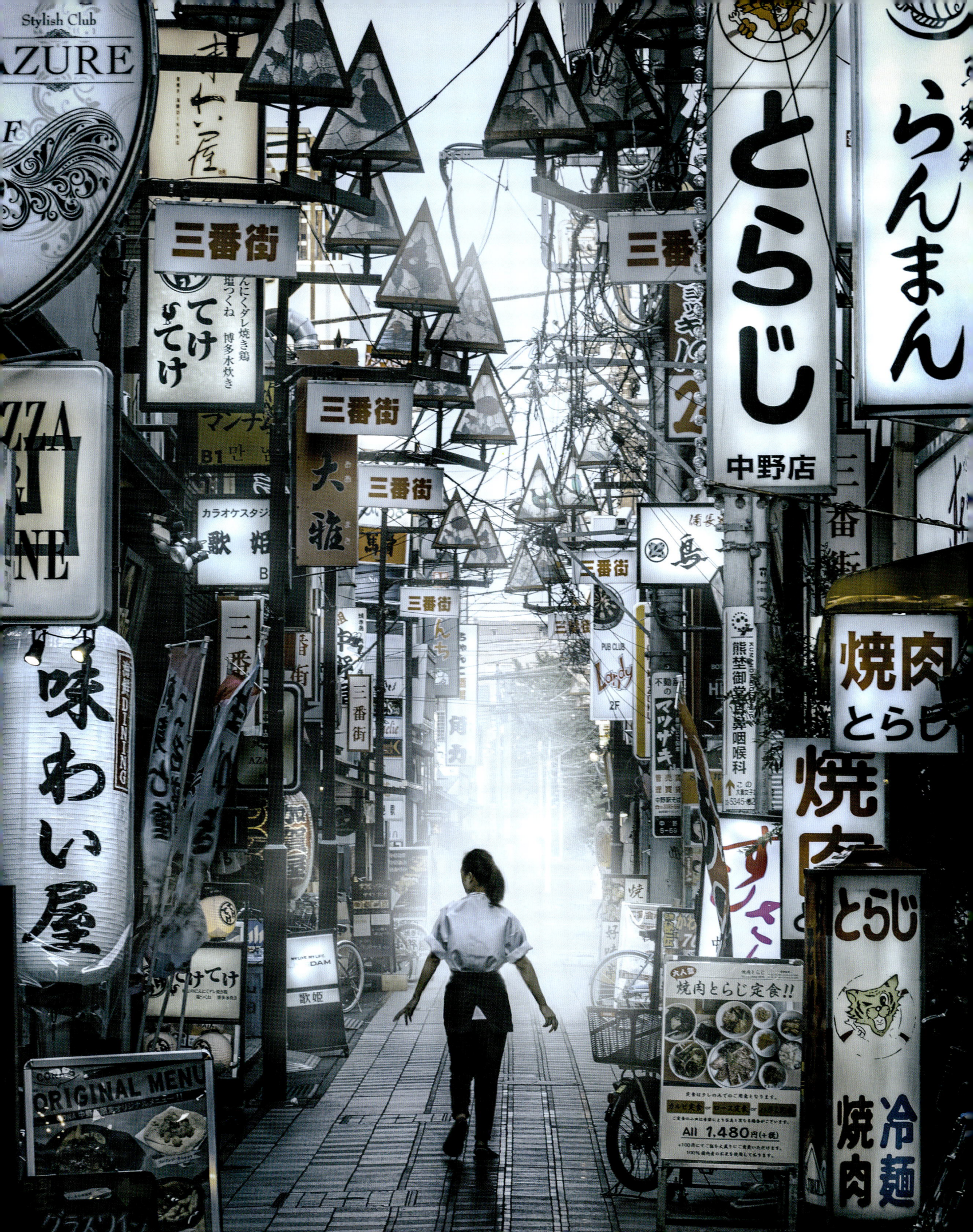

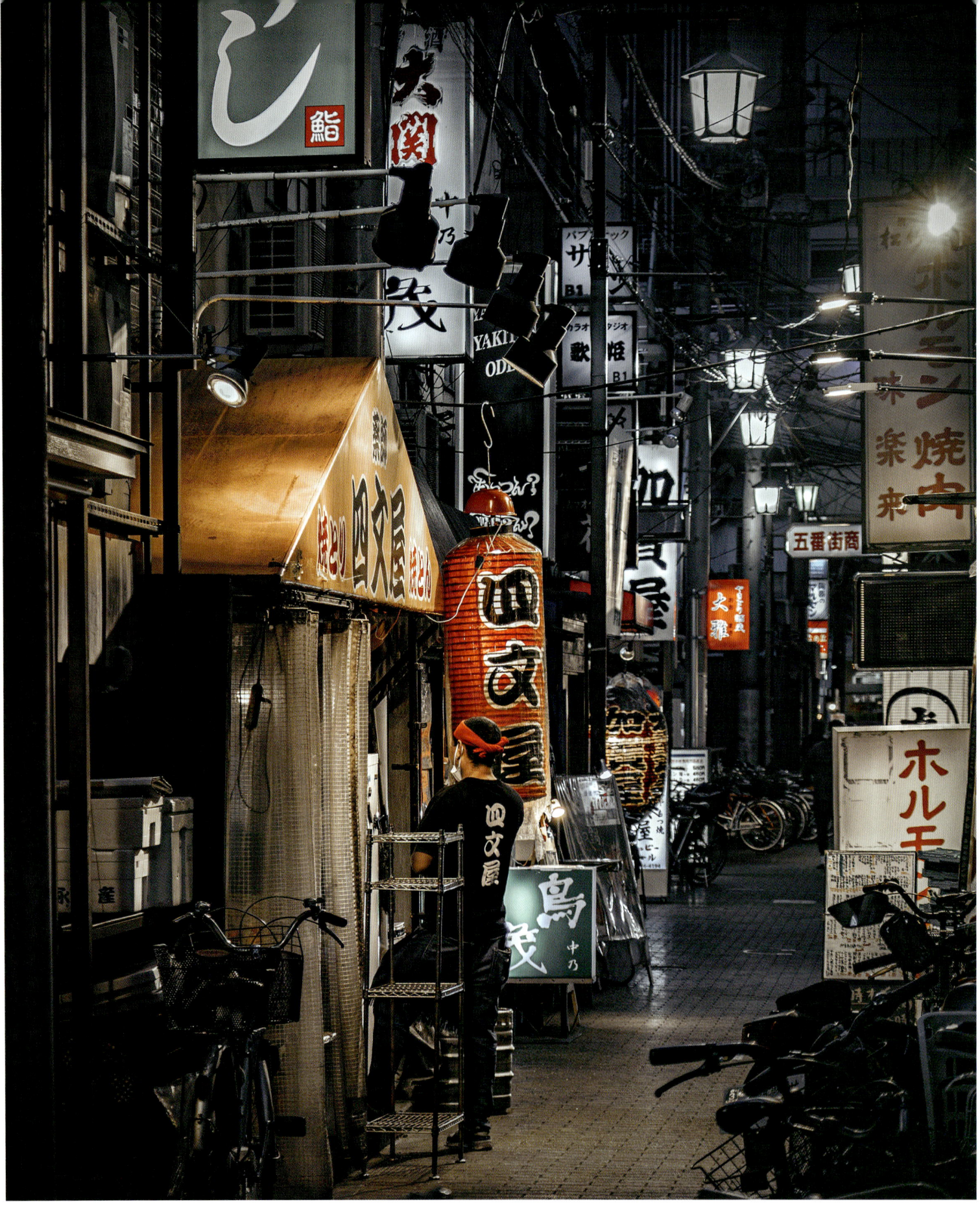

Fifth Avenue Izakaya. Nakano, Tokyo. This yakitori restaurant is in Nakano Gobangai. The distinctive typeface on the sign, lanterns, and T-shirt is called Kantei-ryu, which was originally designed for signs promoting the traditional performing art of Kabuki.

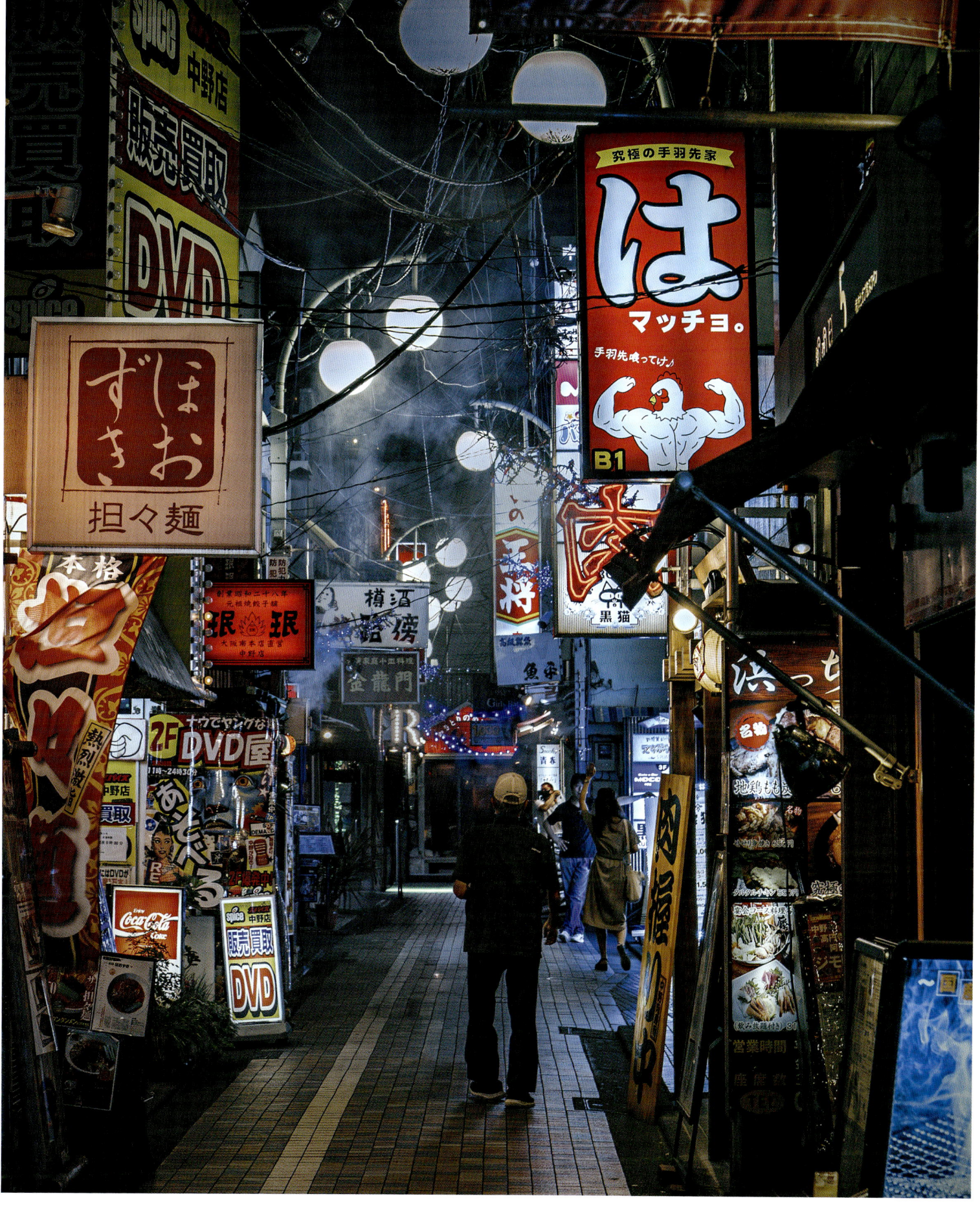

Fantastic Alley. Nakano, Tokyo. This fantastic alley is lined with flashy signs and always filled with yakitori smoke.

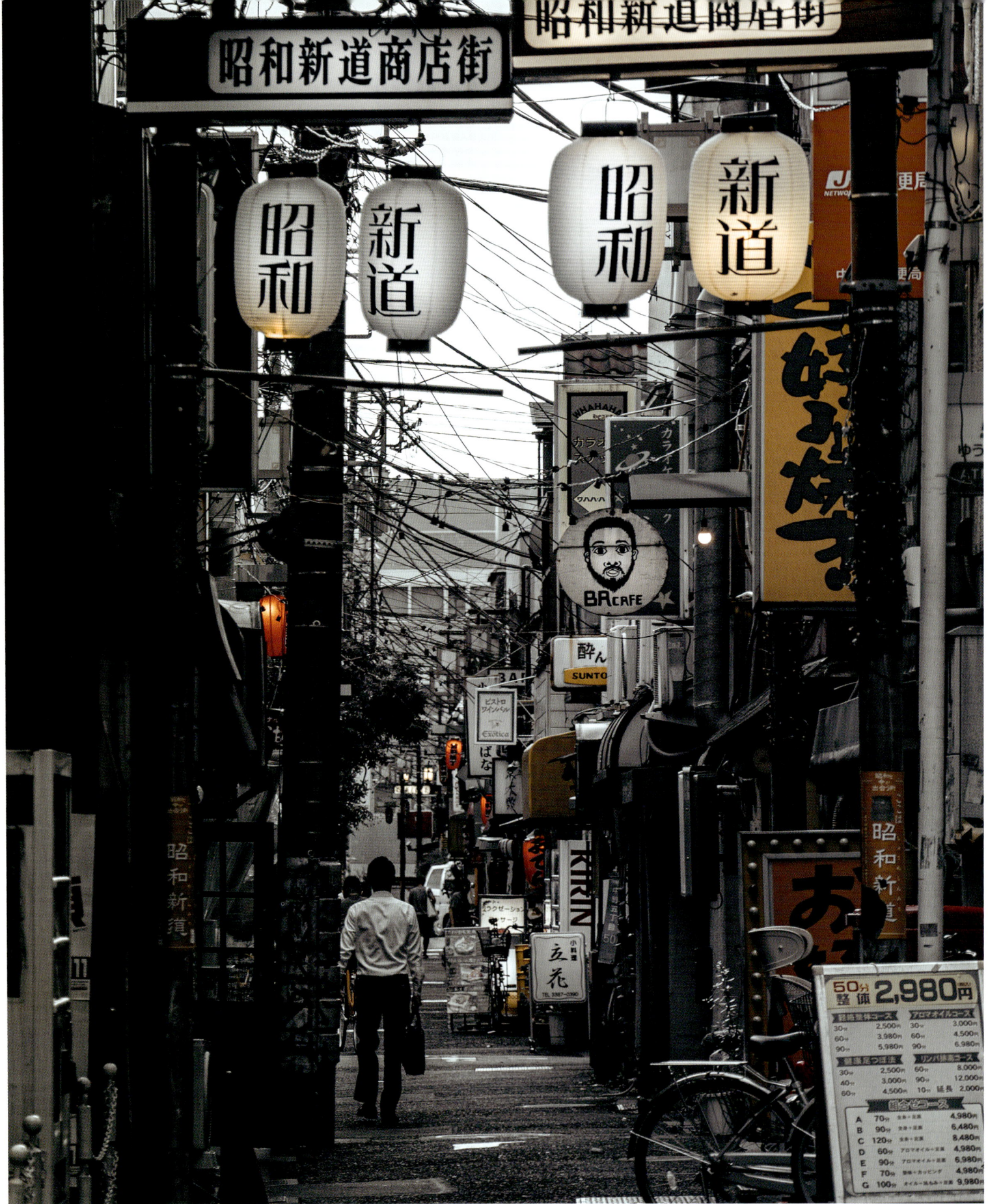

Nostalgic Alley. Nakano, Tokyo. As you proceed deeper and deeper into Nakano's intricate alleyways, you will find this old-fashioned one called Showa Shinmichi.

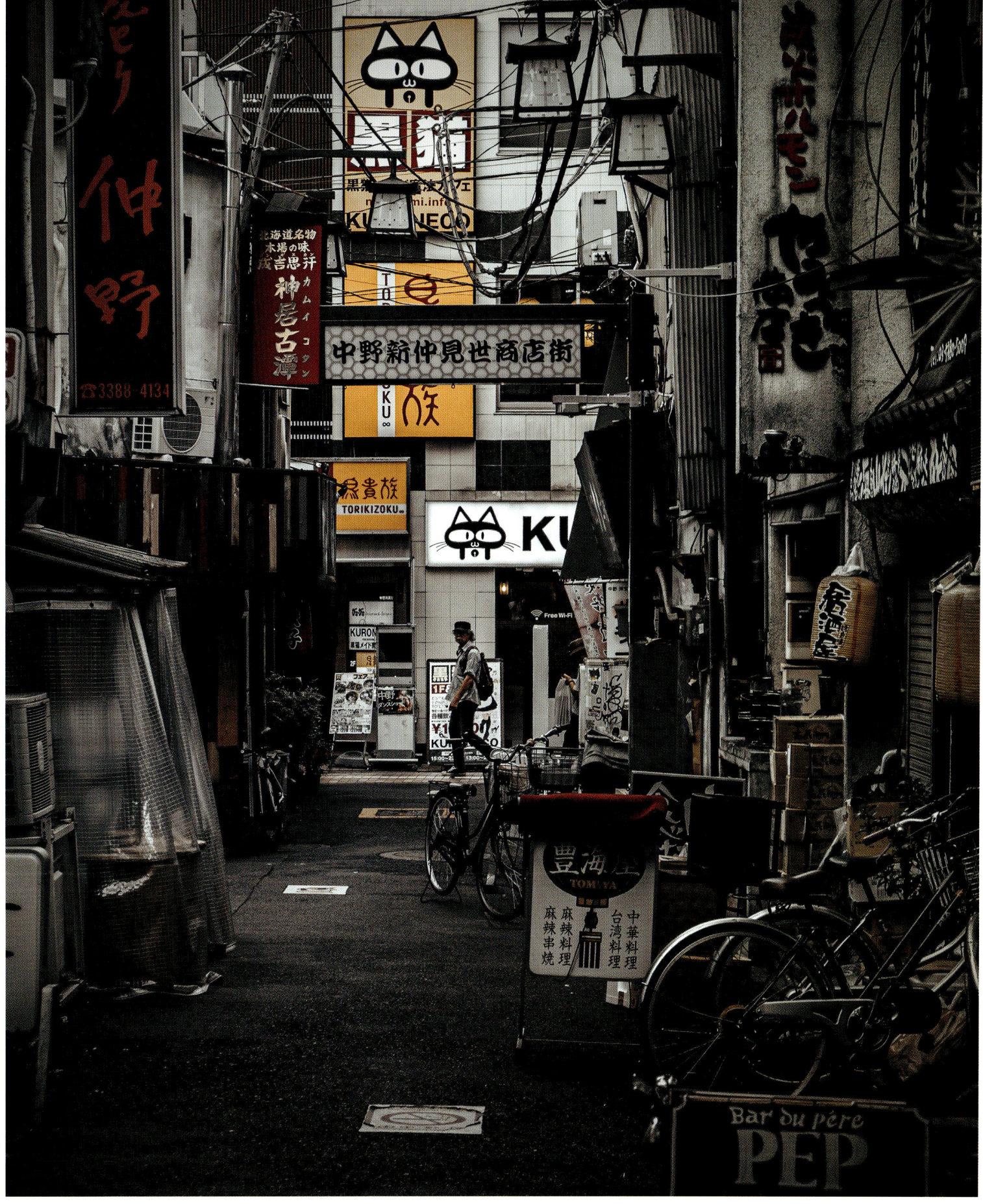

Nakamise Shopping Street. Nakano, Tokyo.
When you step into this shopping street,
it has the appearance of a downtown
side street or back alley, making it feel
strangely nostalgic.

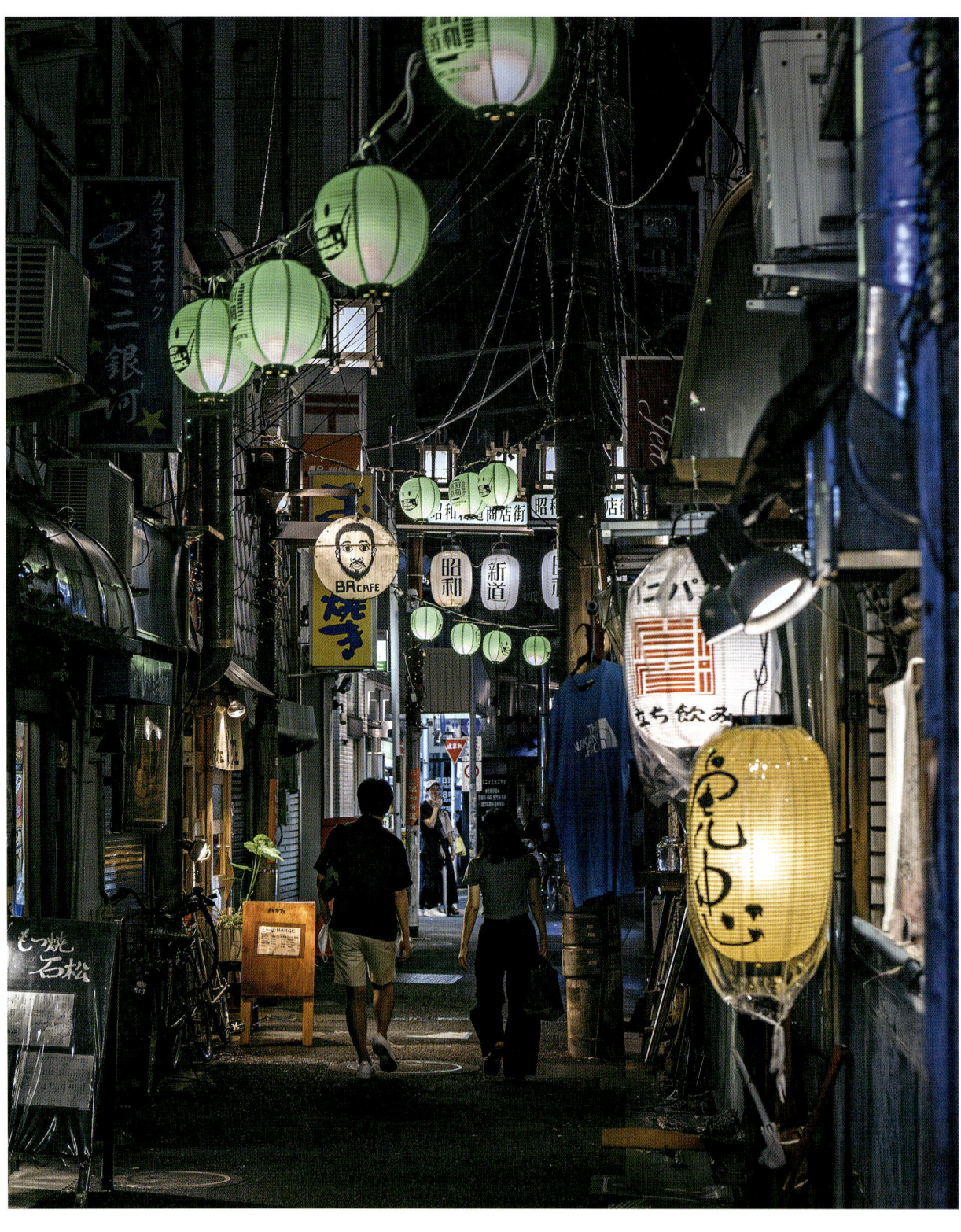

Showa Shindo. Nakano, Tokyo. The comical, green lanterns and the sign with the bearded man make this shopping street memorable.

Tachiaigawa Shopping Street. Tachiaigawa, Tokyo. This shopping street is beautifully lit by colorful lanterns arranged in a zigzag pattern.

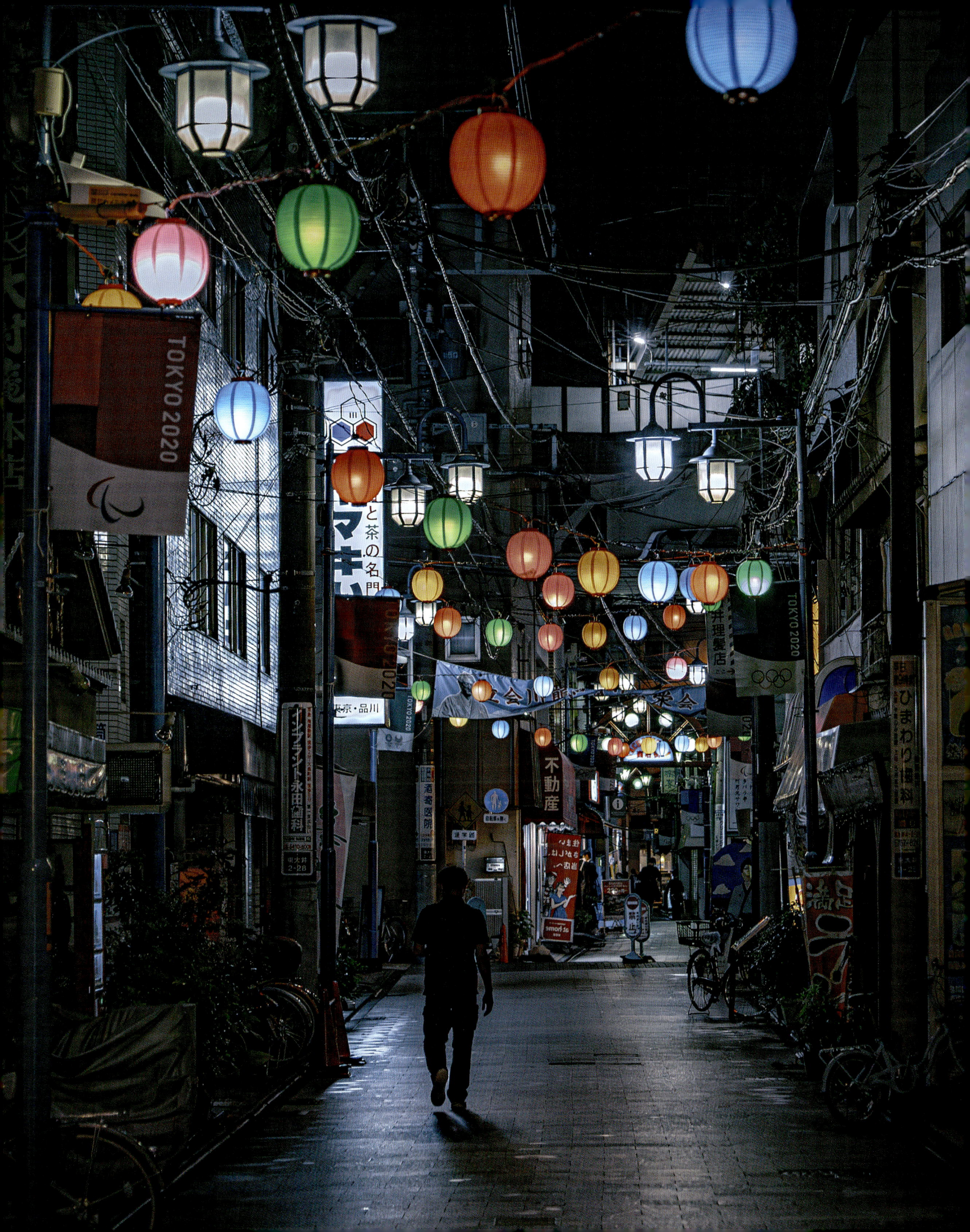

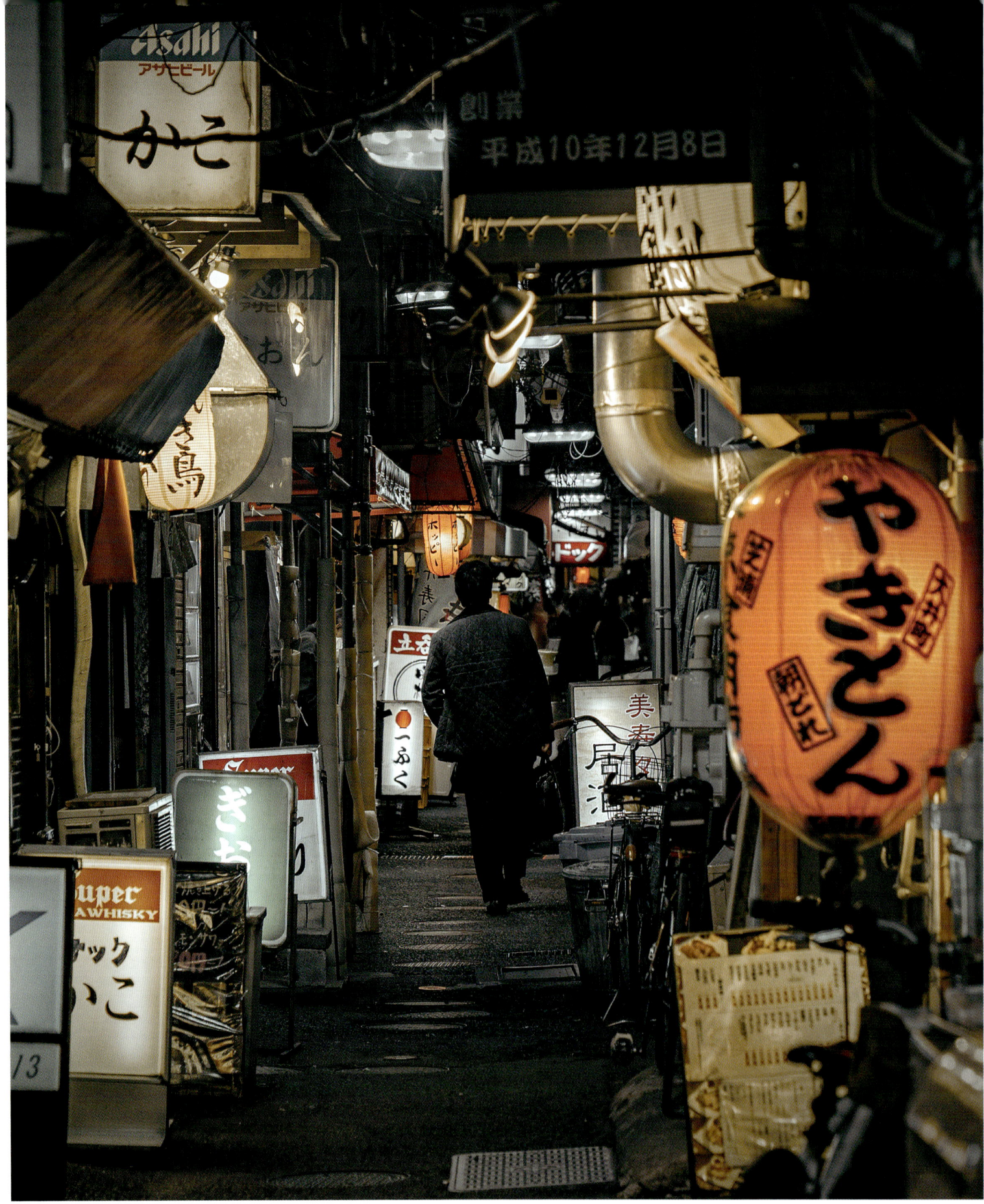

Higashi-koji Restaurant District 1. Oimachi, Tokyo. In this modernized station area, this section has been left behind, with buildings reminiscent of the postwar black market. Small stores line the narrow alleys, stretching from east to west.

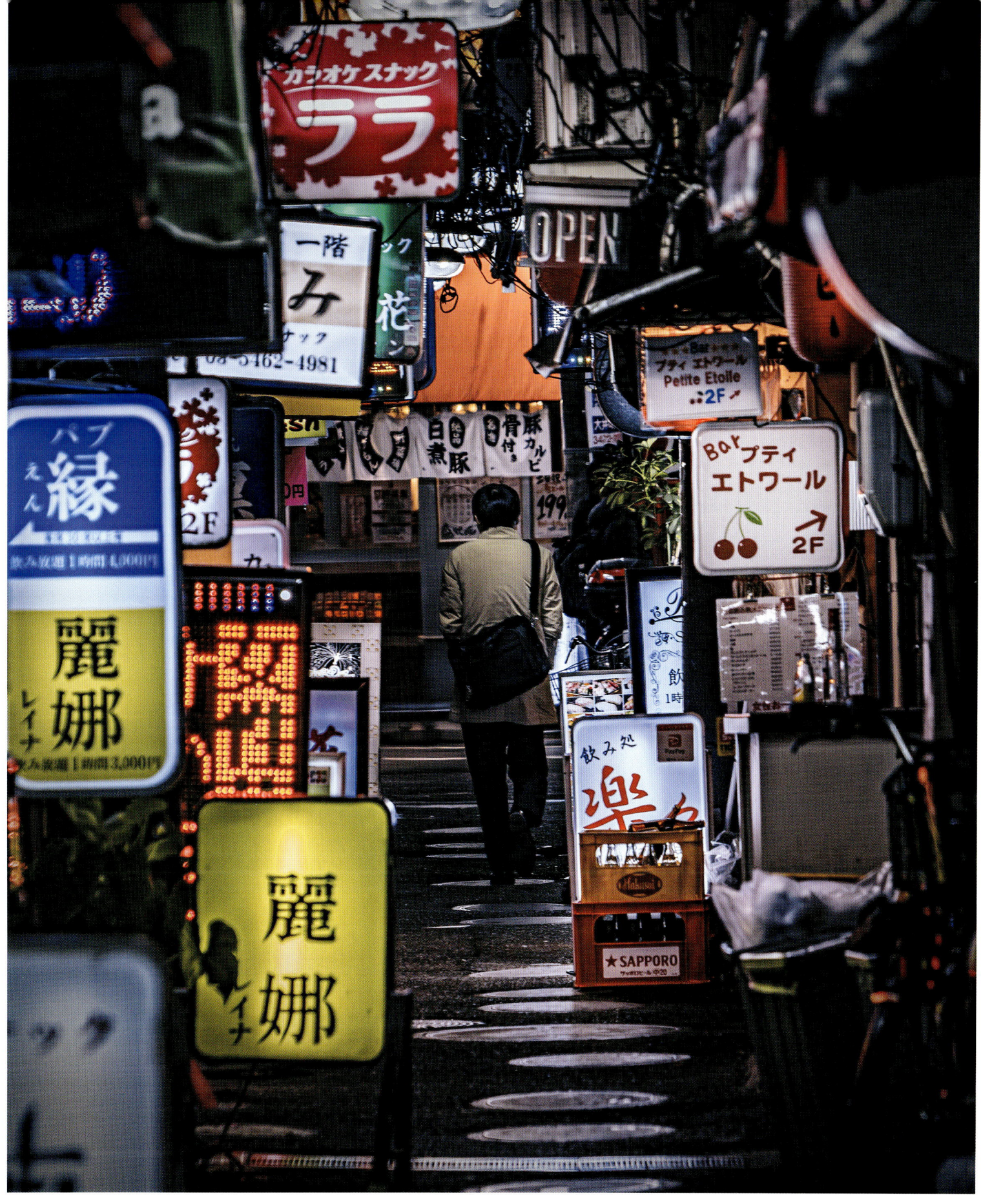

Higashi-koji Restaurant District 2. Oimachi,
Tokyo. This narrow alley is about one hundred
meters long and lined with restaurants.

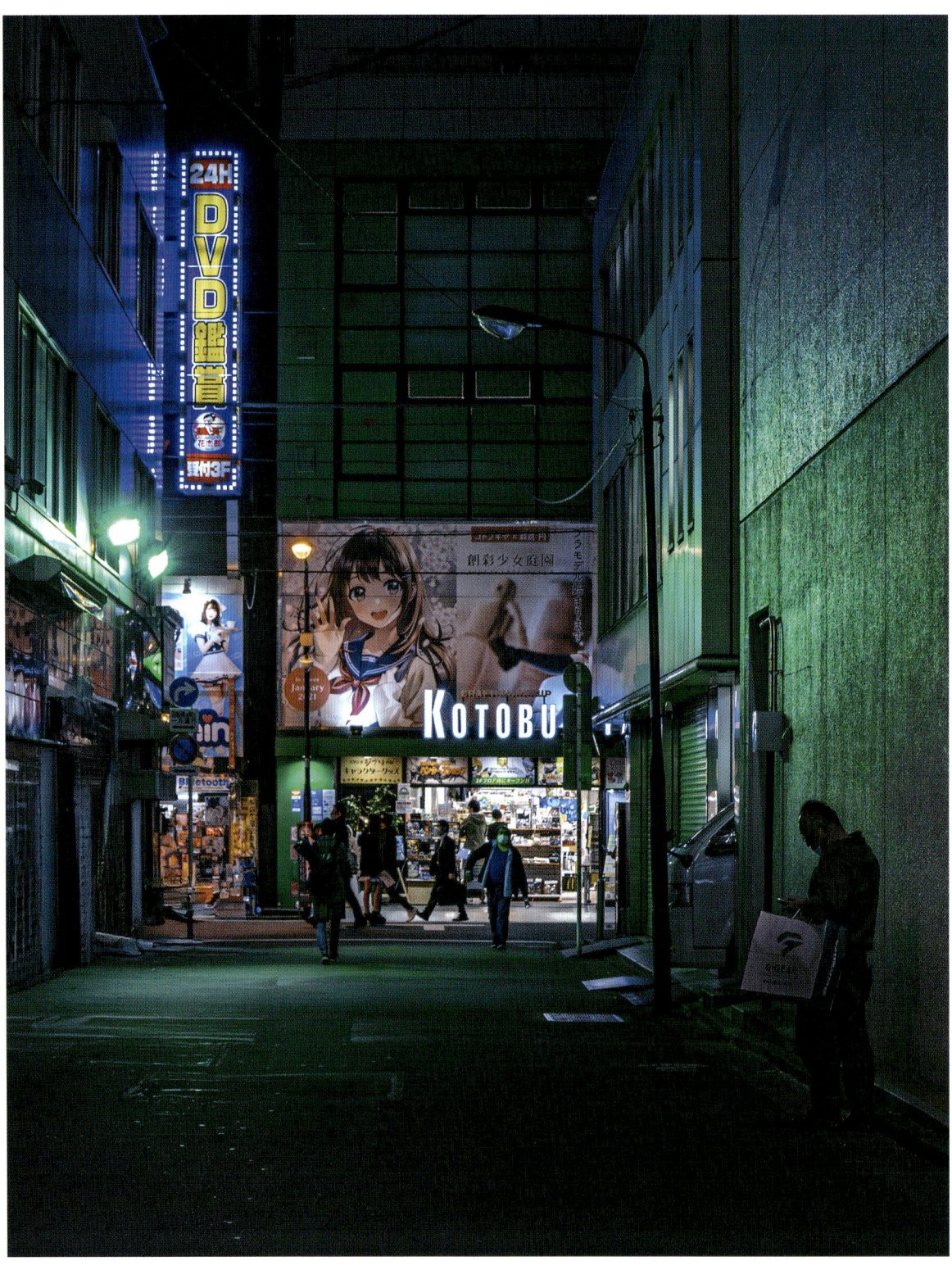

Green Alley. Akihabara, Tokyo. This alley has beautiful green light. The store at the end of the street is an anime character figure store and maid café.

Cyberpunk World. Akihabara, Tokyo. The bustling, neon streets of Akihabara spread out below the railroad tracks.

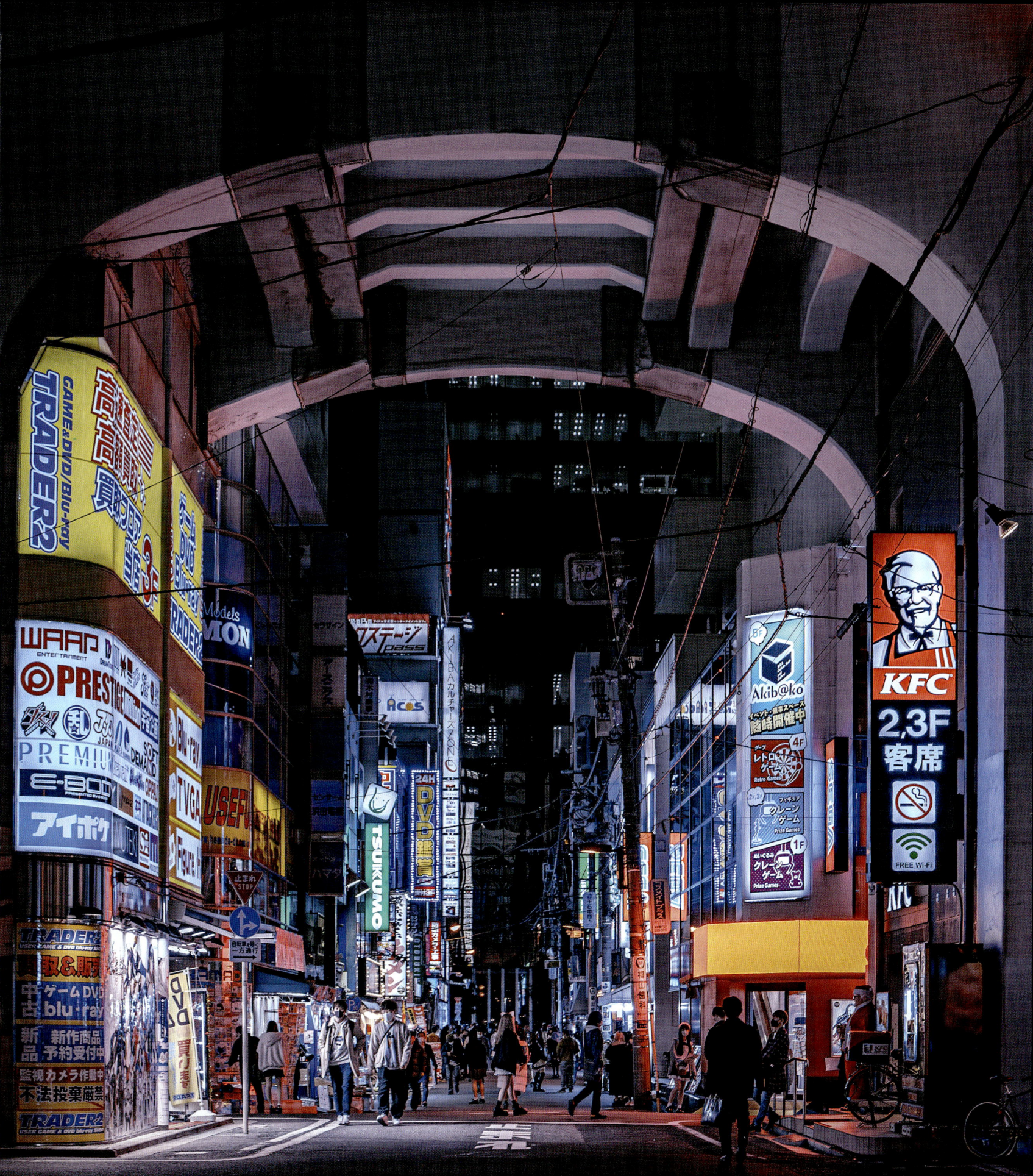

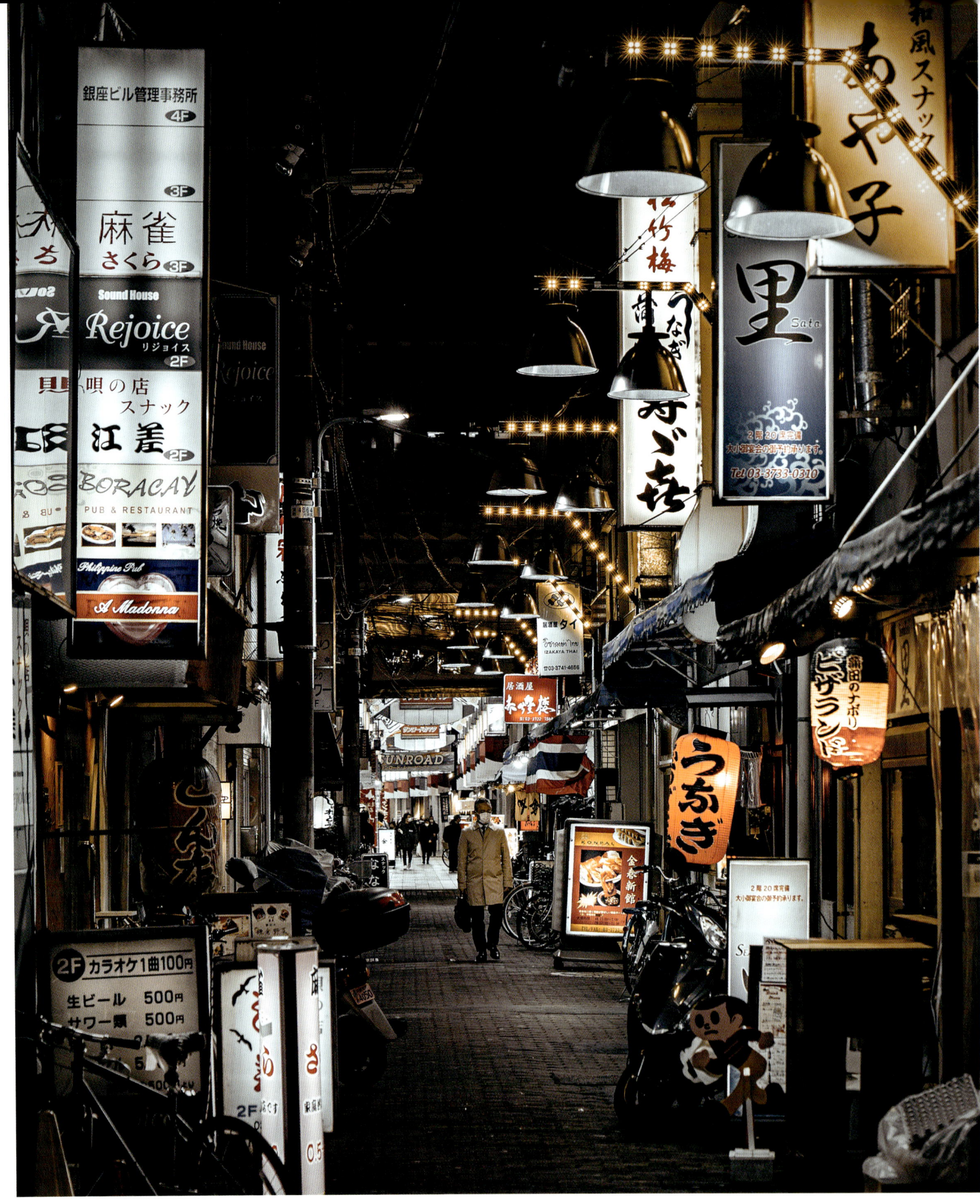

Long Shopping Street. Kamata, Tokyo.
After you exit this arcade, another street
continues on and on.

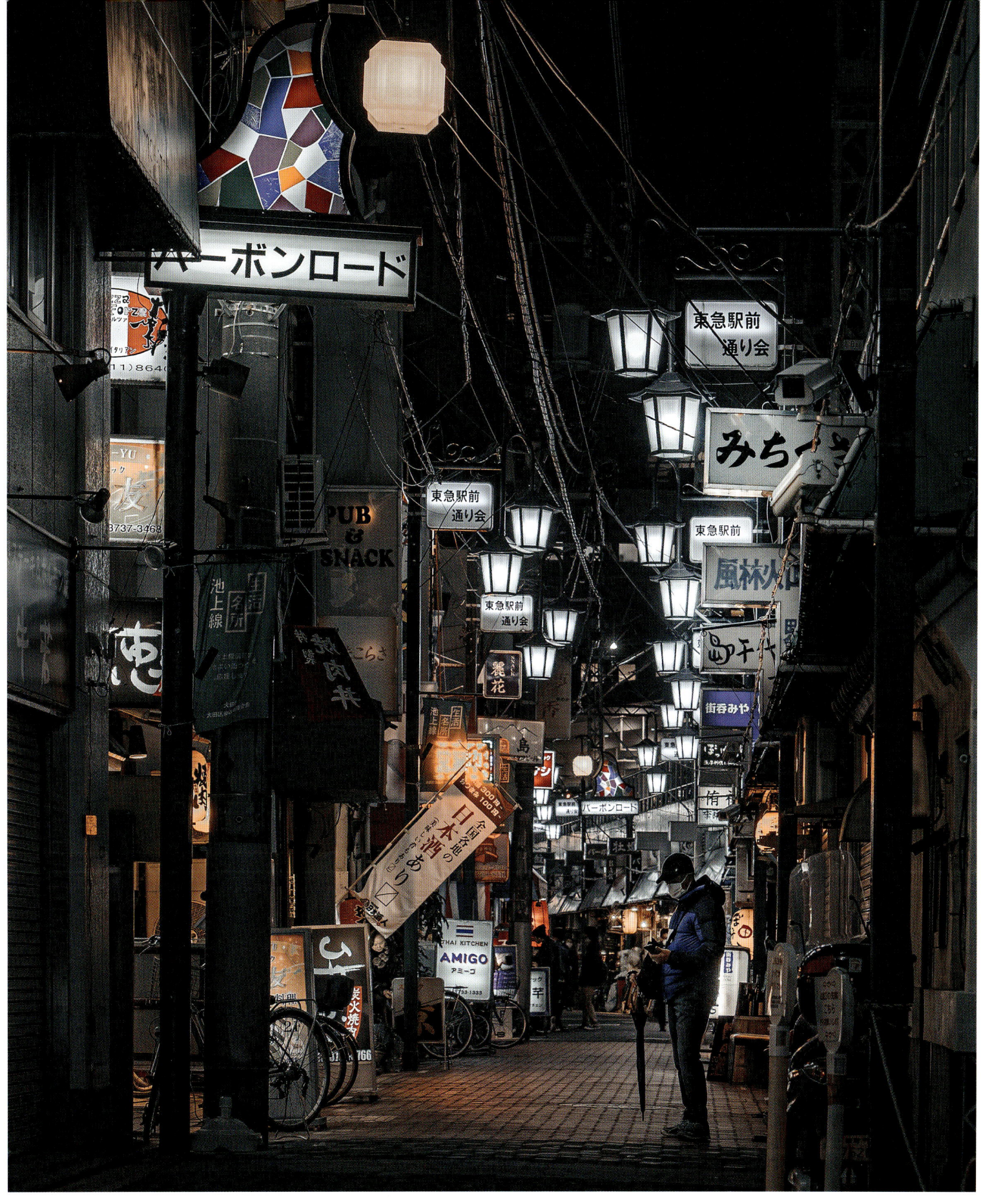

Bourbon Street at Night. Kamata, Tokyo.
When the streetlights are on, this alley
transforms into a charming place.

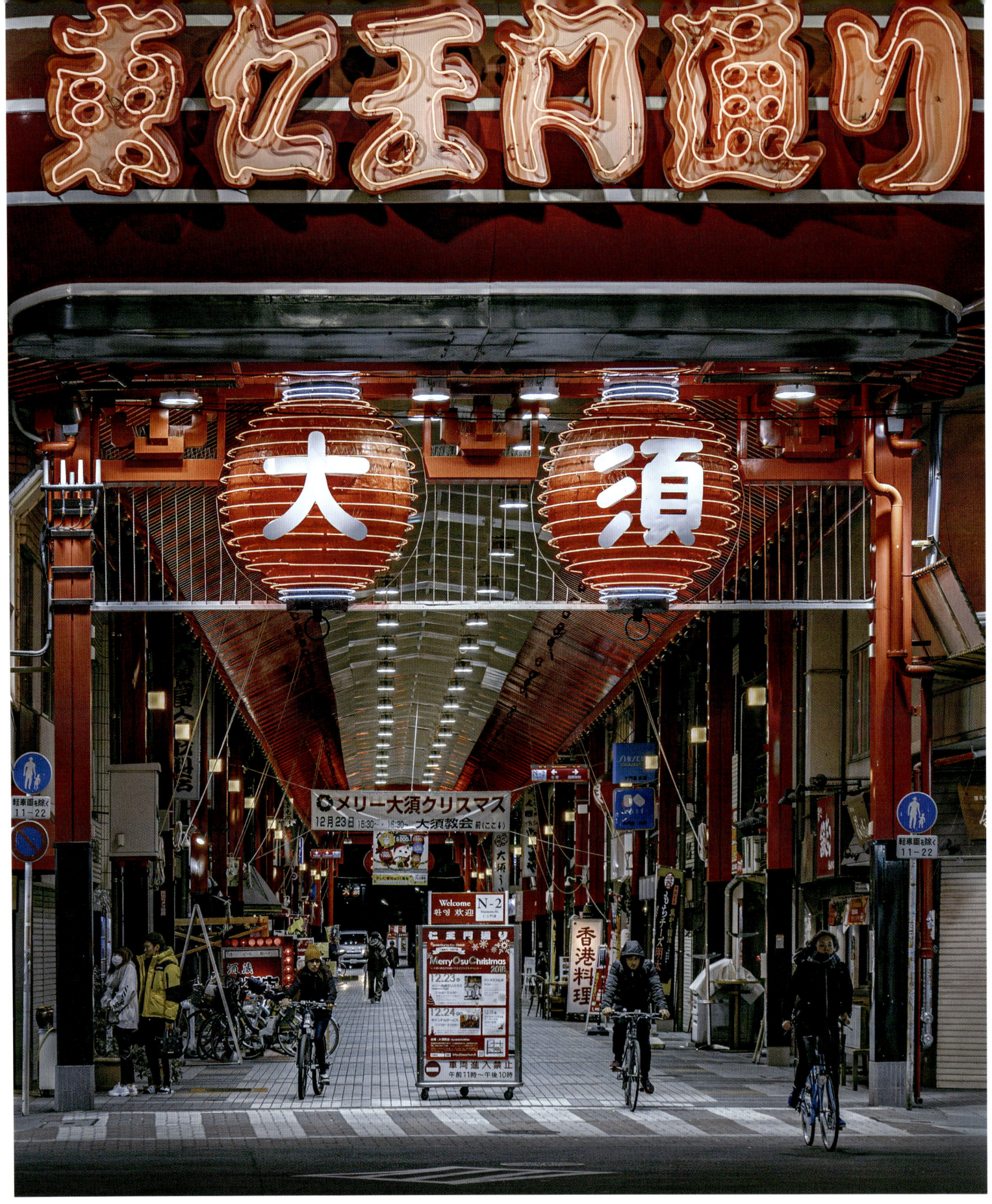

Osu Higashi Niomon Street. Kamimaezu, Nagoya. Although this is a Japanese-style shopping street, it surprisingly has an area with a concentration of international cuisine, attracting foreigners, such as Turks, Brazilians, Vietnamese, and Indians, in search of local delicacies.

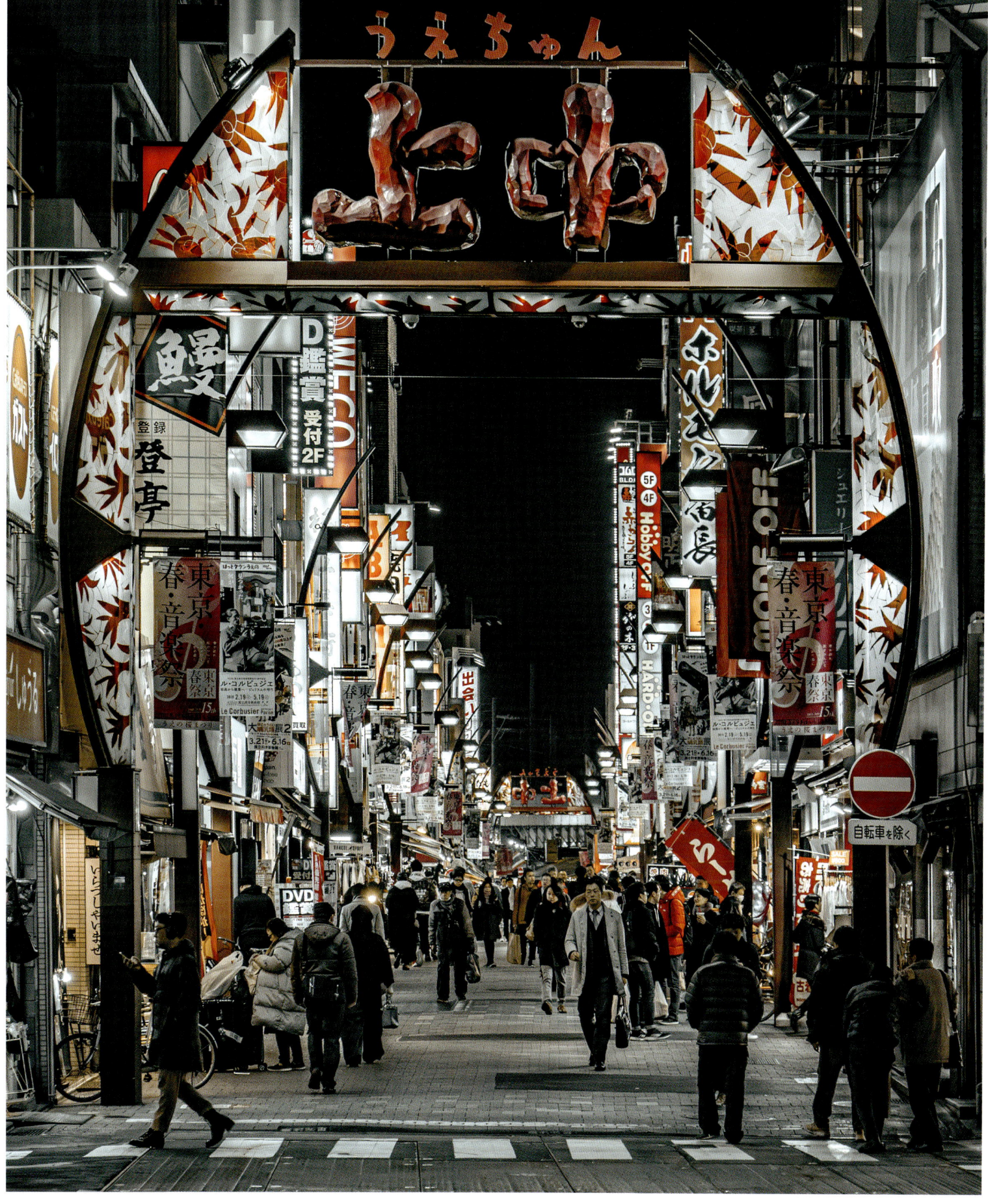

Ueno Naka-dori Shopping Street. Ueno, Tokyo. The Ameya Yokocho shopping district is also known as Uechun, and it is said that stores began to be established here around the beginning of the Edo period.

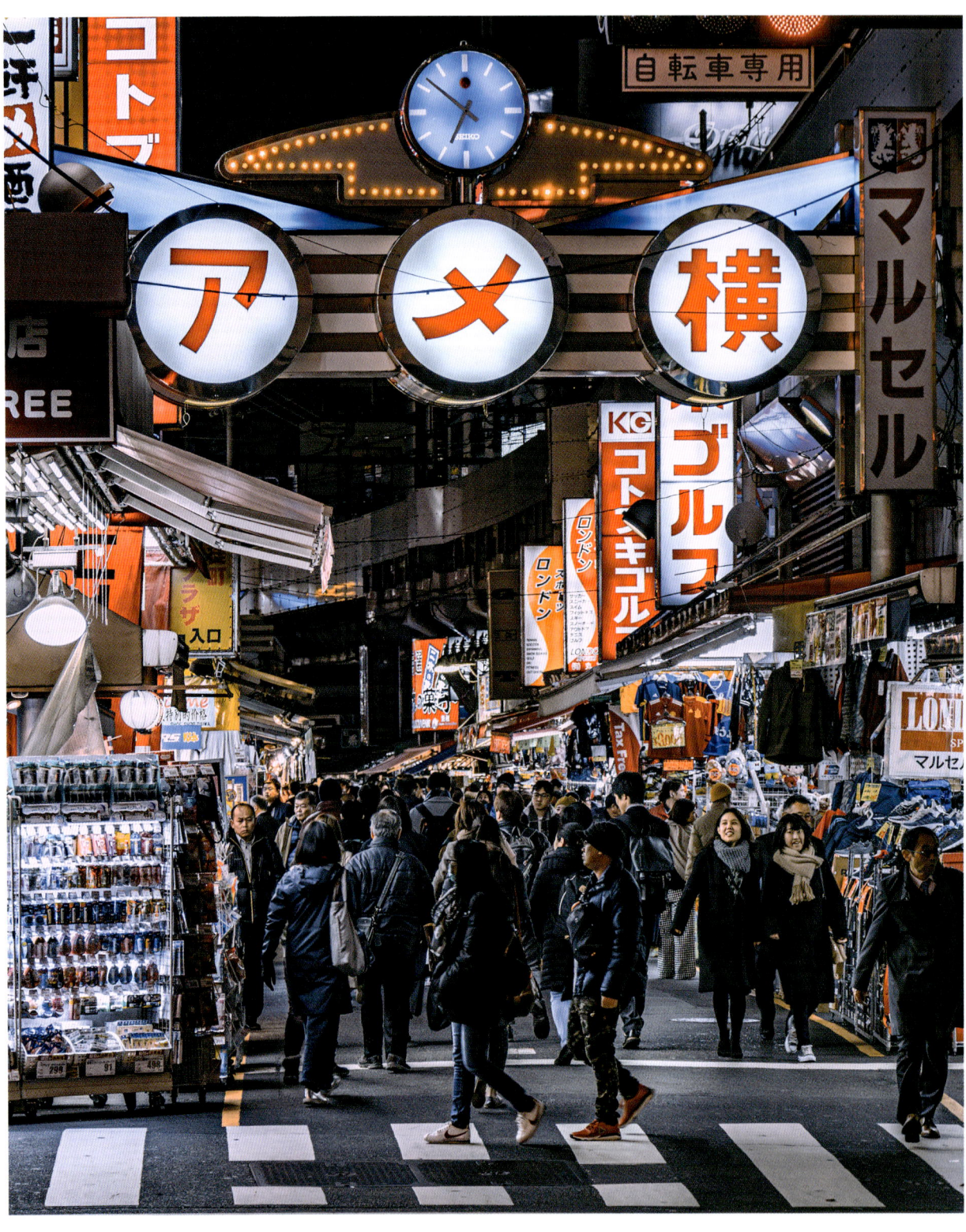

Ameyoko Gate at Night. Ueno, Tokyo. The gate at the entrance to this shopping district is the symbol of Ameyoko. It welcomes the many shoppers who visit this lively street.

Dining District. Ueno, Tokyo. The bustling Ameya Yokocho shopping district also has a vibrant dining scene.

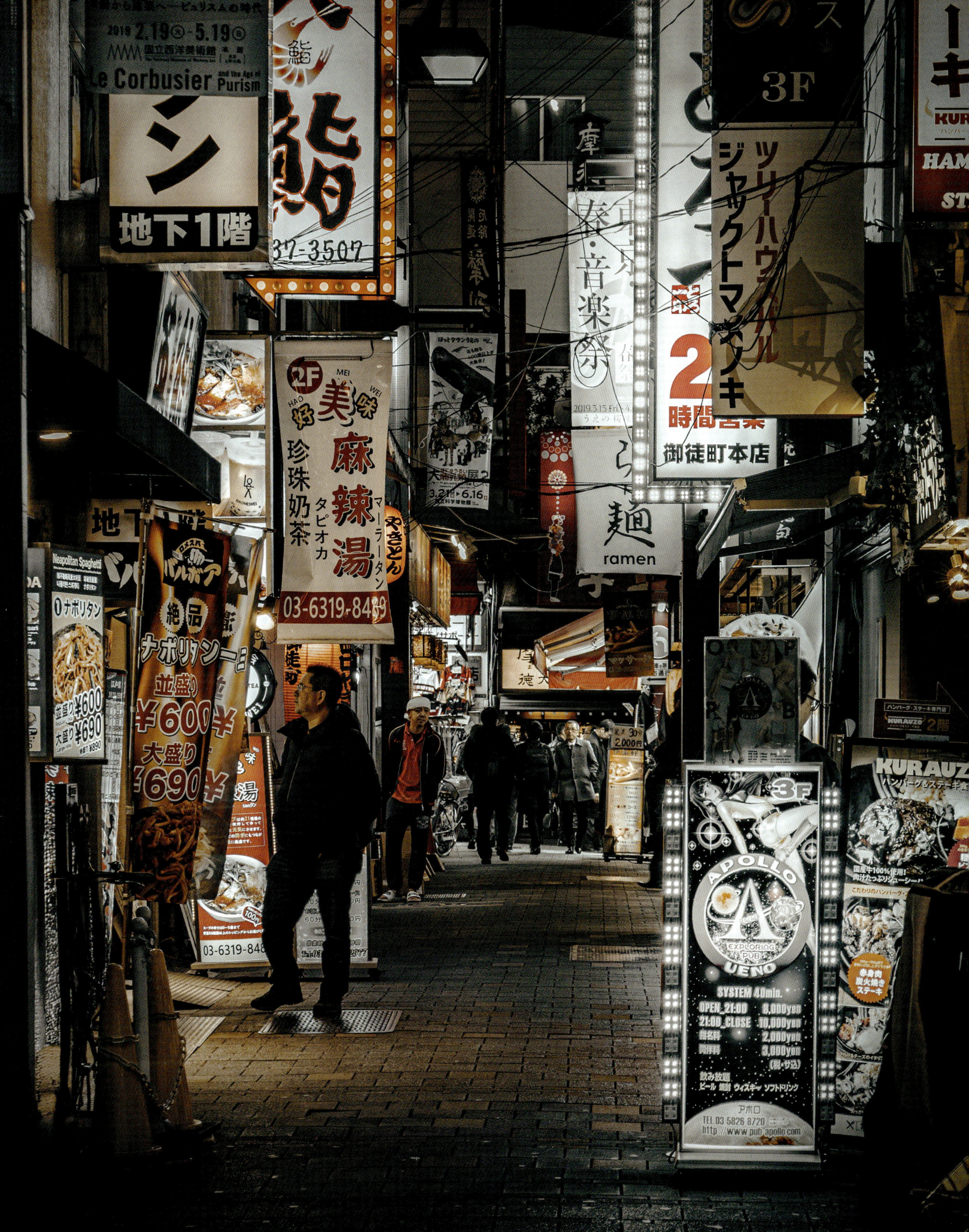

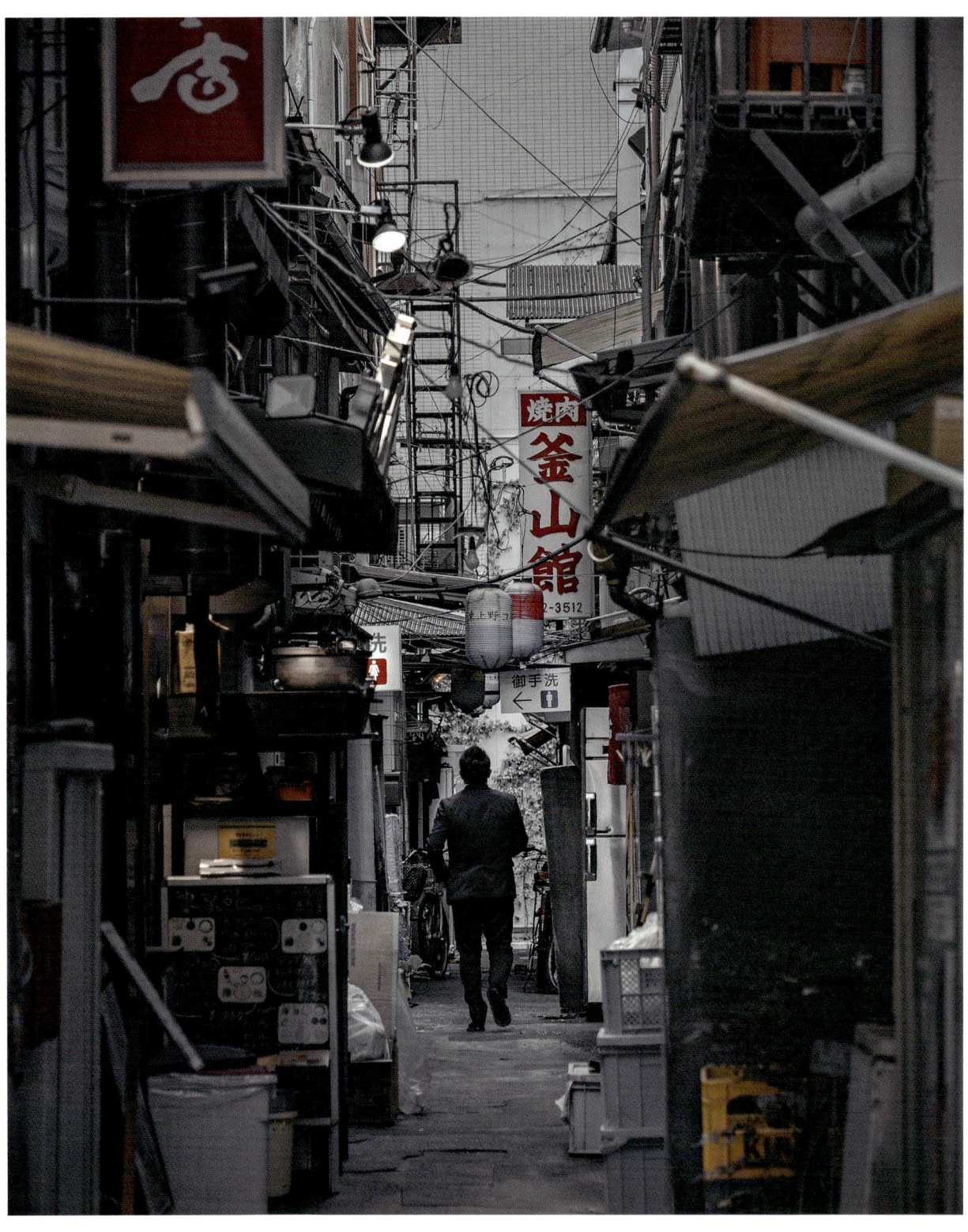

Higashi-Ueno Koreantown. Ueno, Tokyo. This is Tokyo's oldest Koreantown, which has existed since 1948. Otsuka also has a Koreantown, but this one is not concerned with fads and has retained its old-fashioned appearance.

Alley by the Railroad Tracks. Ueno, Tokyo. This alley is below the railroad tracks near Ueno Station. You can't see the end because of the curve, but it continues all the way back.

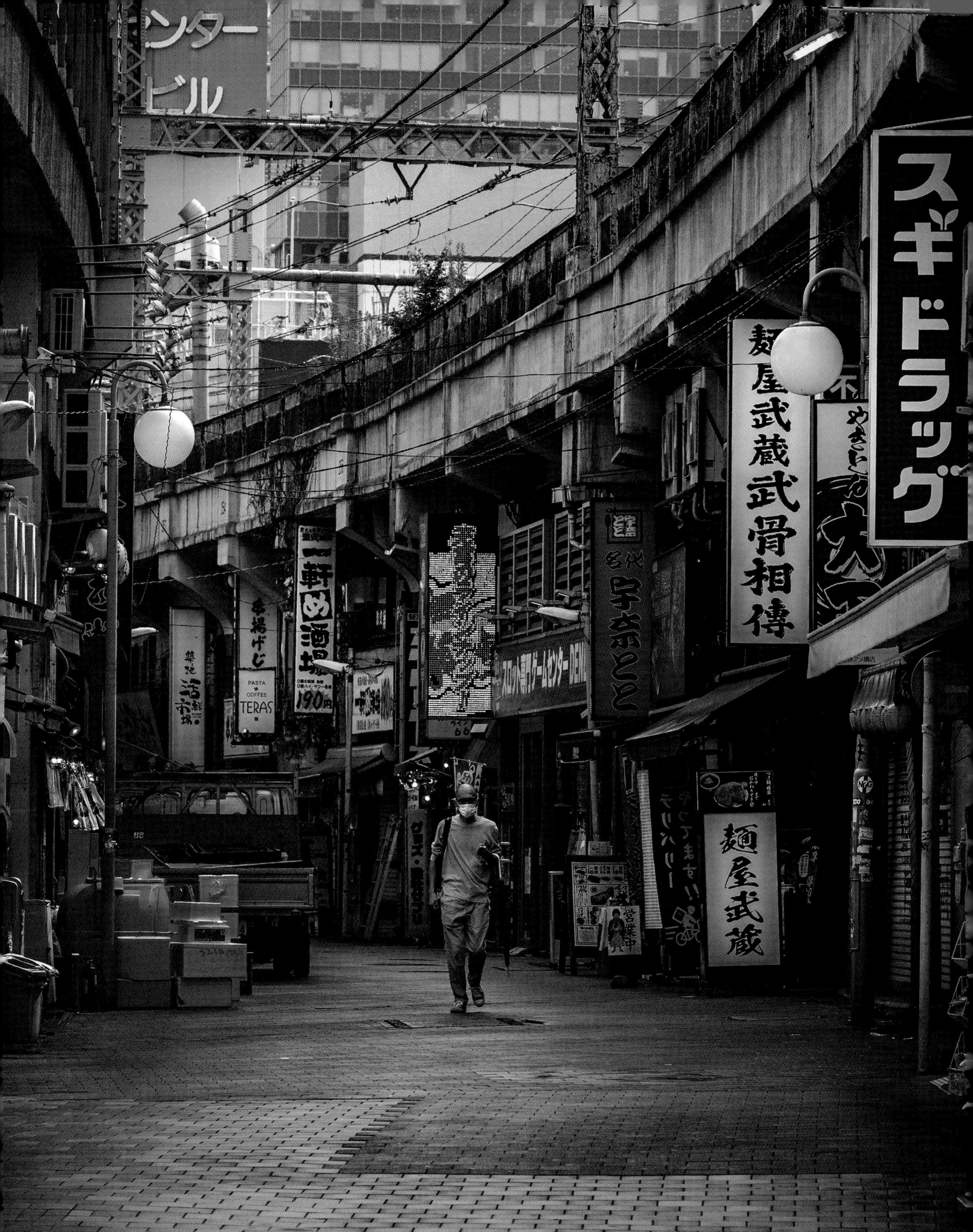

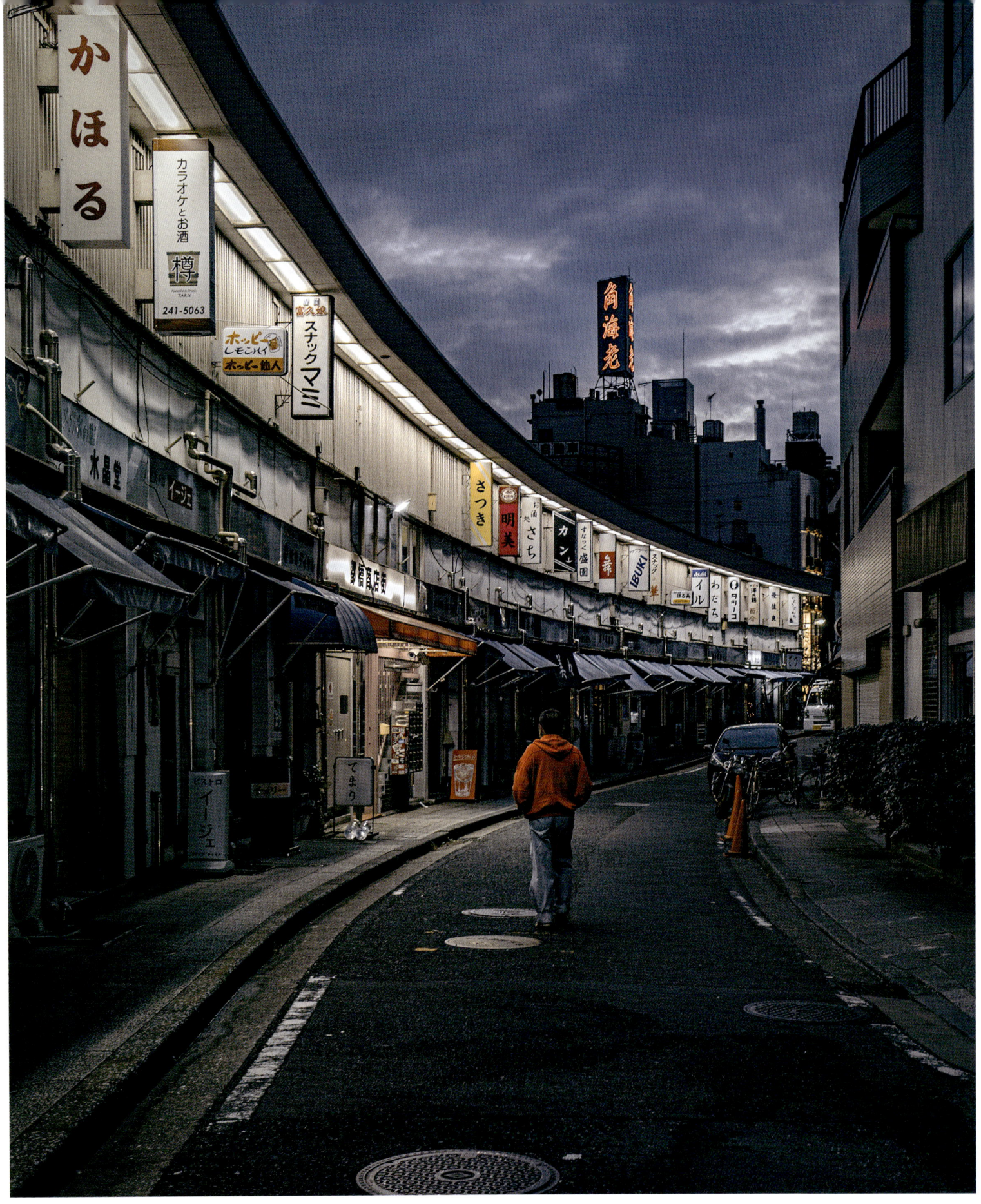

Miyakobashi Shopping Street. Noge, Yokohama. Inside this two-story building that curves along the river are more than sixty stores, including traditional snack and karaoke bars that become crowded in the evening.

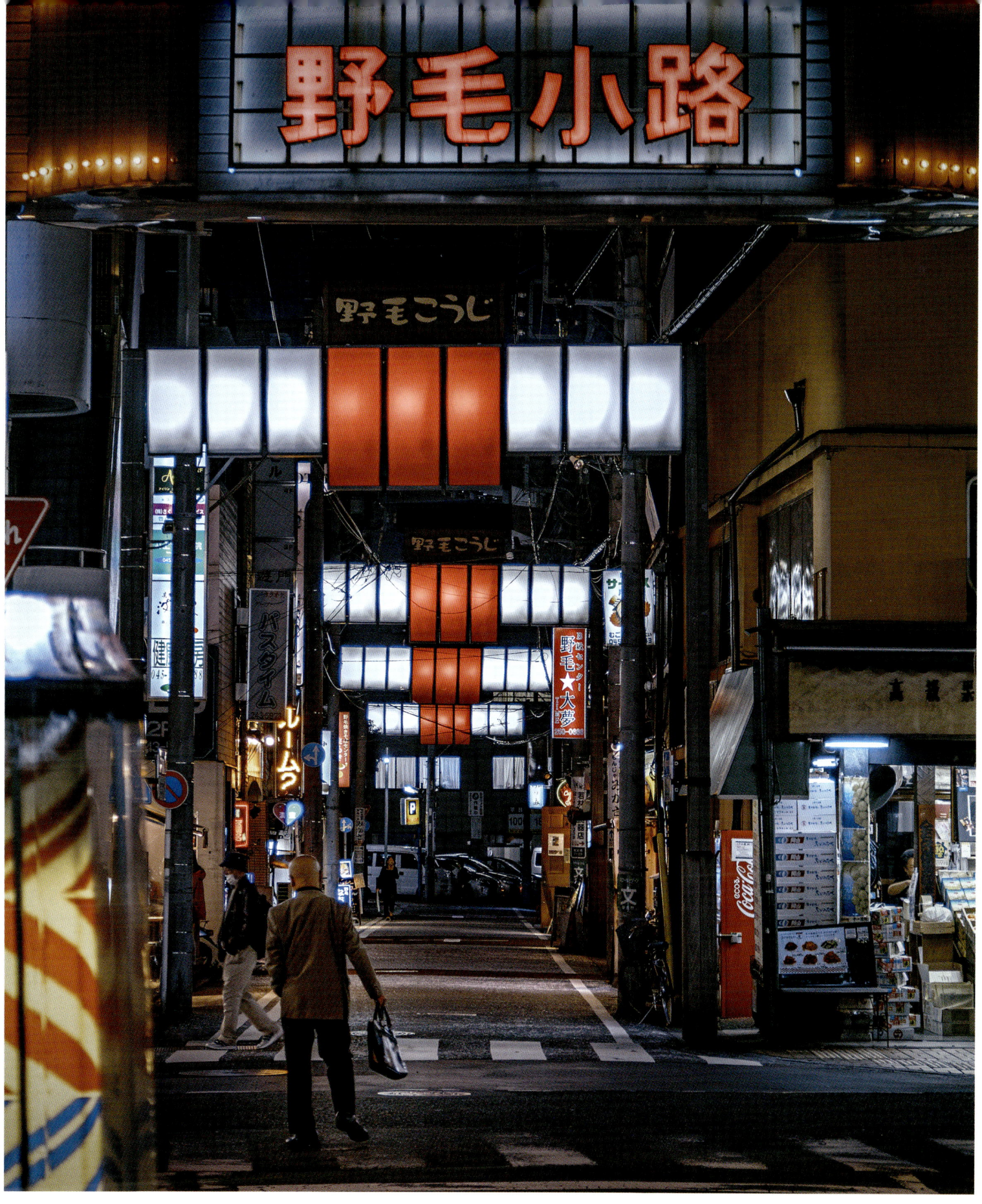

Noge Alley. Noge, Yokohama. Noge, Yokohama's premier drinking district, is a melting pot of food and drink. Numerous izakaya are concentrated in a small area, and once here, you will not be satisfied with just one place but will be tempted to visit a number of these curious spots.

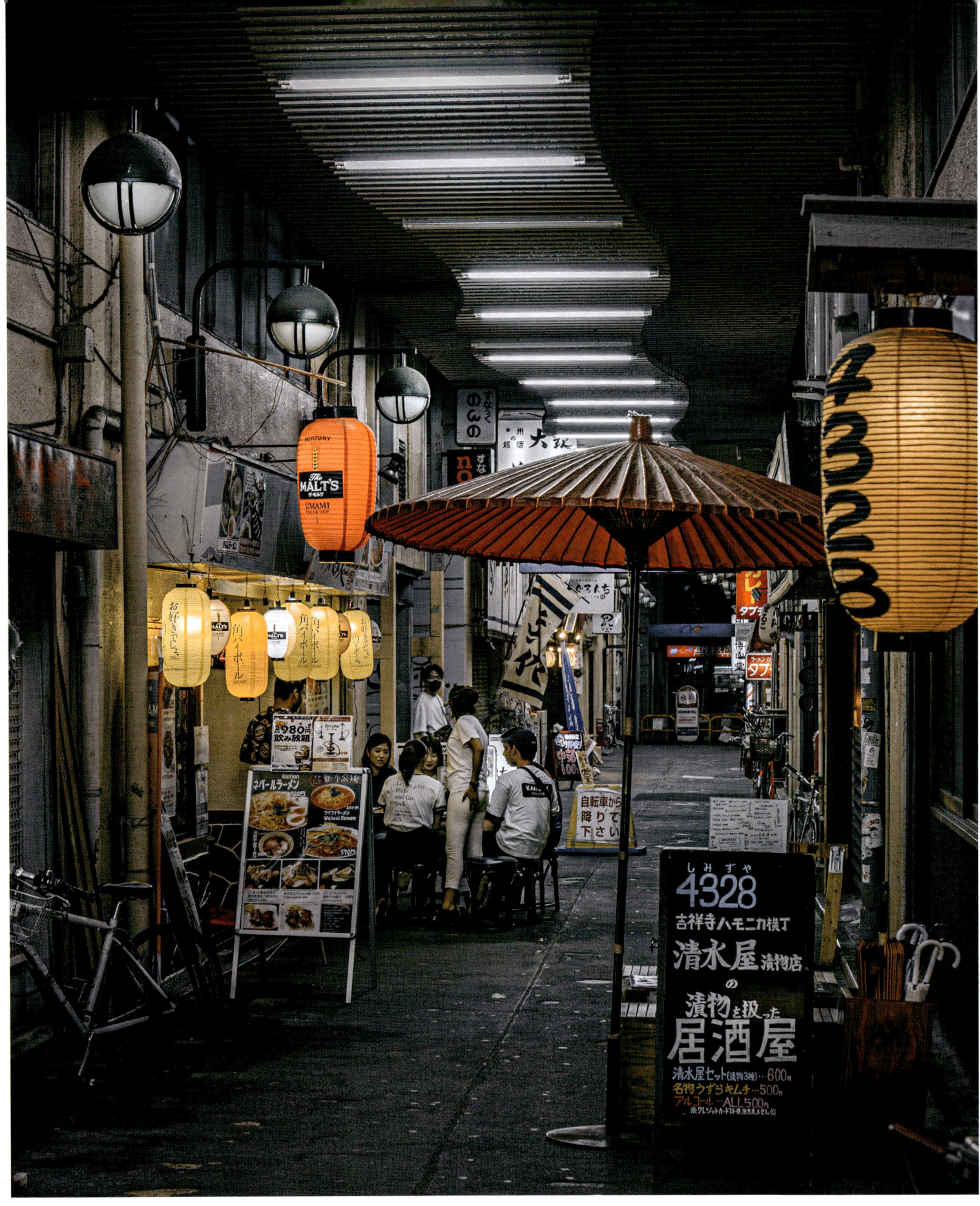

Koenji Street. Koenji, Tokyo. This izakaya is highlighted by the impressive light fixture, which looks like a flowing river.

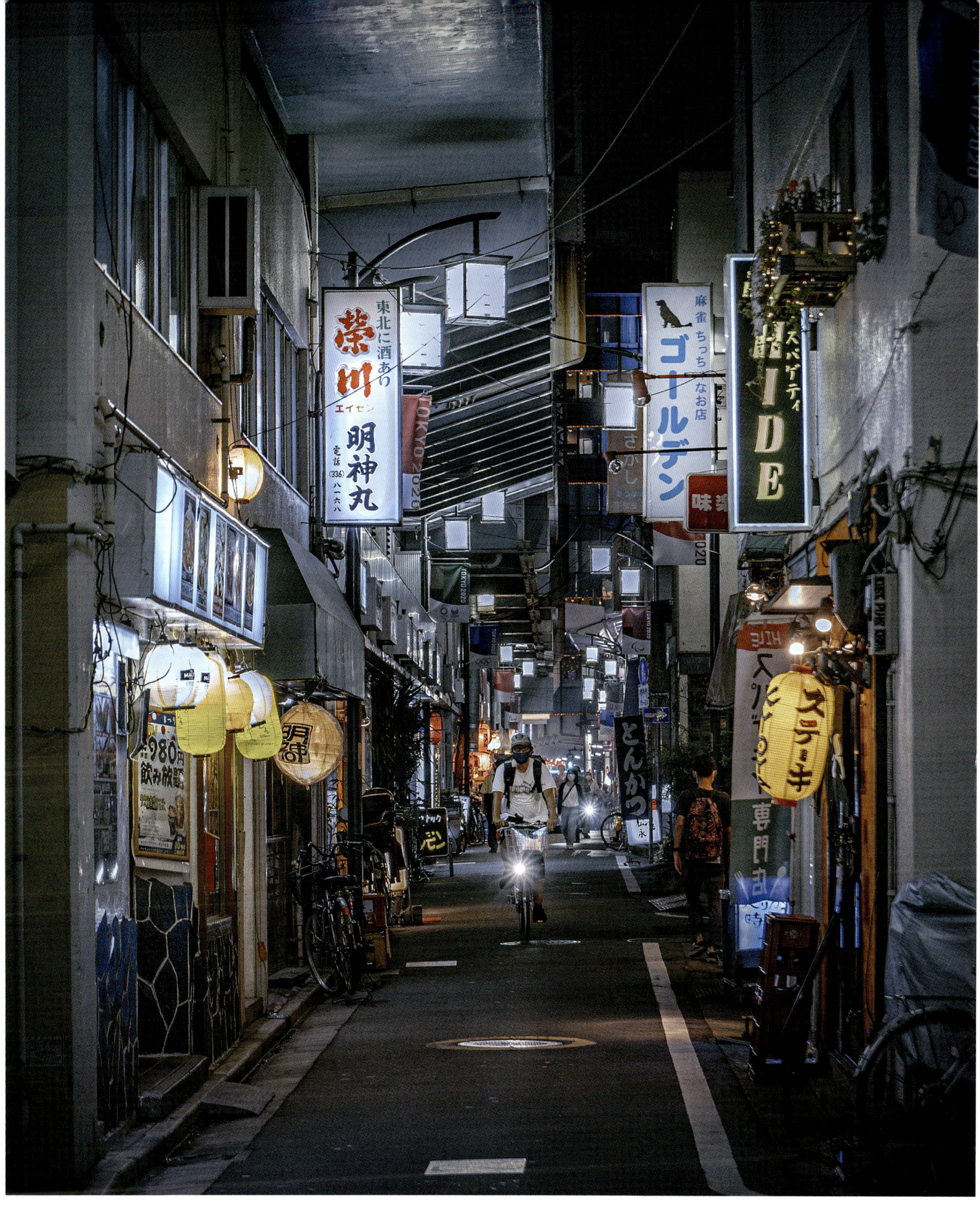

Under-the-Tracks Izakaya. Koenji, Tokyo.
Izakaya lined up under railroad tracks, like
here, is not uncommon in Japan.

Izakaya as Rain Shelter. Sangenjaya, Tokyo.
This is one of my favorite alleys found in the
untouched Triangle Zone. I hope it remains as
it is forever.

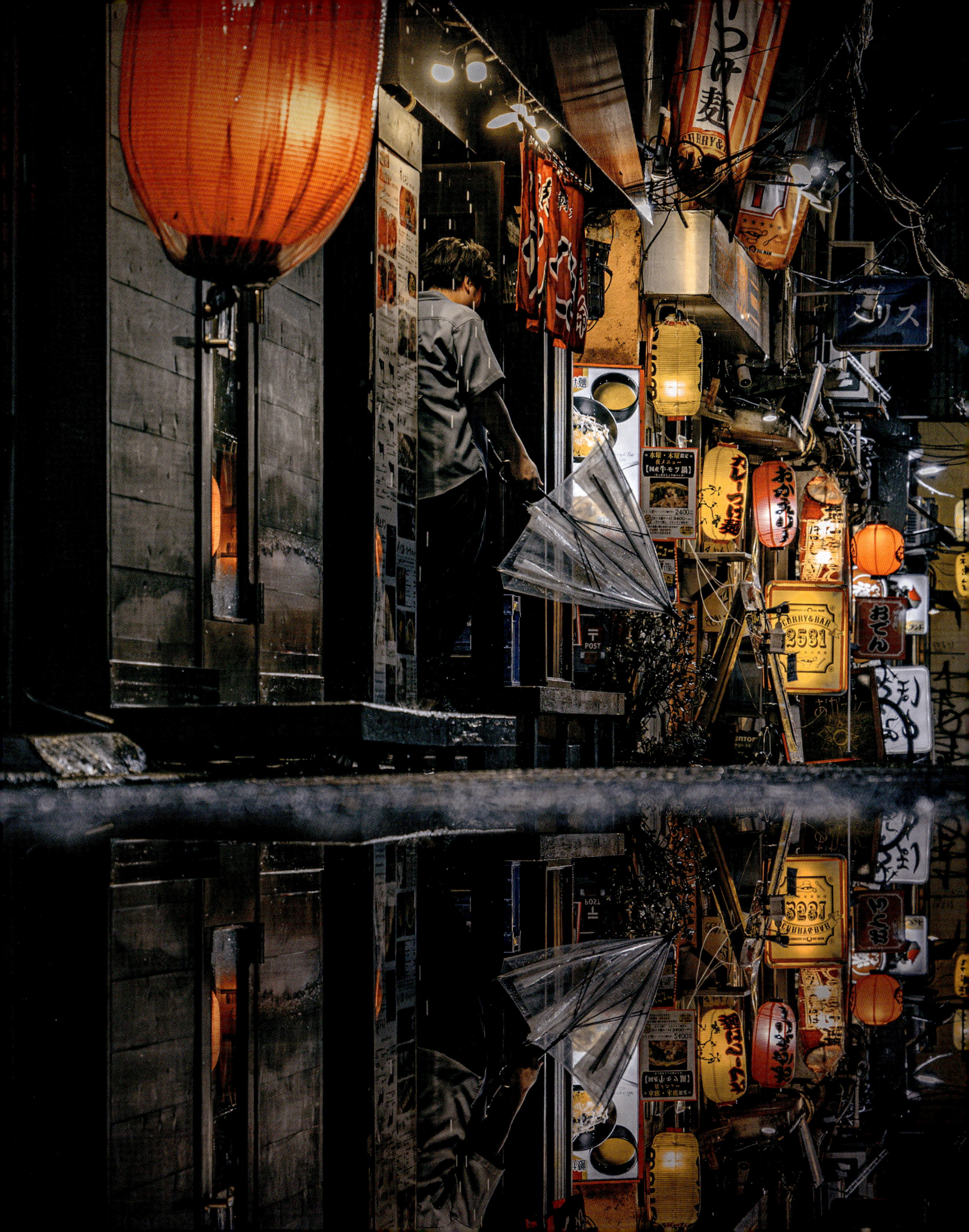

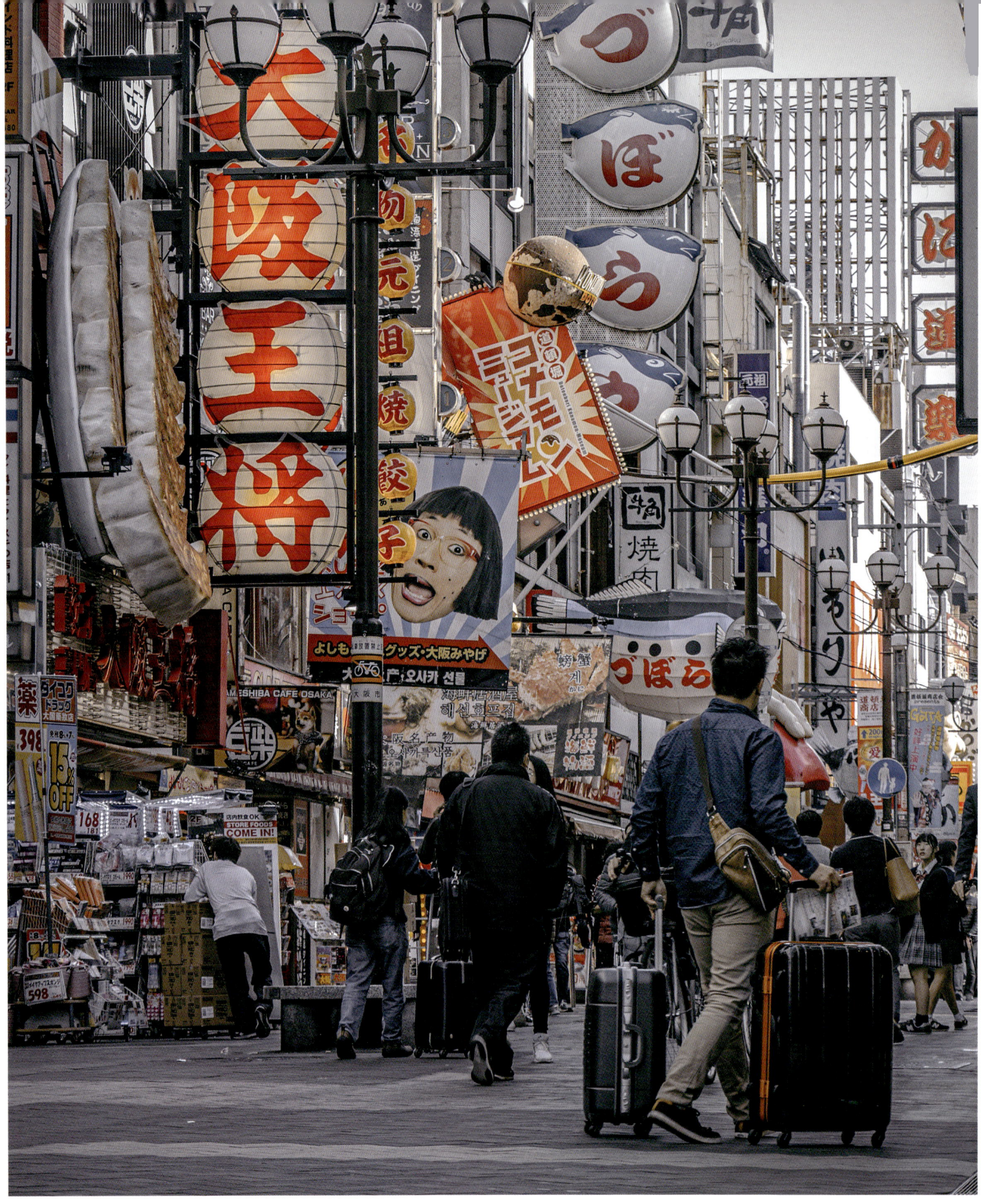

Vibrant Dotonbori. Namba, Osaka. Osaka is famous for its food, and many tourists visit Namba for its food culture. One of the most unique features of restaurants here are the huge three-dimensional signs featuring giant crabs, octopuses, dumplings, and more. The blowfish restaurant in the center of the photo is now closed.

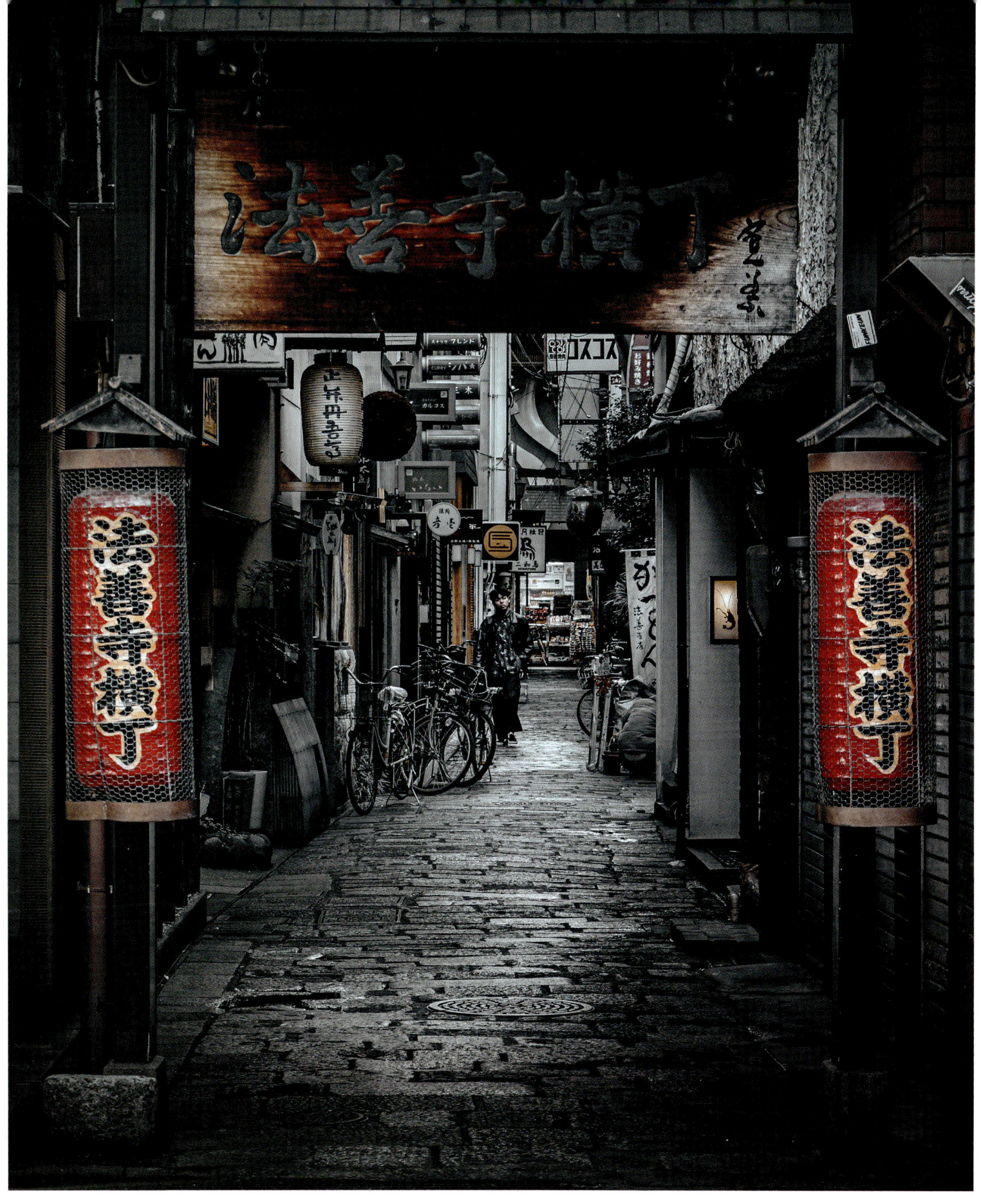

Hozenji Yokocho. Namba, Osaka. Though Hozenji Yokocho is located in the bustling downtown section of Minami, it has a serene atmosphere. This area originally was the grounds of a temple.

Nanchi Nakasuji Shopping Street. Namba, Osaka. Nicknamed Nannaka, this shopping street is approximately 160 meters long and begins just outside of Namba Station.

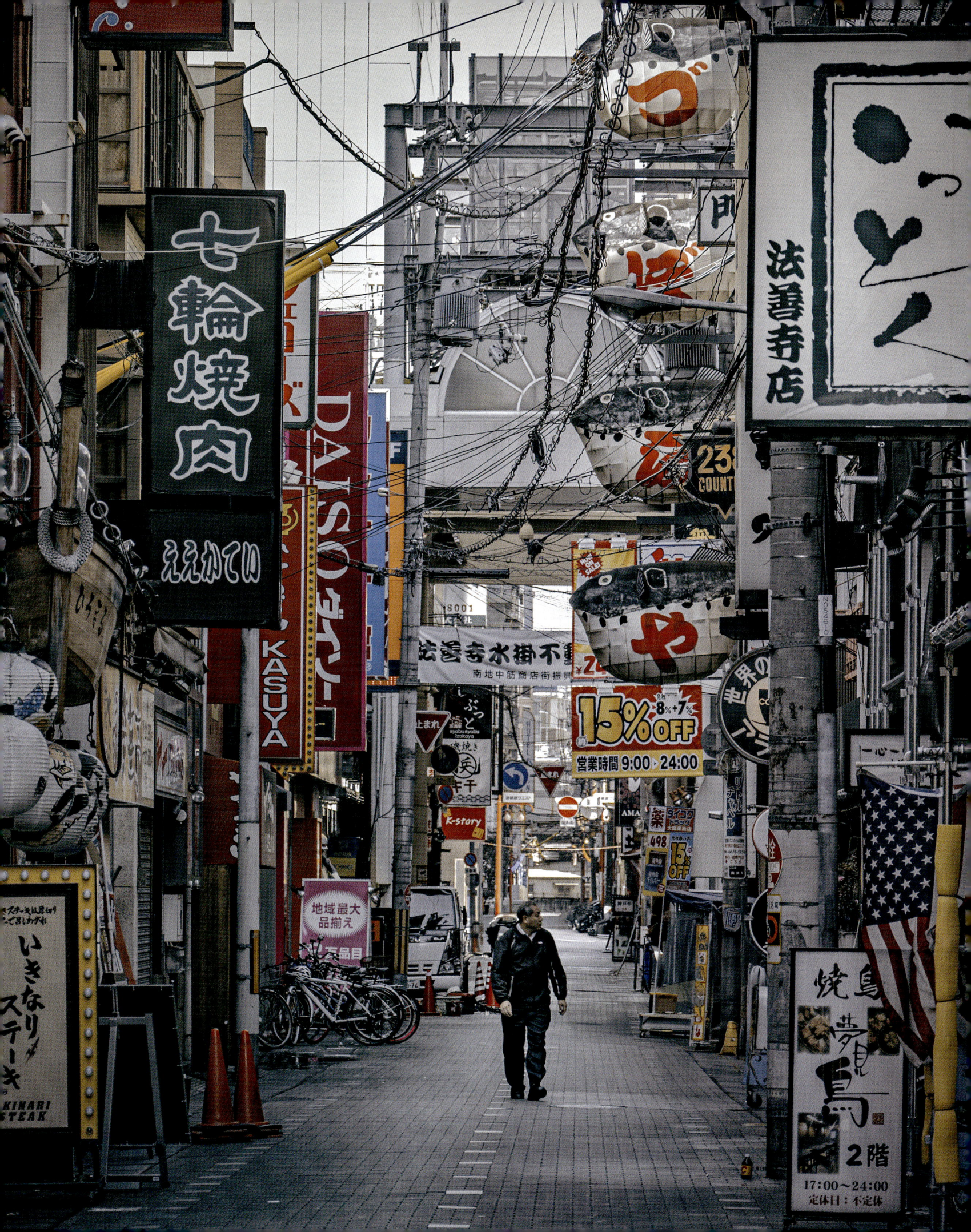

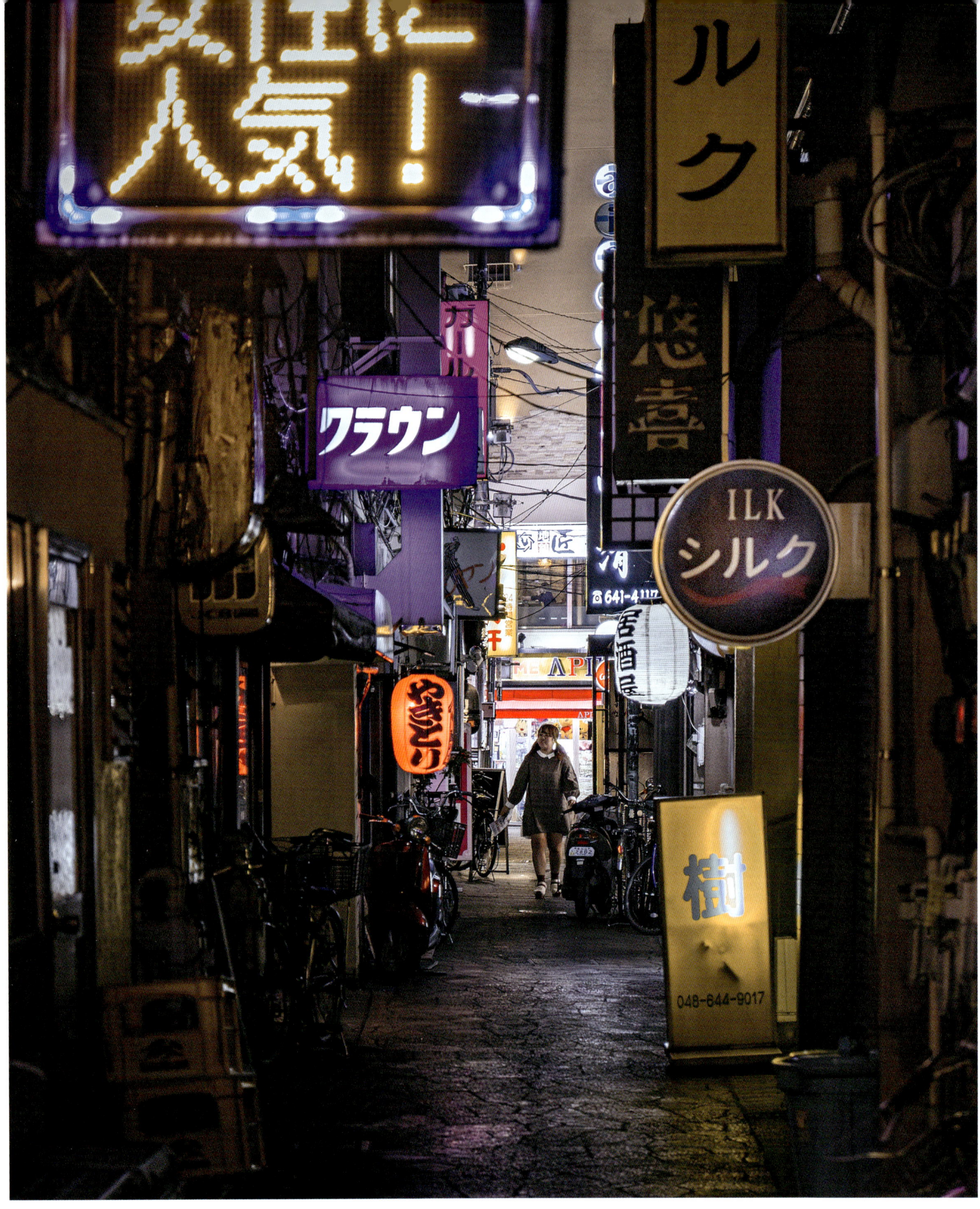

Alley in Nakamachi. Omiya, Saitama. A little south of the east exit of Omiya Station, there is this nice alleyway that intersects with the train station. It is a place that has retained a tasteful, nostalgic atmosphere.

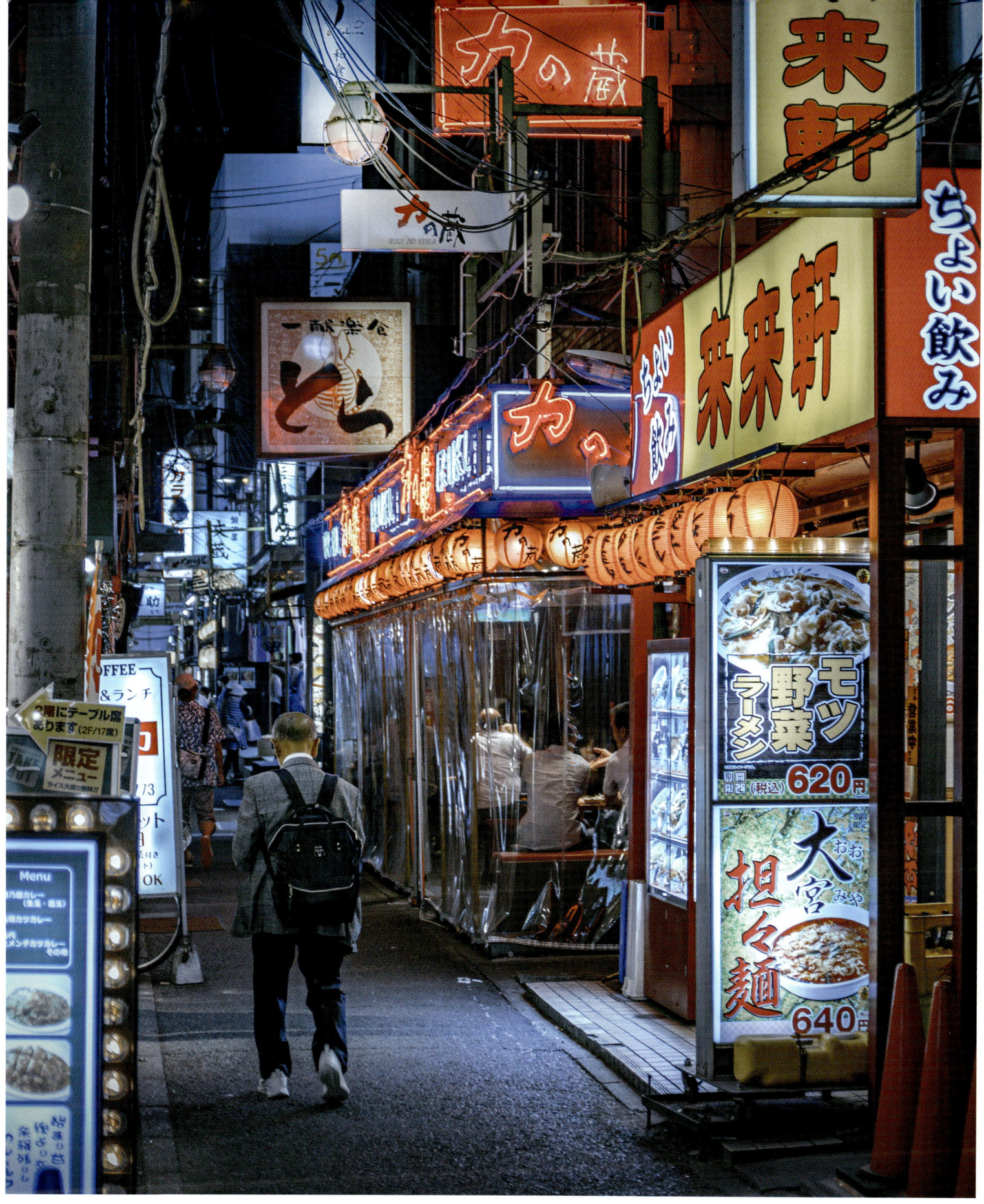

Minami Ginza. Omiya, Saitama. Commonly known as the Nangin Restaurant District, this area has lots of small stores and tenant buildings that line the narrow, old-fashioned alleys.

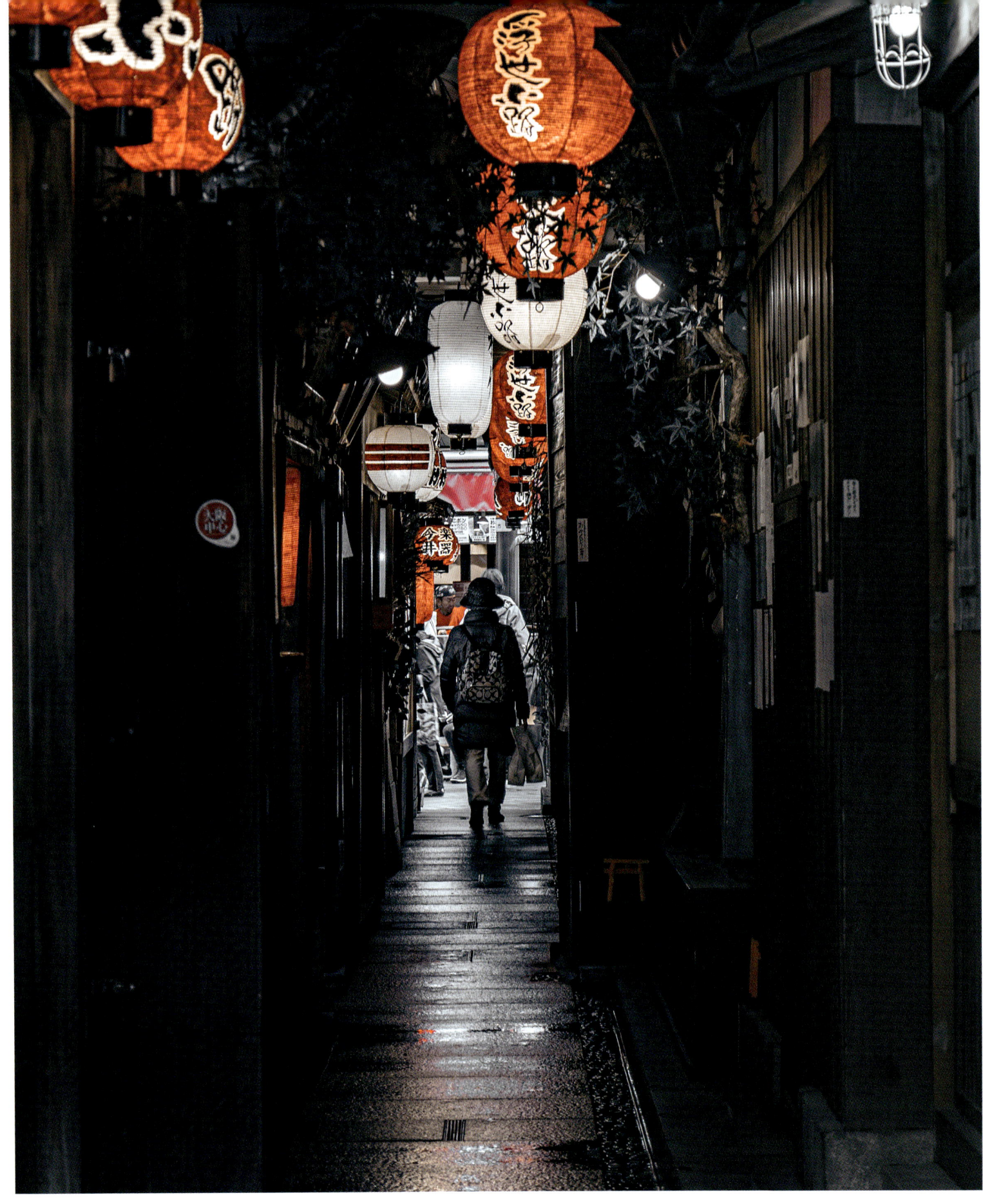

Ukiyo Koji. Namba, Osaka. This small,
inconspicuous alley is next to a ramen
restaurant famous for its dragon sculpture.

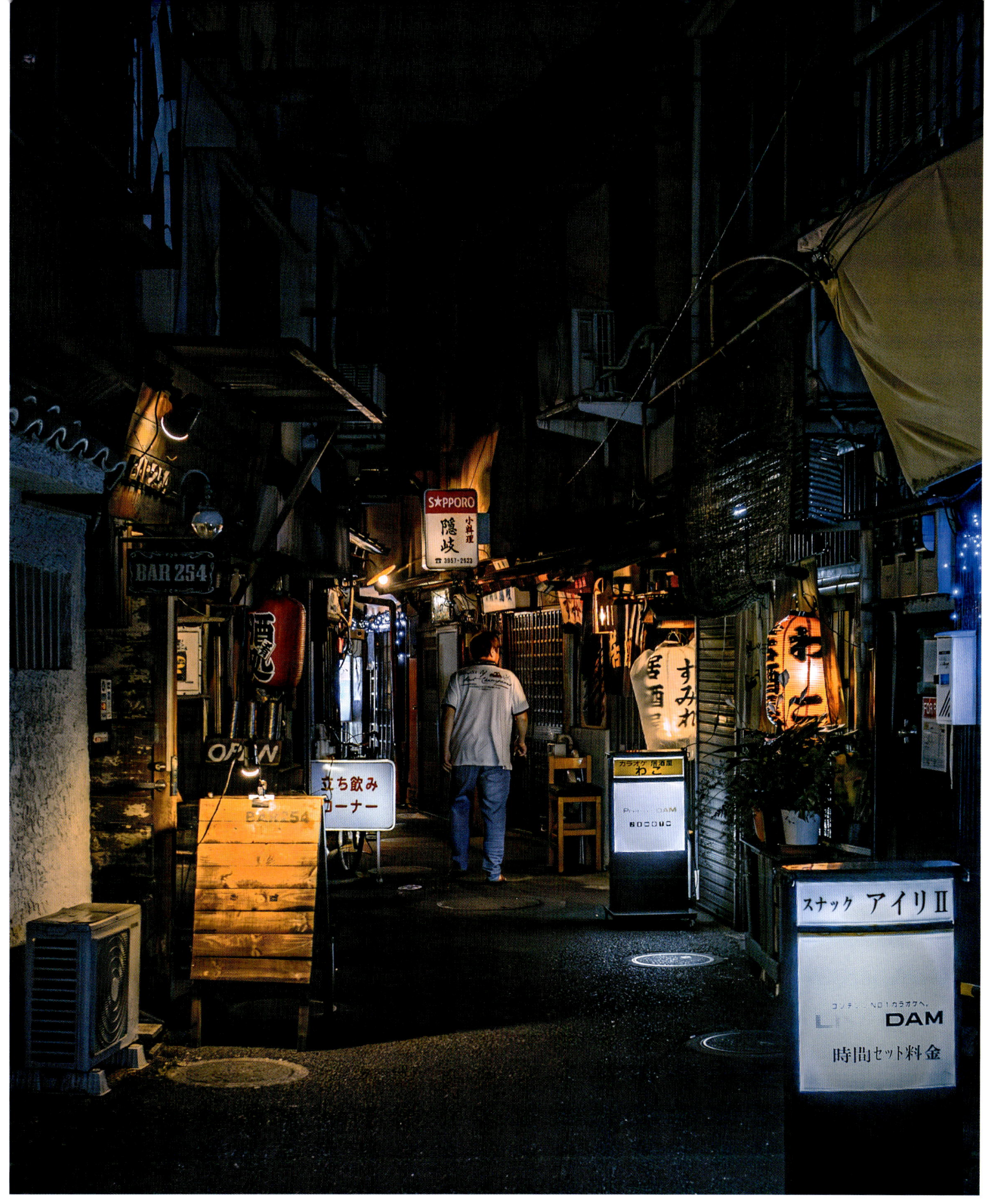

Dead End. Oyama. This is an unusual alleyway where the path gets narrower the deeper you go.

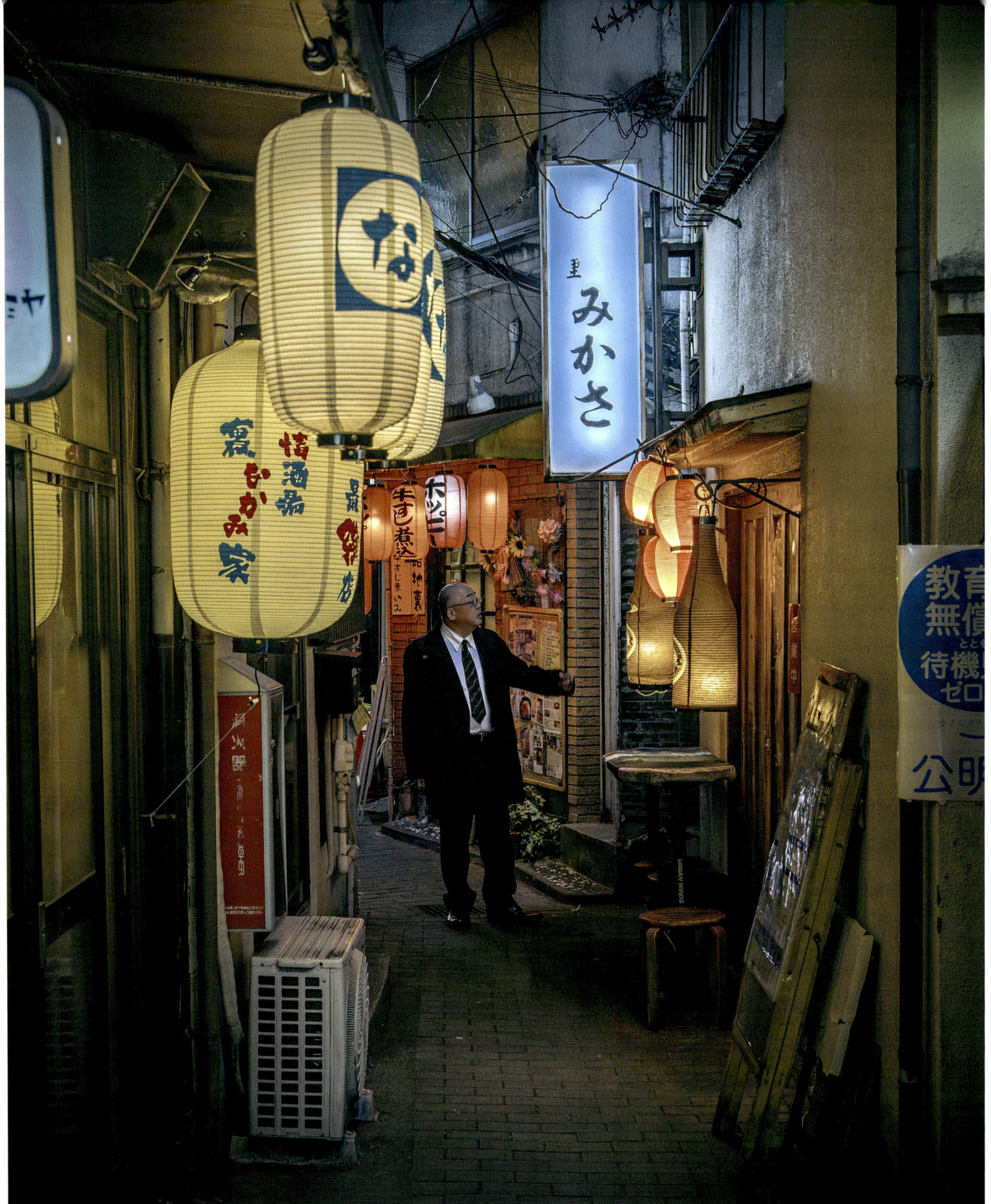

Maze in Front of Shinagawa Station.
Shinagawa, Tokyo. Entering a gap between
buildings in front of Shinagawa Station, in
the heart of the city center, you come upon
an incredibly narrow alleyway of izakaya.

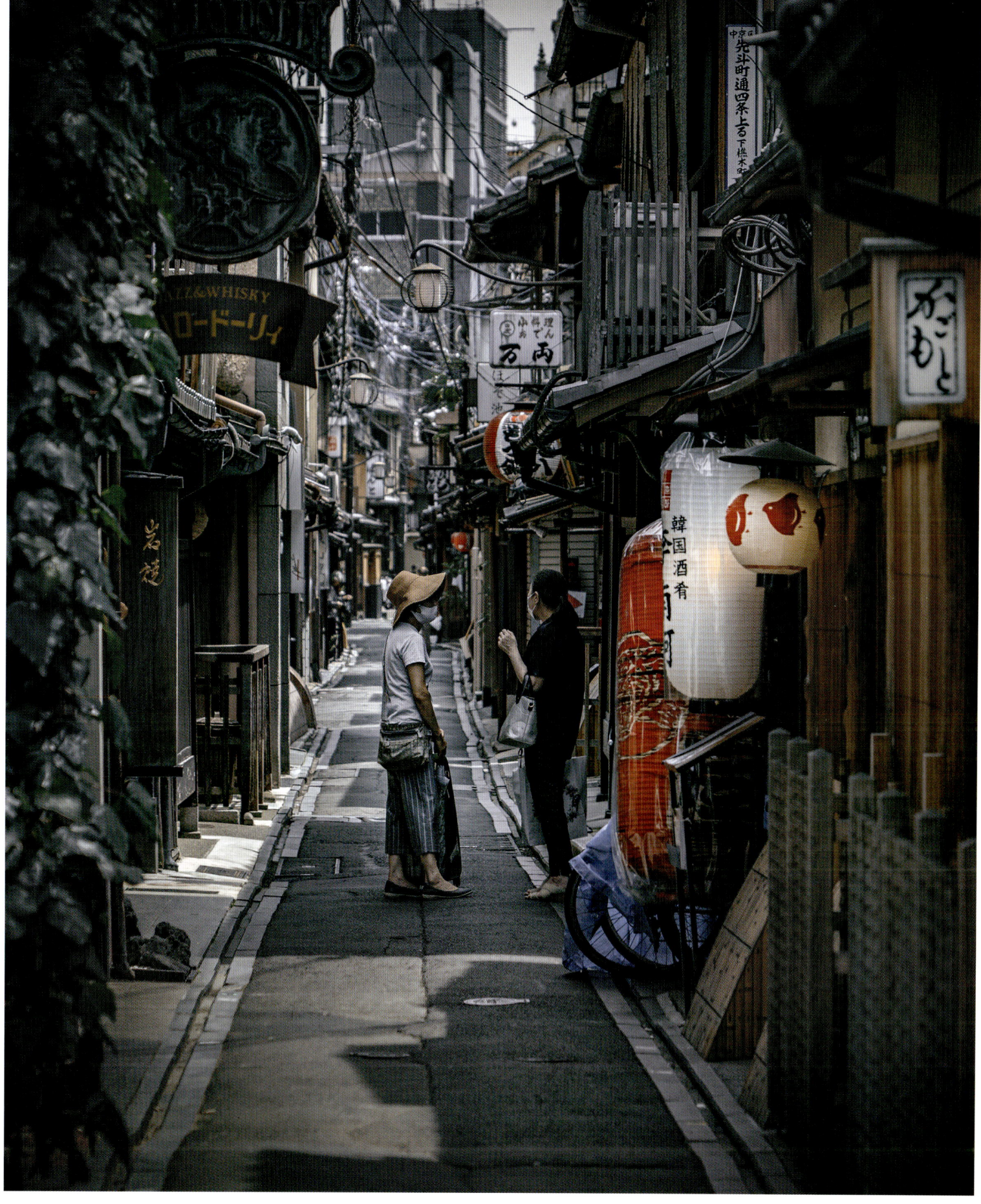

Pontocho Alley. Kyoto. Ponto-cho is Kyoto's *hanamachi* (flower district) where traditional stores are crammed together. The narrow alleys, which are different from those of Gion, Kyoto's geisha district, arouse the curiosity of tourists.

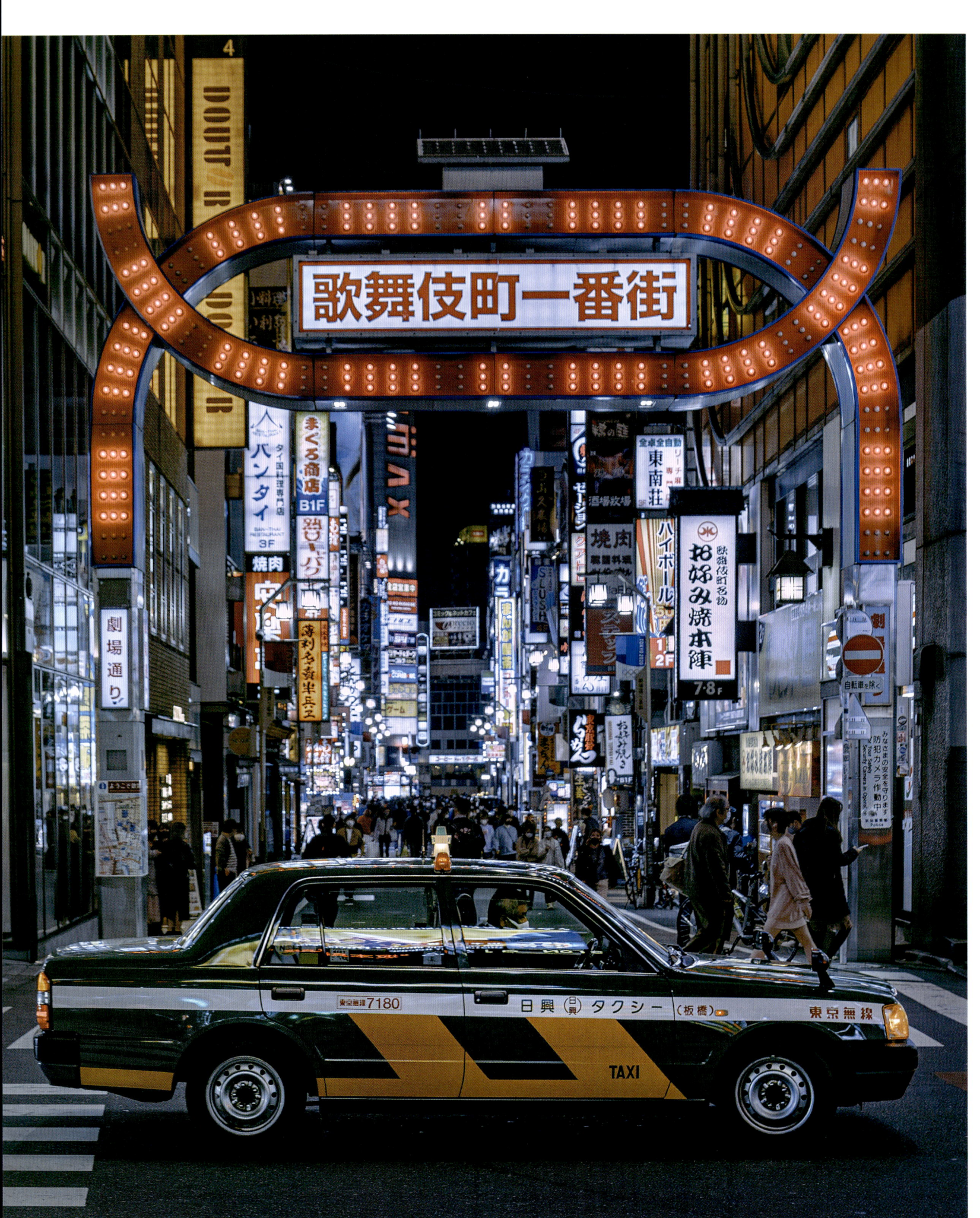

都市景観

The Japanese language is said to be the most difficult language in the world. One of the features of Japan's urban landscape is the concentration in a small space of signs written in various languages—hiragana, katakana, kanji, and English abound throughout the city.

It is also interesting to note that each area has its own distinct purpose. For example, Shinjuku Kabukicho is one of the largest entertainment districts in Asia, Akihabara is a mecca for electronics and otaku, and Ueno Ameya Yokocho is lined with many grocery stores.

In this section, I bring you the energy of these unique cities through my photographs.

Kabukicho Gate. Shinjuku, Tokyo. Kabukicho is Asia's largest entertainment district. Nowadays, it is safe to some extent, but it used to be very unsafe.

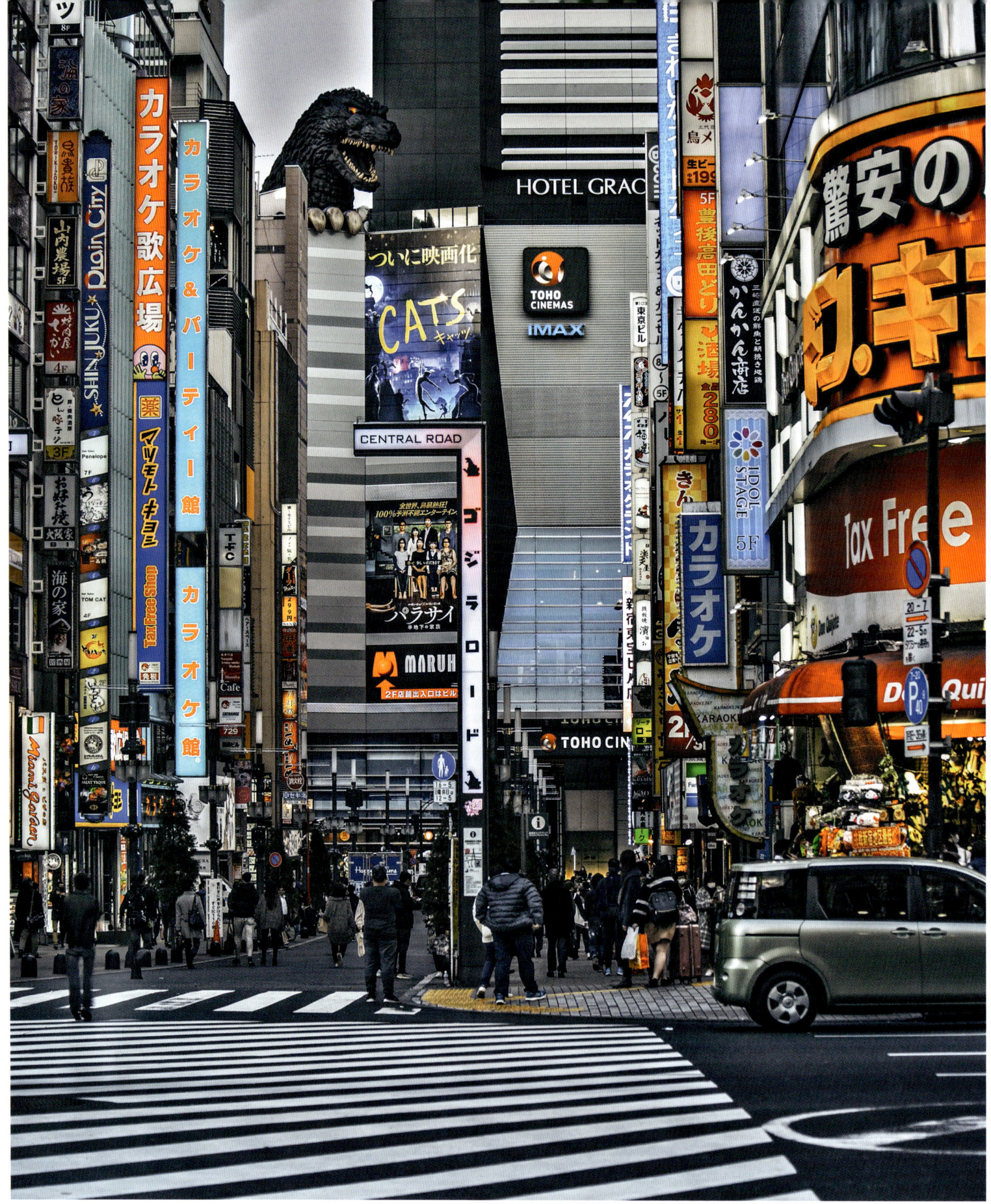

Godzilla Road in the Daytime. Shinjuku,
Tokyo. In 2016, Central Road in Kabukicho
was renamed Godzilla Road, to coincide
with the release of the movie *Shin Godzilla*.

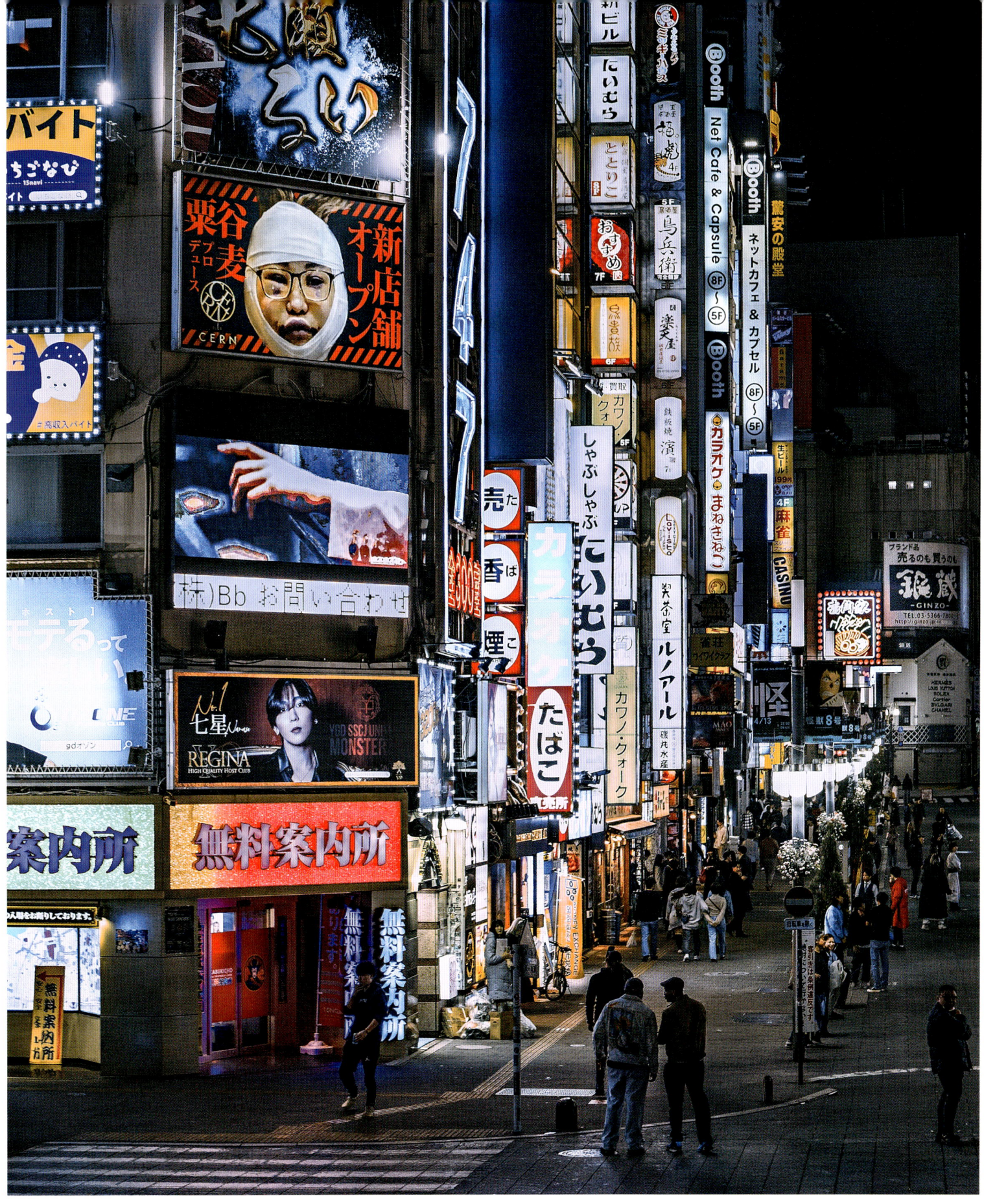

Neon Signs on Central Road. Shinjuku,
Tokyo. This is a scene unique to Kabukicho,
where a variety of neon signs for
restaurants, clubs, karaoke, and other
venues line the streets.

Godzilla Road from Above. Shinjuku, Tokyo.
This is the view from the third floor of the
building where Godzilla is located.

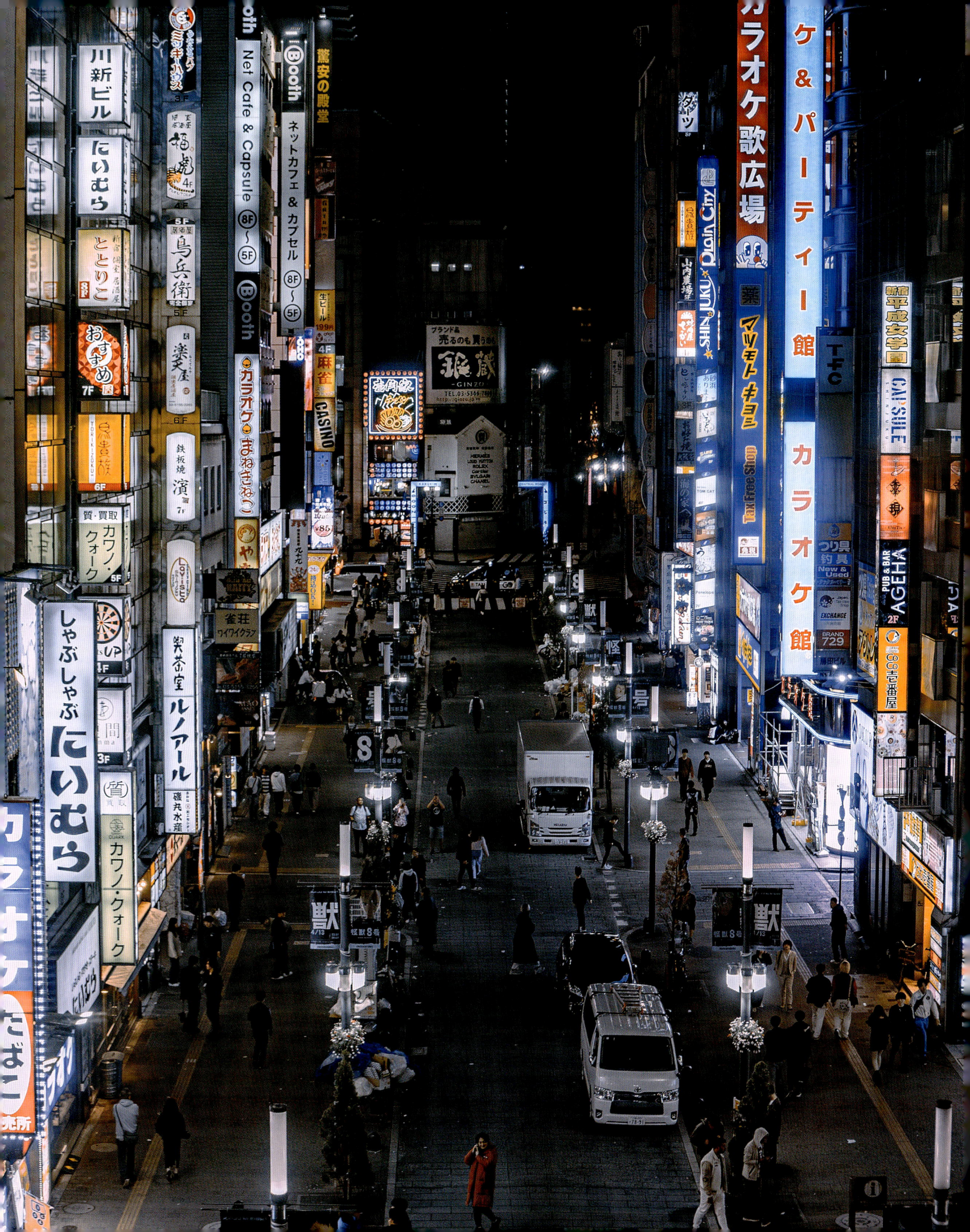

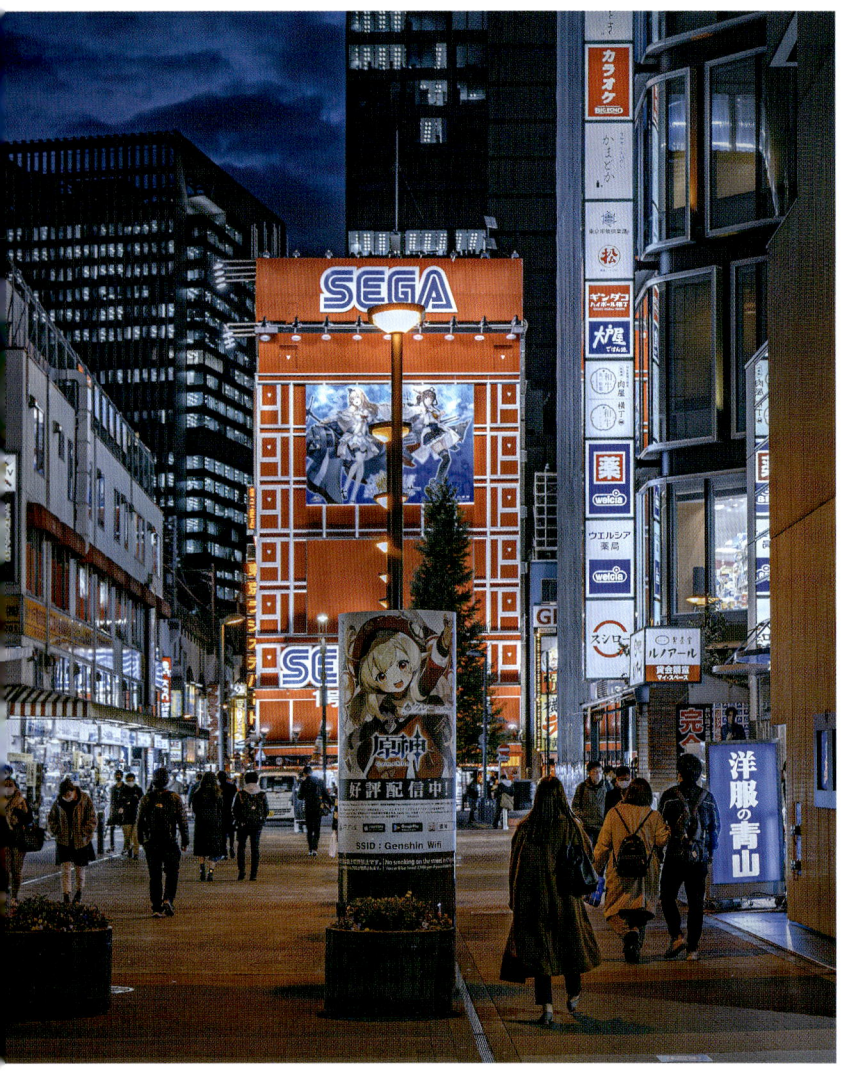

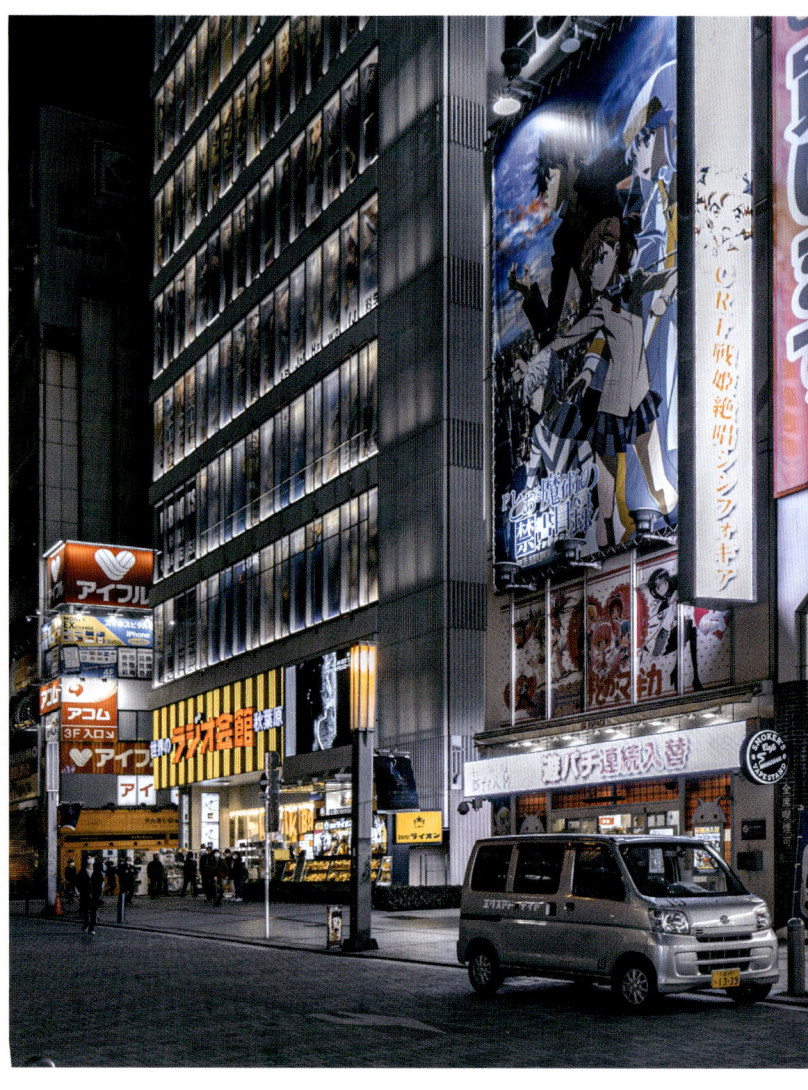

The Red Building. Akihabara, Tokyo. When this photo was taken, the building was owned by SEGA.

Radio Kaikan. Akihabara, Tokyo. Radio Kaikan, a popular shopping complex with an impressive yellow neon sign, is still going strong.

VOLKS Akihabara. Akihabara, Tokyo. Opened in 2014, VOLKS Hobby Paradise was popular with hobbyists in Japan and from around the world, but it is now closed.

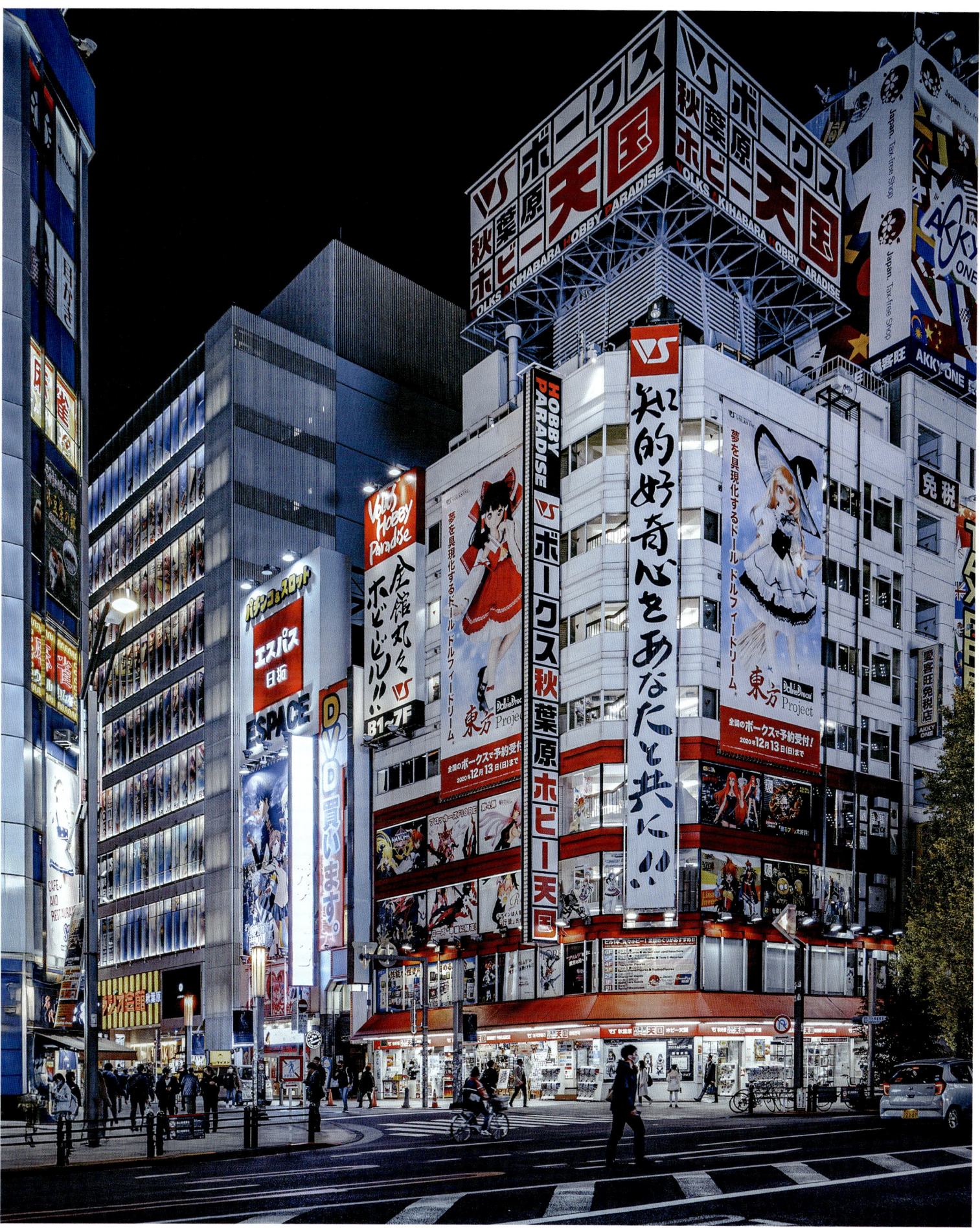

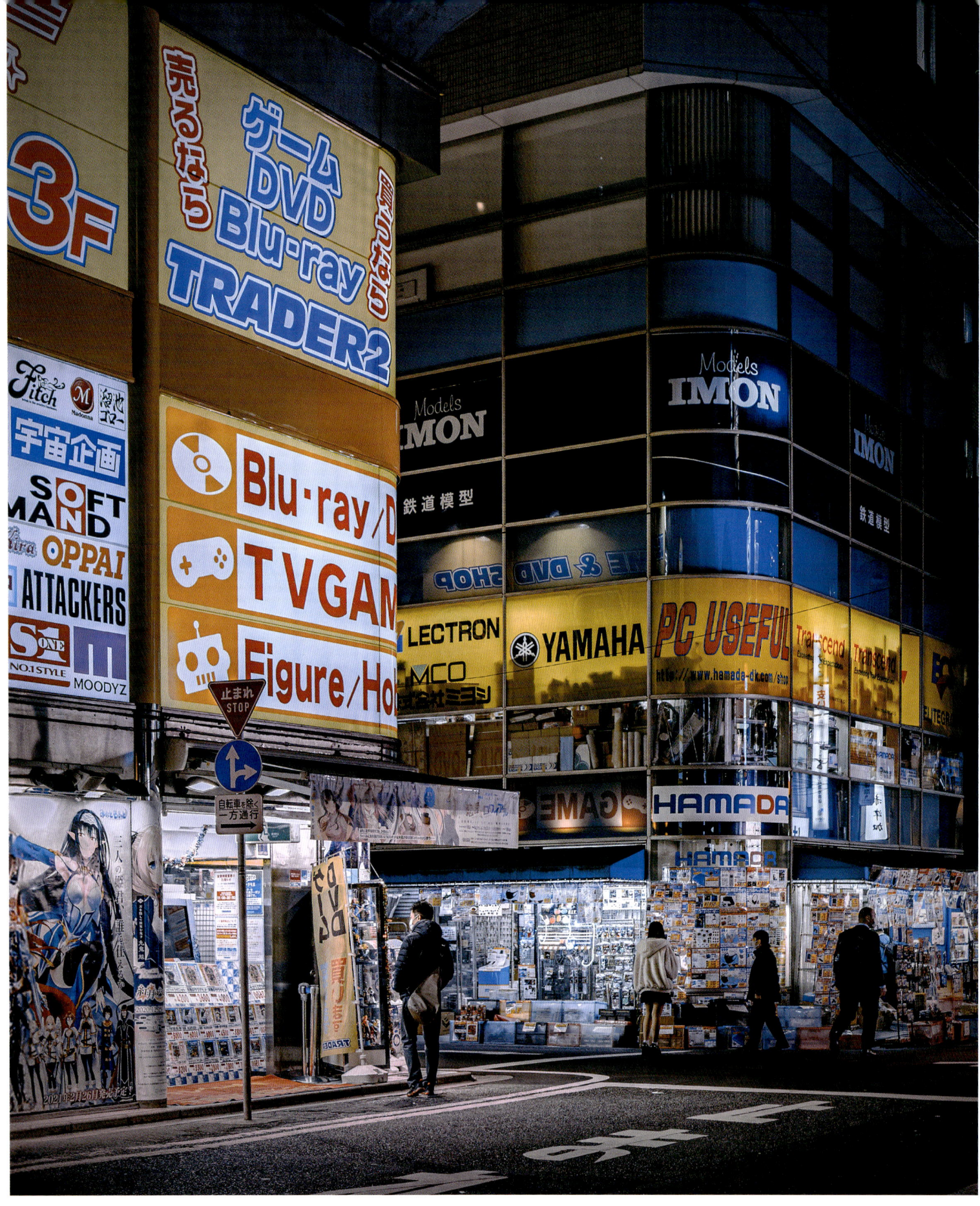

Electronic Stores. The store on the left is a game store and the one on the right is a used computer store. The woman standing in front of the store is handing out maid café flyers. This shot is symbolic of Akihabara.

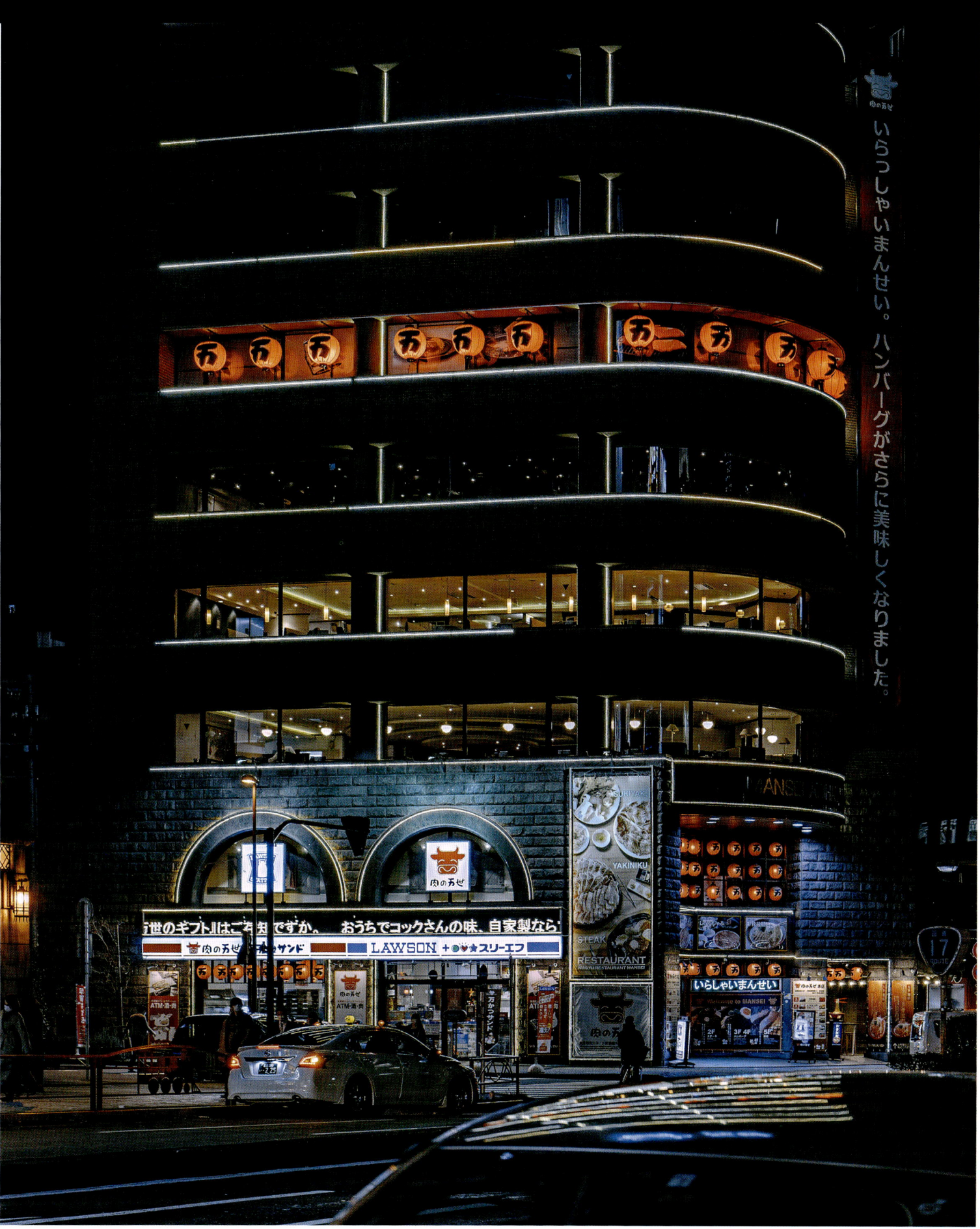

いらっしゃいまんせい。ハンバーグがさらに美味しくなりました。

Sukiyaki Restaurant. Akihabara, Tokyo. The neon lights and lanterns, which are often overlooked, are fascinating when you look closely at them.

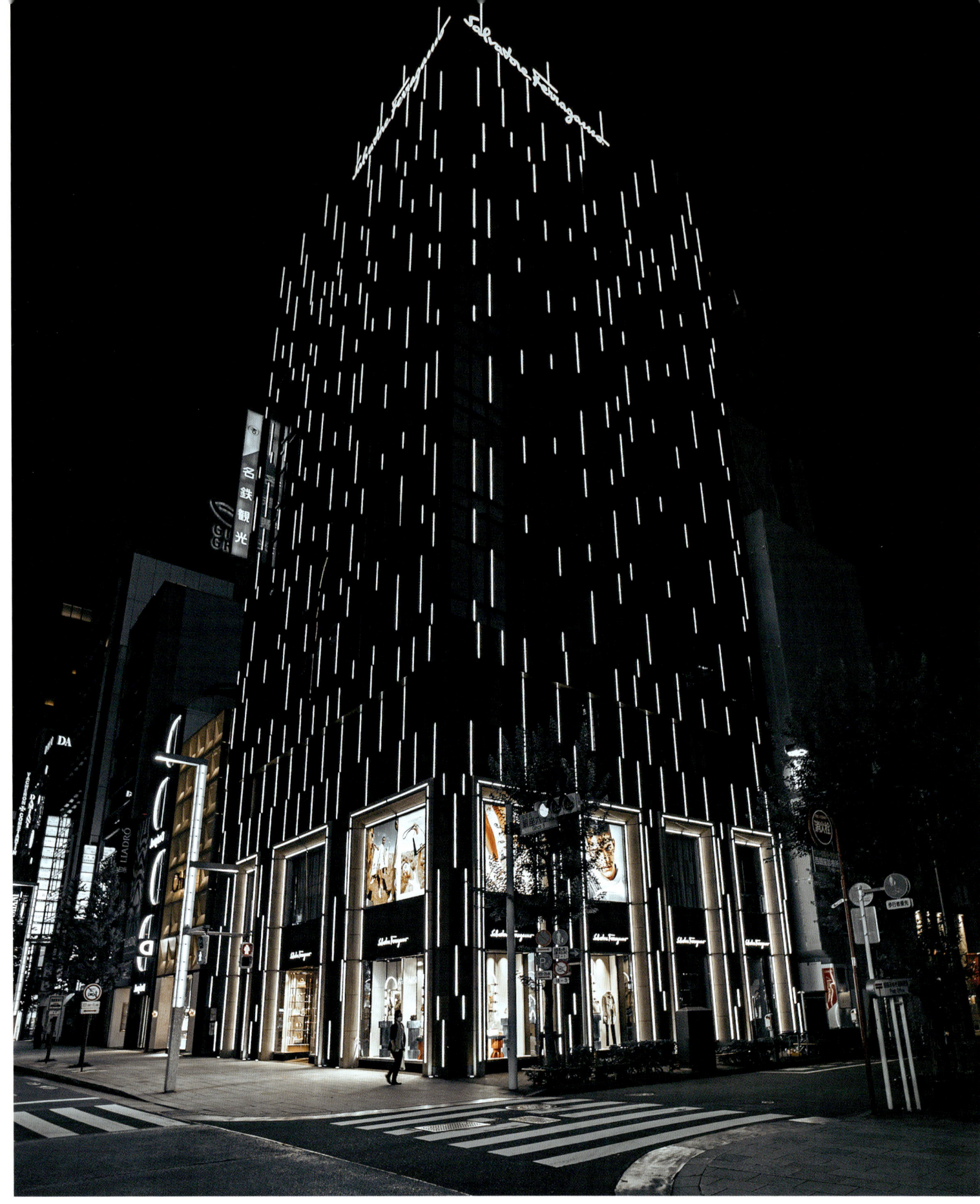

Beautiful Building. Ginza, Tokyo. Ginza
is lined with numerous well-designed
buildings, such as this Ferragamo store.

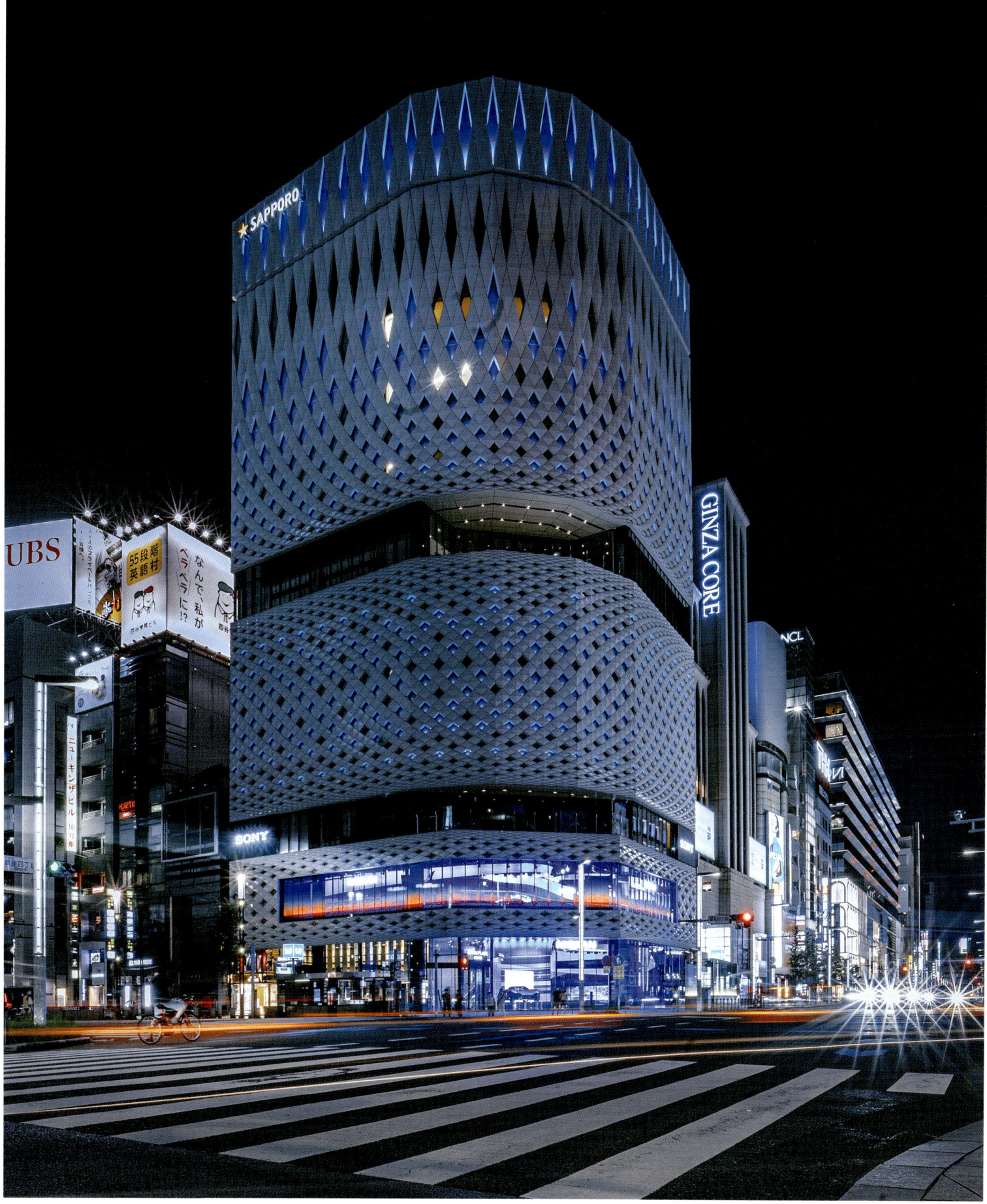

Ginza Place. Ginza, Tokyo. This photo was taken with a tripod and long exposure. Long-exposure photography is a technique in which the shutter speed is slowed down and light is shone on the camera's sensor for a long period of time to capture lights as trails.

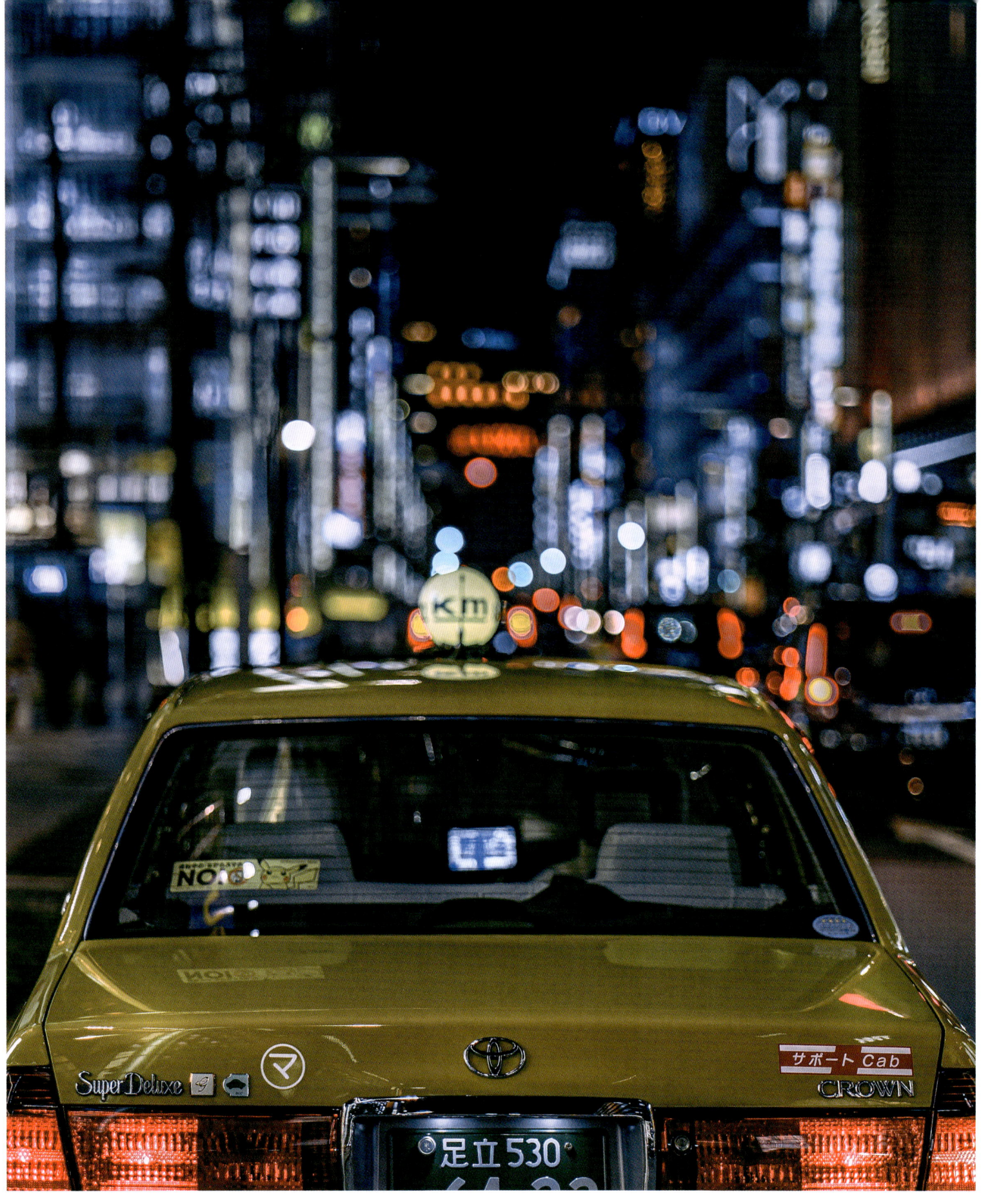

Chuo-dori Street. Ginza, Tokyo. This street is filled with incredible lights. When you open the camera's aperture and focus on the foreground, you can take a "bokeh" picture like this one.

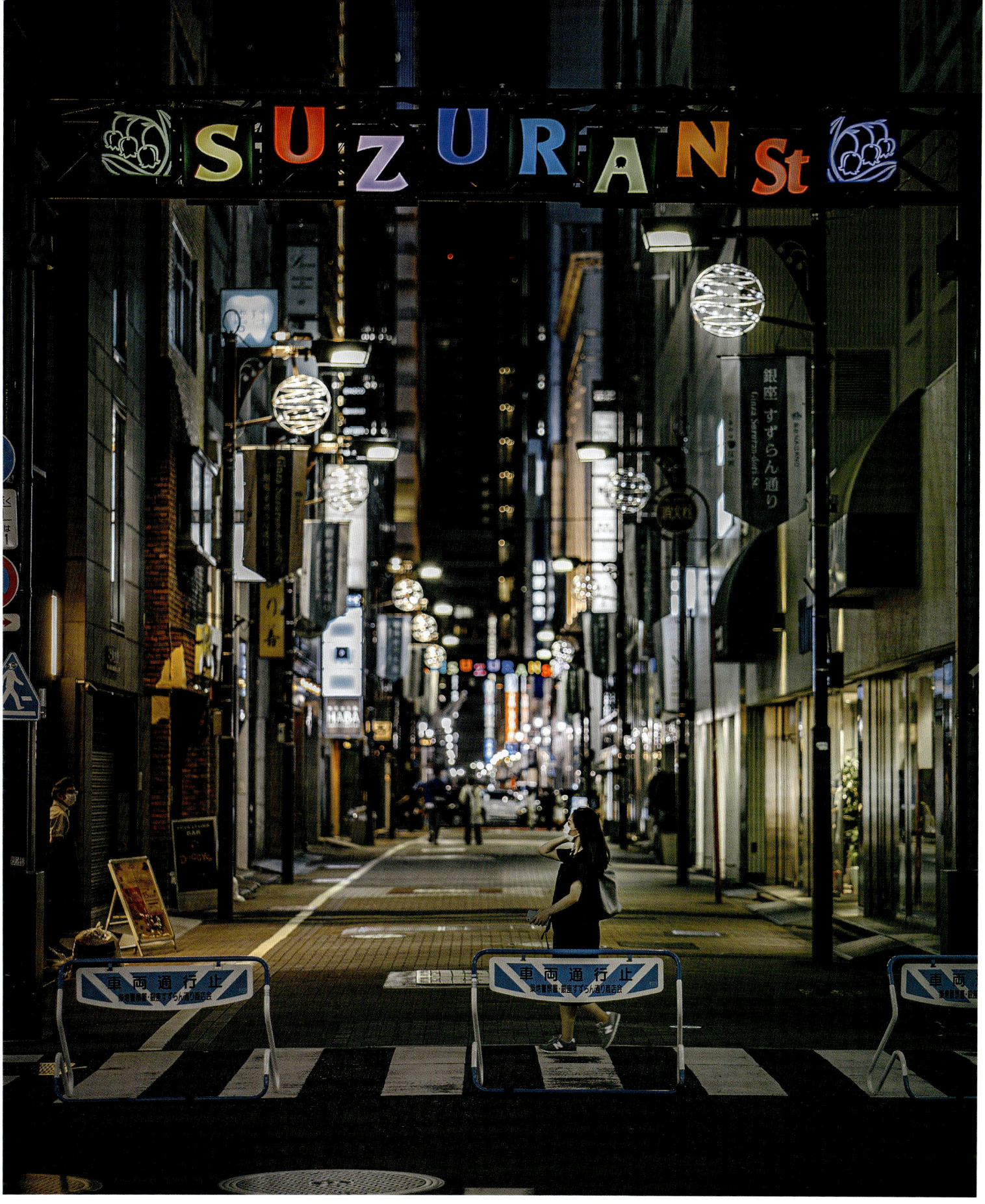

Suzuran (Lily of the Valley) Street. Ginza, Tokyo. This street is lined with charming stores, including high-end boutiques, historic companies, and long-established restaurants.

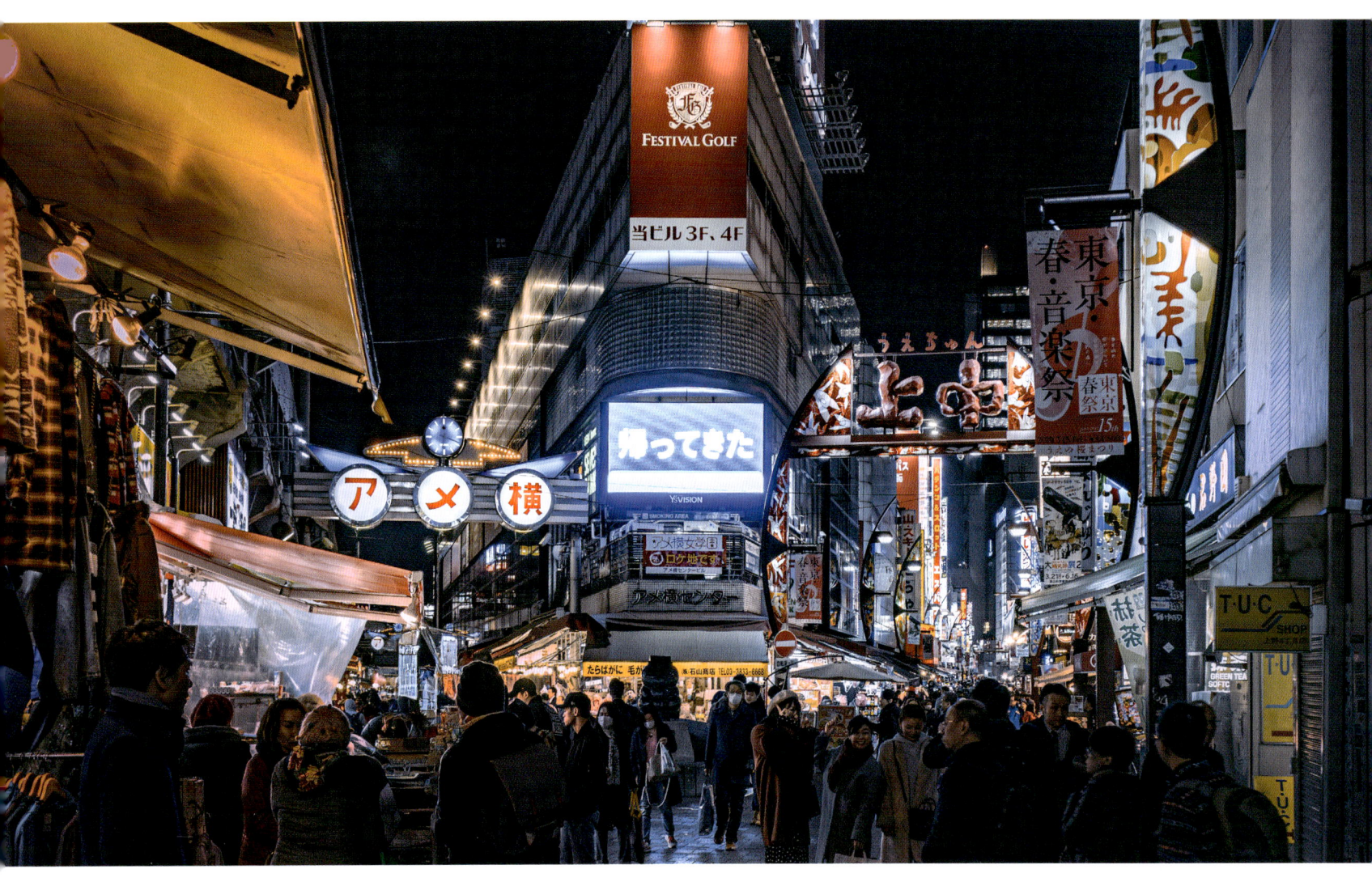

Ameyoko Center Building. Ueno, Tokyo. This is the symbolic building of Ameya Yokocho, which houses stores selling food, clothing, shoes, cosmetics, sporting goods, and more.

Ameya Yokocho. Ueno, Tokyo. The Ameya Yokocho shopping district is situated between buildings, such as the Yodobashi Camera Multimedia store, and railroad tracks.

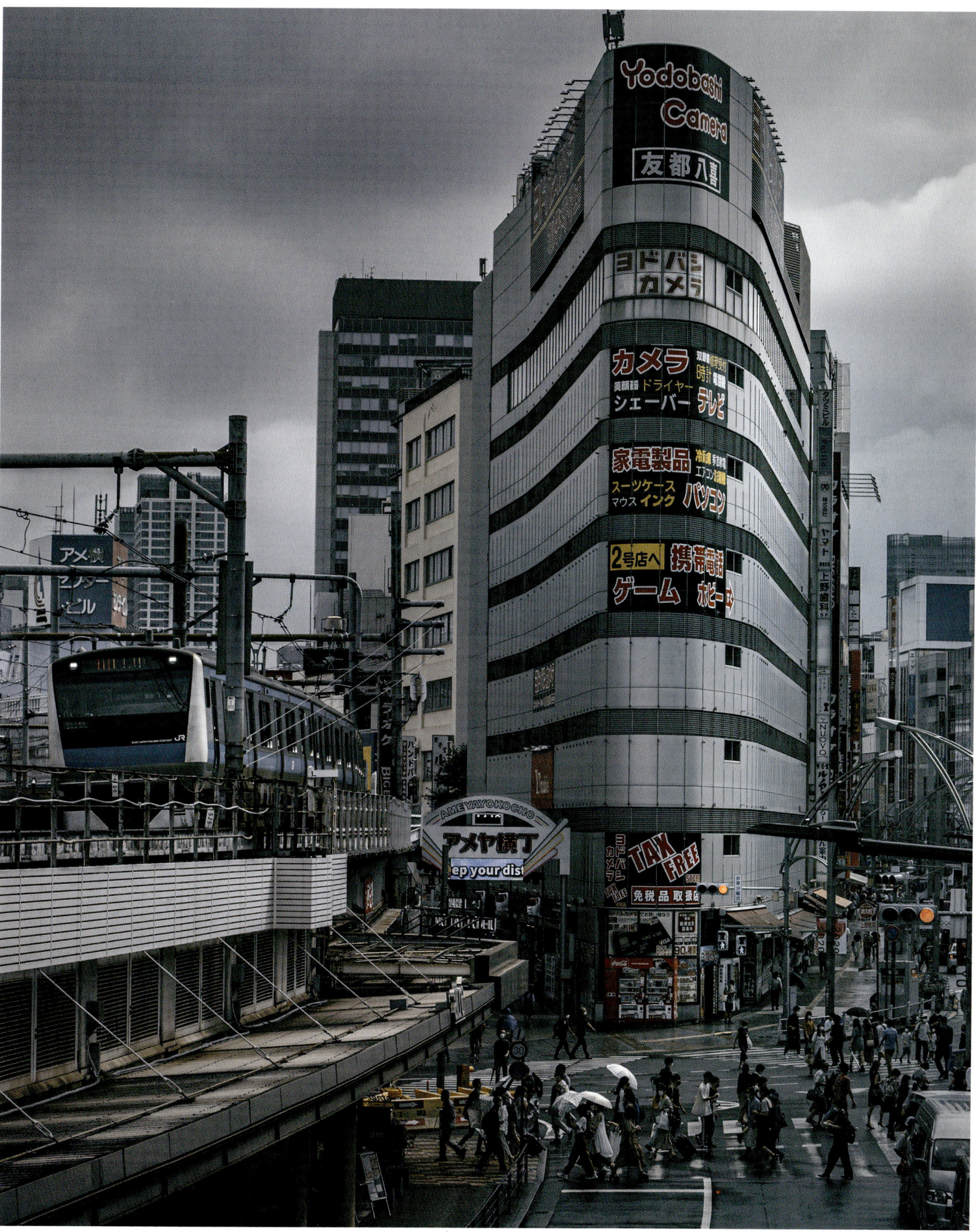

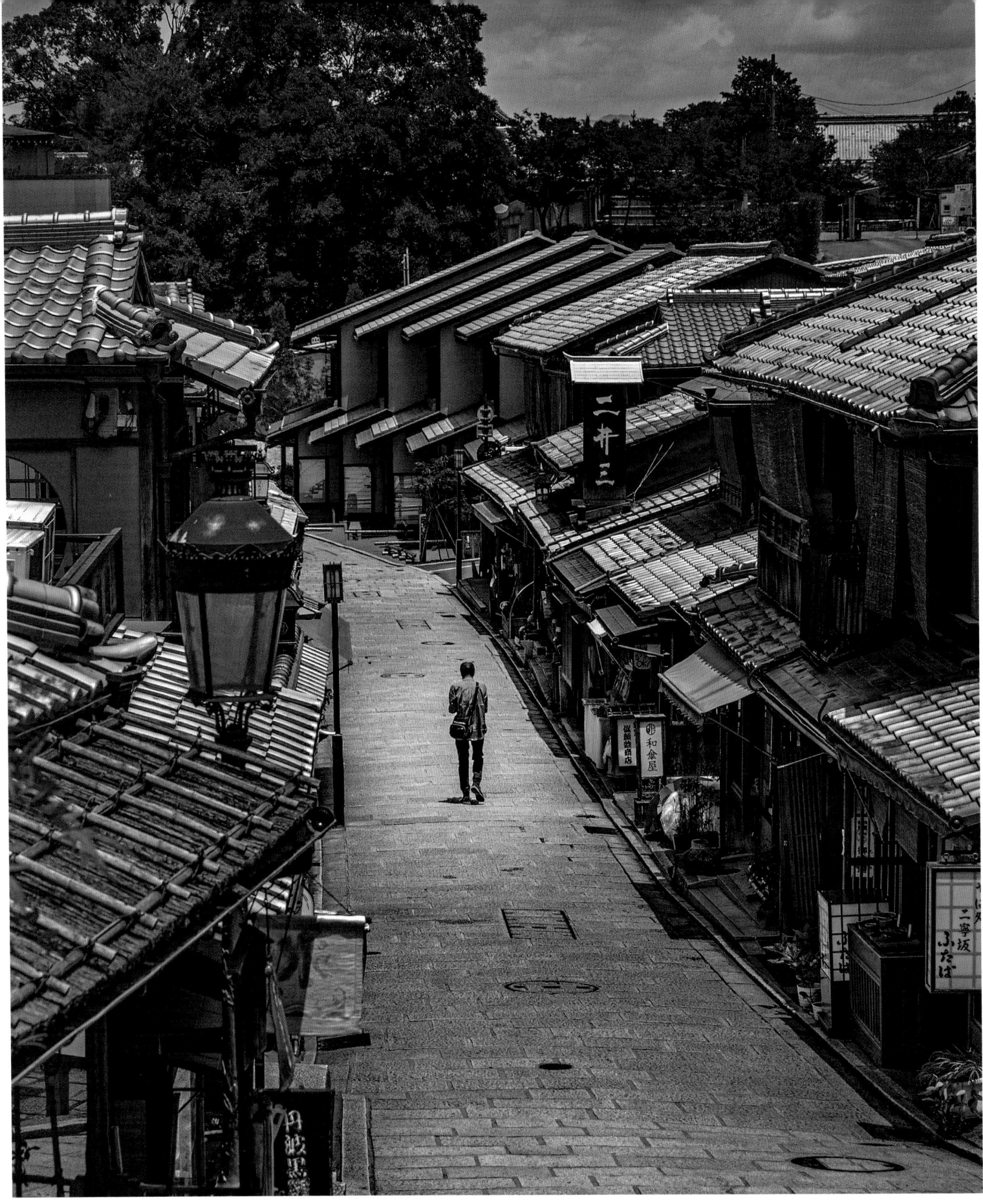

Ninenzaka (Hill of Two Years). Kyoto. The legend is if you stumble and fall here, you will die within two years (*ninen*), which is thought to have been passed down from generation to generation as a warning to be careful on the stone-paved slope.

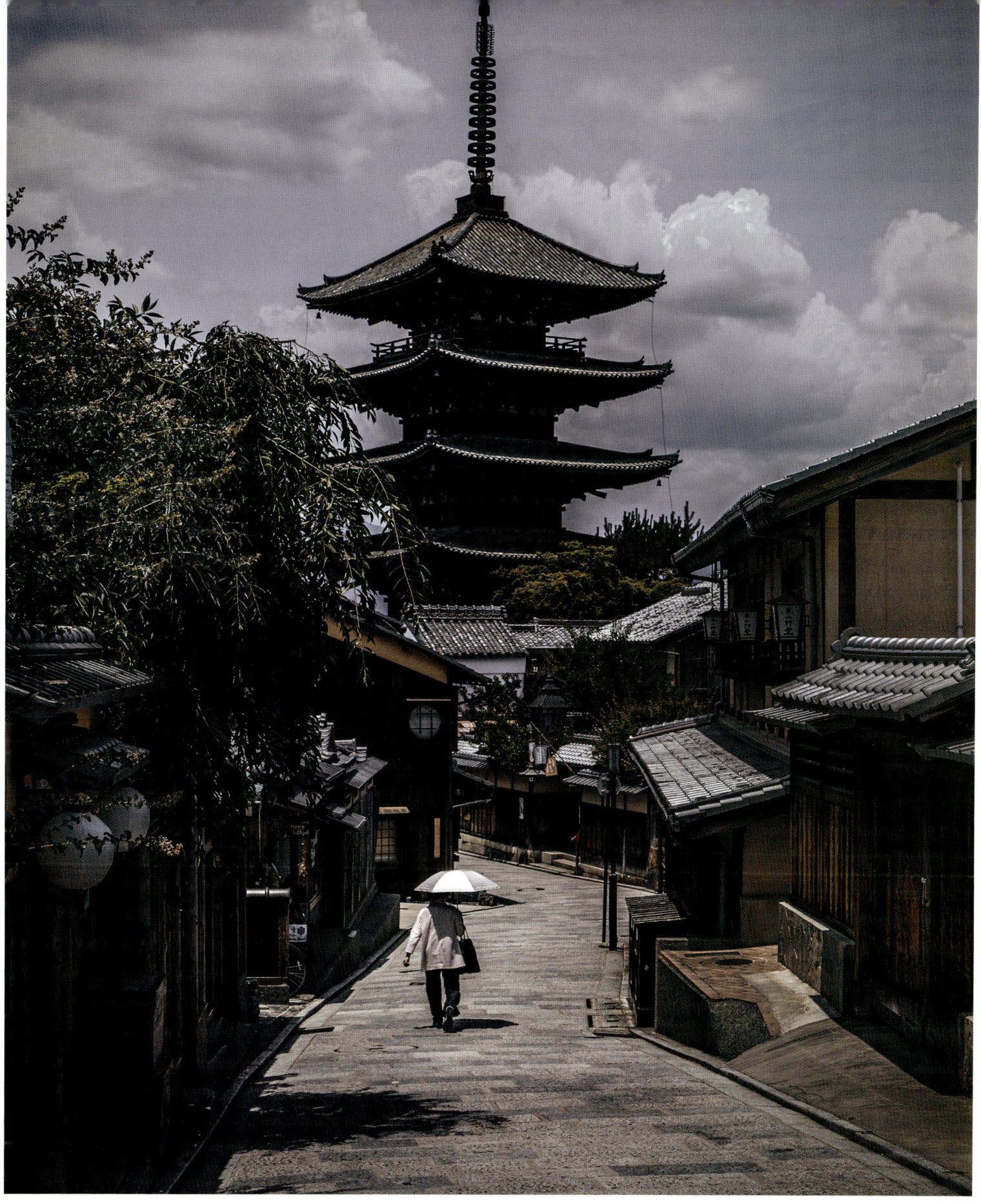

Woman with a Parasol. Kyoto. Shot in the strong midsummer sun, this photo taken from the top of the hill on Yasaka-dori shows a wonderful view, with both sides of the street lined with buildings typical of Kyoto.

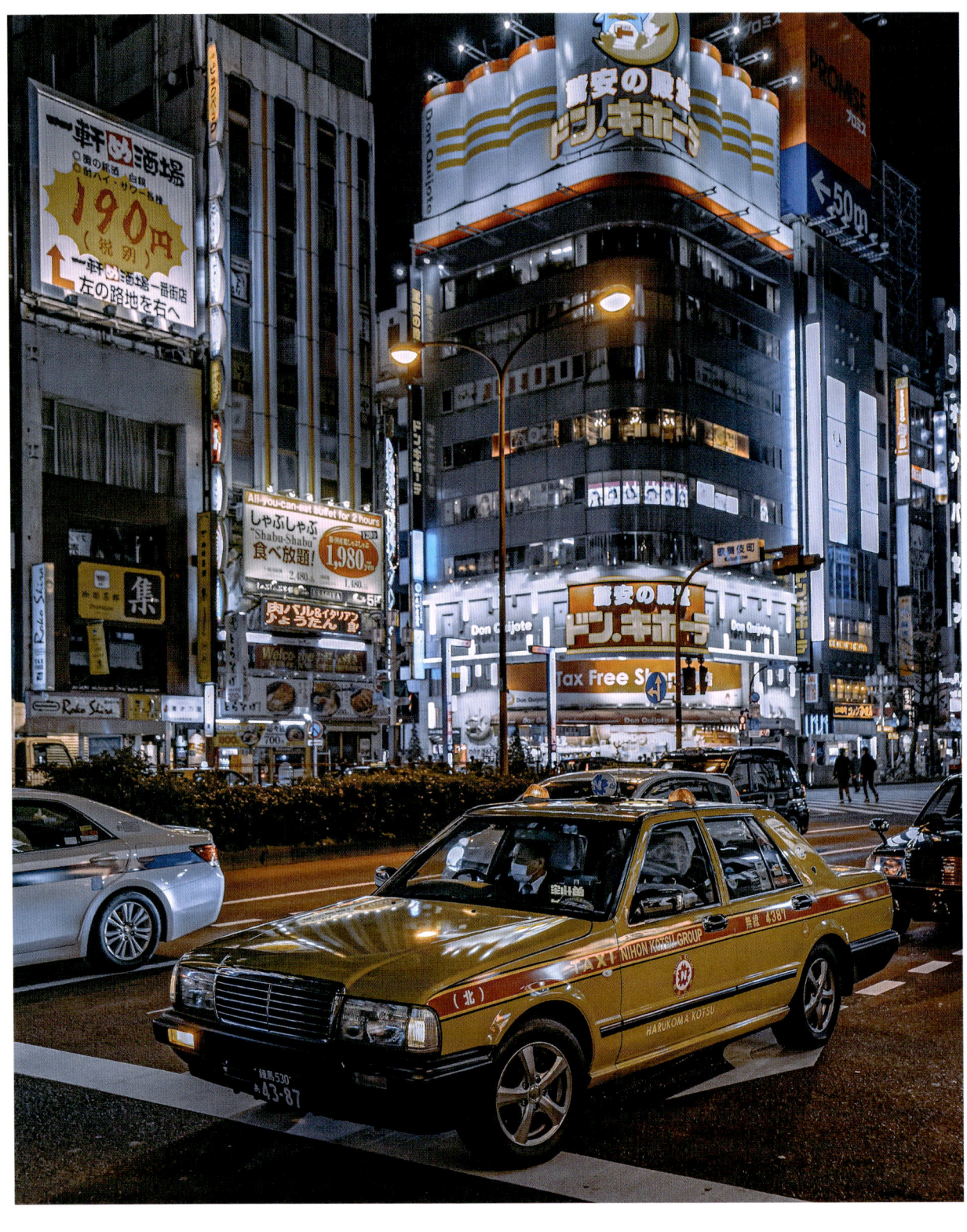

Cab on Shinjuku Street. Shinjuku, Tokyo.
The neon lights of Kabukicho reflect nicely
on this recently washed taxi.

The Beauty of Crossing. Omiya, Saitama.
Omiya Arche's intersecting escalator lights
are quite beautiful.

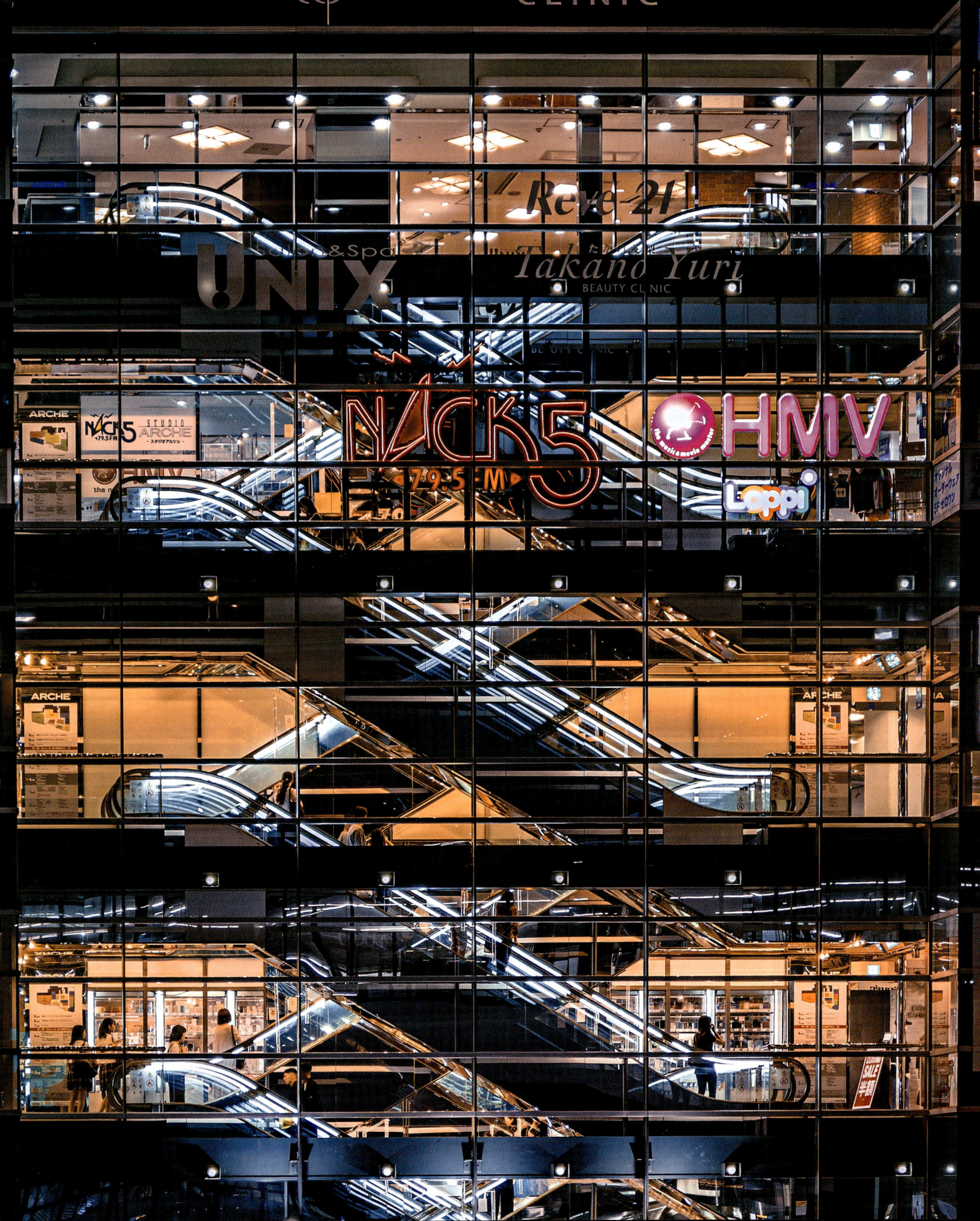

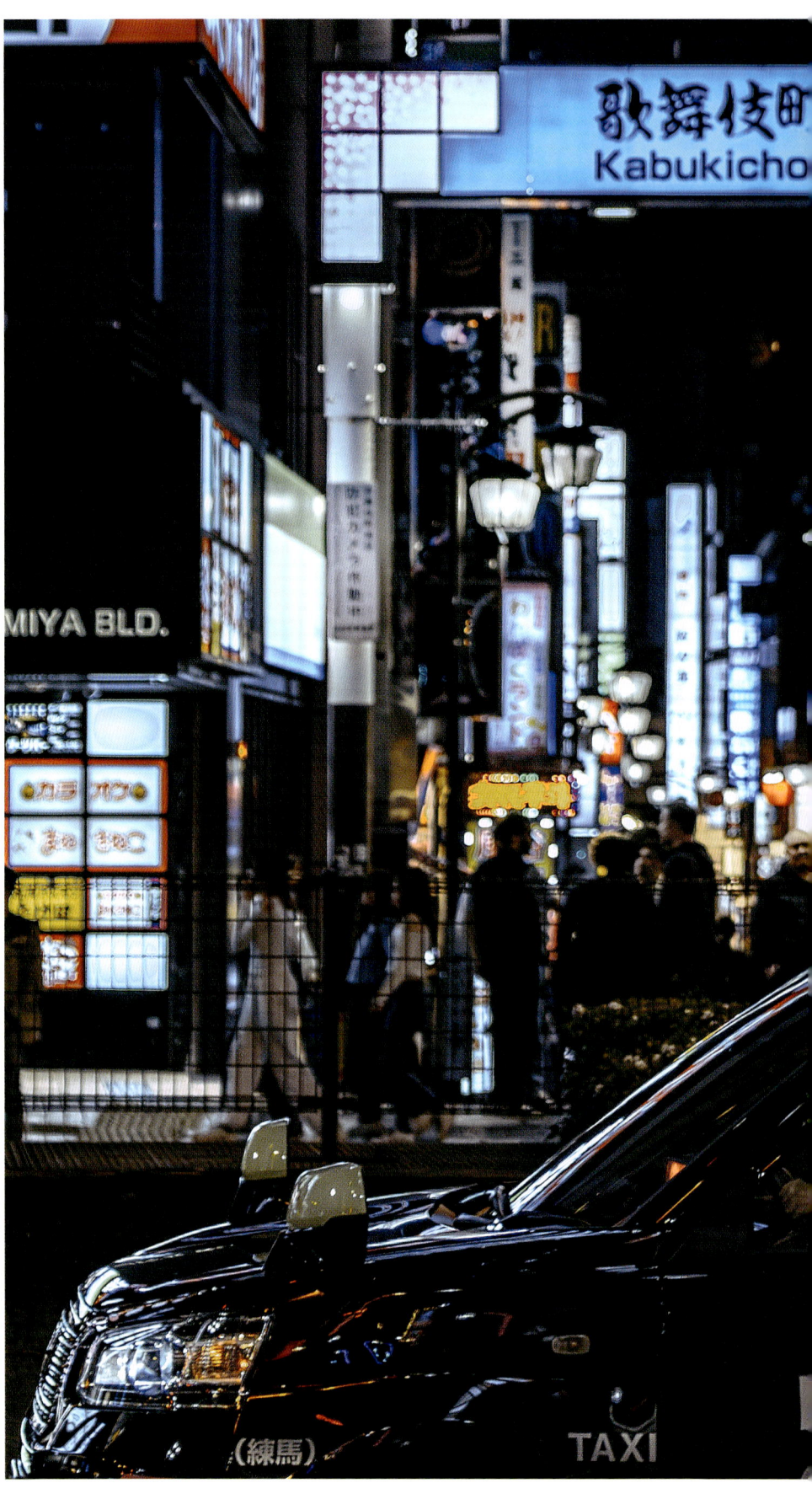

Sakura Street. Shinjuku, Tokyo. This street, lined with cabarets, host clubs, and adult entertainment establishments, is illuminated with neon lights and creates a scene that symbolizes Kabukicho.

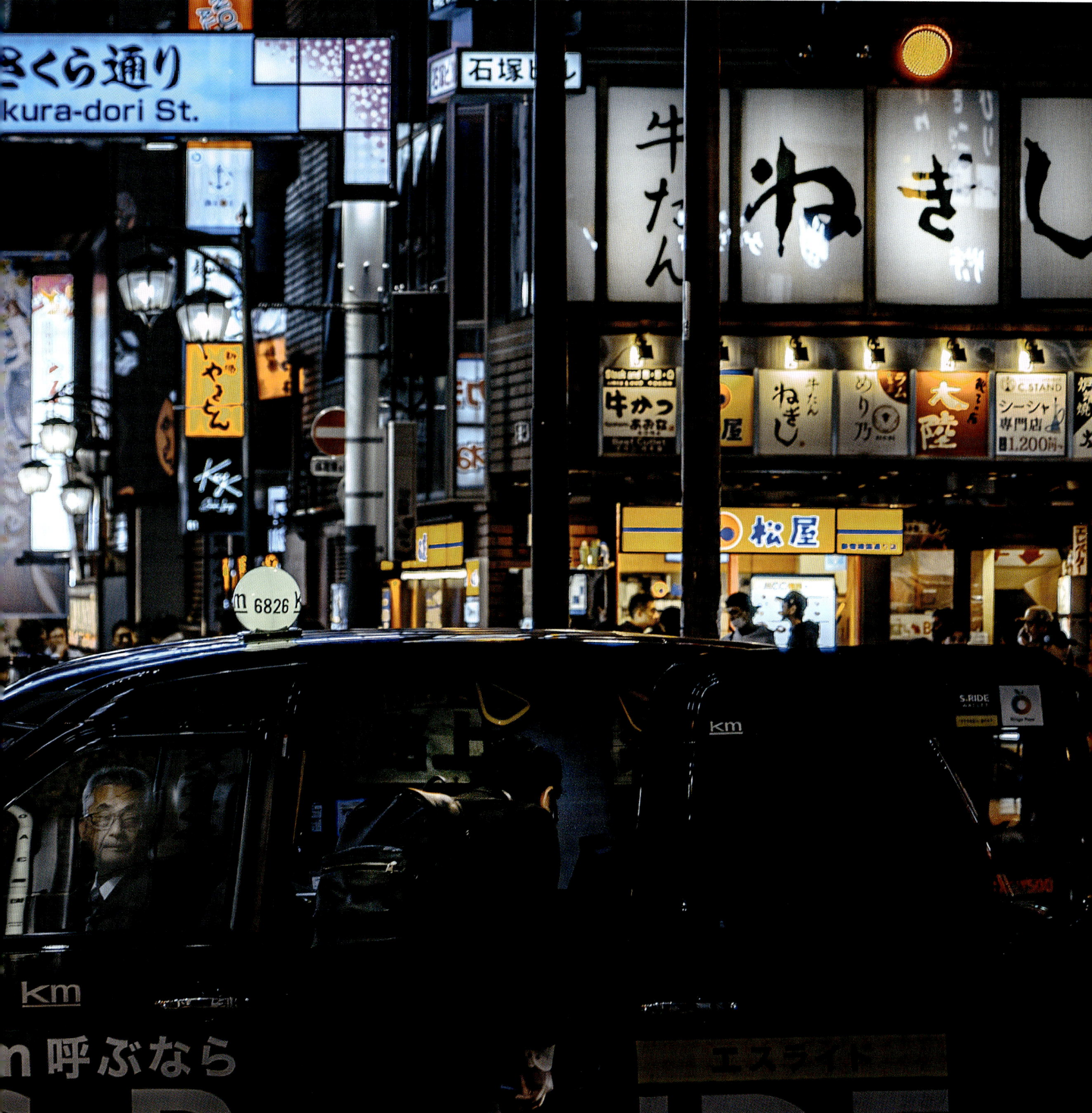

Namiki Street. Ginza, Tokyo. This famous avenue is more attractive to photograph in cold seasons when the leaves have fallen.

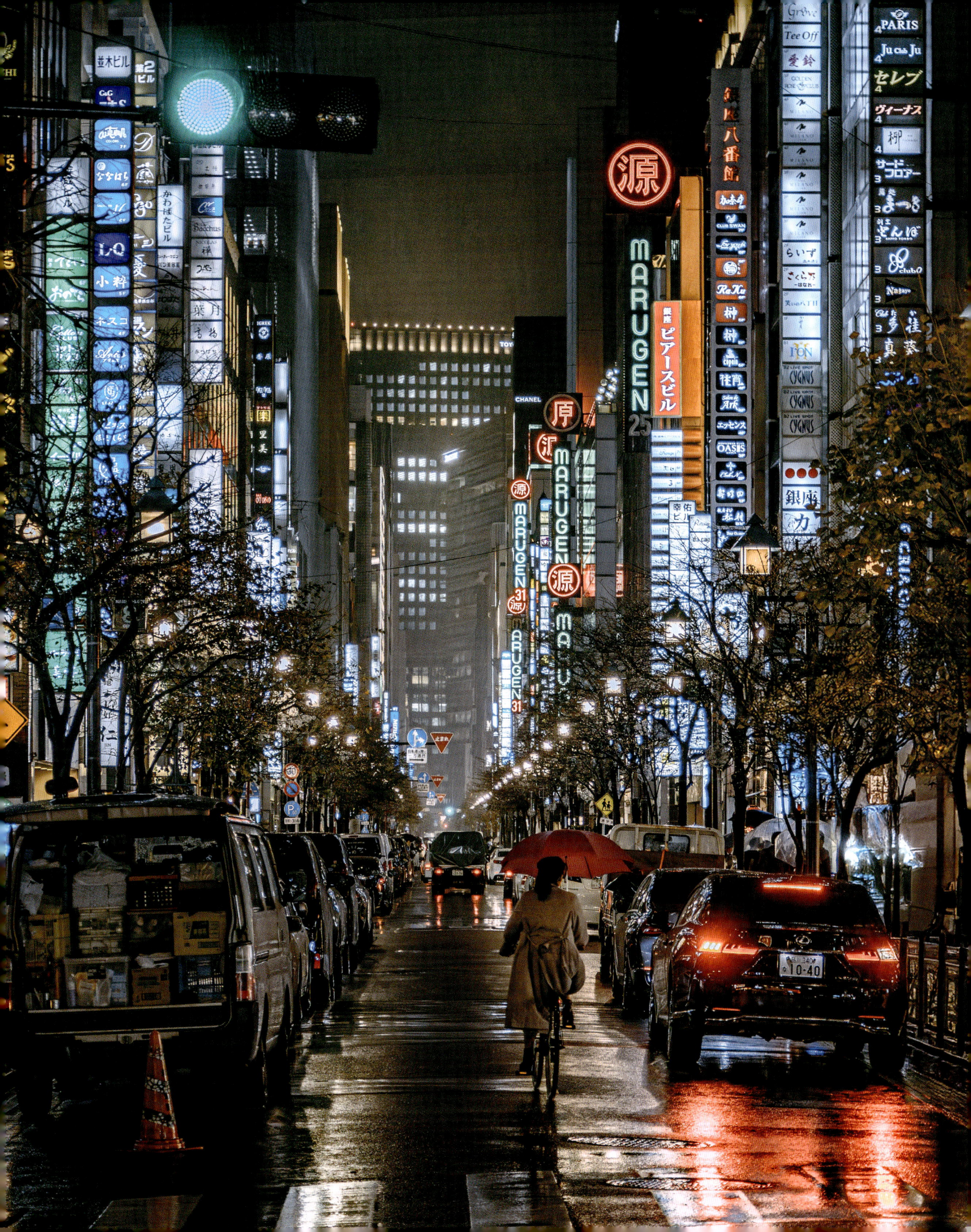

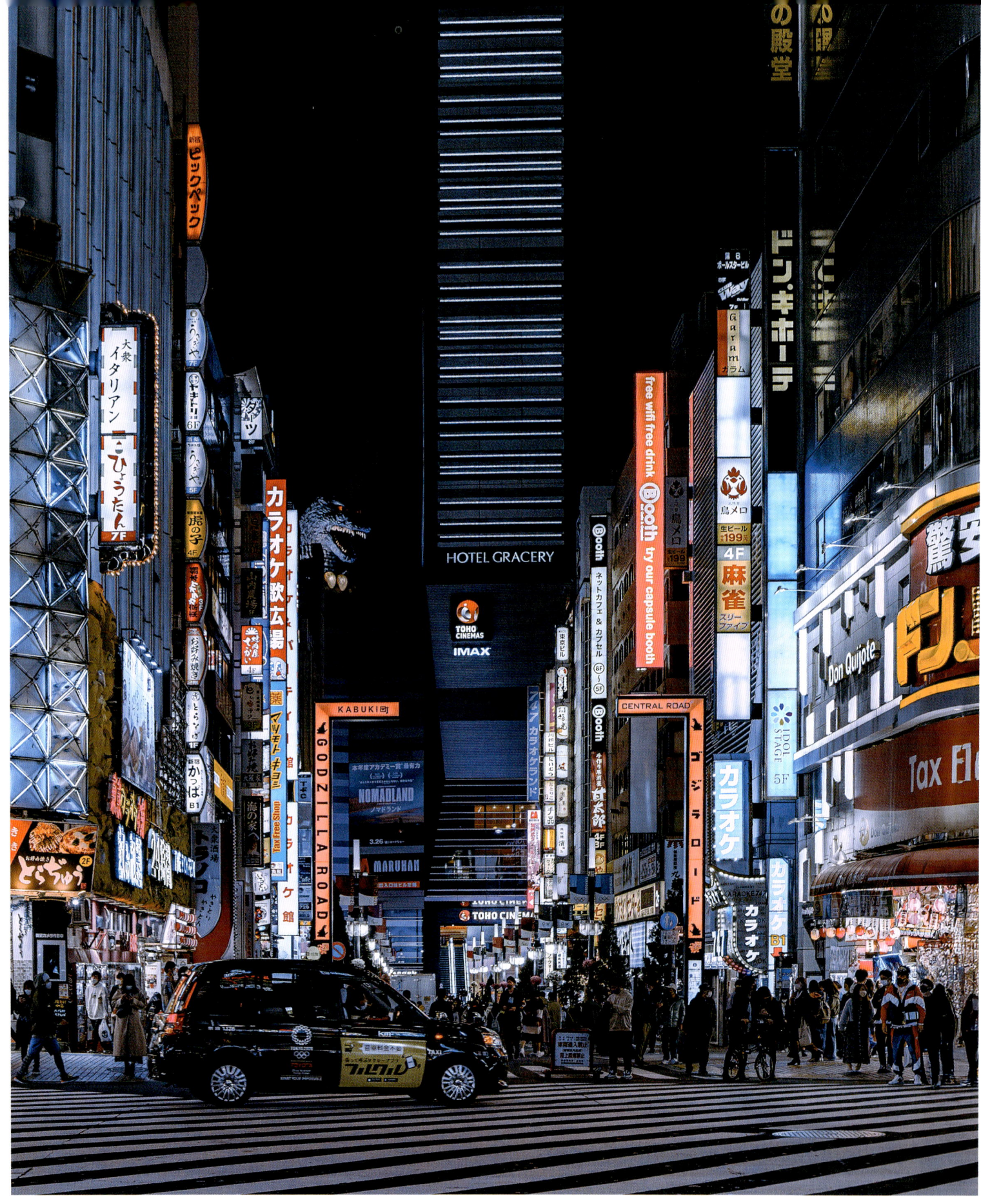

Godzilla Road at Night. Shinjuku, Tokyo.
Godzilla Road (Central Road) stretches north
to south between Yasukuni Street and the
Shinjuku Toho Building.

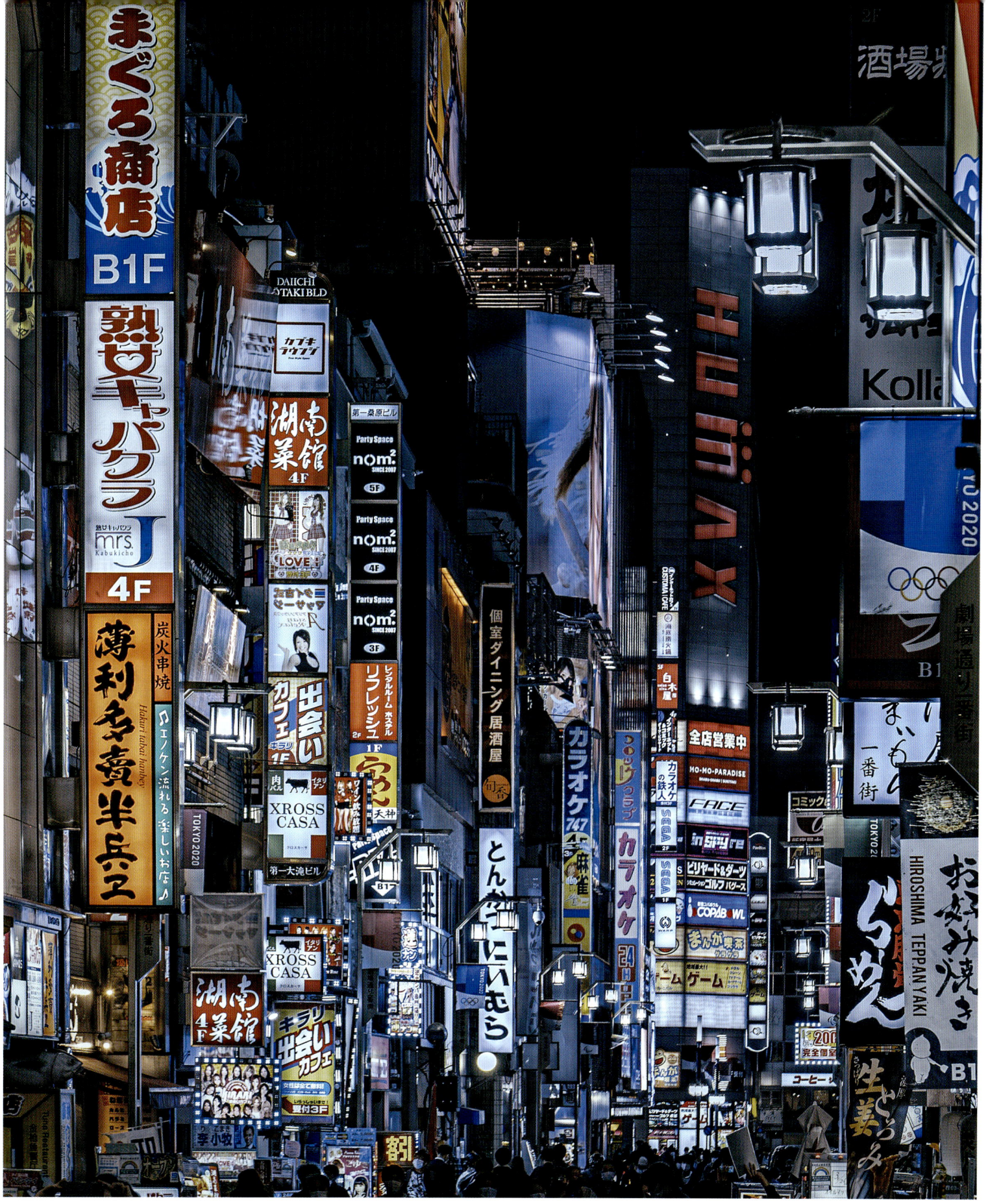

Neon Lights in Kabukicho. Shinjuku, Tokyo. Kabukicho is also known as "the town that never sleeps" or "the nightless city," as it is a busy entertainment district with a constant flow of people enjoying restaurants and nightlife venues from late night to early morning.

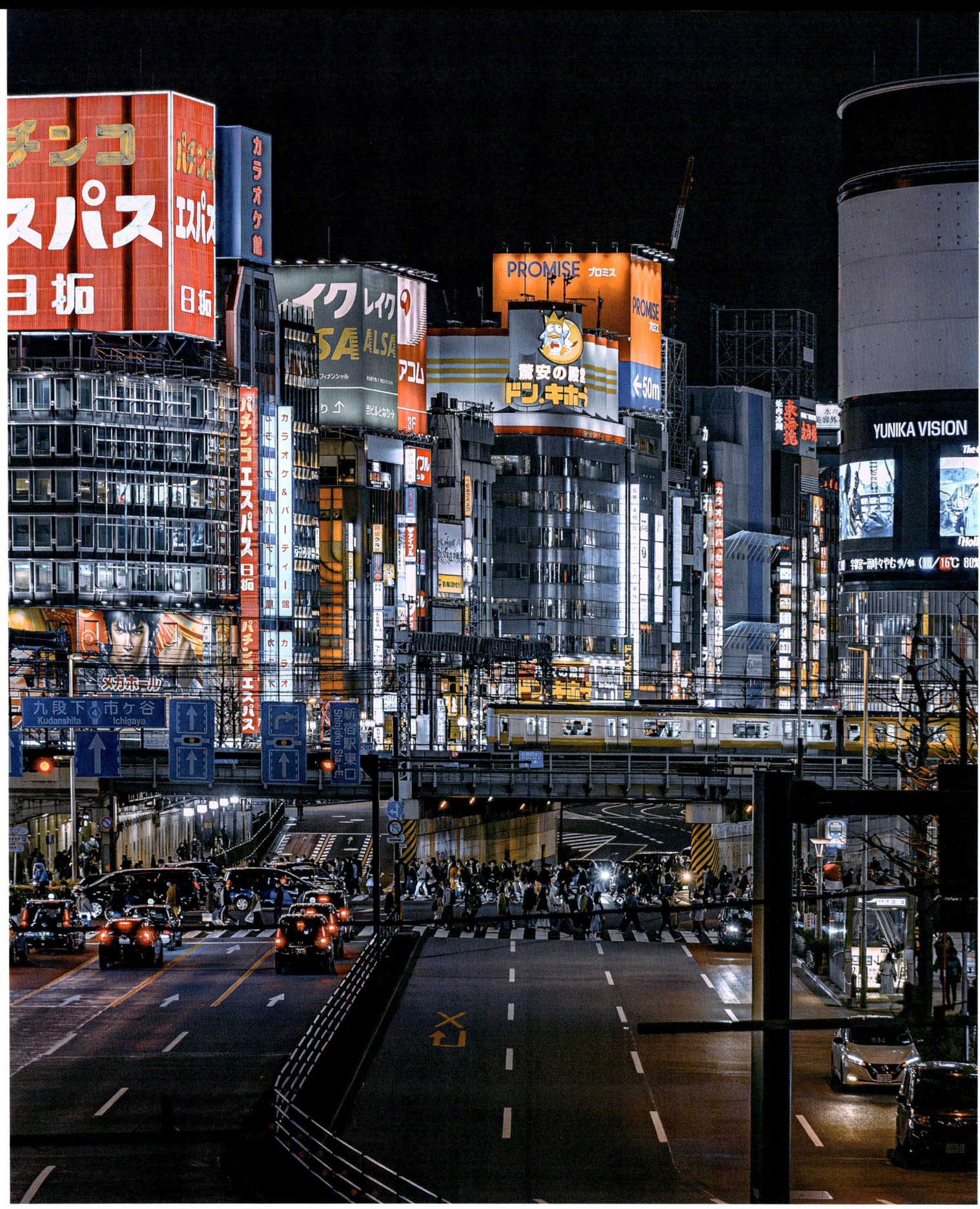

View of Shinjuku from the Pedestrian Bridge.
Shinjuku, Tokyo. From the pedestrian
bridge near the west exit of Shinjuku Station,
you can photograph the stunning neon
backdrop. The view from here is filled with
the energy of Shinjuku at night.

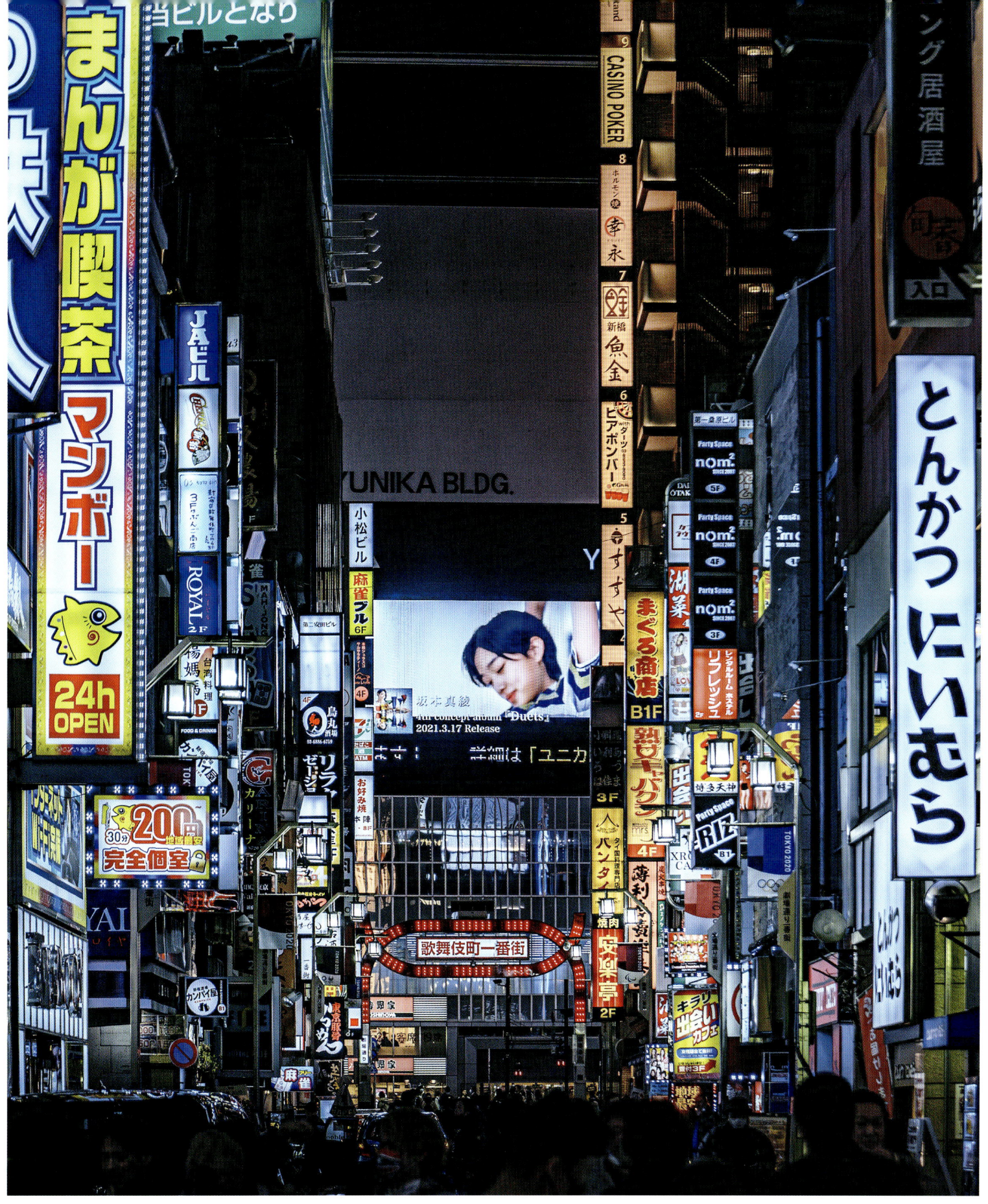

Inside Kabukicho Gate. Shinjuku, Tokyo. At night, the energy of Kabukicho reaches its peak. This photo captures the enthusiasm of the people passing by.

Chinatown East Gate. Chinatown, Yokohama. The guardian deity of Choyomon, the gate that welcomes the sunrise, is a blue dragon.

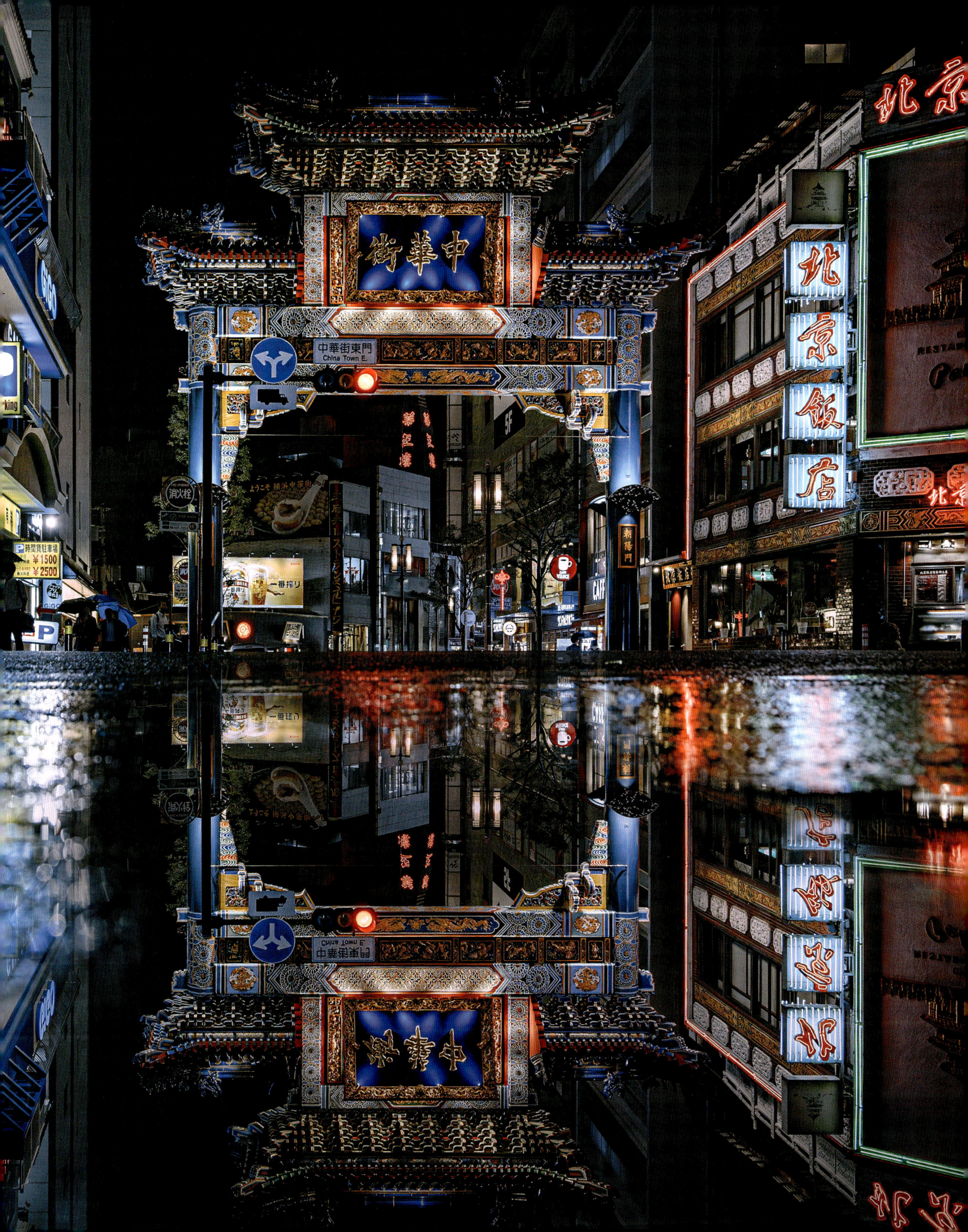

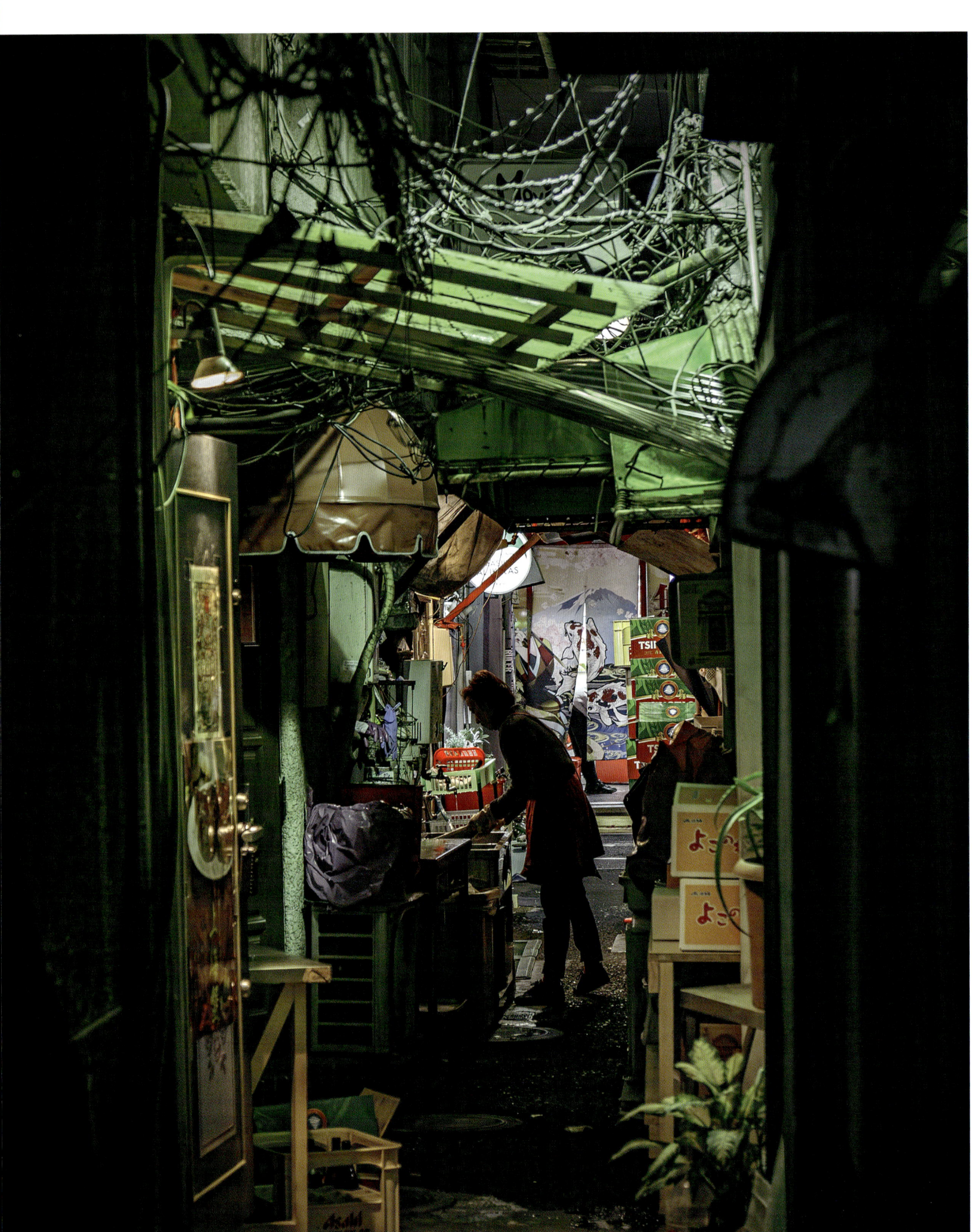

無秩序

Many visitors to Japan may feel uncomfortable seeing power lines all over the streets. In developed countries, burying power lines has become the "norm," as some people believe that utility poles and power lines make the landscape look bad. For example, when one wants to clearly view or photograph a historical or famous landmark, having utility poles around it will not only block the view but also make it look less elegant.

However, some street photographers, including me, feel this is what makes Japanese cities unique and exciting. Behind buildings in the city center are electric wires, condenser units, exhaust ducts for ventilation fans, and other things that support and comfort people's livelihoods.

Shanghai Restaurant. Shinjuku, Tokyo. In the middle of glittering Kabukicho is this restaurant with a bizarre menu that includes grasshoppers, cicadas, spiders, centipedes, and even snakes and scorpions.

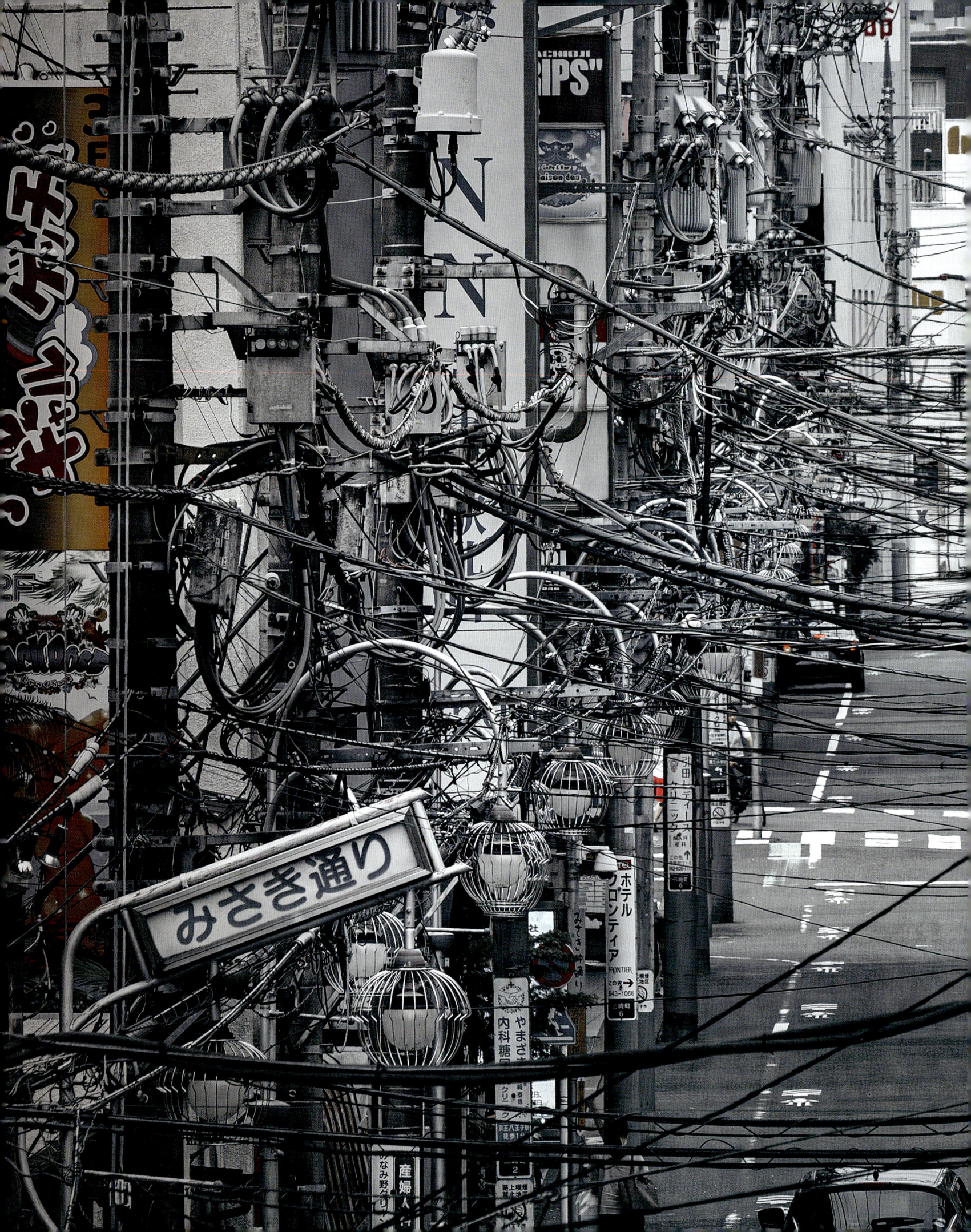

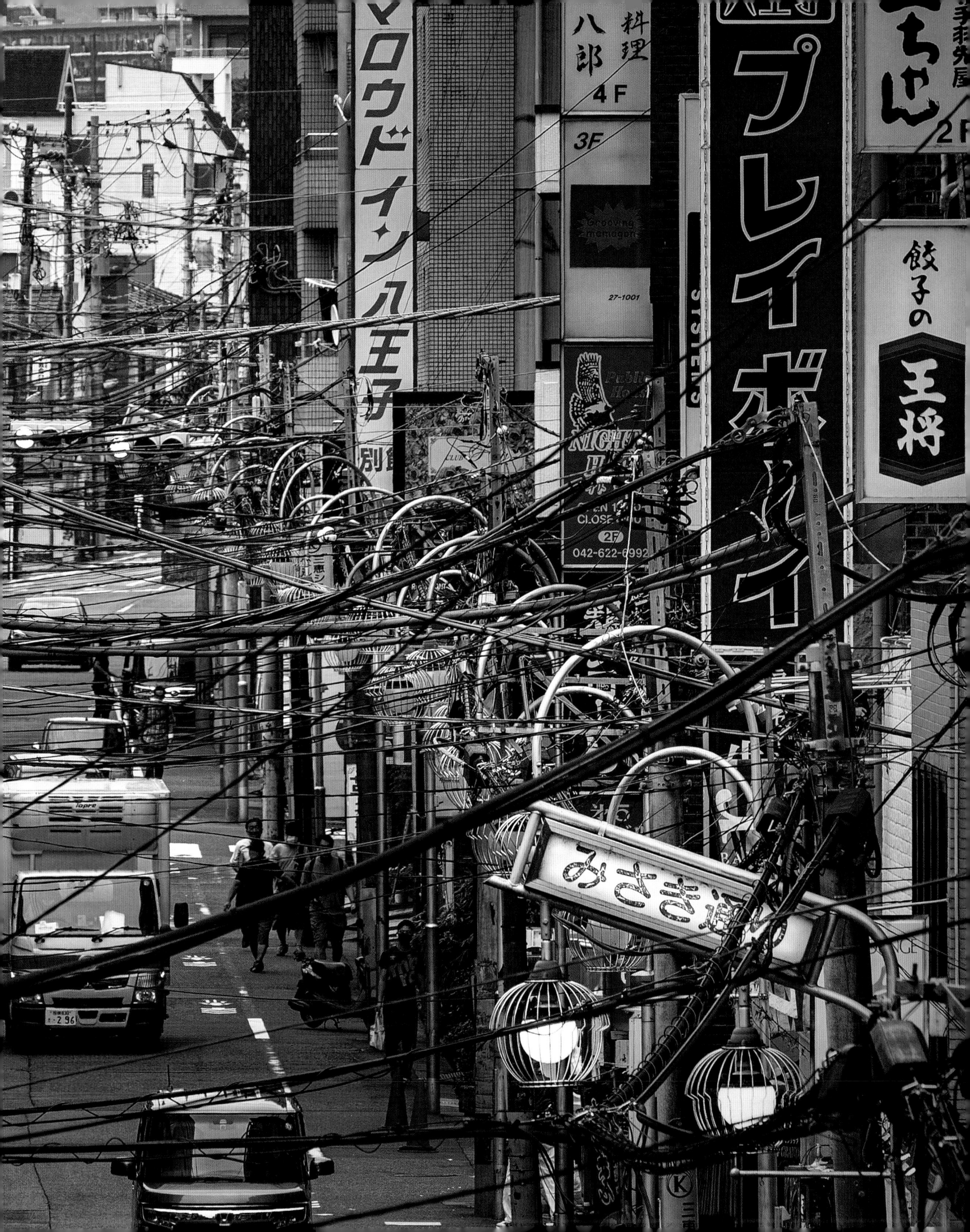

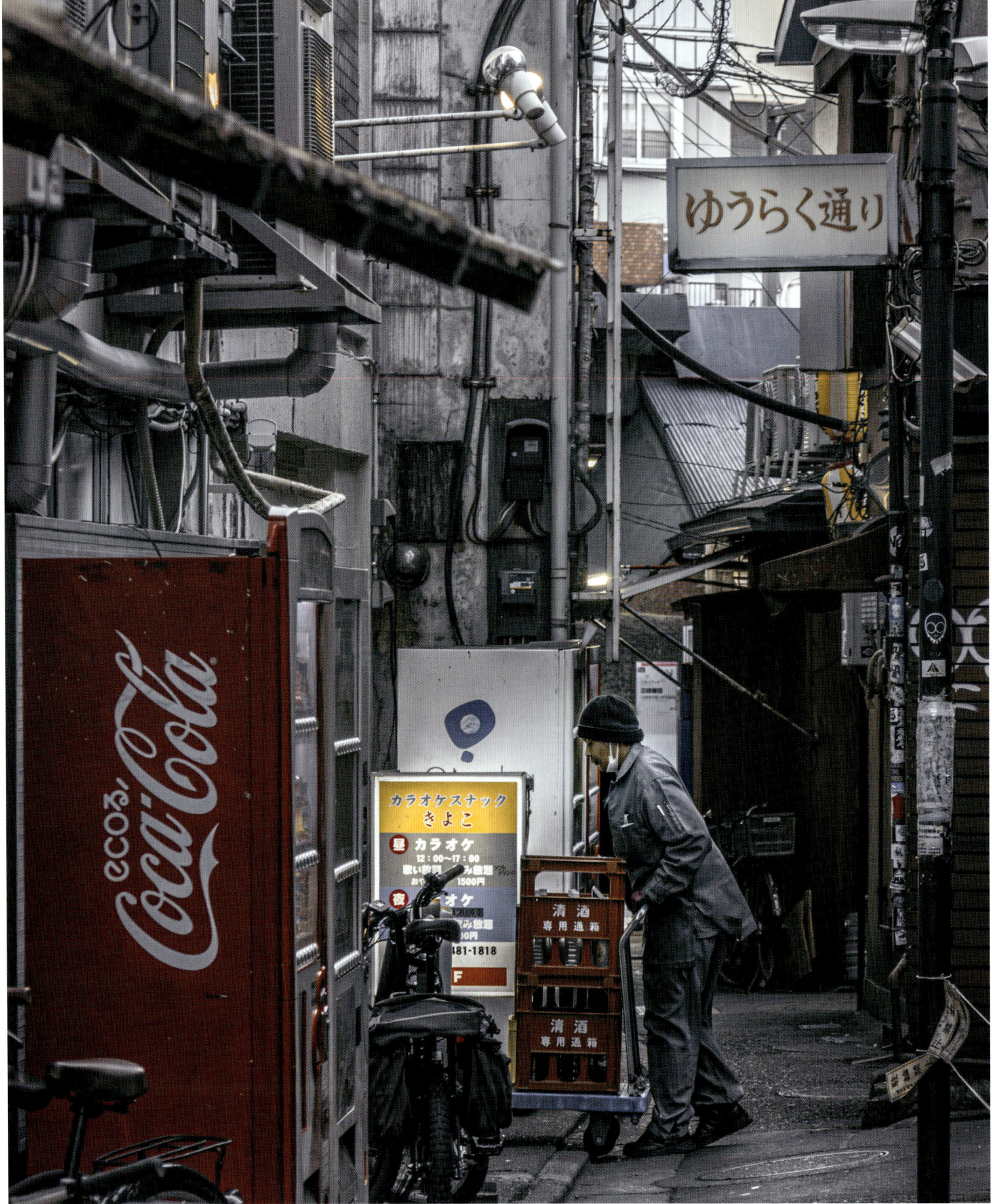

previous spread **Electric Wire Scenery in Misaki-cho.** Hachioji, Tokyo. The wires lining this street near Hachioji Station are unpopular with the locals and will eventually be buried underground.

Karaoke Snack Bar. Sangenjaya, Tokyo. Yuraku Street is located at the far end of Sangenjaya's Triangle Zone. Sake is delivered to the bar every evening.

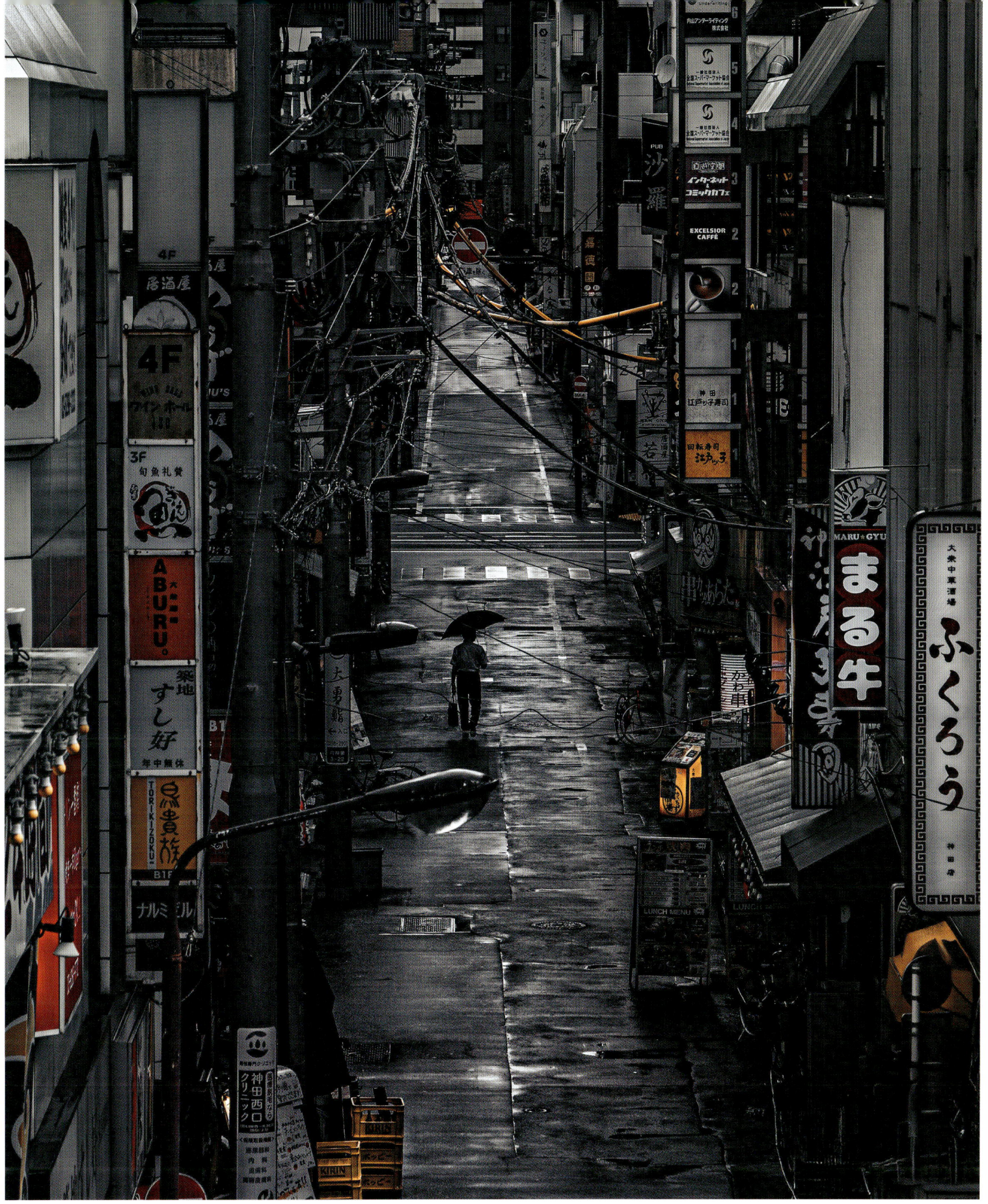

Light and Shadow. Kanda, Tokyo. Rainy days make for special photos. This one was taken with a zoom lens from the platform at Kanda Station

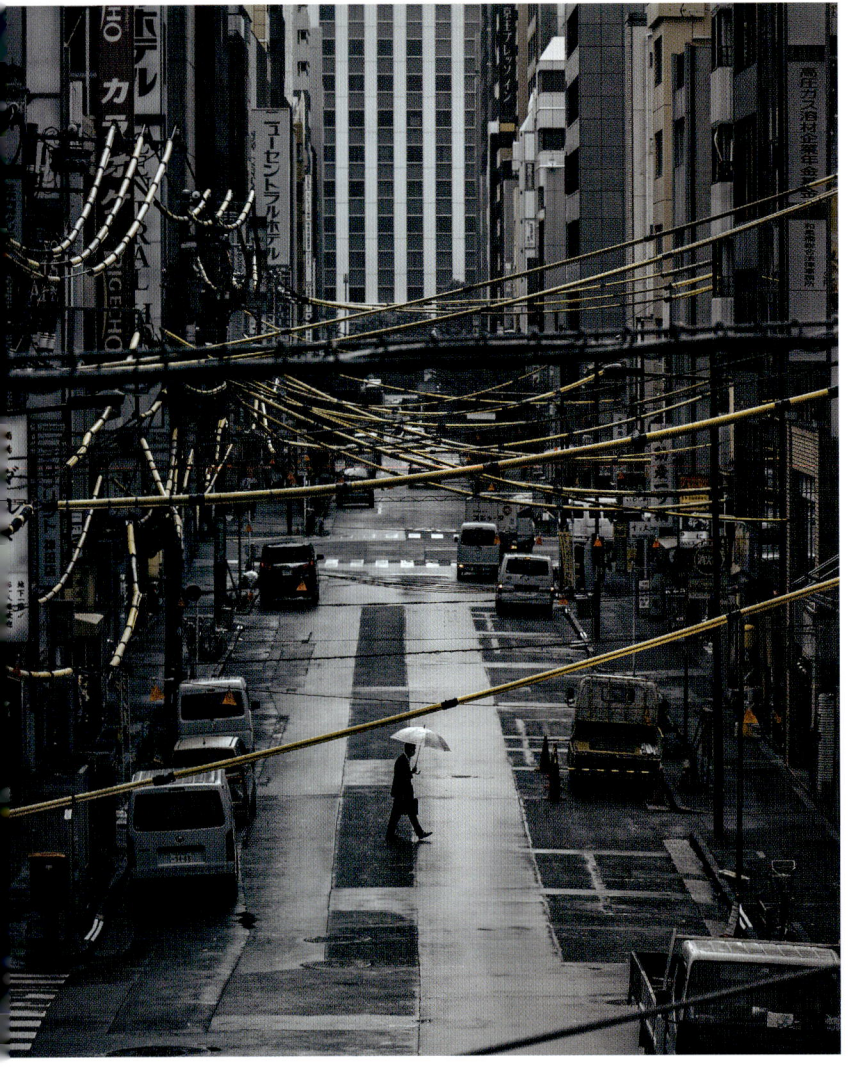

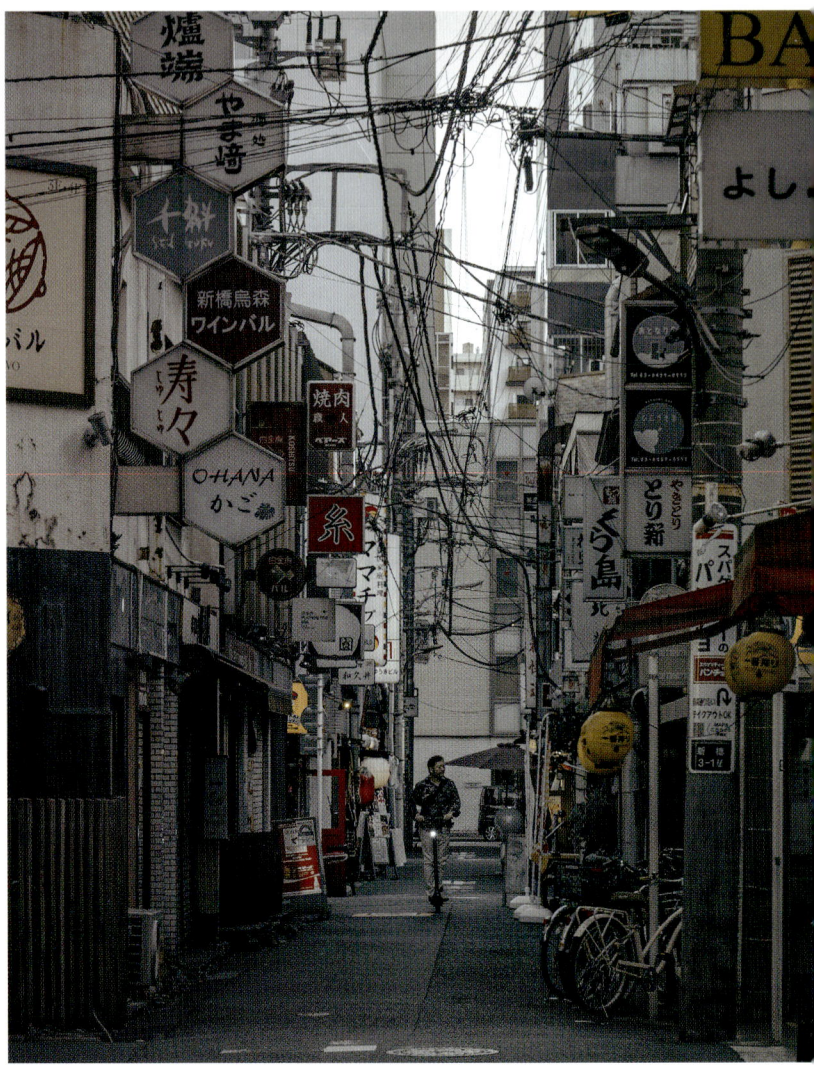

Tacho Odori Avenue. Kanda, Tokyo. The yellow covers on the wires were supposed to be removed after construction, but for some reason they have been left in place.

Alley with Hexagonal Sign. Shinbashi, Tokyo. I like the hexagonal sign in this alley and often take pictures of it. Since it is daytime, the irregularly placed power lines are clearly visible, creating an even better scene.

Tanuki Street. Asakusa, Tokyo. *Tanuki* translates to "raccoon," and there are various legends and beliefs about raccoons in Japan.

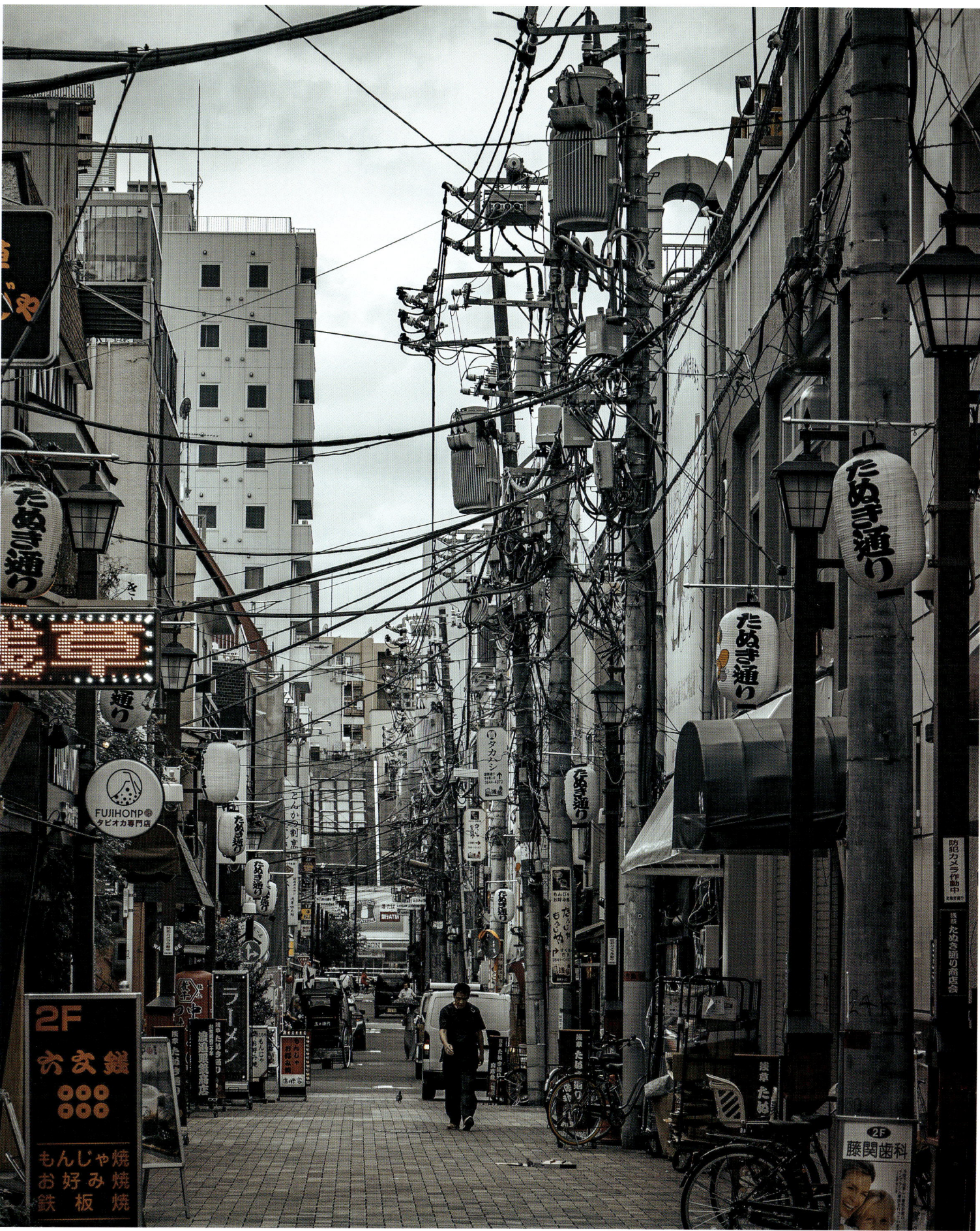

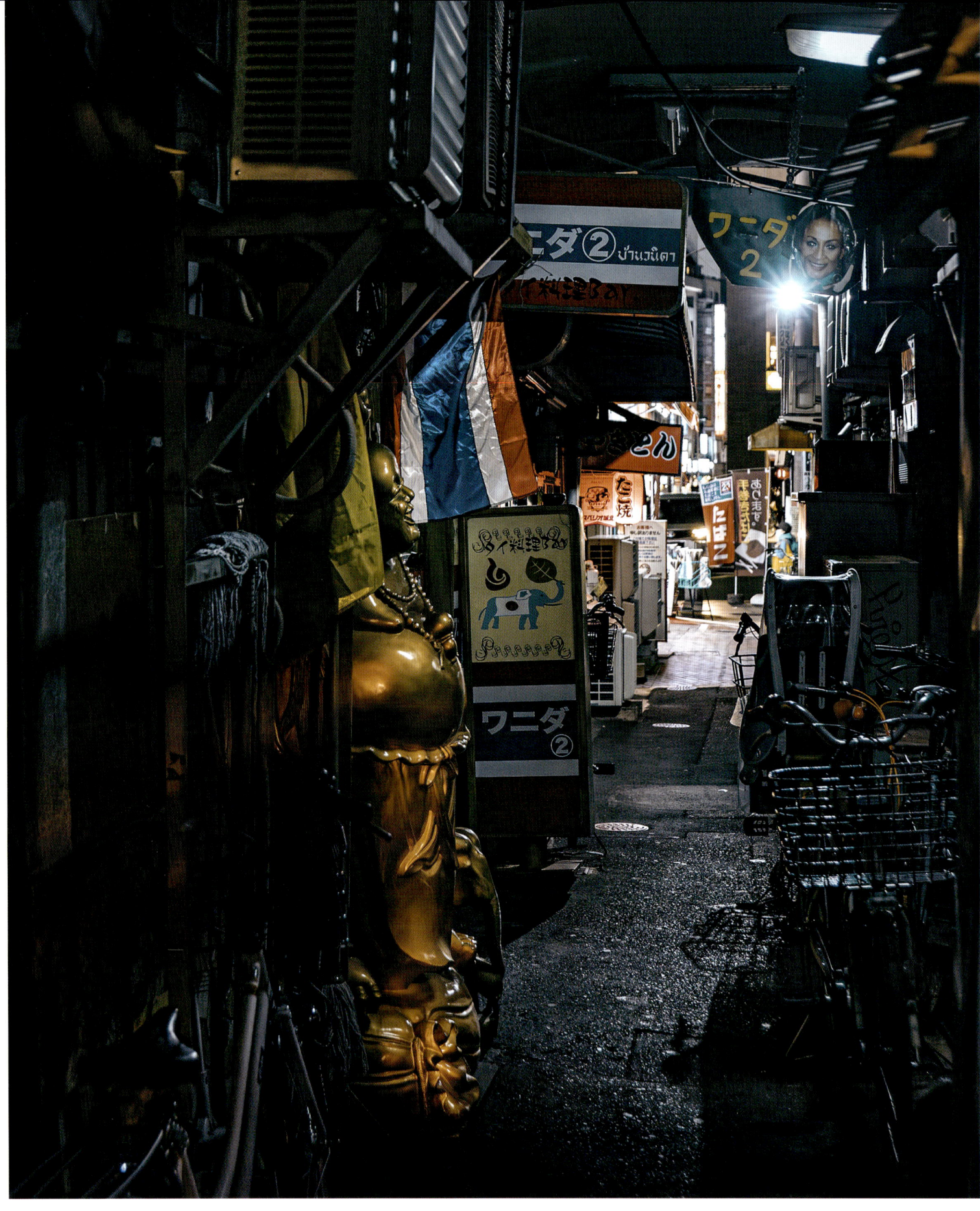

Thai Restaurant Alley. Akabane, Tokyo.
A golden statue stands out in the darkness
and chaos of the alleyway.

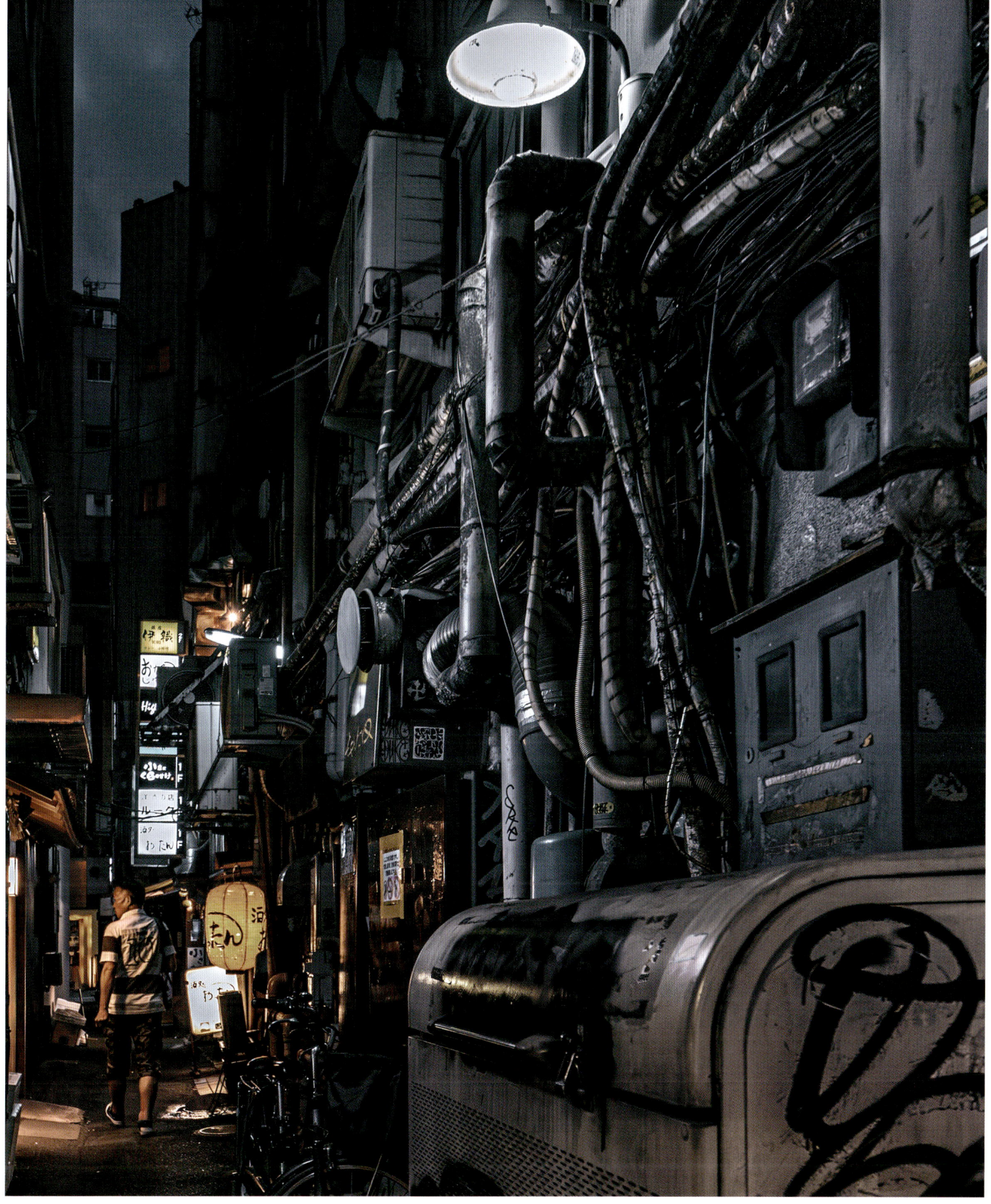

Back Alleys of Ginza. Ginza, Tokyo. Even modern buildings in Ginza have chaotic scenes like this behind them.

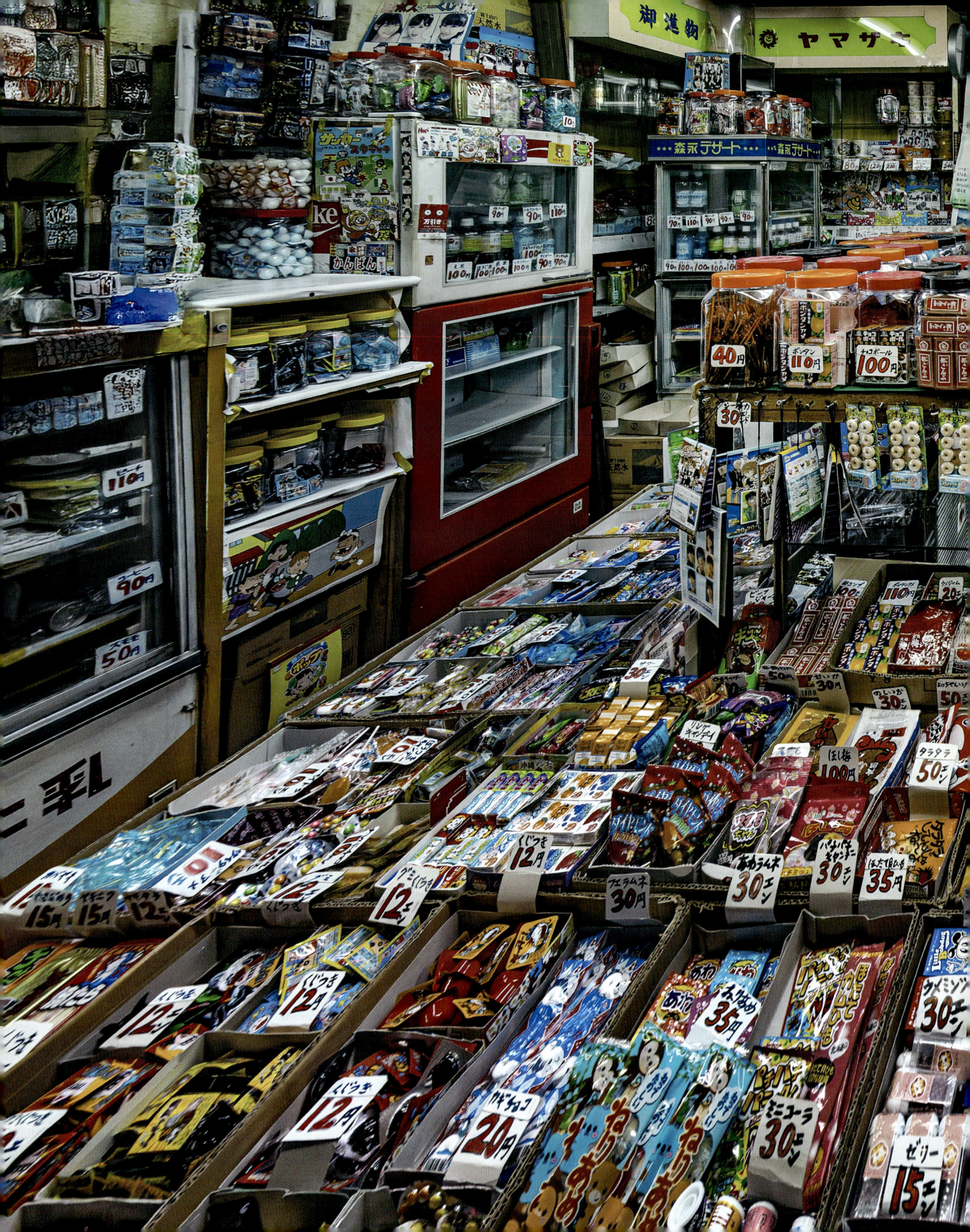

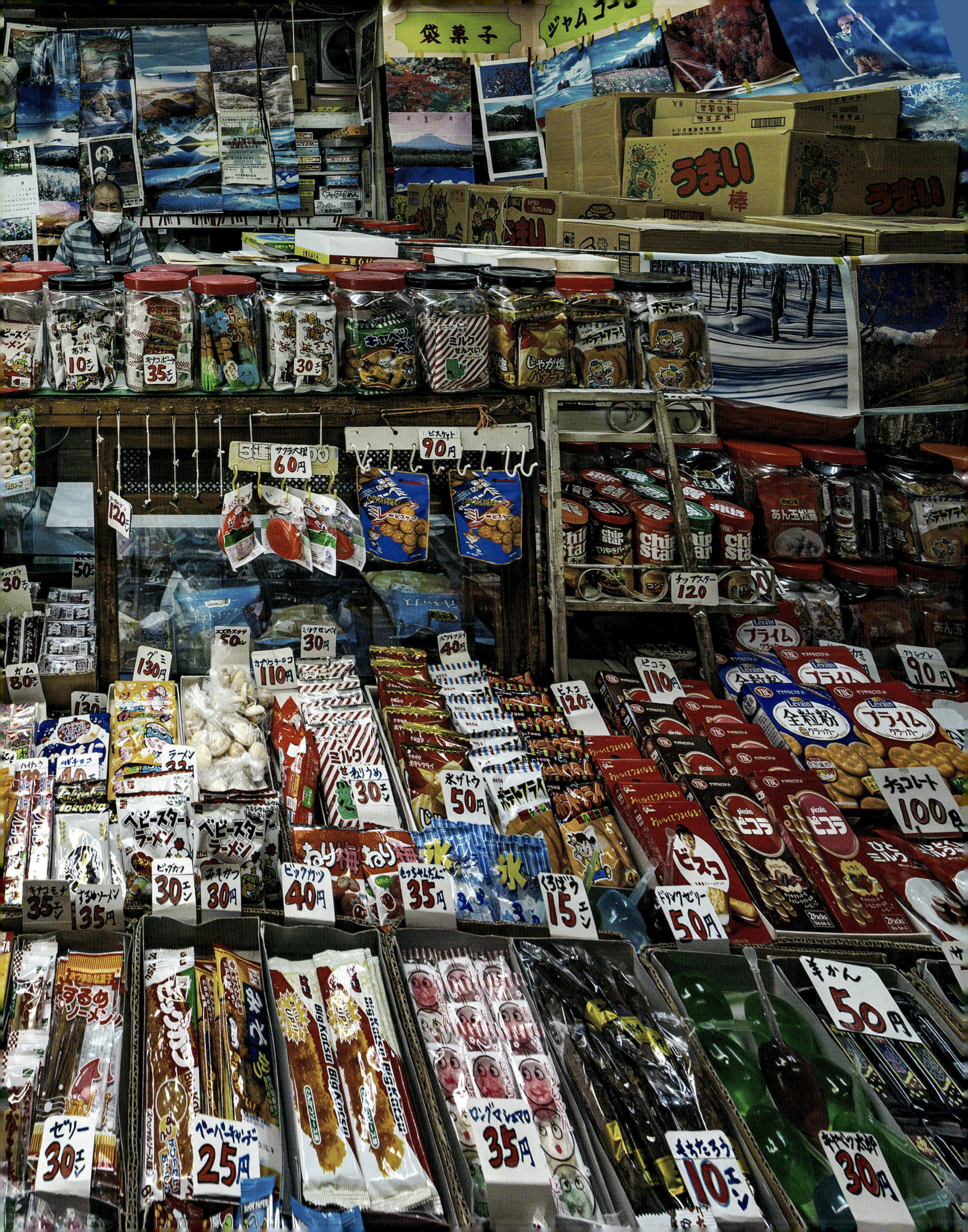

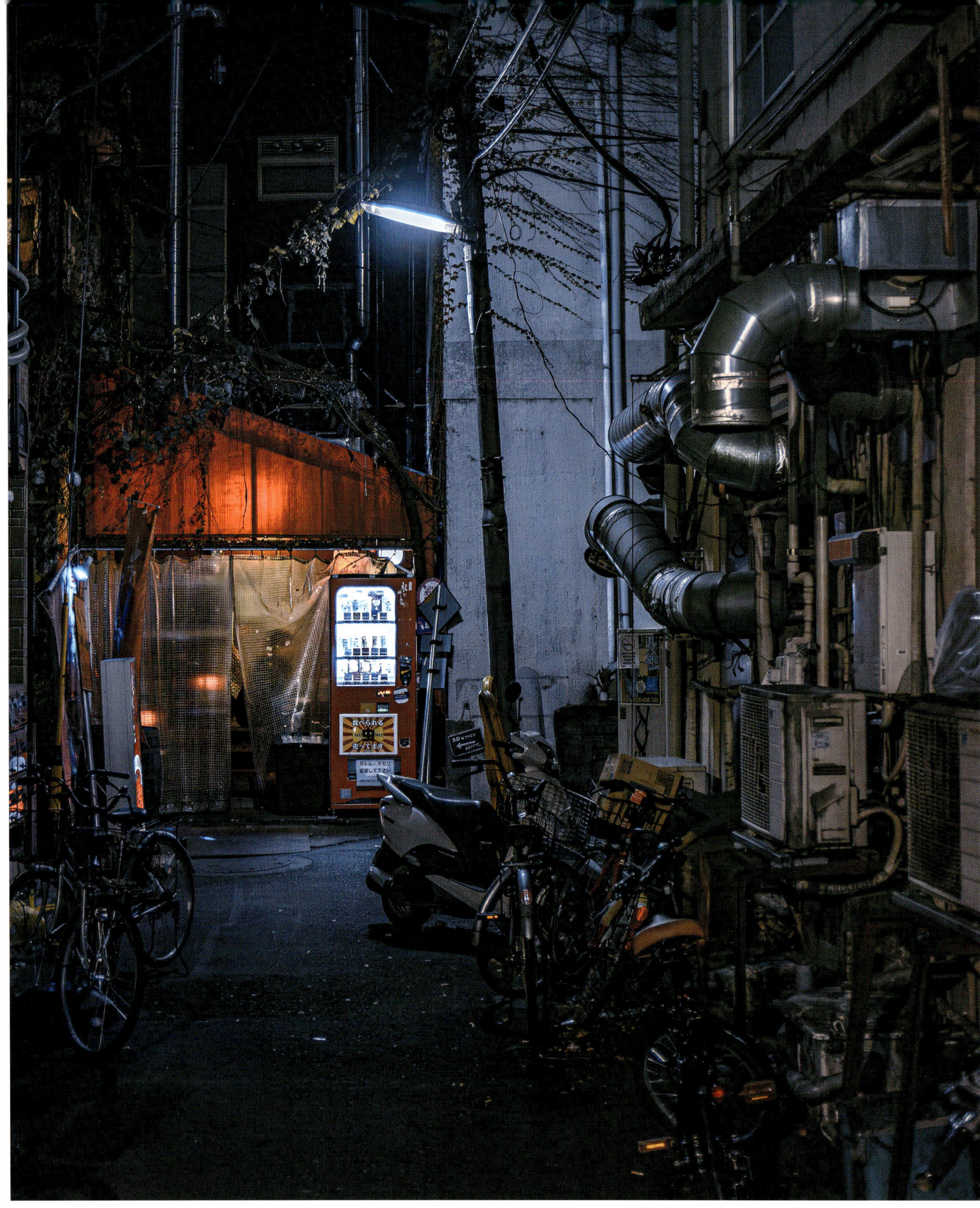

previous spread **Old-Fashioned Candy Store**. Tokyo. The owner of this store is ninety-five years old, but he was very energetic and willing to be photographed. When a girl came in to buy something, he greeted her with a big smile, which I found to be quite impressive.

Insect Vending Machine. Takadanobaba, Tokyo. This is a back alley where few people pass. Grass is tangled in the wires, and the exposed pipes and condenser units are intriguing. Even more surprising is the restaurant in the back that specializes in insects, reptiles, and wild animals. A vending machine in front of the store sells "insect ingredients."

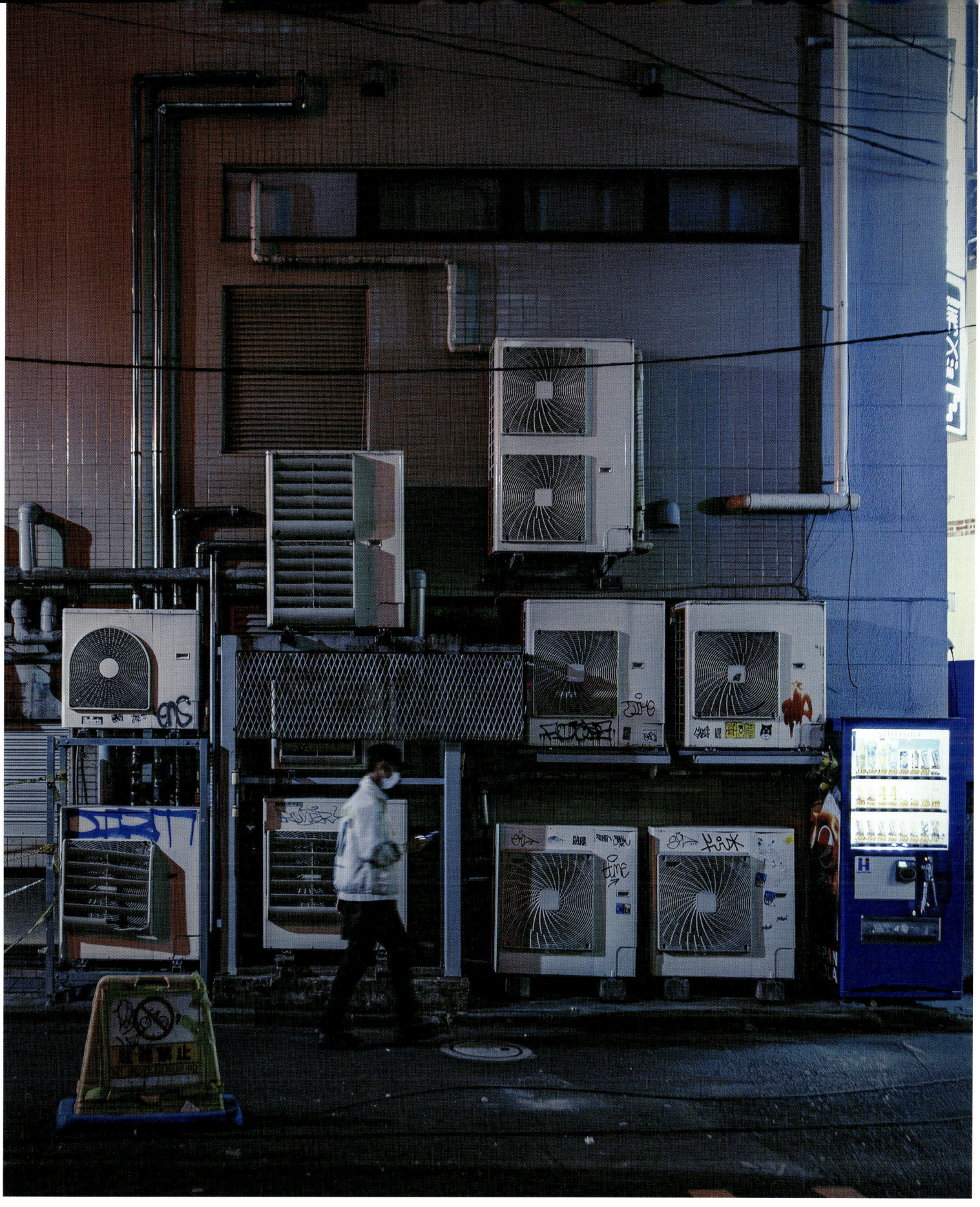

Condenser Unit Next to Soba Noodle Shop.
Shibuya, Tokyo. If you go around the side of a
building, you will encounter this type of scene,
which plays an indispensable role in making
people's lives comfortable.

Wall of Toys. Nakano, Tokyo. When surrounded by toys piled without any gaps in between them, one is struck by a strange sensation.

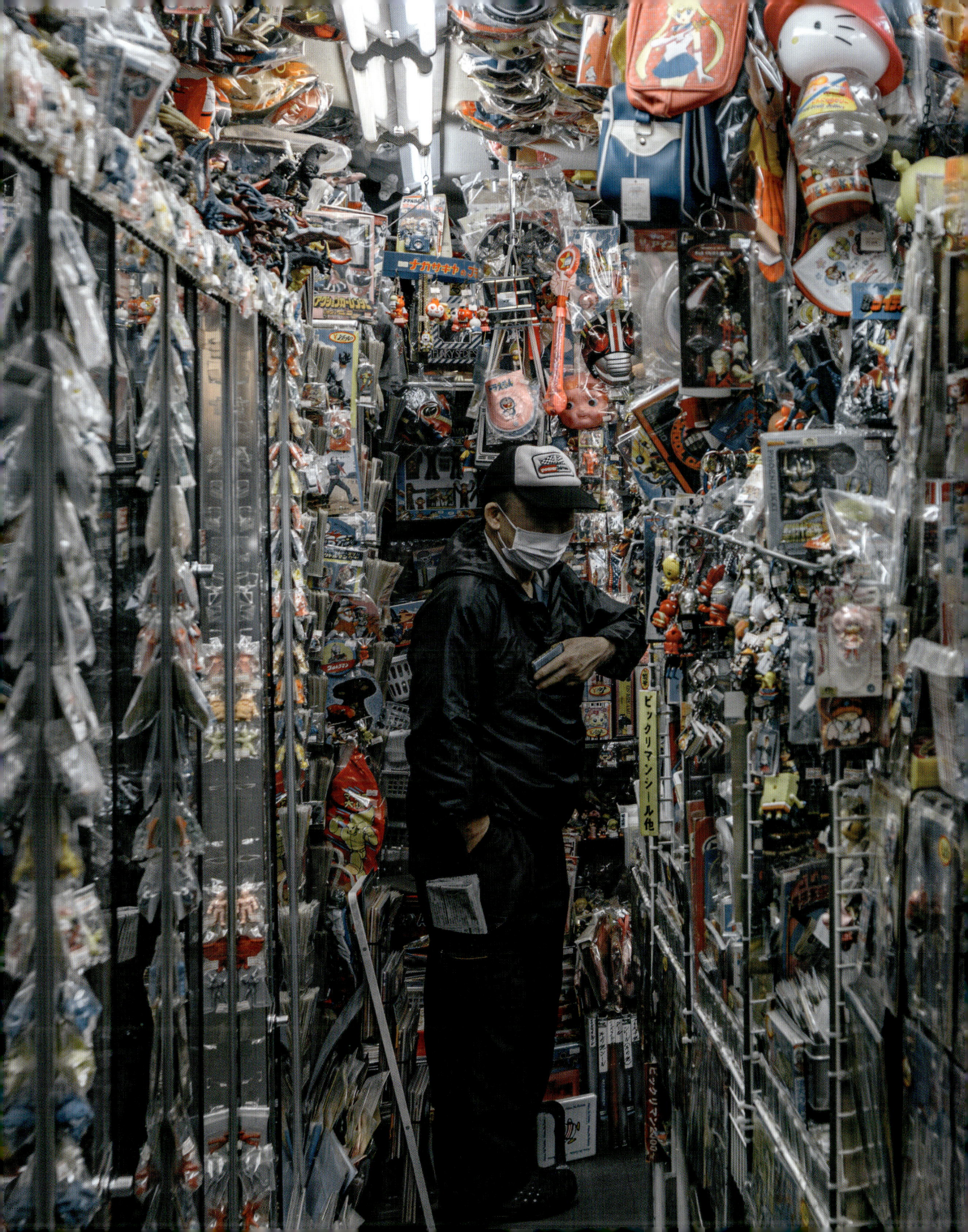

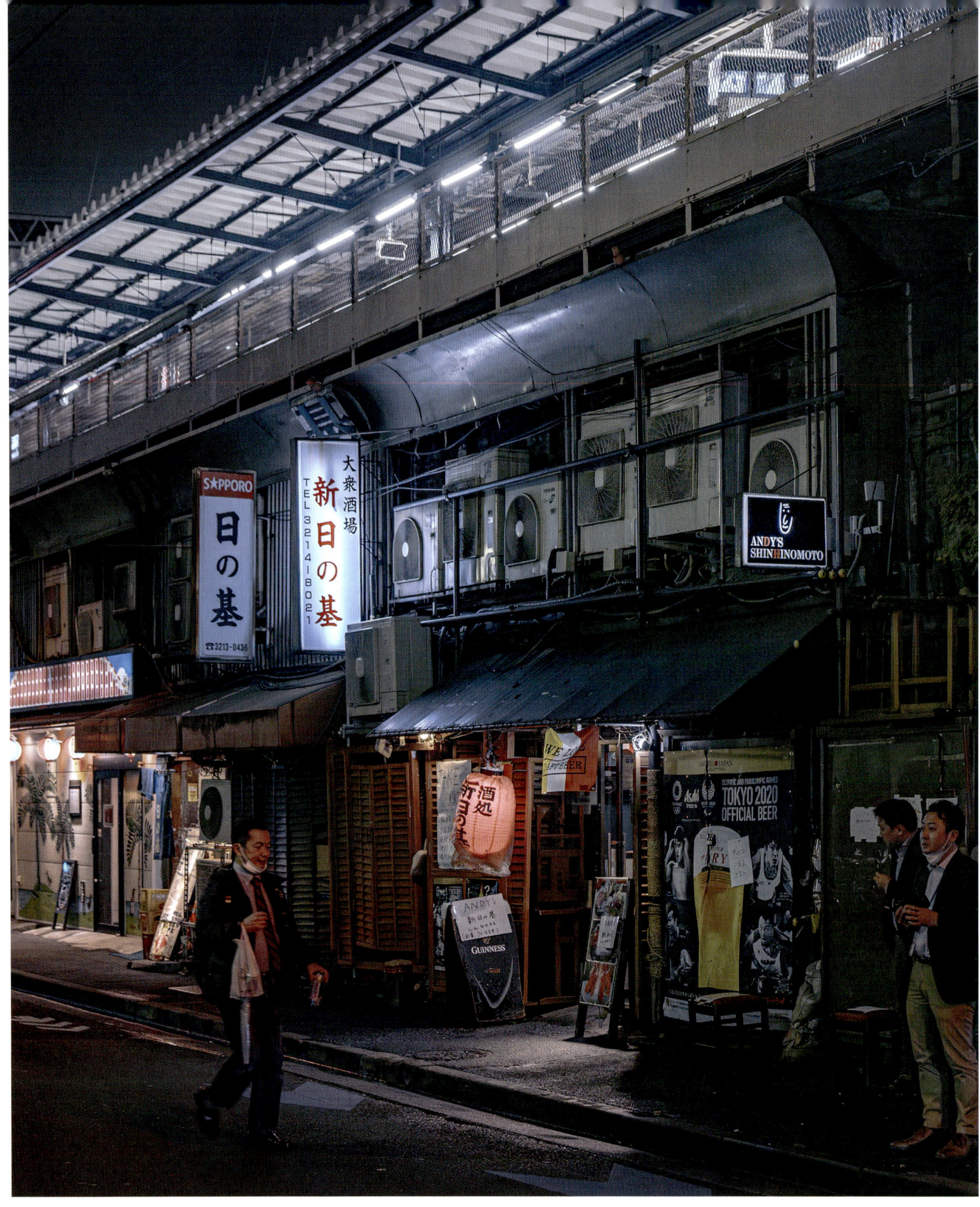

Izakaya Under the Platform. Yurakucho, Tokyo. At the top is the platform of Yurakucho Station and below it is an izakaya with many air conditioner units. A unique place.

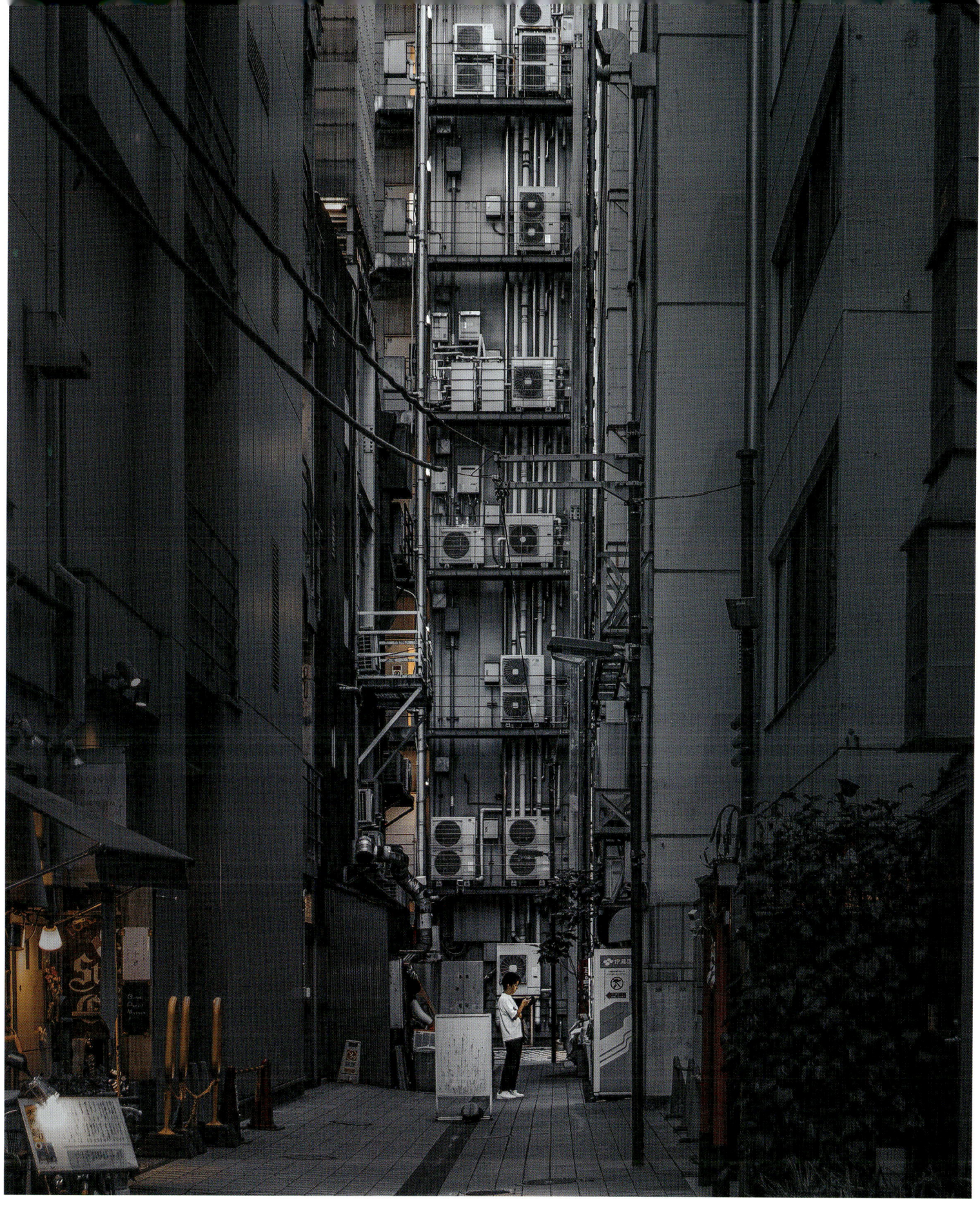

Condenser Units. Ginza, Tokyo. These air-conditioner units are nicely lined up along the back of this long, narrow building.

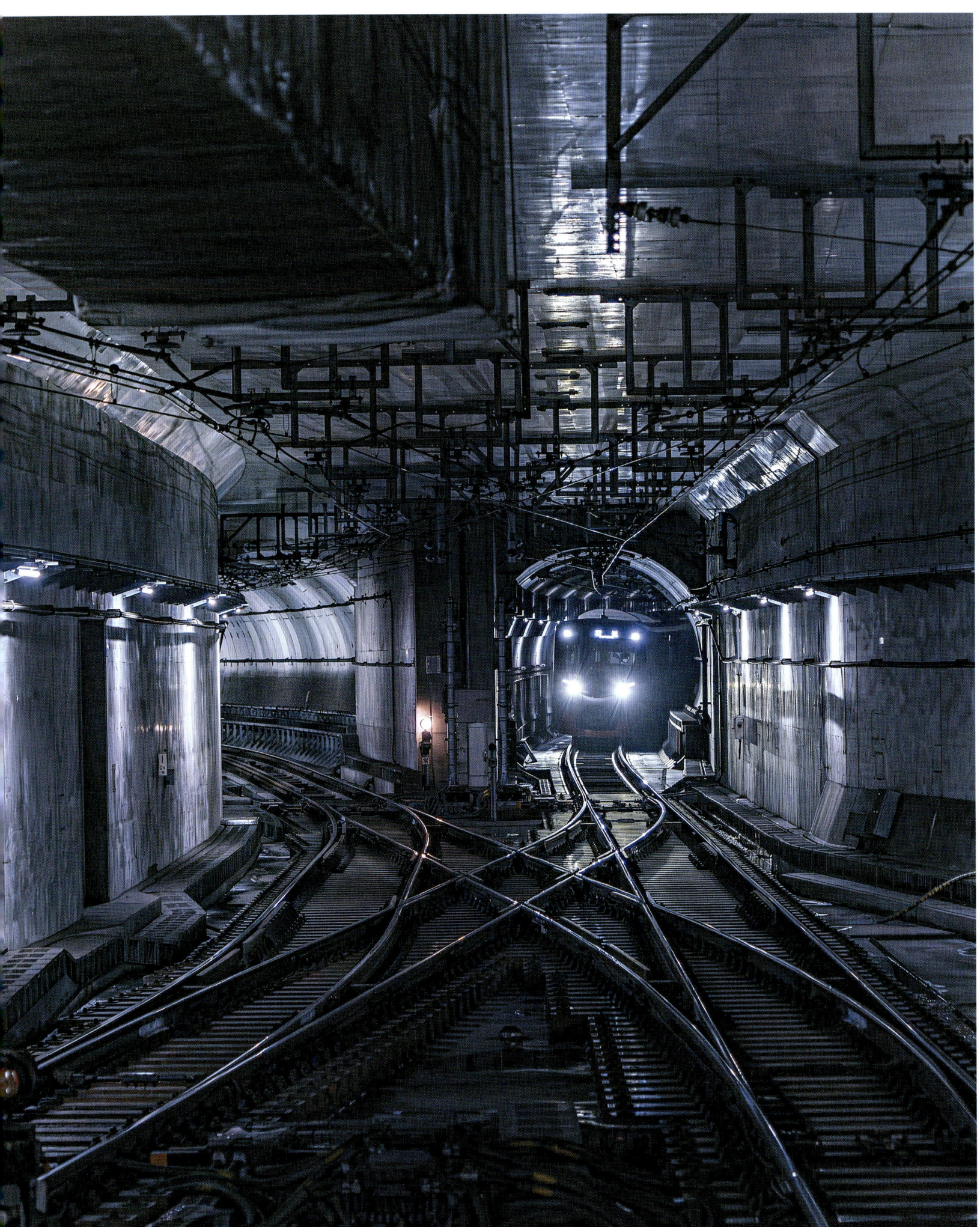

社会基盤

Japan has modern architecture and state-of-the-art transportation systems, but there are also older, classic buildings and vehicles that contrast with them.

I enjoy photographing the juxtaposition of new and old, and this distinction is especially evident in the photos in this section.

Twin Tunnels. Chofu, Tokyo. This photo was taken from the platform of Chofu Station. The complex intersecting tracks and twin tunnels make this scene special.

133

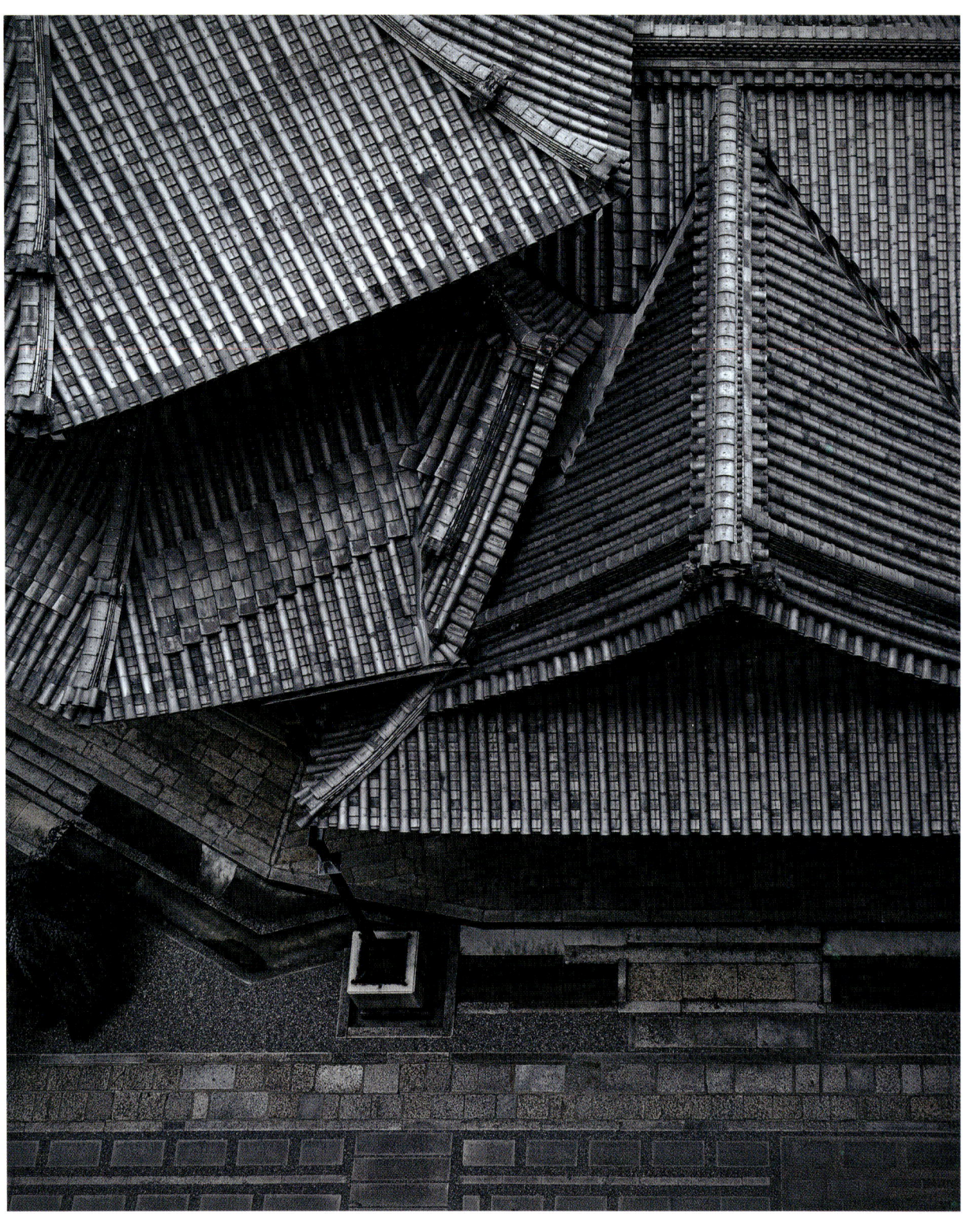

The Beauty of Tile Roofs. Kyoto. This is a bird's-eye view of Choho-ji Temple (Rokkaku-do) from an adjacent building.

Nakagin Capsule Tower. Shinbashi, Tokyo. This apartment building was designed by the late Kisho Kurokawa, a famous and brilliant architect. It was a beautifully designed complex with a unique collection of capsule-shaped dwellings. It was demolished in 2022 because of deterioration.

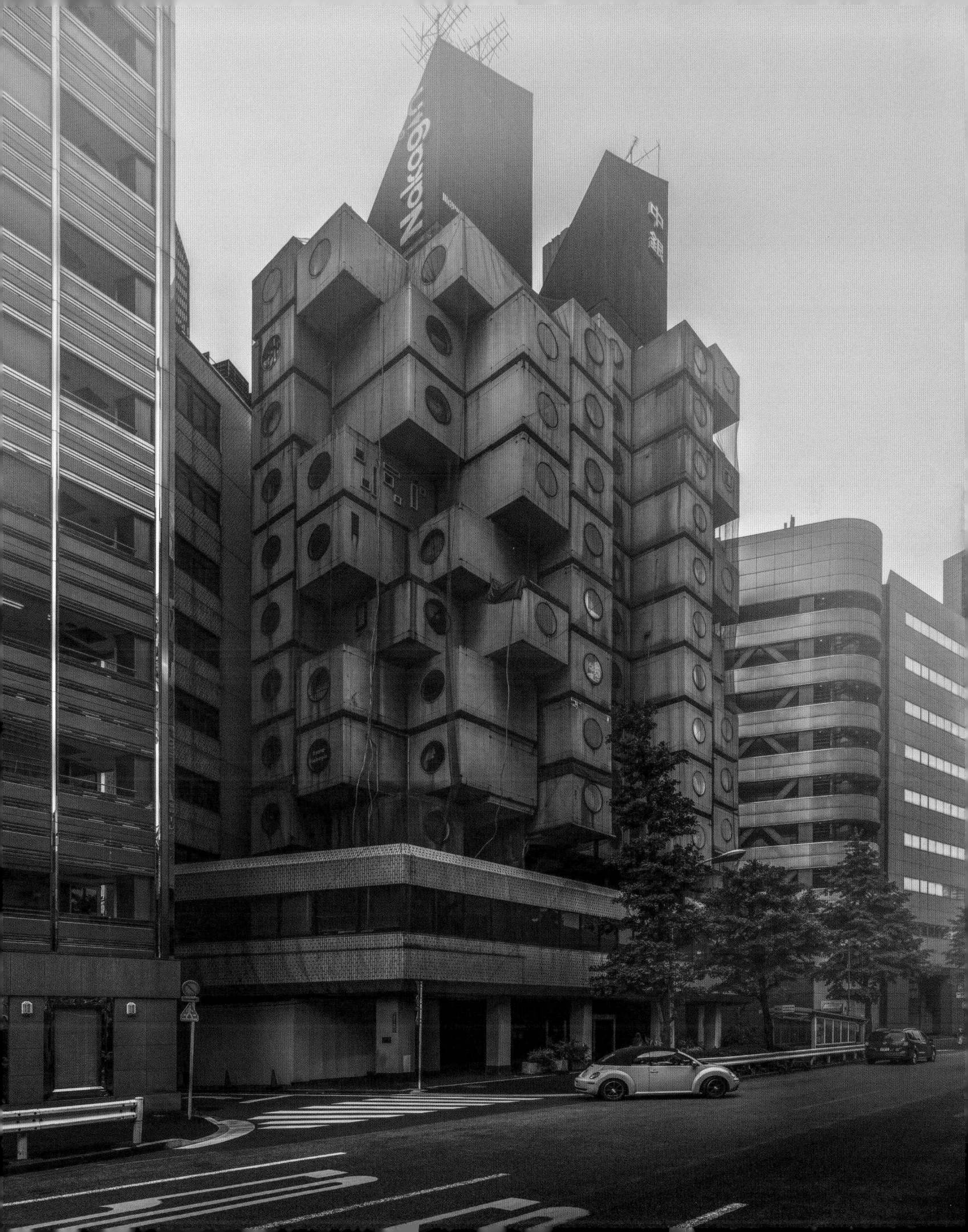

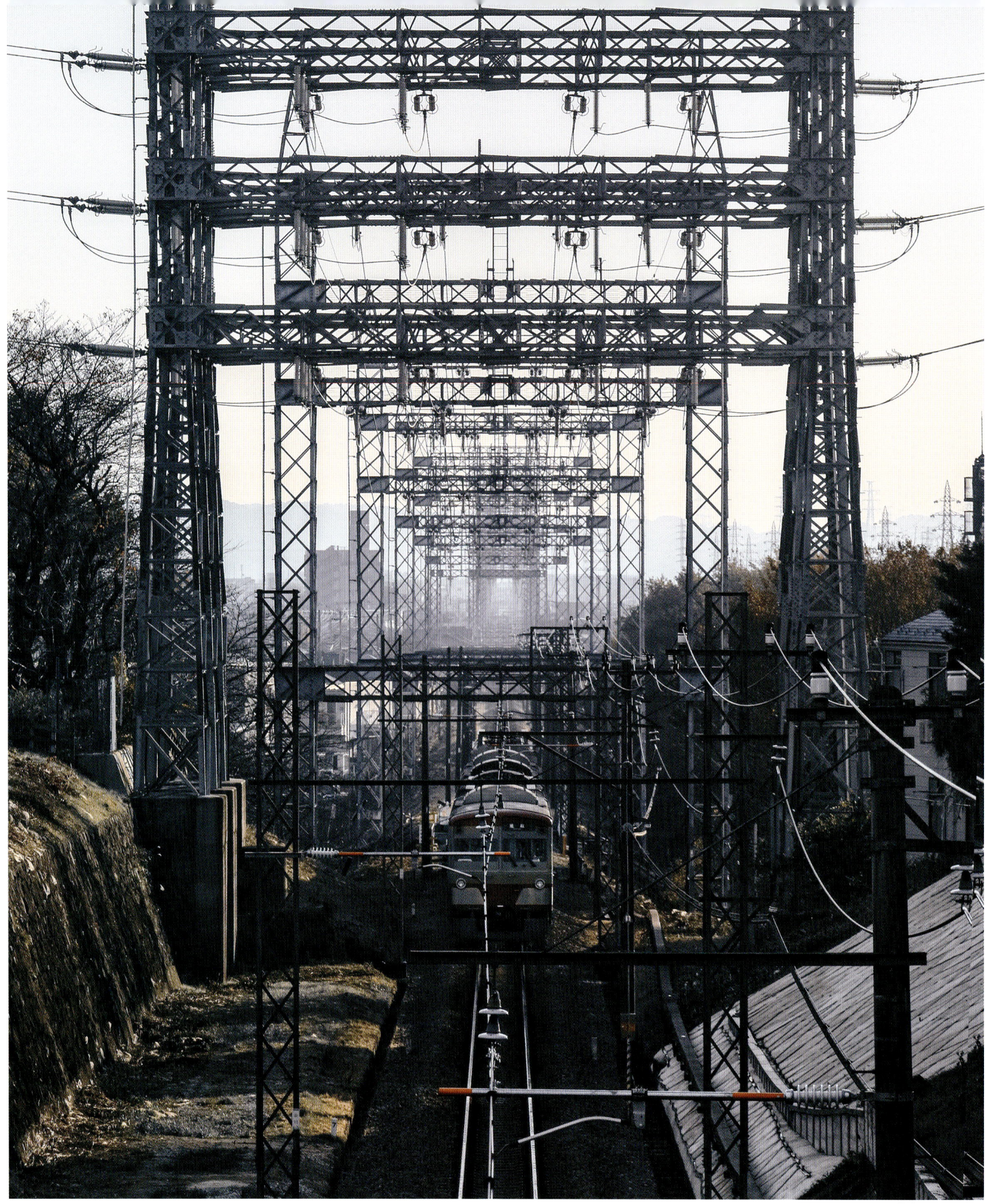

Seibu Tamagawa Line. Koganei, Tokyo.
Shin-Koganei Station is a great spot to utilize
the compression effect of a telephoto lens.
Mostly newer yellow trains pass by, but
occasionally you see the older red ones.

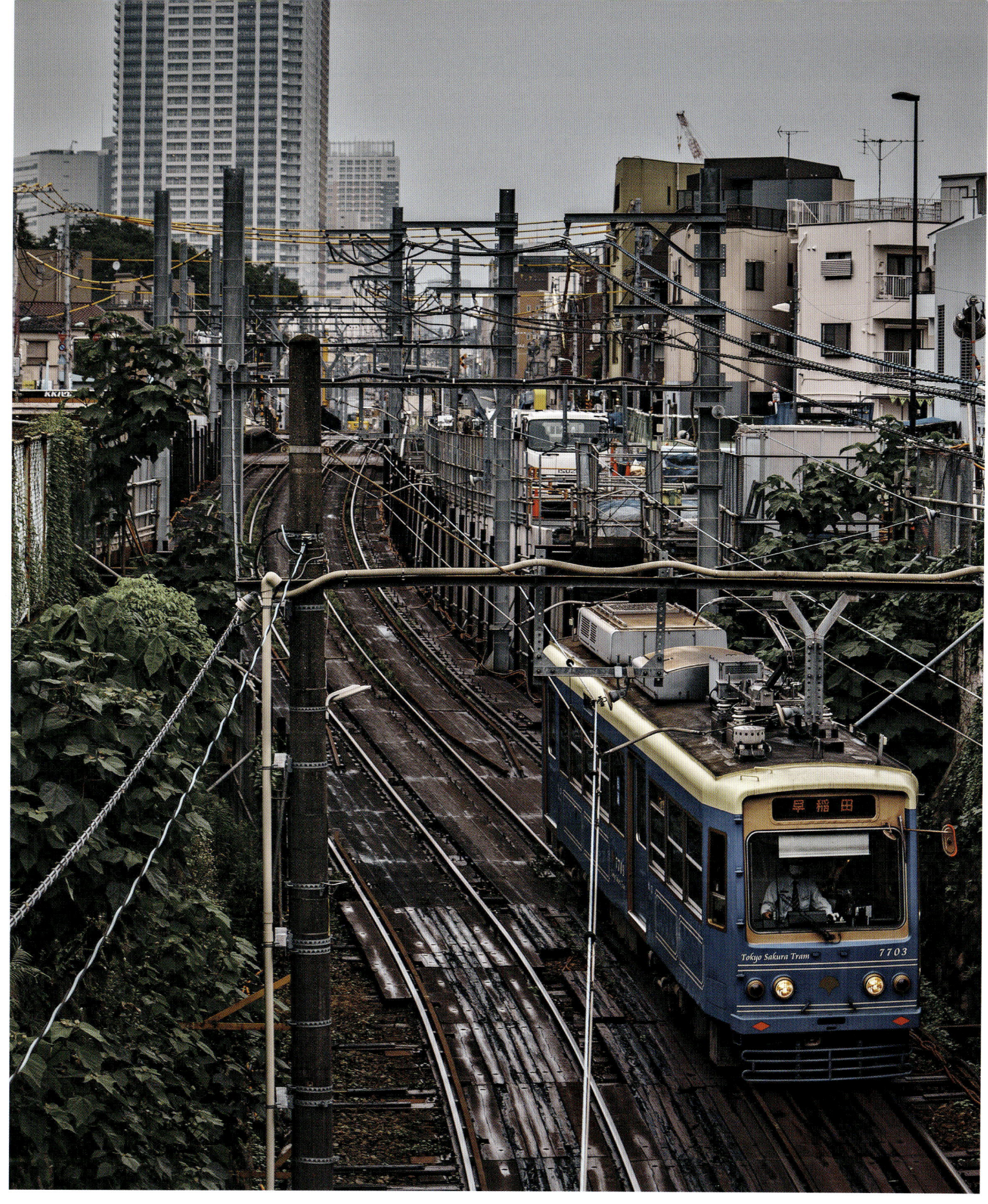

S Curve. Shinjuku, Tokyo. This shot from a bridge highlights the lovely one-car 7700.

Station Corridor. Iidabashi, Tokyo. Iidabashi
Station was designed by architect Makoto
Watanabe, who incorporated computer
programs into the design.

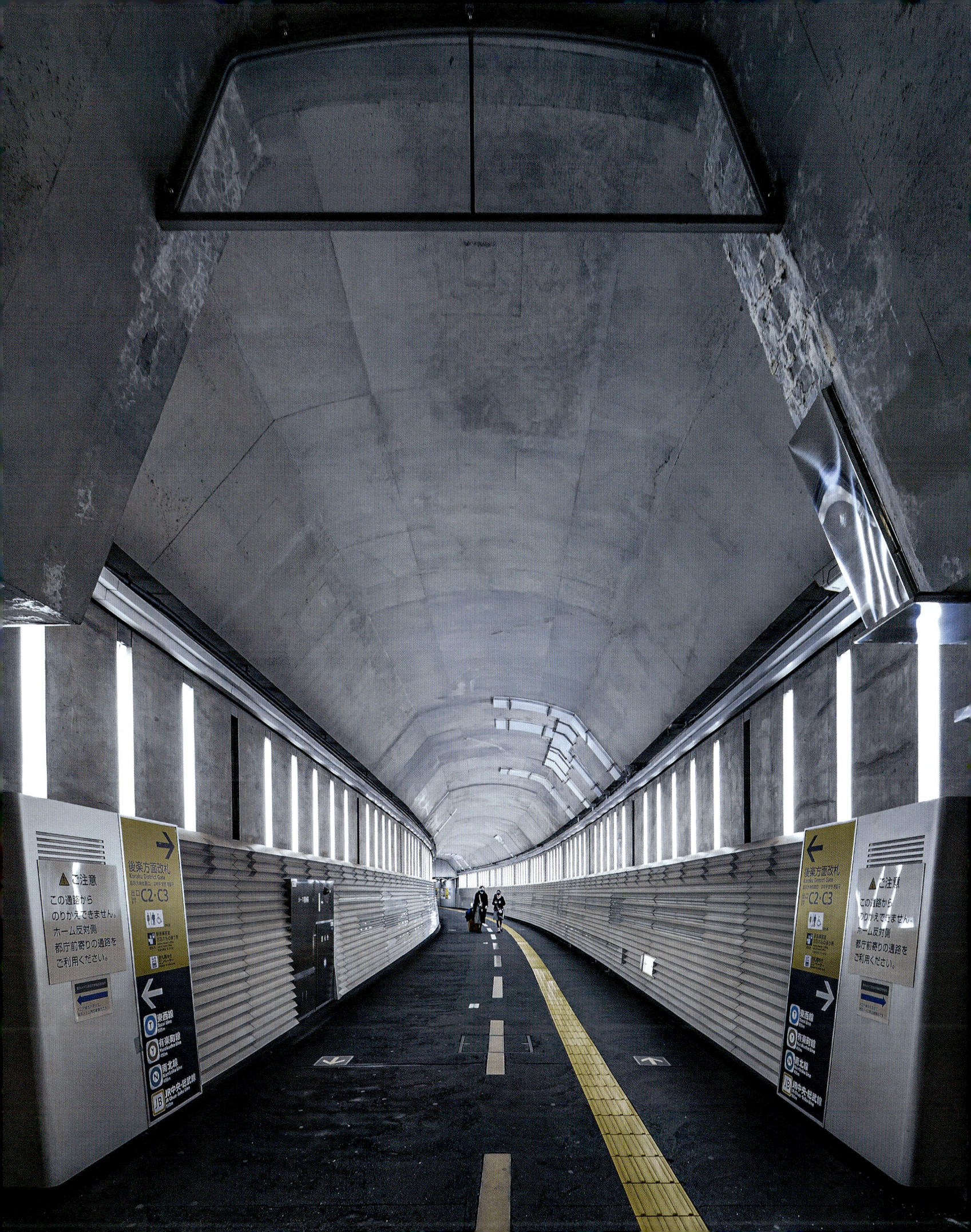

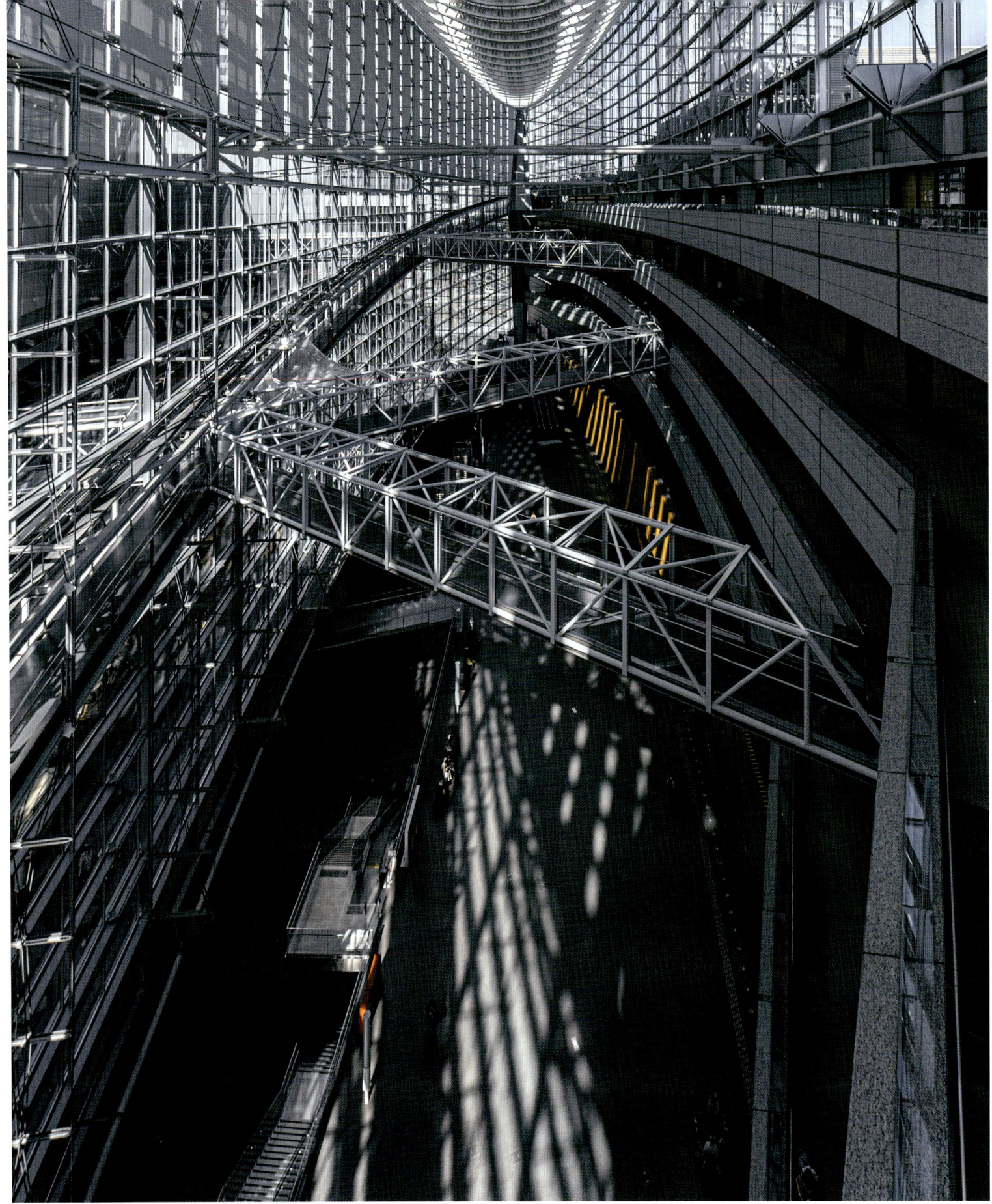

Tokyo International Forum, First Floor.
Yurakucho, Tokyo. Looking down from the
first floor, the light and shadows that pass
through the glass onto the floor create
interesting patterns.

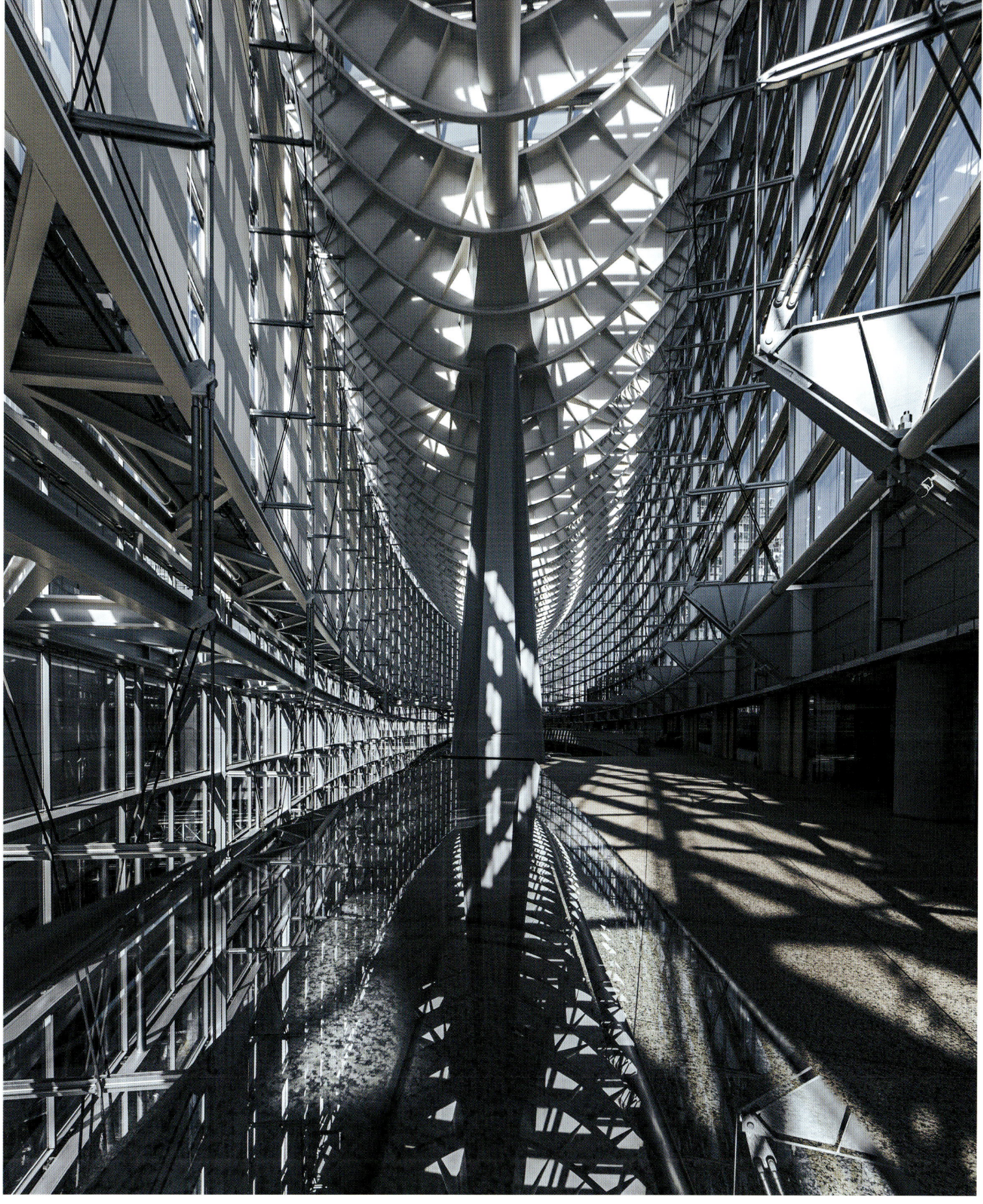

Tokyo International Forum, Second Floor.
Yurakucho, Tokyo. The glass atrium of this public cultural center has an exposed structure that resembles the skeleton of a ship.

Ginza Line, Shibuya Station. Shibuya, Tokyo. The platform of this train station, which was renovated in 2020, features an open space with no pillars and a continuous line of steel roof with an arched structure. It makes you feel as if you are inside the body of a giant whale or dinosaur.

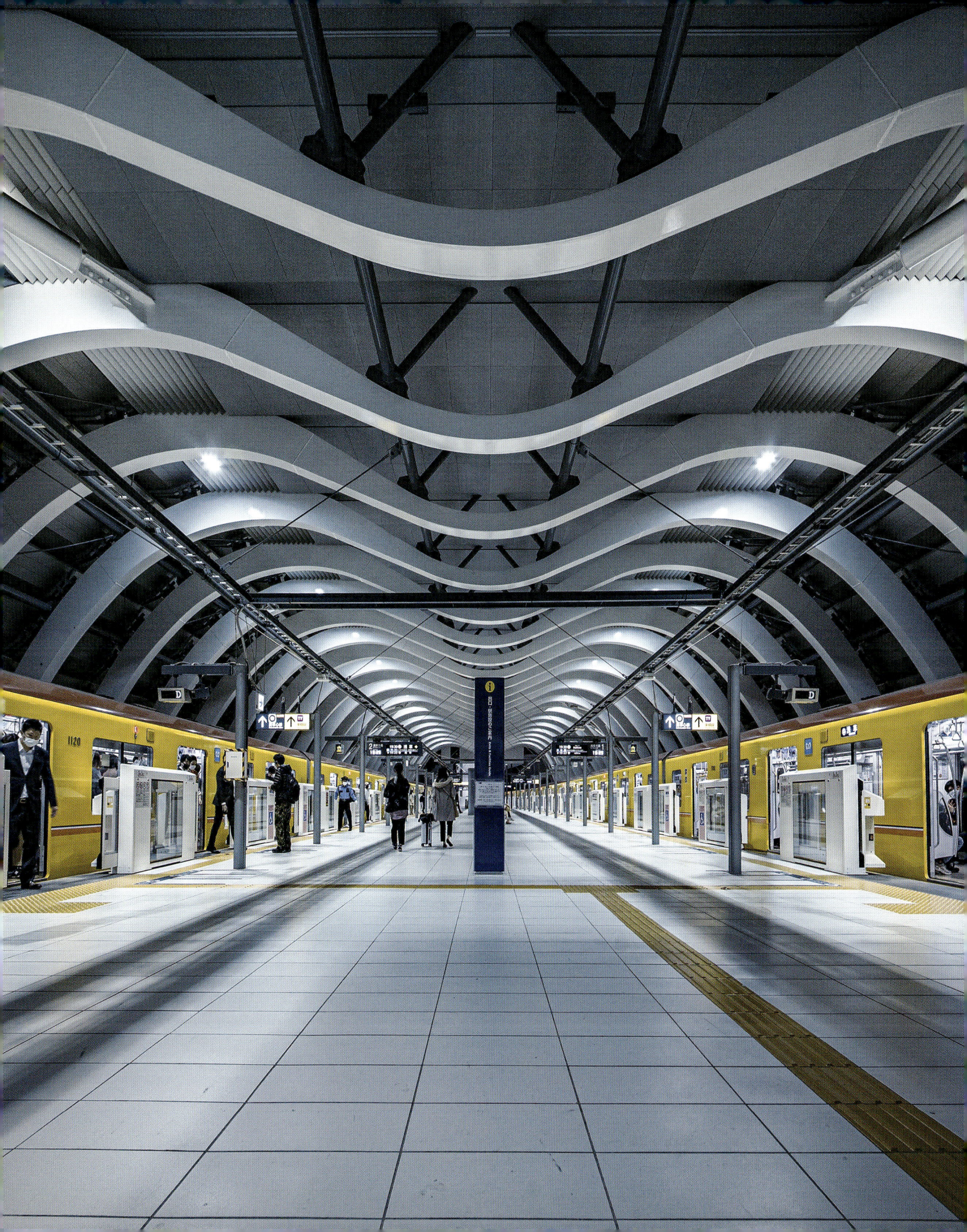

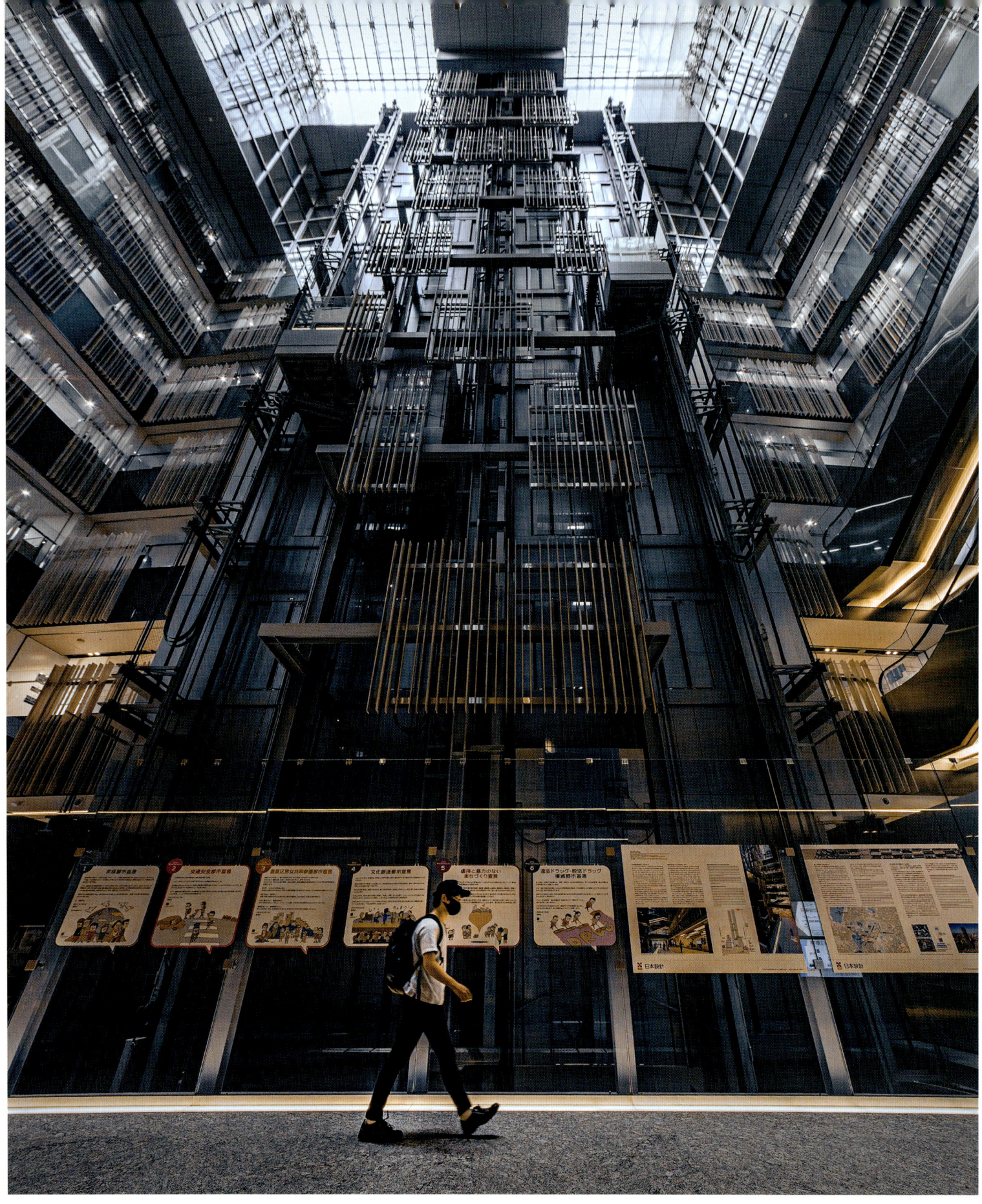

Toshima Ecomusée Town. Toshima, Tokyo.
This building was jointly designed by
renowned architects Kengo Kuma and Nihon
Sekkei and is the first condominium building
in Japan to house both government offices
and residential apartments.

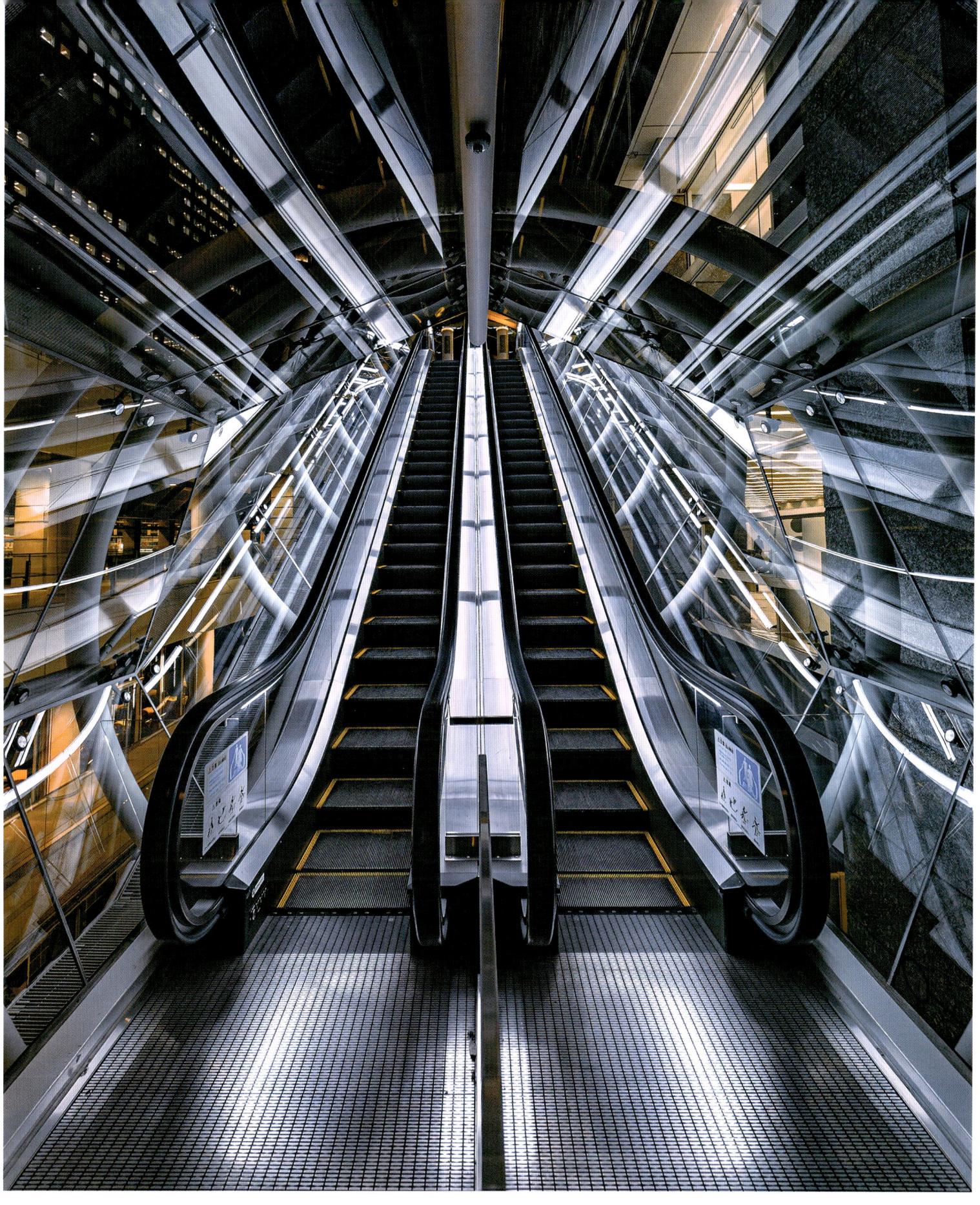

An Escalator Somewhere. Shinagawa, Tokyo. The light reflecting on the glass is very beautiful. It looks futuristic.

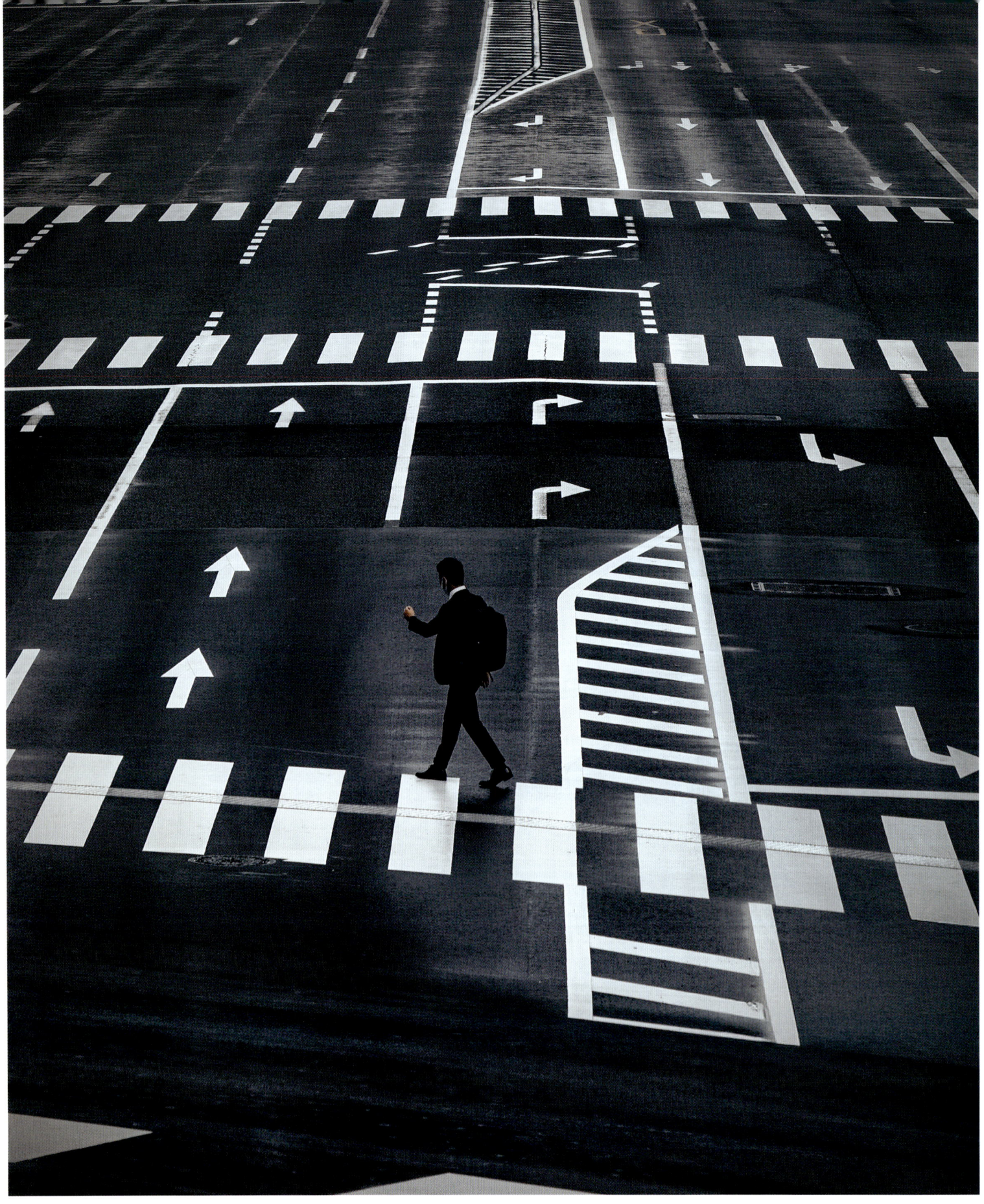

Empty Lot. Ueno, Tokyo. This photo was taken from the pedestrian bridge at Ueno Station. It was a rare scene with no cars because it was dawn.

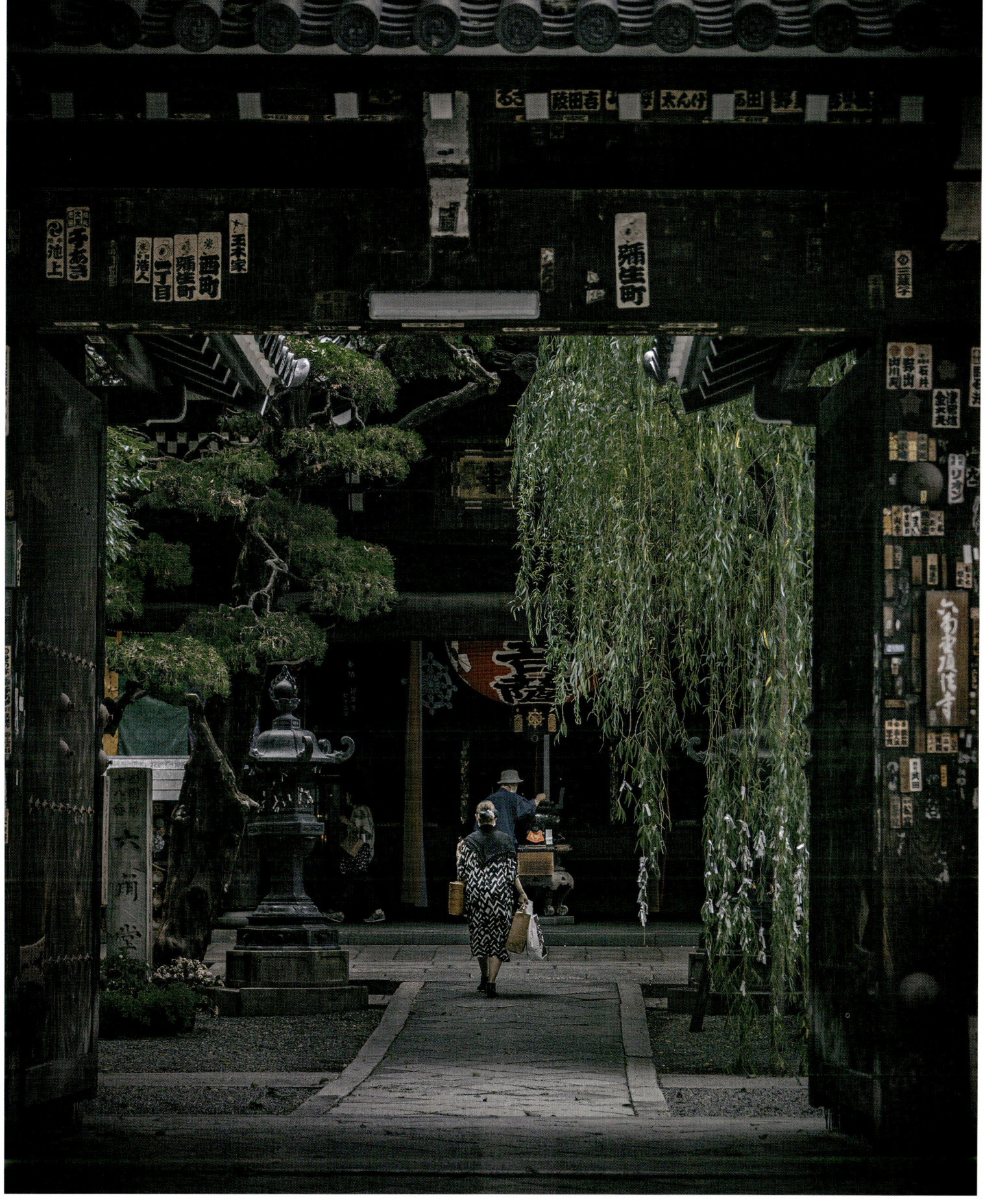

People Worshipping. Kyoto. Choho-ji Temple (Rokkaku-do) is said to be the birthplace of *ikebana* (flower arranging).

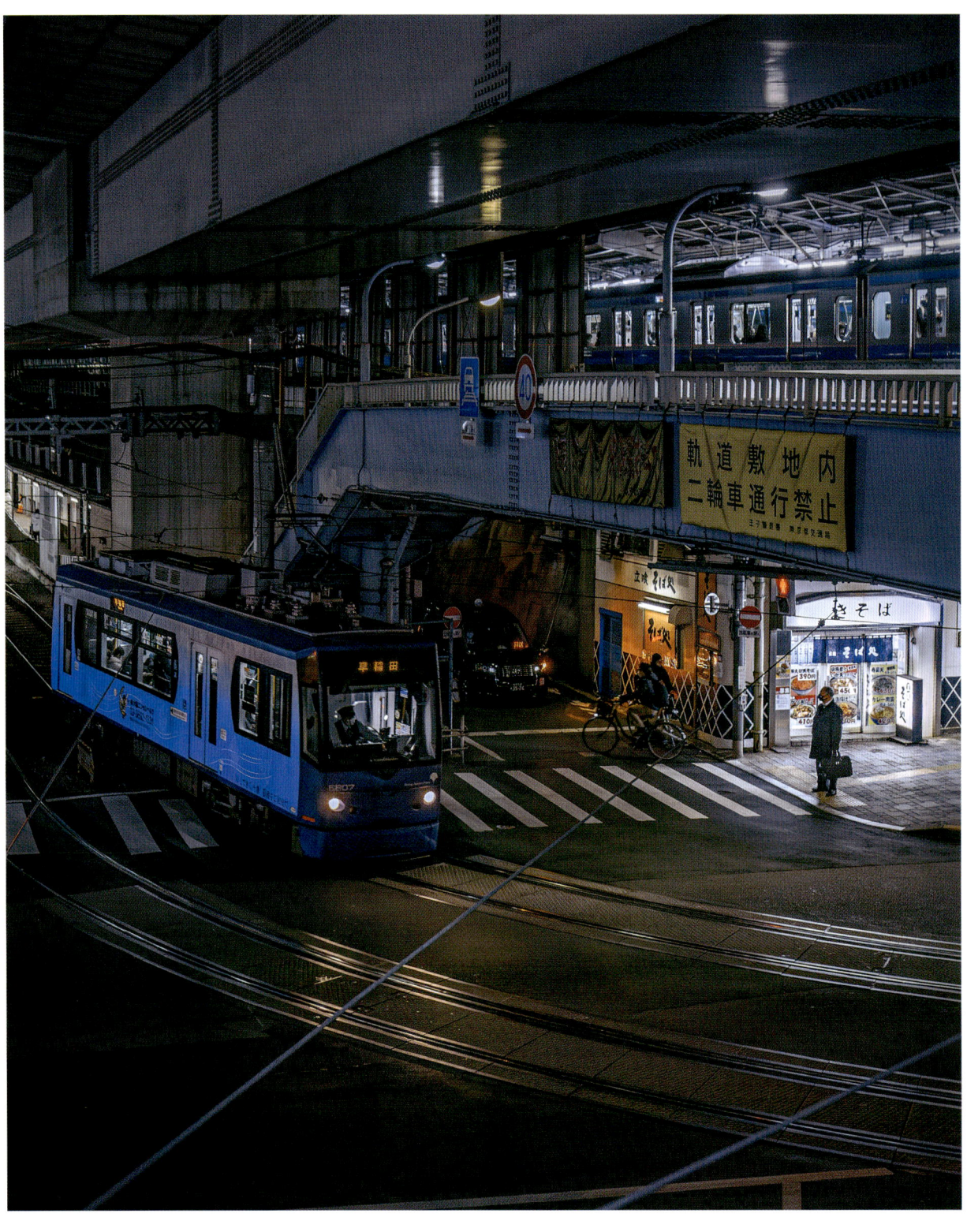

Oji Station. Oji, Tokyo. The Toden Arakawa Line (Tokyo Sakura Tram) is the only streetcar currently in operation in Tokyo.

Blue Meter. Ginza, Tokyo. The colorful lights behind this parking meter complement it nicely.

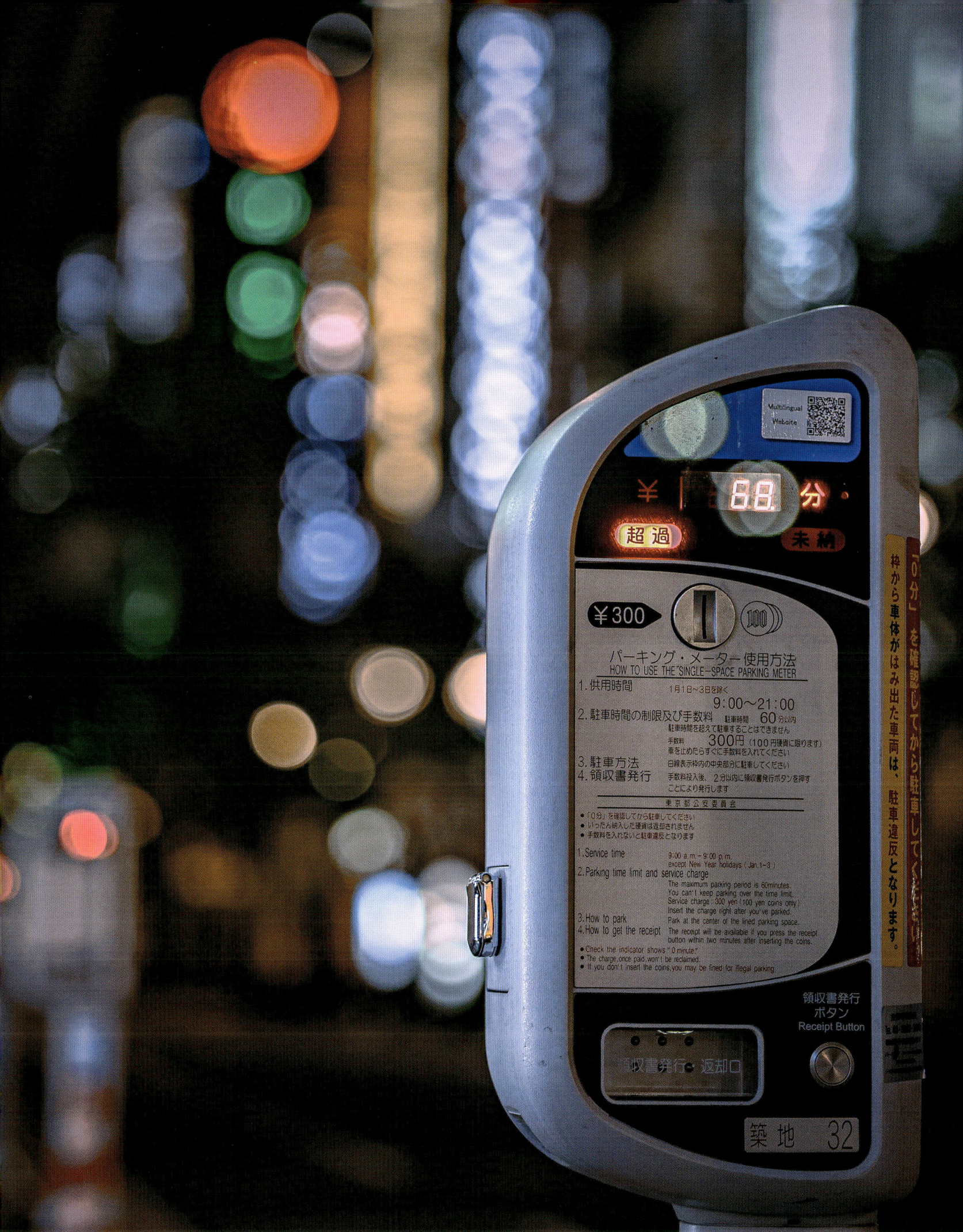

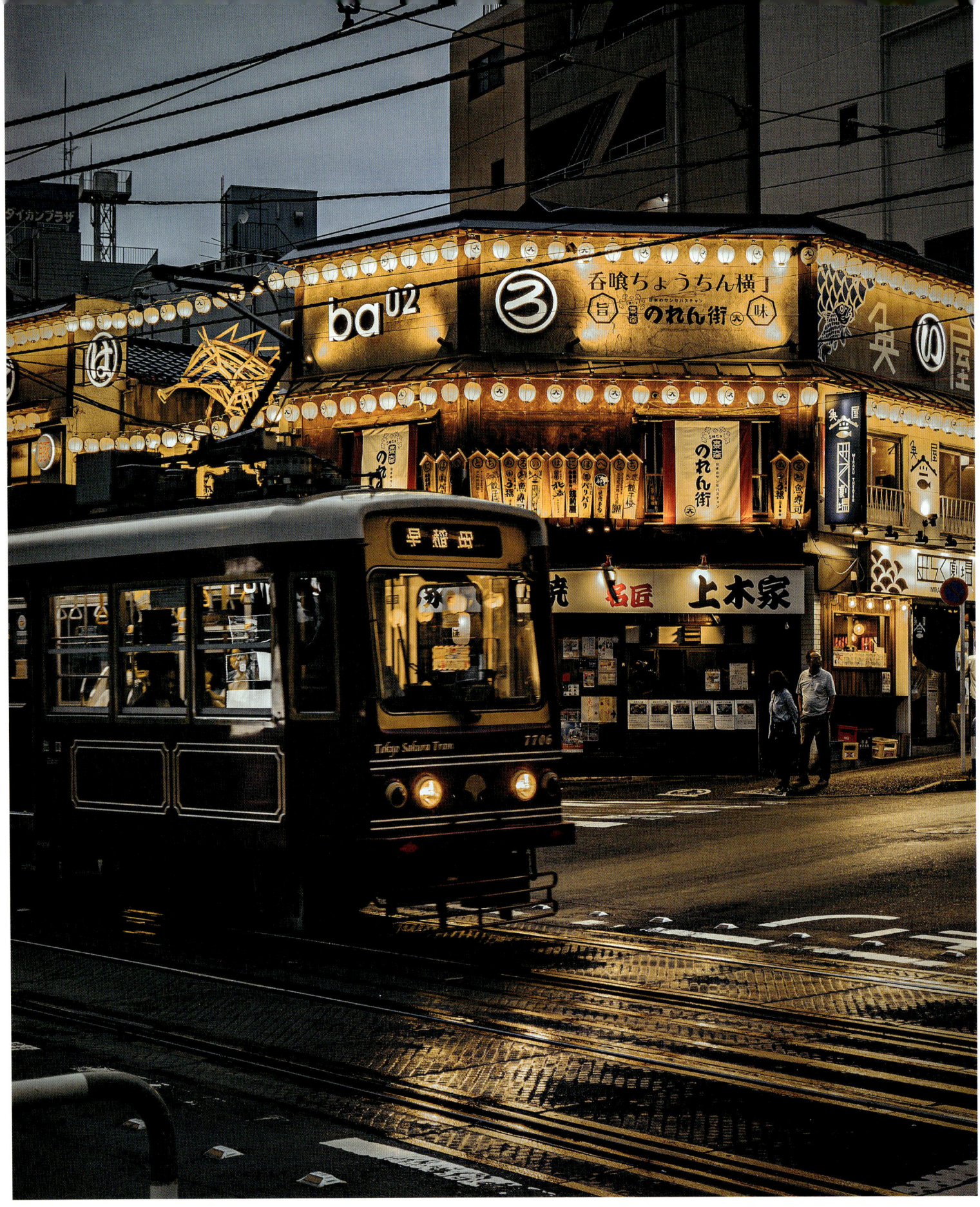

Tramway and Izakaya. Otsuka, Tokyo. The streetcars come and go frequently, making for some impressive photo opportunities.

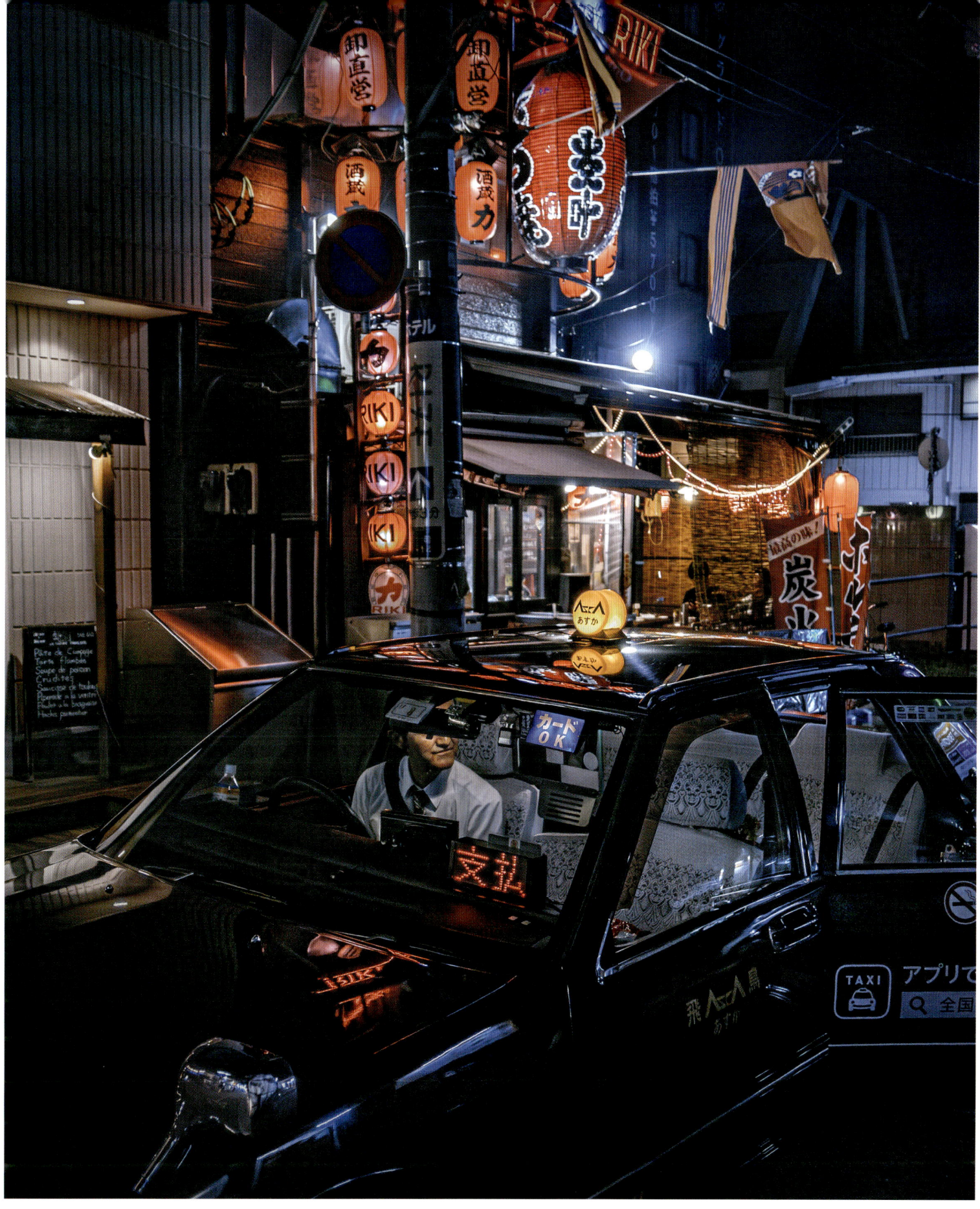

Red Lanterns and Cab. Omiya, Tokyo.
The red lights of the lanterns reflect
on the black body of this taxi dropping
off a customer.

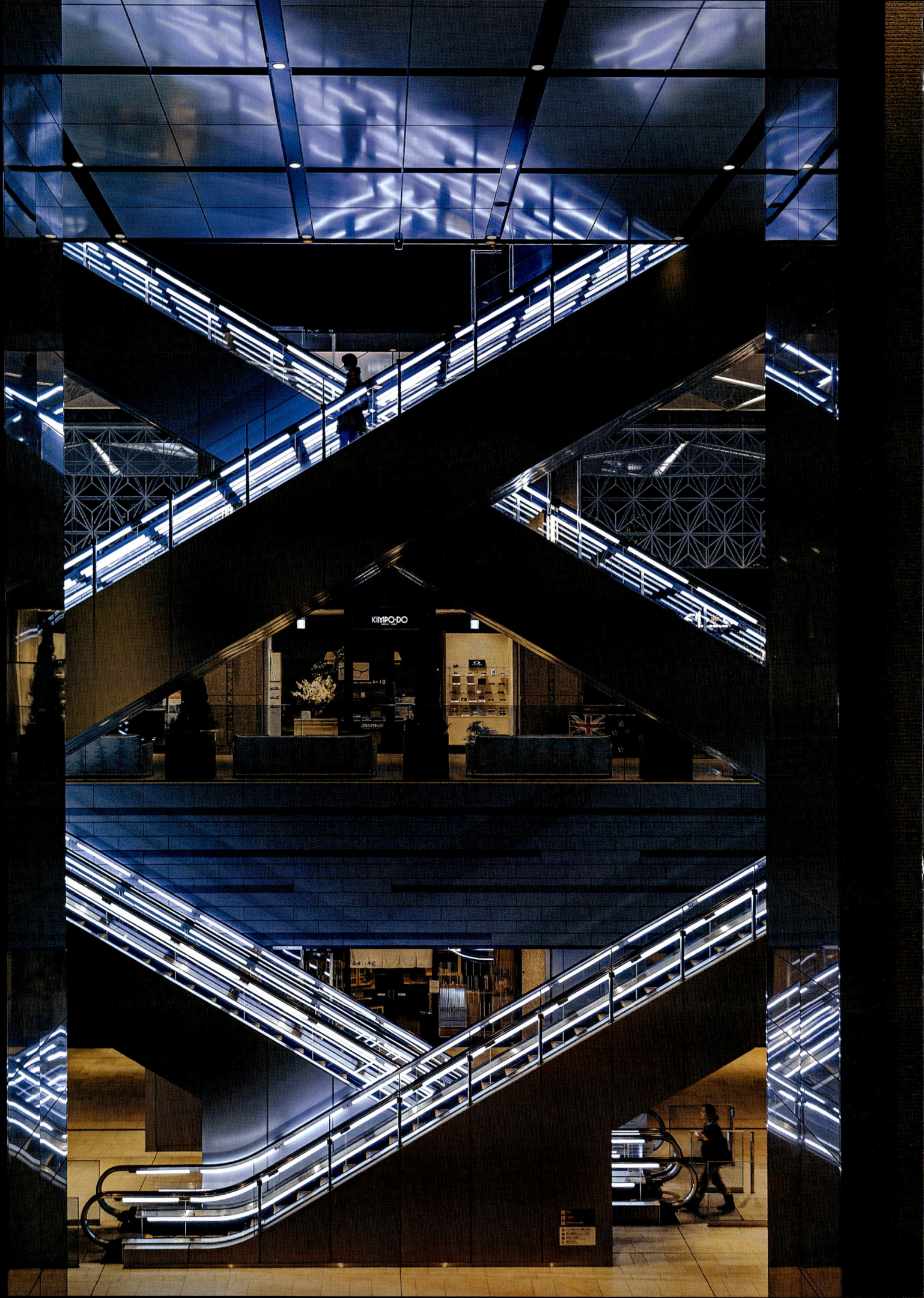

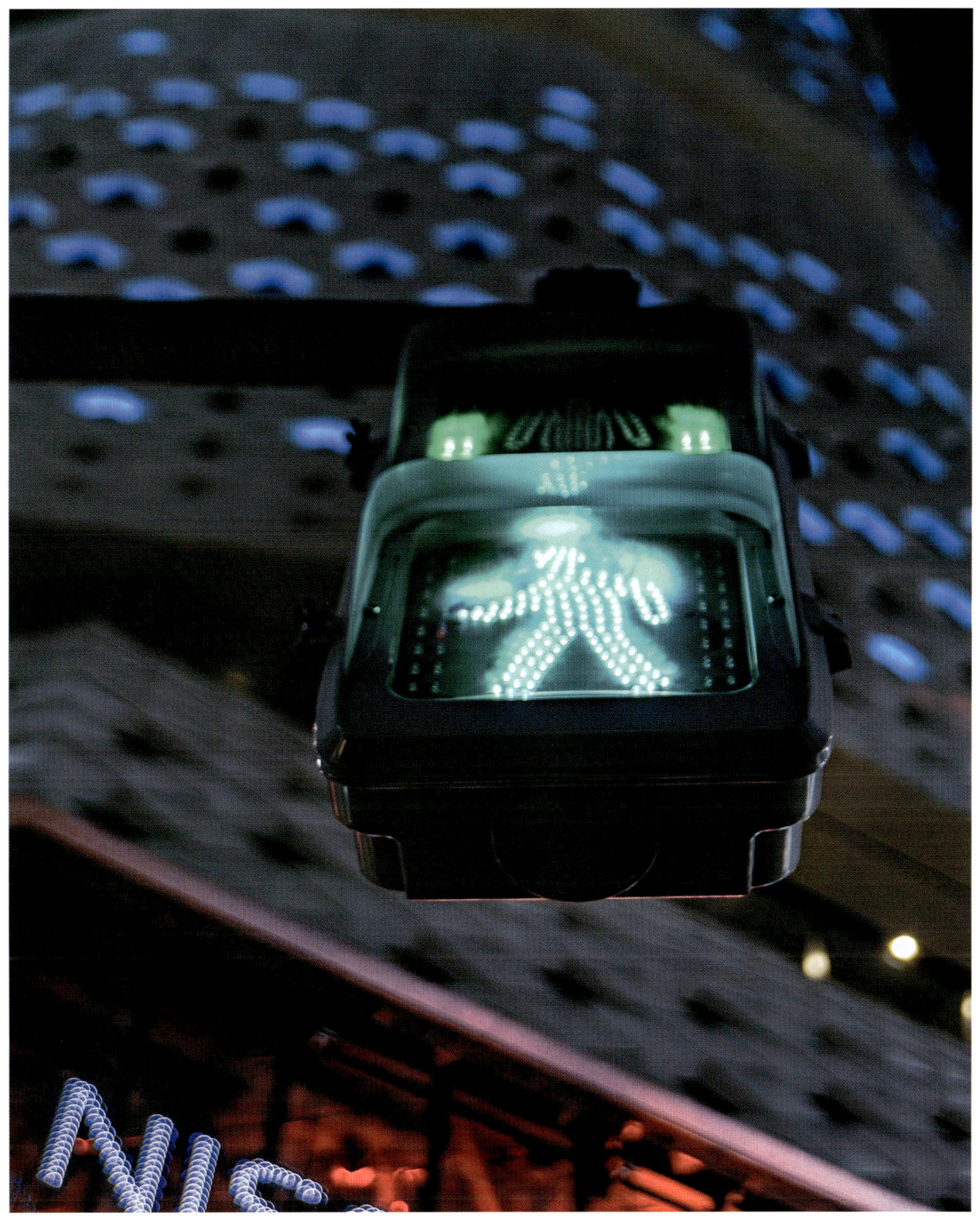

The Cross. Kyobashi, Tokyo. Beautifully lit escalators crisscross in this atrium.

Walk. Ginza, Tokyo. A close-up of a pedestrian signal.

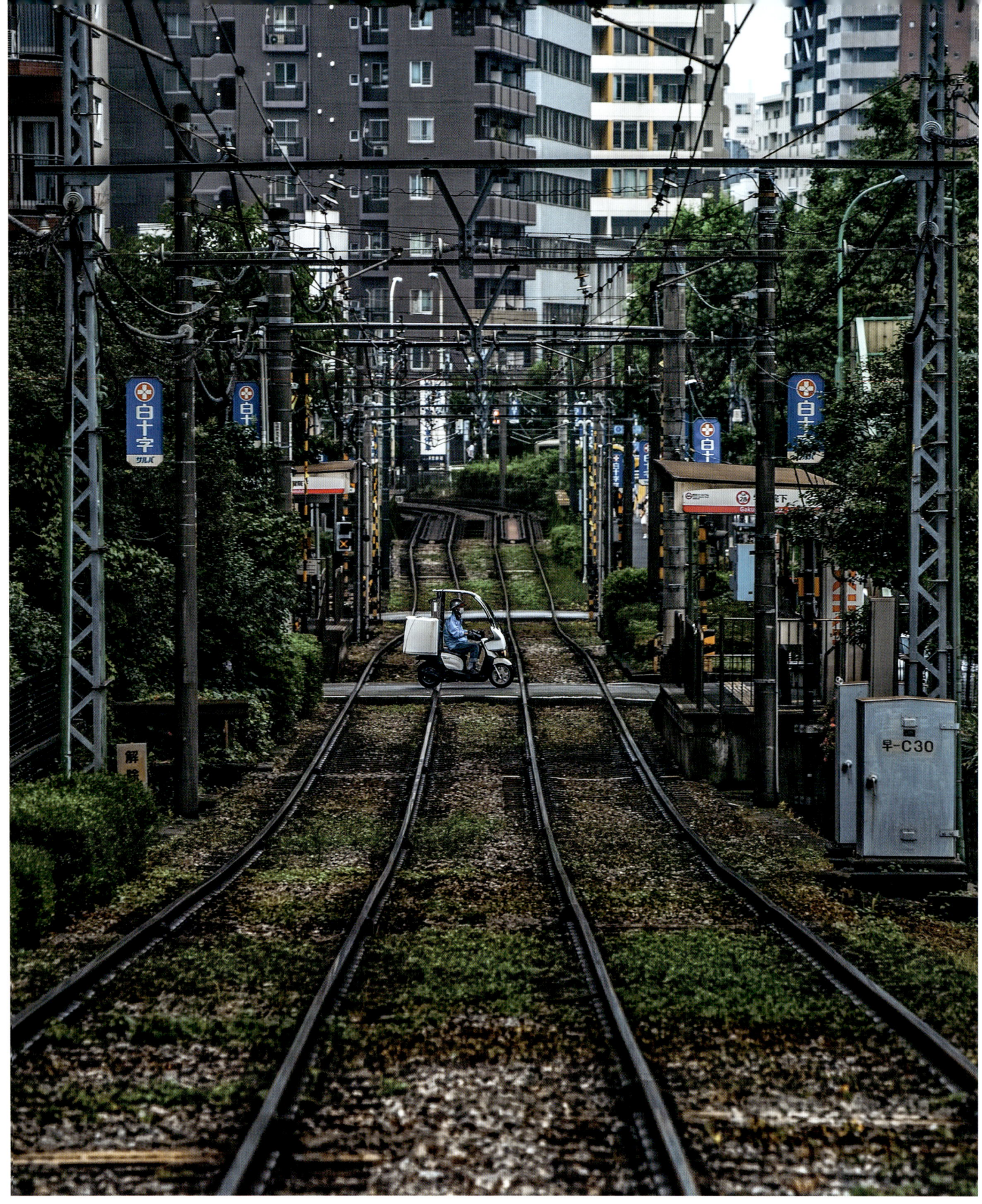

Toden Arakawa Line. Shinjuku, Tokyo. At its peak, Tokyo had forty streetcar lines. Today, only the Toden Arakawa Line remains.

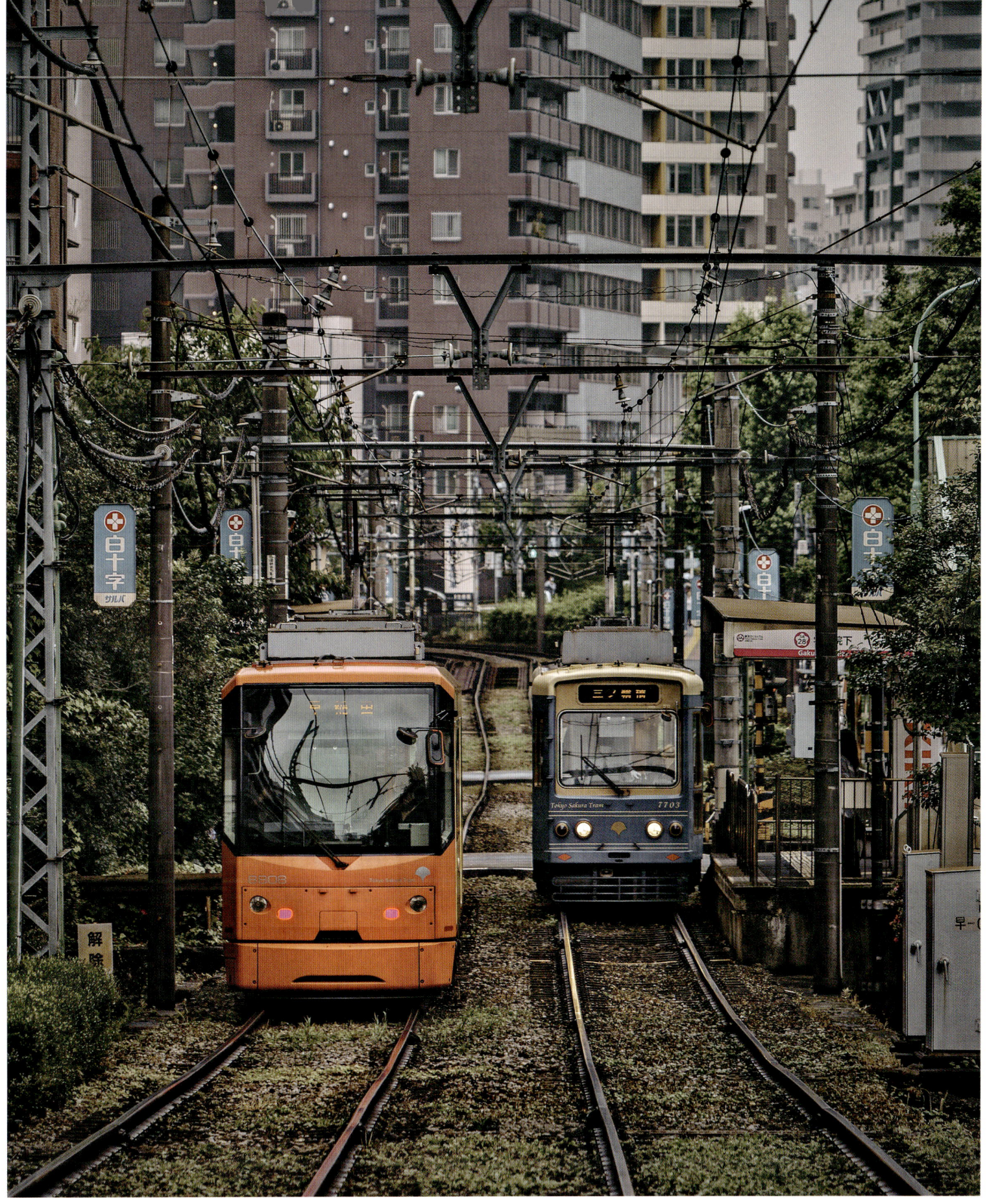

Gakushuinshita Station. Shinjuku, Tokyo. The orange car is the 8800 model, which was designed to be environmentally friendly, saving about 20 percent of the energy of conventional trains.

8500 and 9000 Models. Shinjuku, Tokyo. This line is commonly known as the Sakura Tram. There are many different models of cars of various ages used on this line. The one on the right is the 8500, and the other is the 9000.

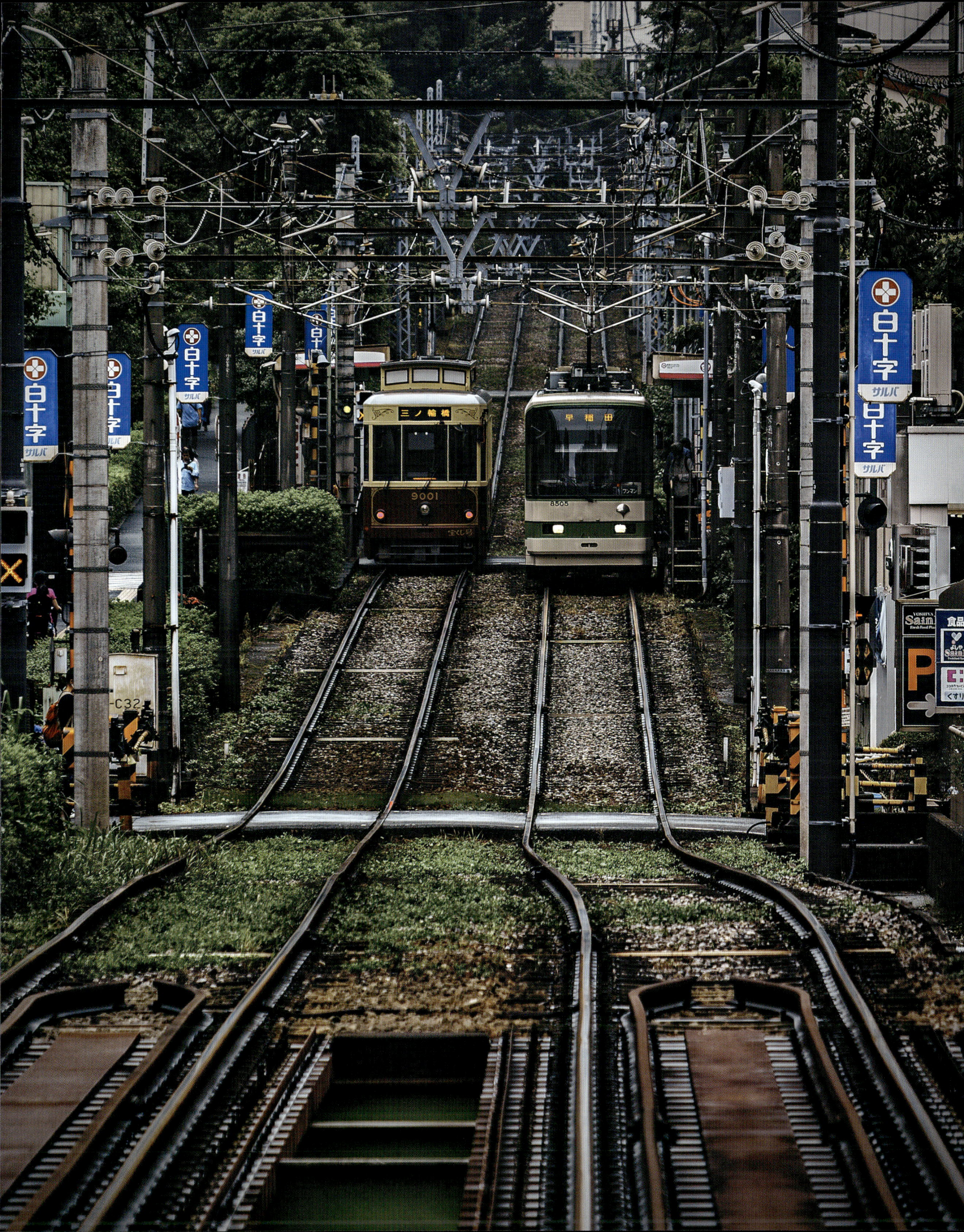

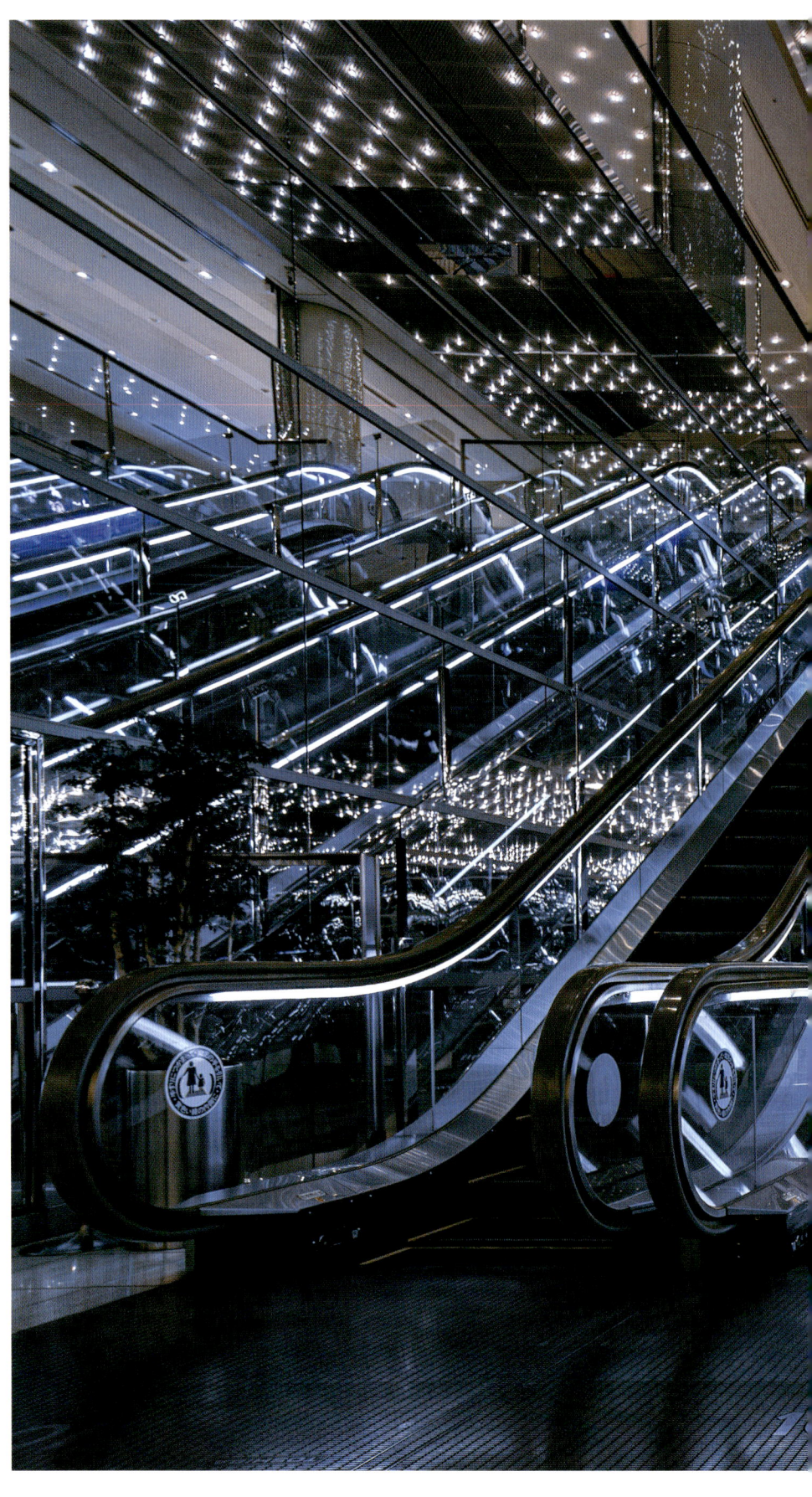

The Most Beautiful Escalators in Japan.
Yurakucho, Tokyo. At least I think they are
the most beautiful. Unfortunately, it is now
prohibited to take photos here.

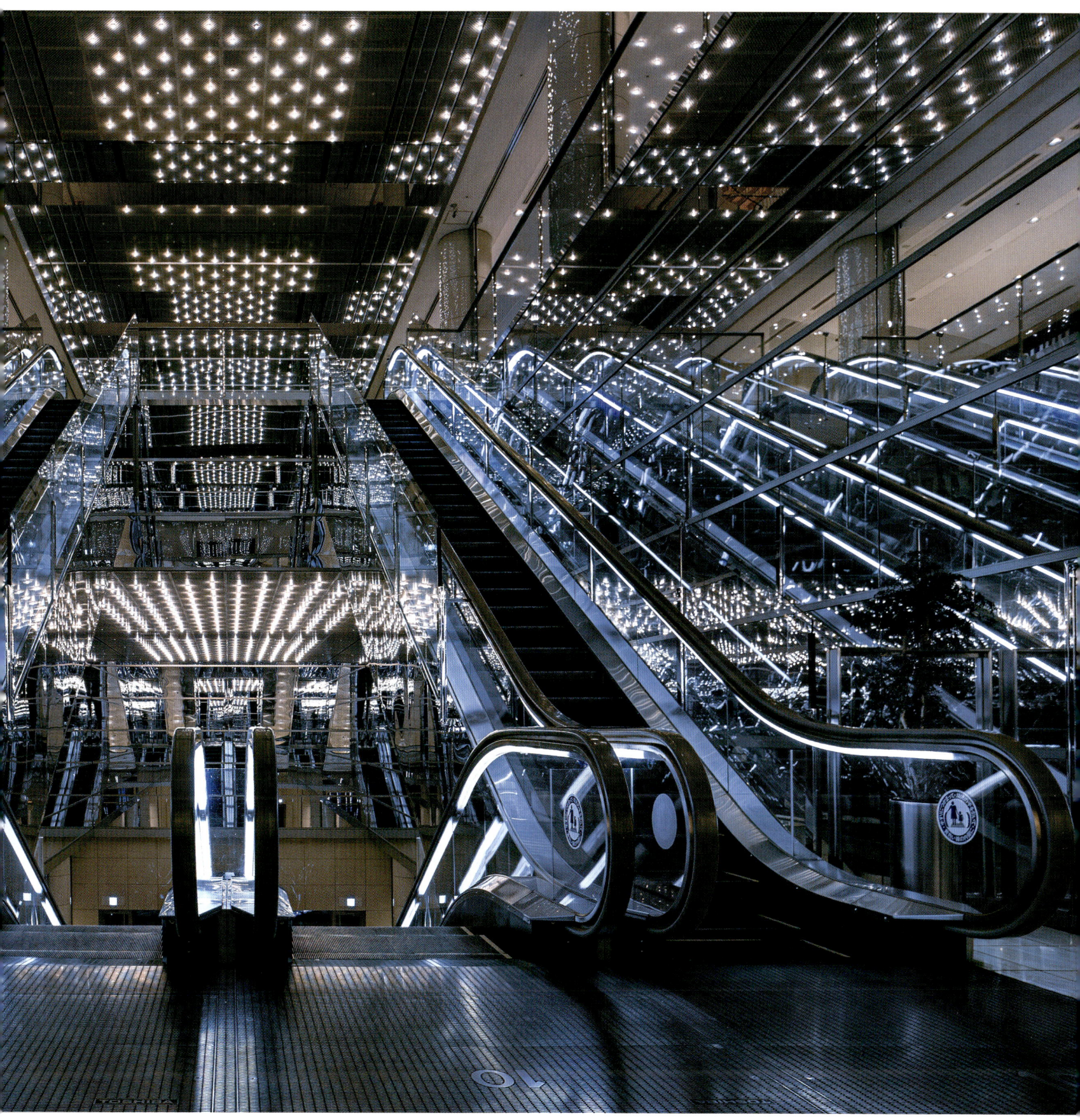

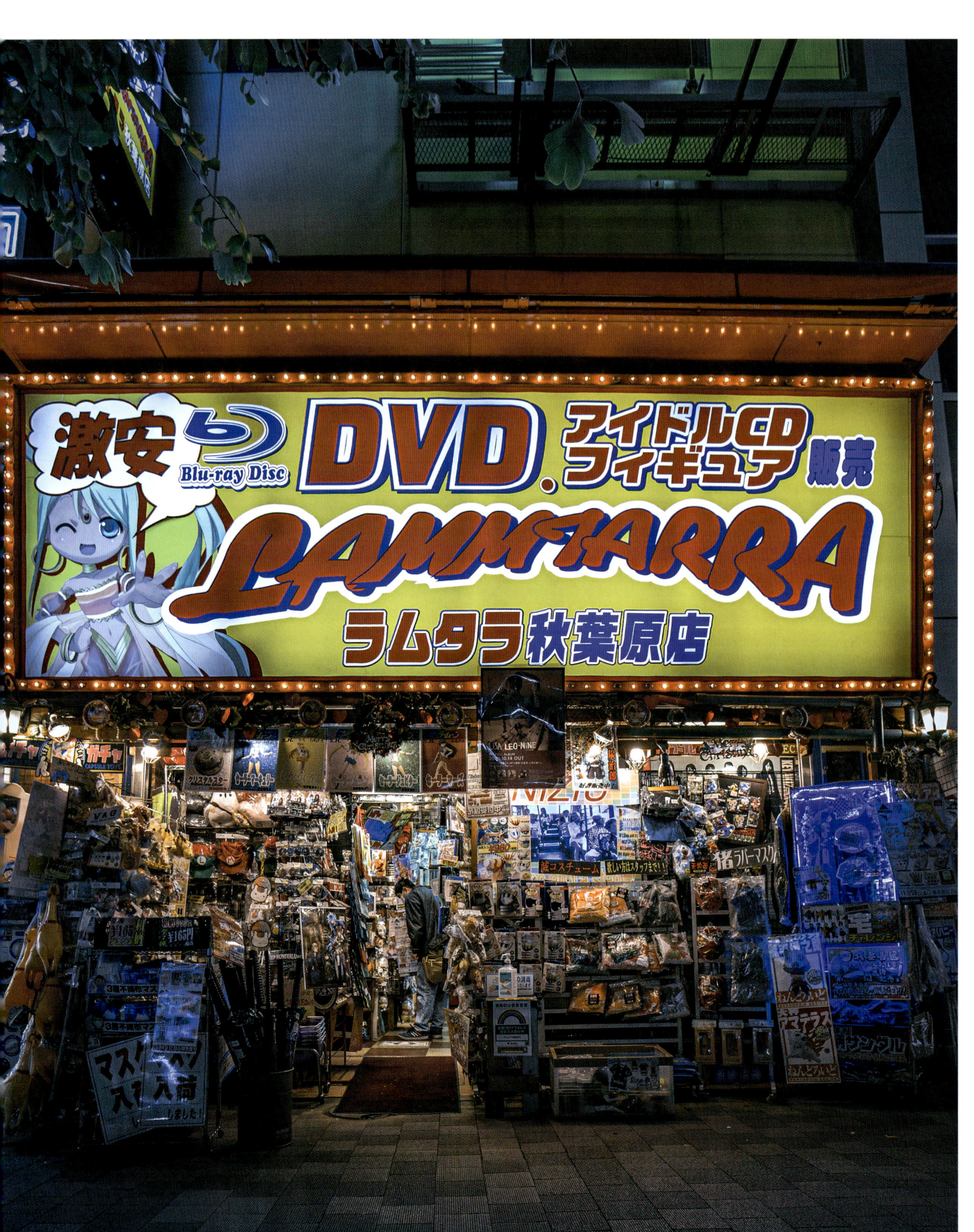

店先

Japanese cities have a unique landscape with a mix of Western and ancient Japanese culture on every street. So, when I am out taking photographs, I am much more attracted to traditional Japanese storefronts than the newer, more sophisticated ones.

More than anything, I love to capture the energy of the variety of people who work at and visit these places.

Anime Character Store. Akihabara, Tokyo. This store is packed with products related to anime characters. The store's signage and lights create a unique ambiance.

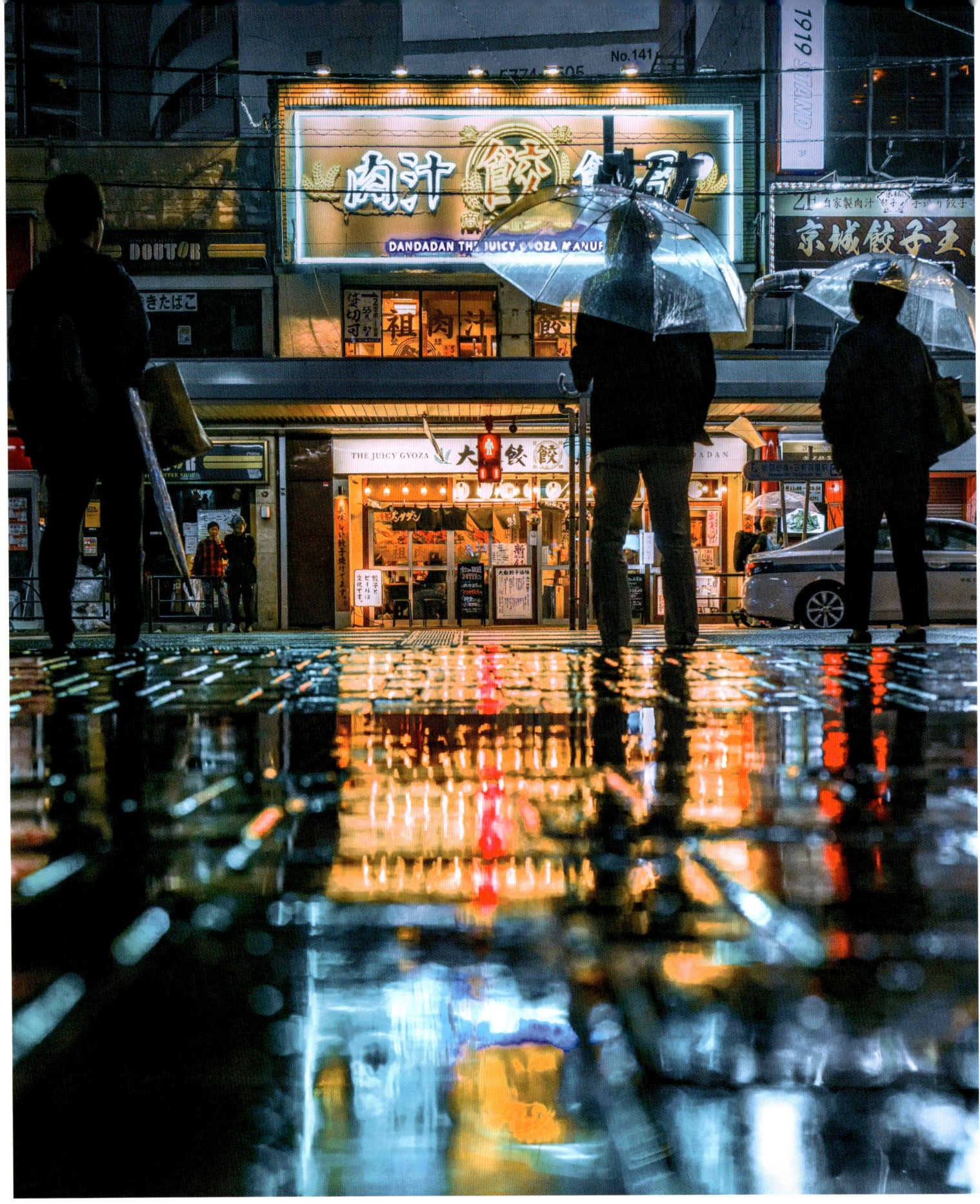

Waiting for the Signal. Sangenjaya, Tokyo.
We can find beauty even in everyday
moments, such as the reflection of neon
lights on the wet road.

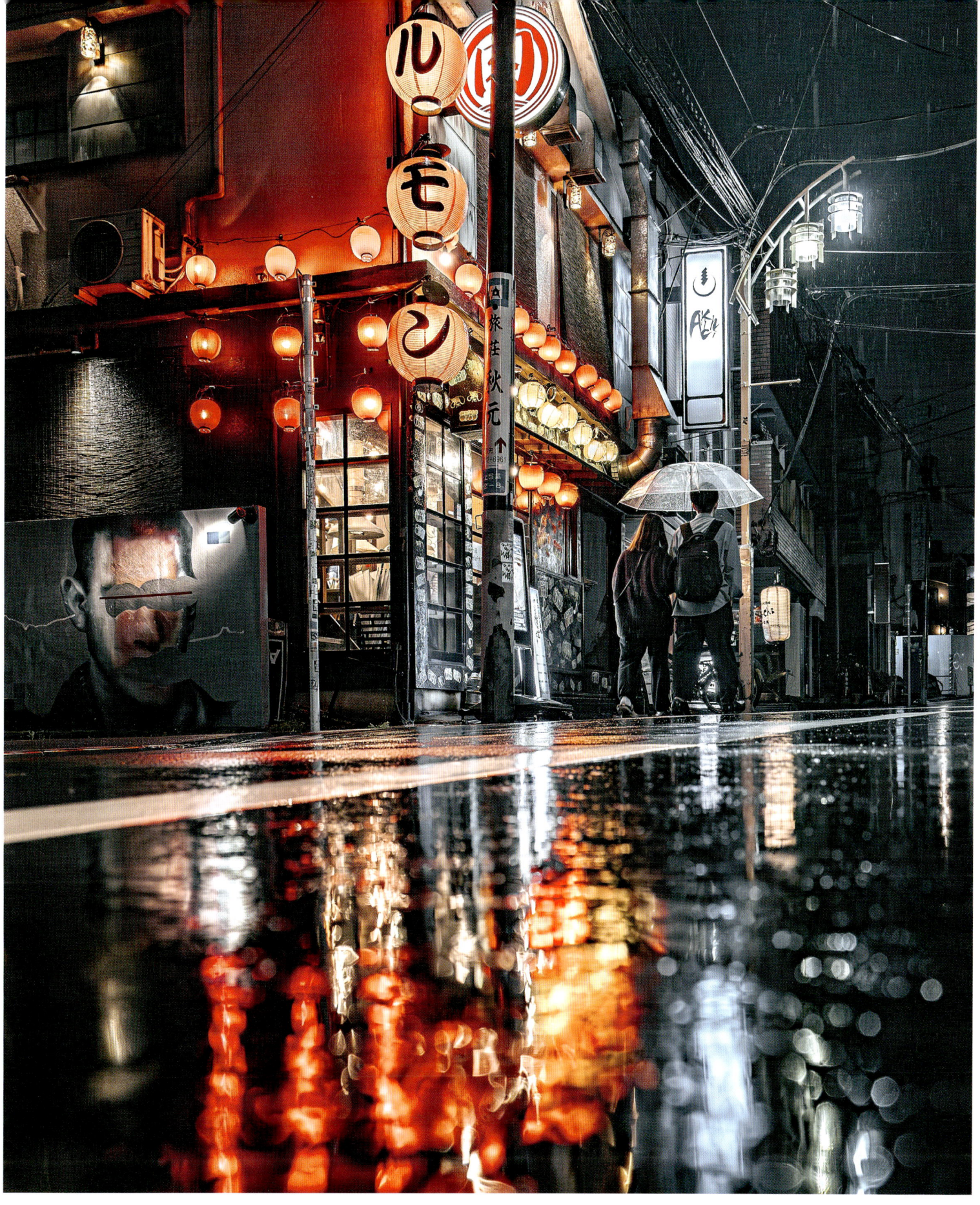

Izakaya on a Rainy Night. Nakameguro,
Tokyo. On rainy nights, you can take a
photo like this by holding the camera close
to the road surface.

Yakiton Restaurant. Asagaya, Tokyo. Although many people hesitate to visit this restaurant because of its plastic greenhouse appearance, it is an excellent restaurant with sixty outlets throughout Japan. Yakitori and yakiton are inexpensive and can be taken to-go.

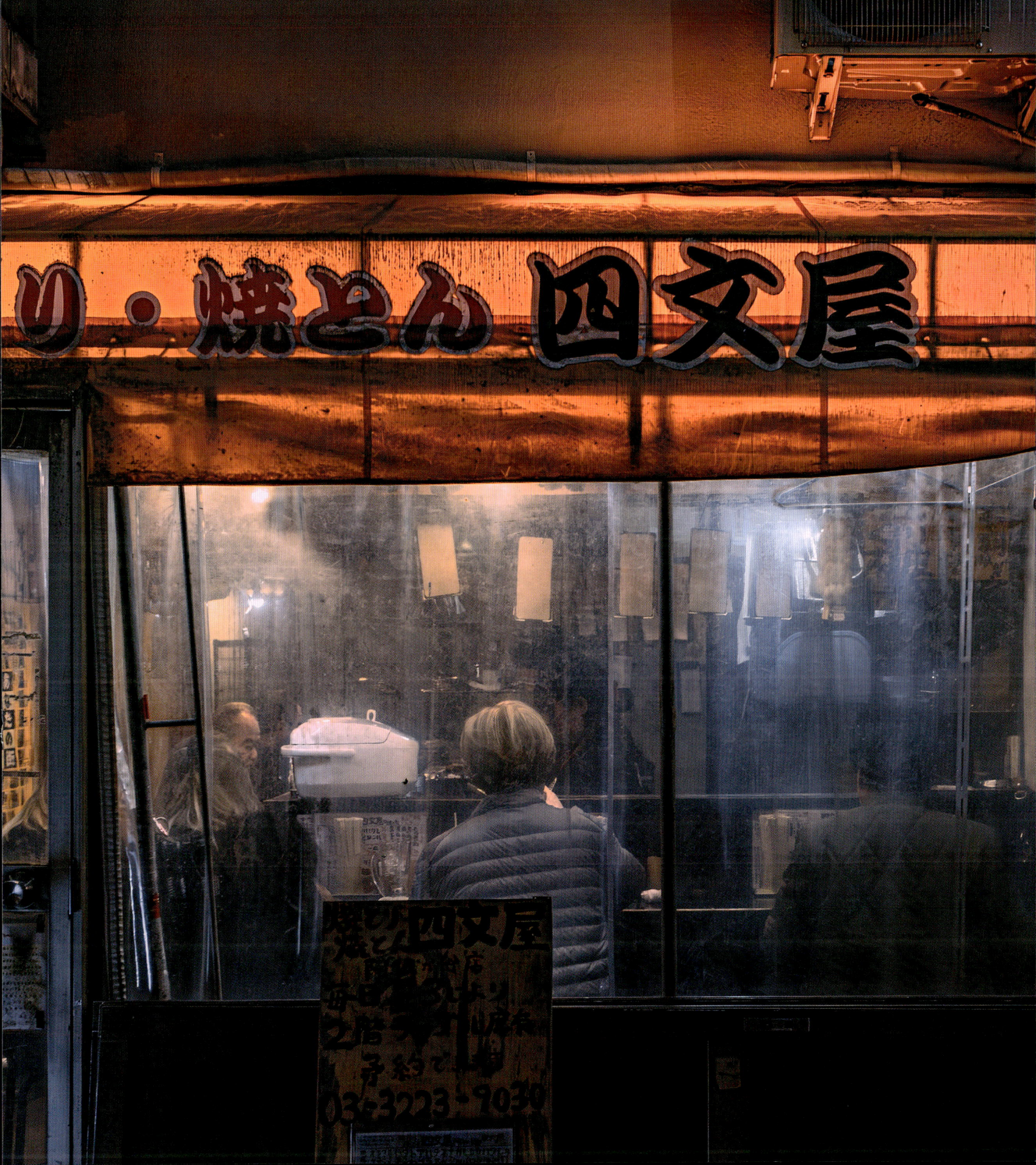

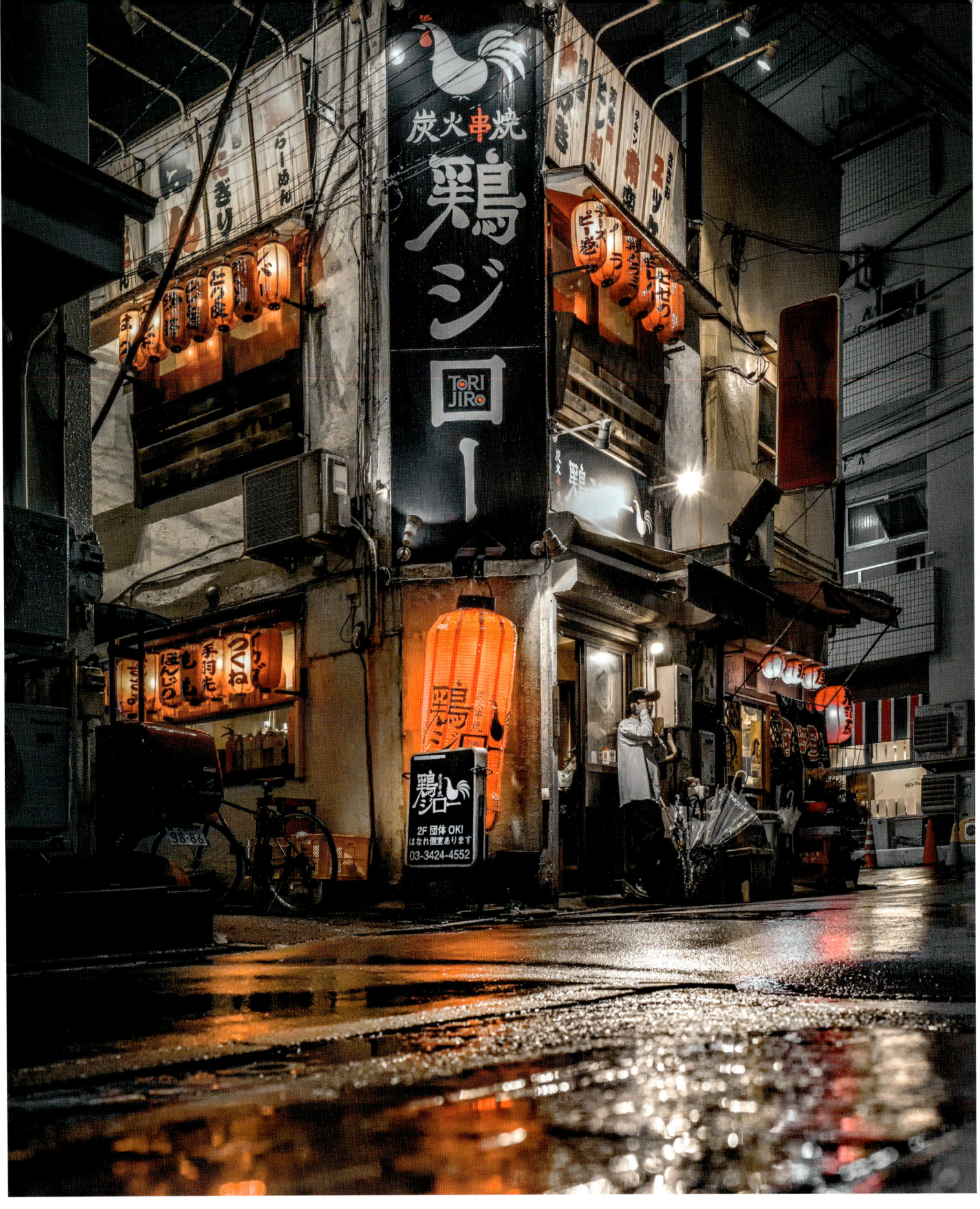

Grilled Chicken Restaurant. Sangenjaya, Tokyo.
When I take photos of storefronts, my favorite
shots are of their corners. This restaurant looks
like it was made for this purpose.

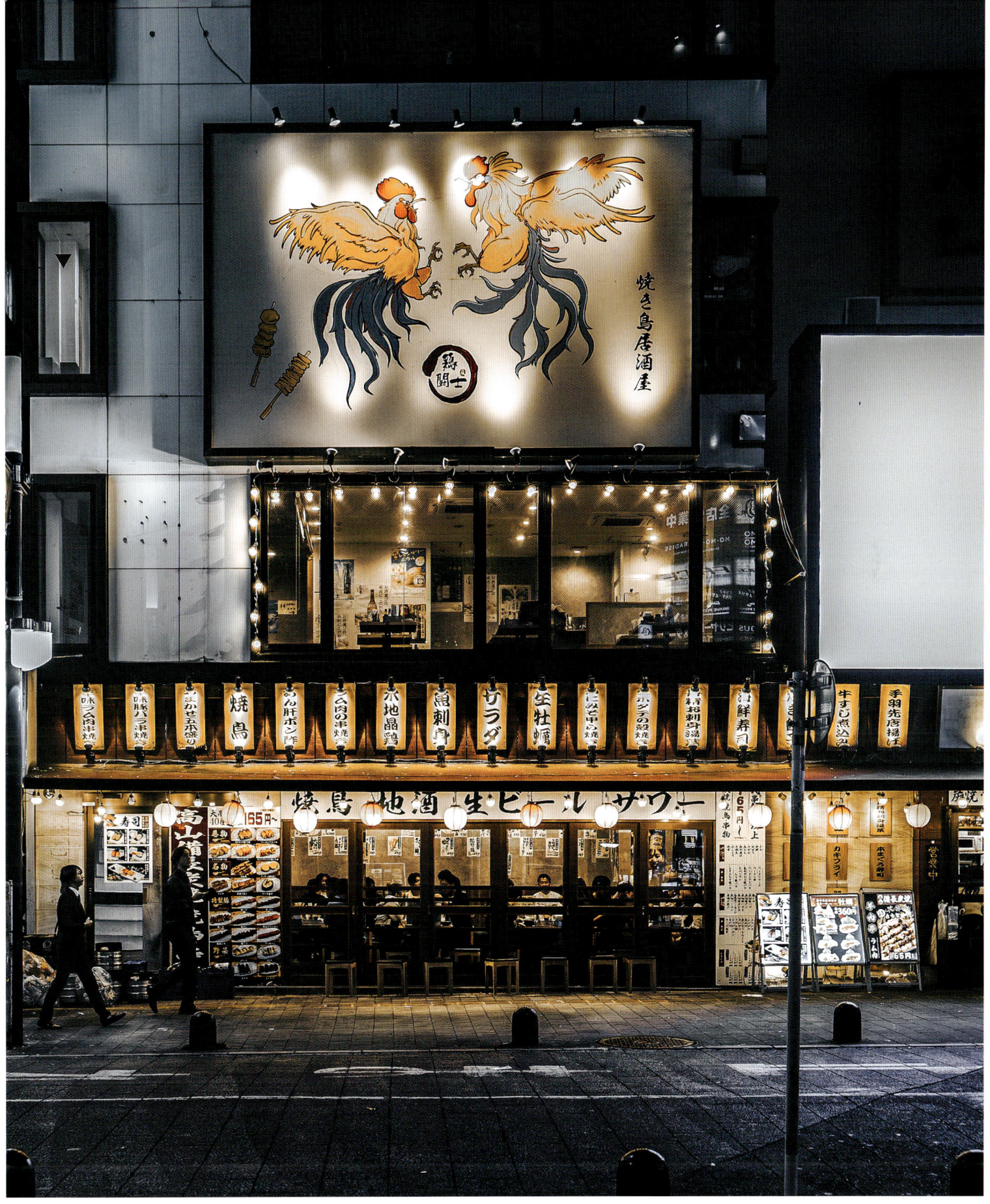

Yakitori Restaurant in Kabukicho. Shinjuku, Tokyo. Located in front of the Godzilla Building (see page 86) and open twenty-four hours a day, this restaurant is always crowded with tourists from abroad.

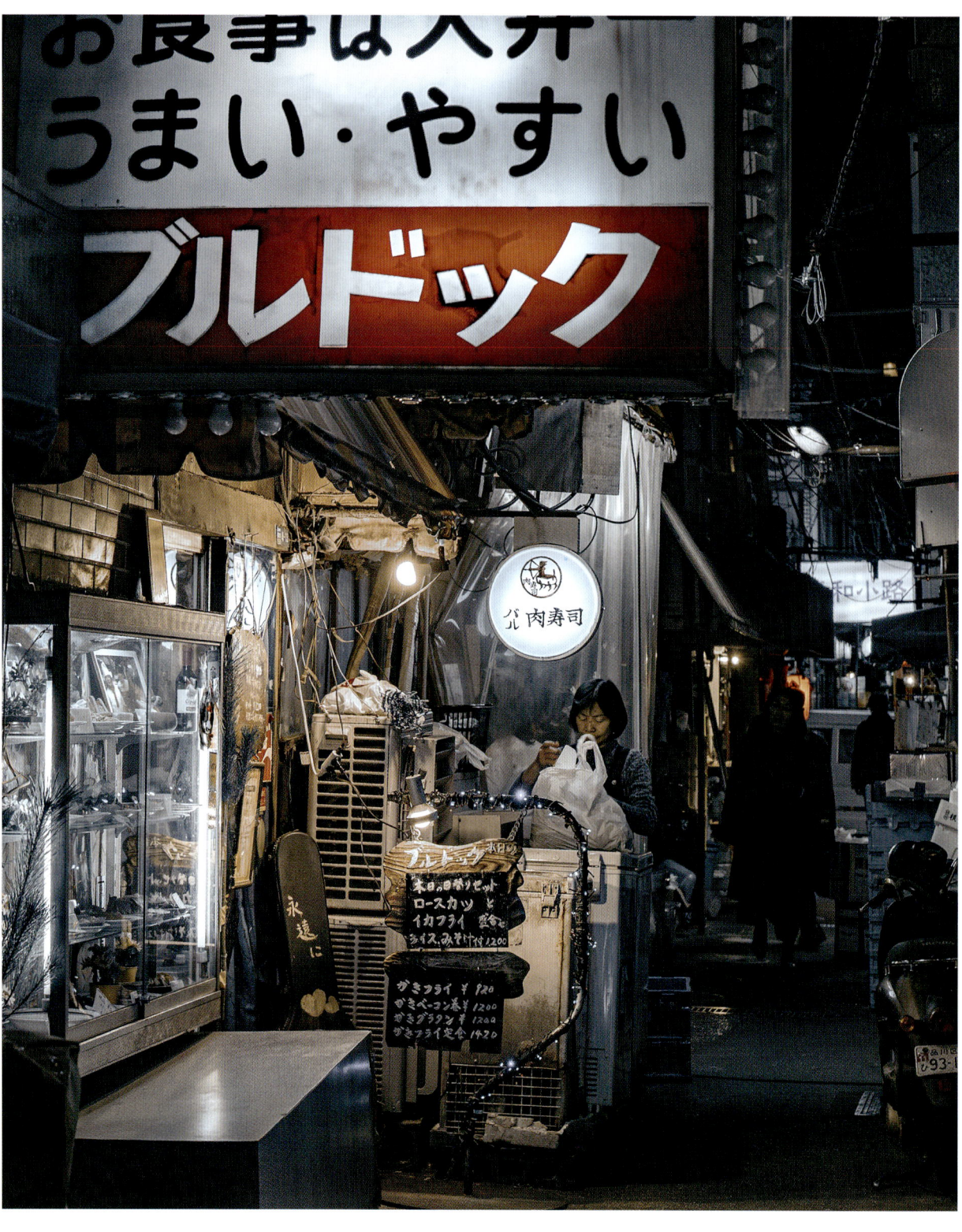

Popular Restaurant. Oimachi, Tokyo. This restaurant was destroyed in a fire in 2023, and although it reopened, its unique, nostalgic ambiance (fortunately captured here before the fire) is gone.

Warm Light Reflected. Ningyocho, Tokyo. Rain casts a spell on the usually dingy roads, making the reflection of warm light quite beautiful.

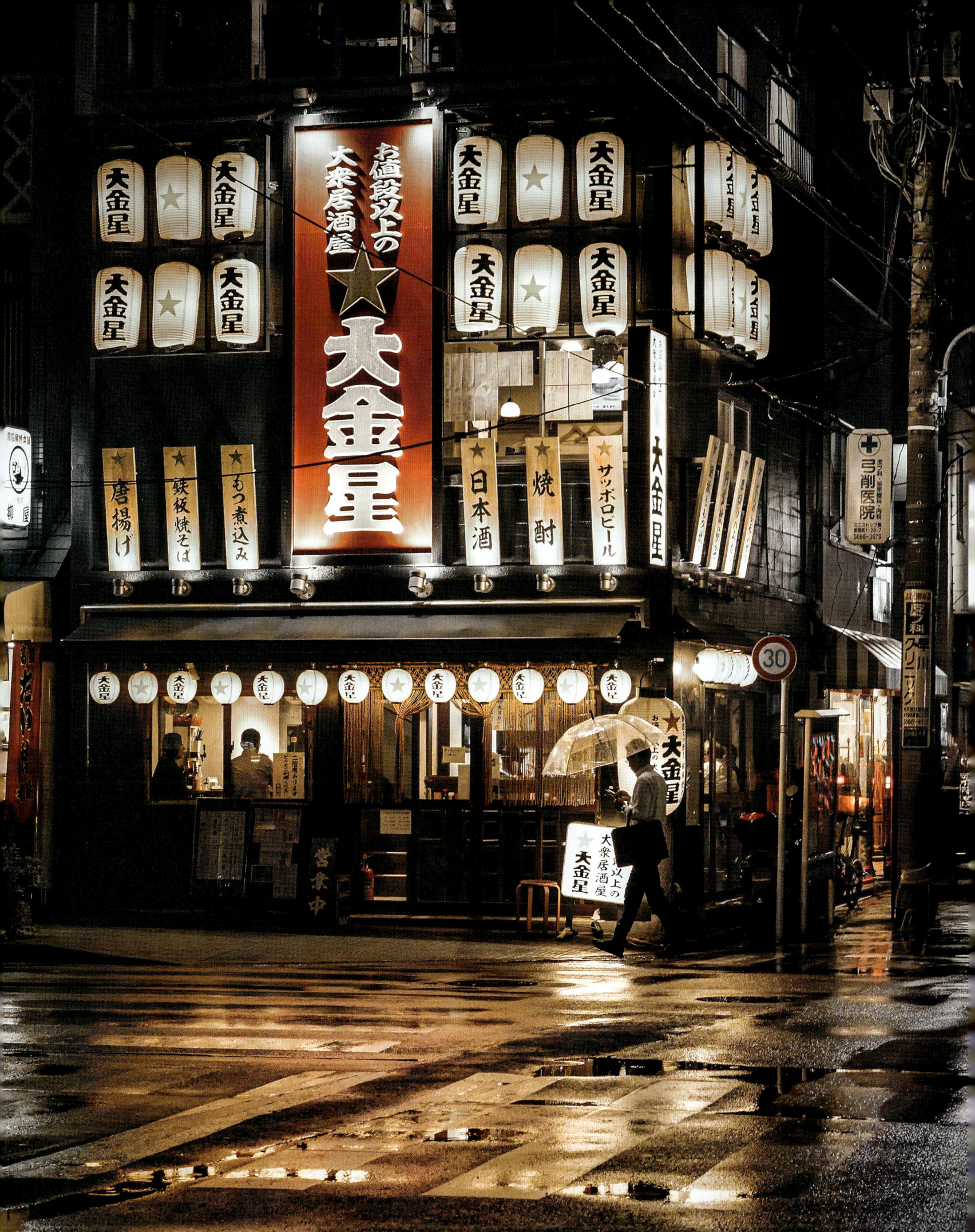

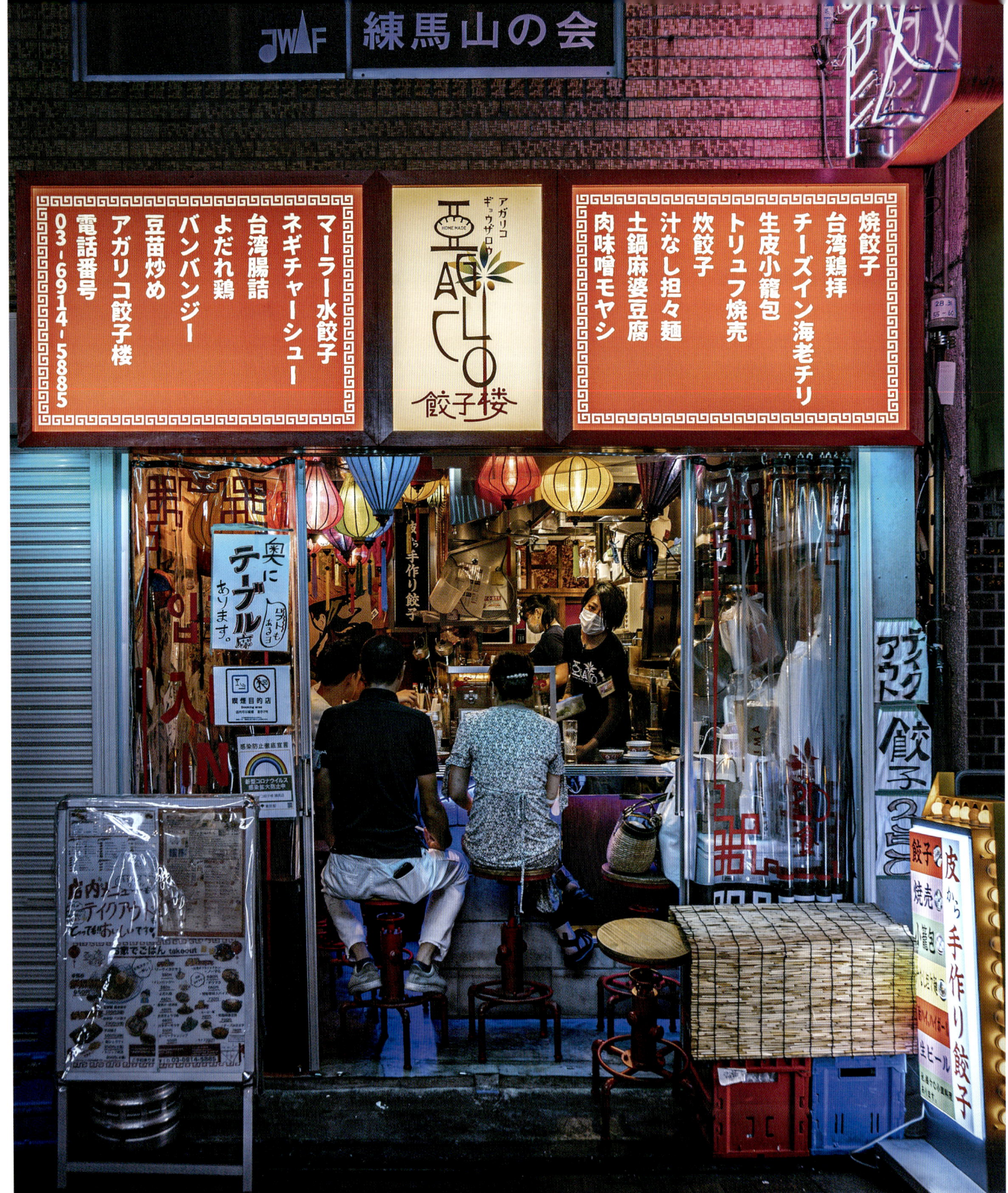

Handmade Dumpling Restaurant. Nerima, Tokyo.
The pink and blue neon lights and lanterns create
a beautiful yet mysterious atmosphere.

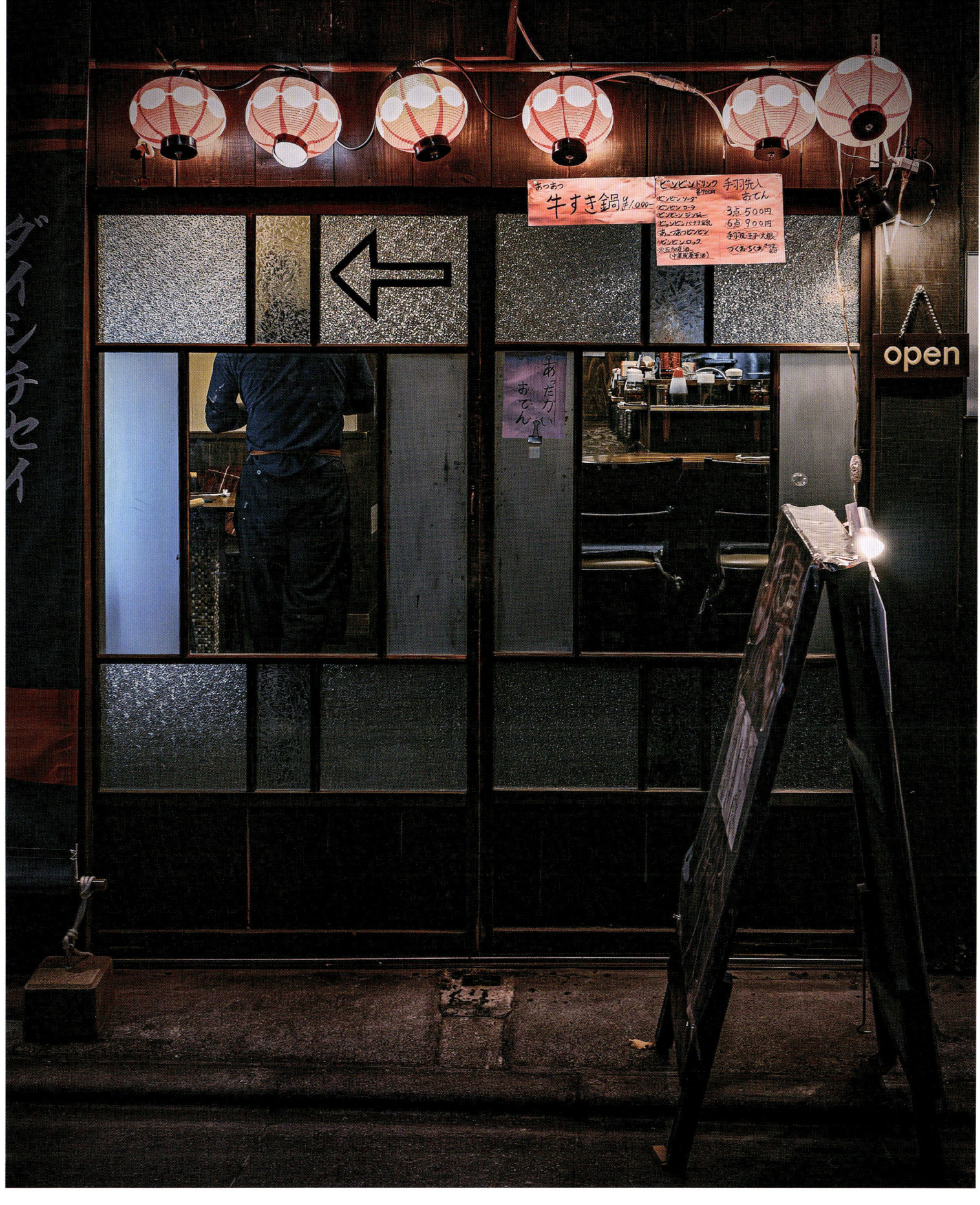

A Little Drink. Asagaya, Tokyo. This stylish izakaya, located on Star Road, was renovated from an old, private house. The handmade retro windowpanes are rarely seen anymore.

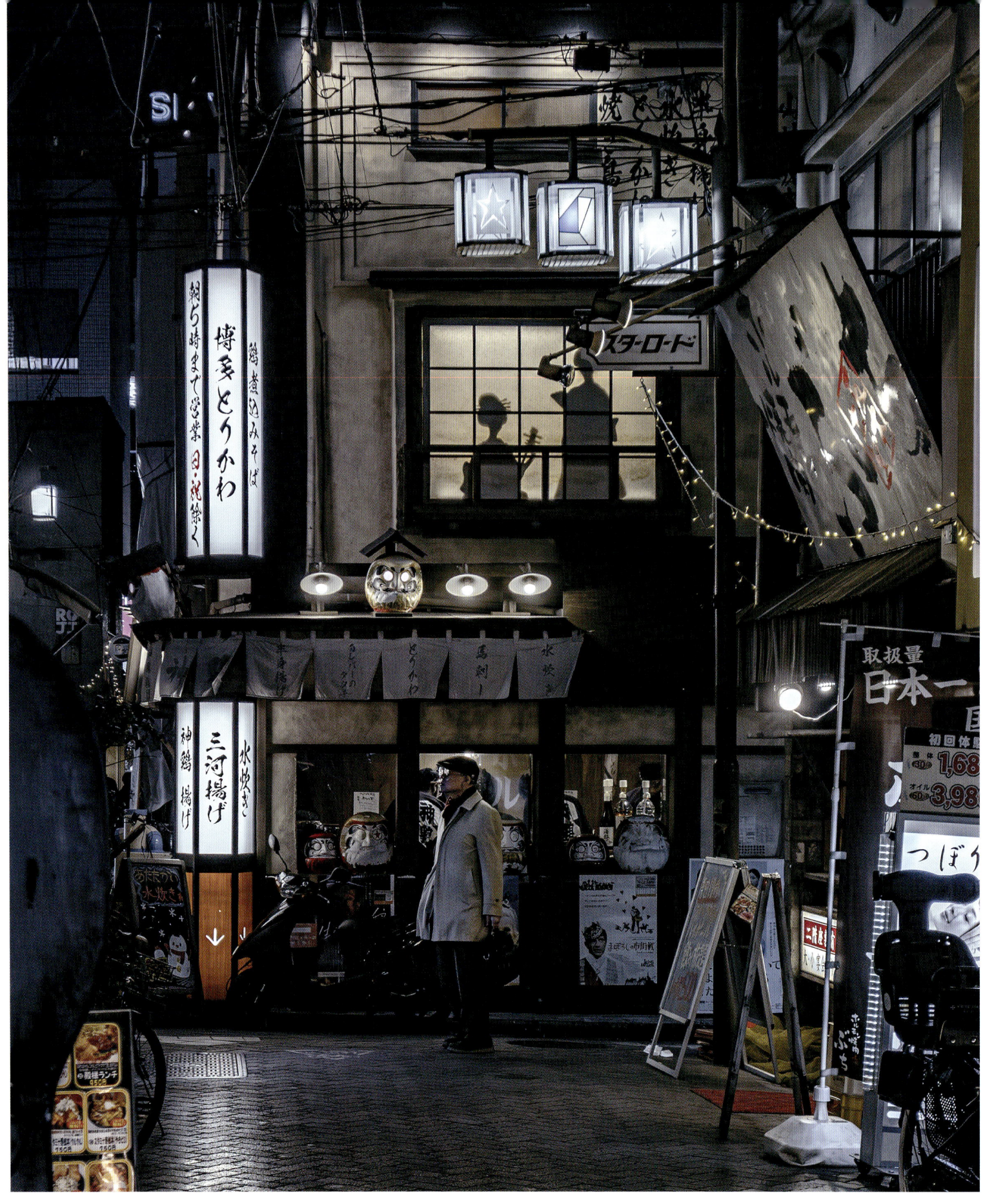

Star Road at Night. Asagaya, Tokyo. This chicken restaurant has a chic effect on shoji paper of a shadow of a geisha playing a shamisen.

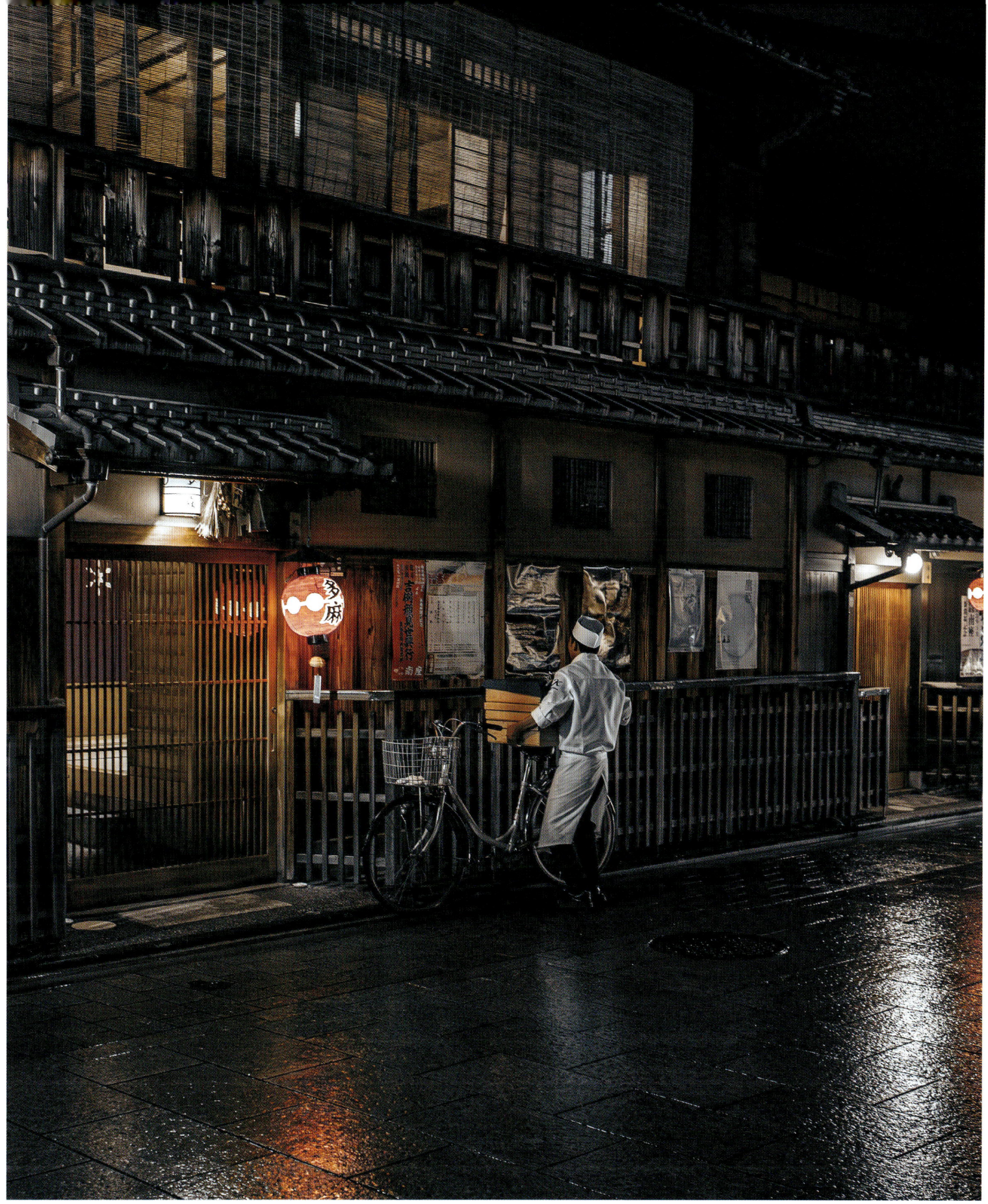

Evening Delivery. Kyoto. Many of Kyoto's traditional teahouses (*ochaya*) do not allow visitors to enter without an introduction. Ochaya is a place where geisha entertain wealthy merchants with singing, playing, and dancing.

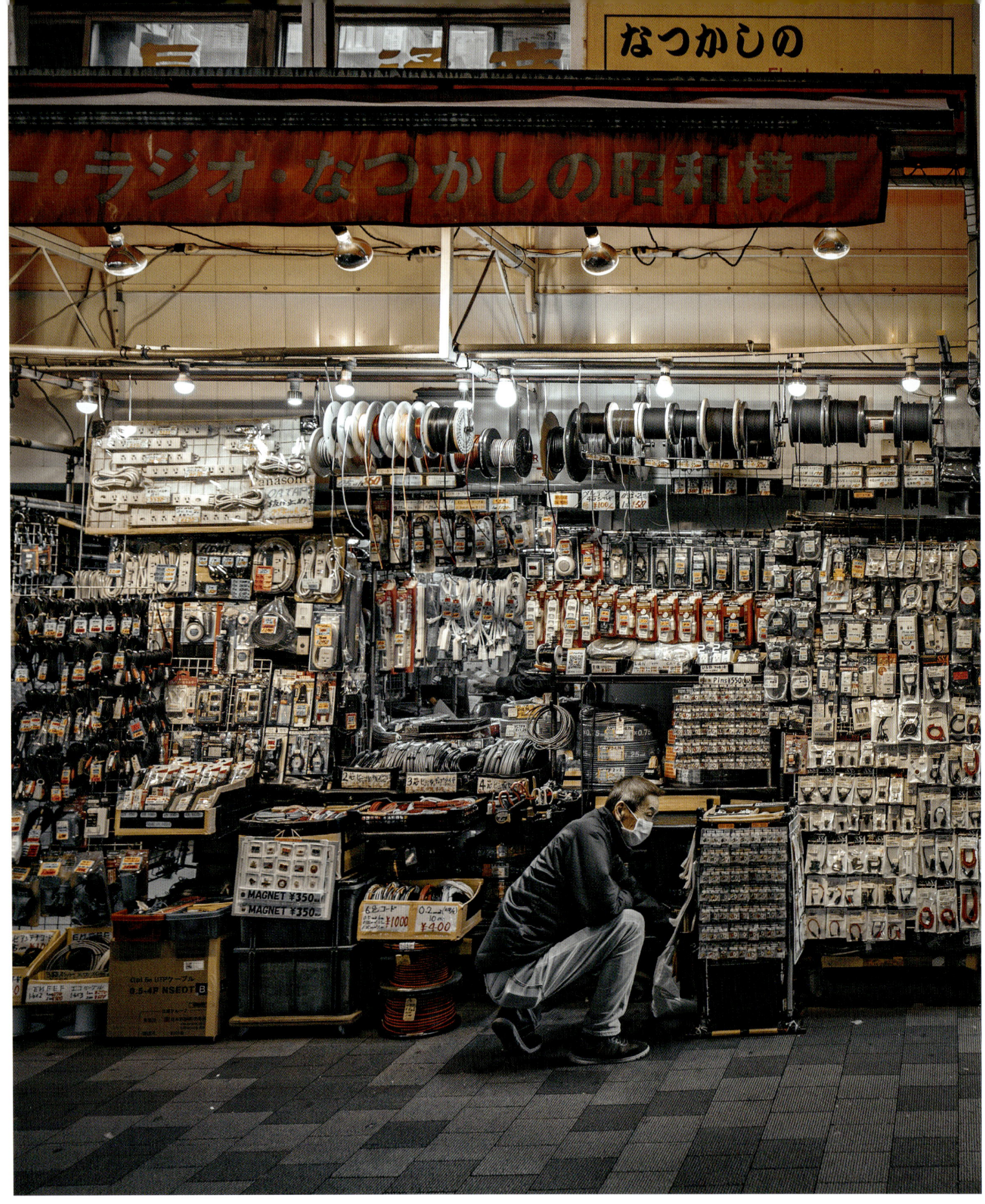

Cable Shop. Akihabara, Tokyo. This store that specializes in electronic cables and power strips is a vestige of the good old days of Akihabara.

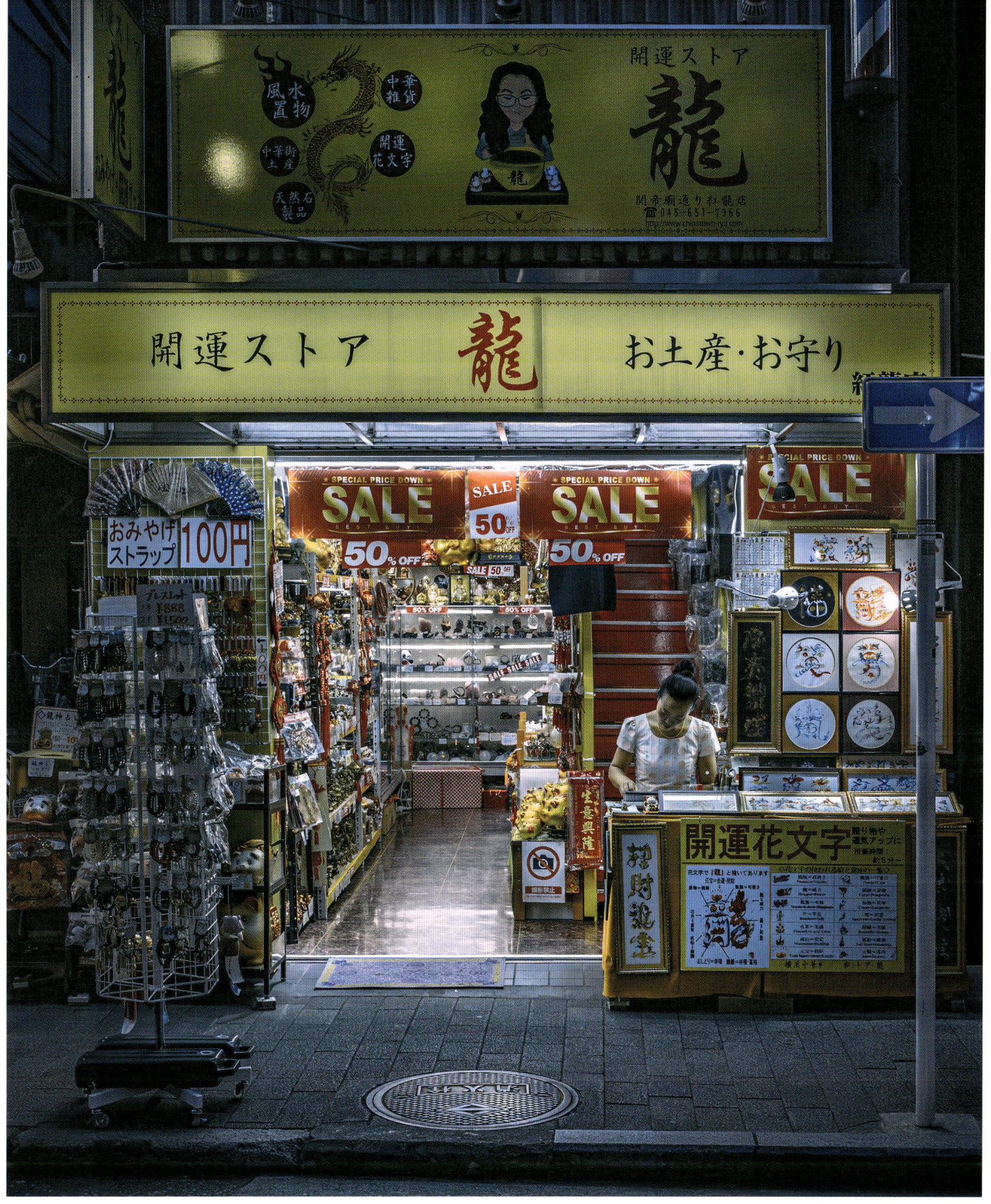

Good Luck Store. Chinatown, Yokohama. This store offers a traditional Chinese art form in which customers can have their names or favorite kanji characters turned into beautiful characters decorated with flower illustrations.

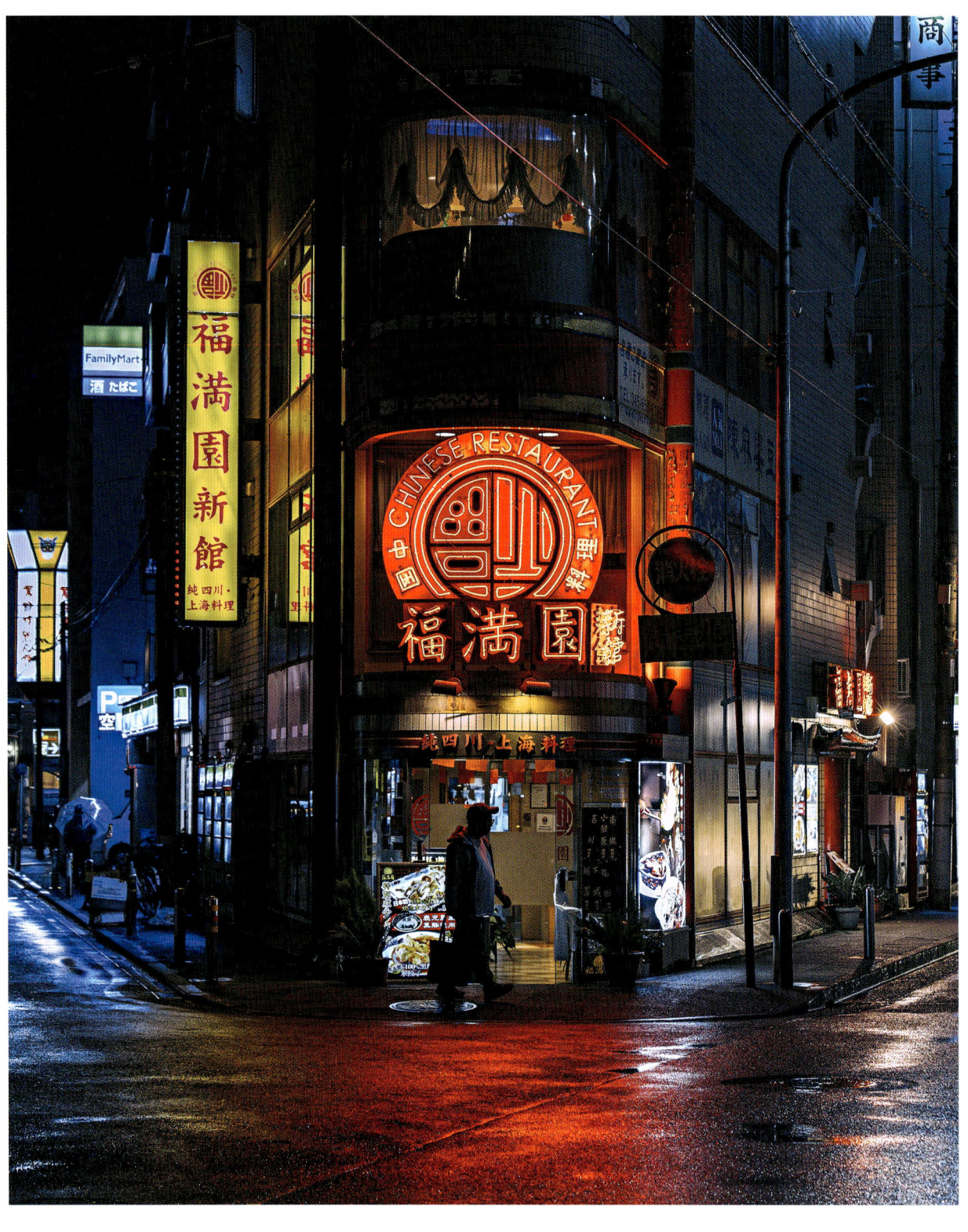

Beautifully Designed Chinese Restaurant. Chinatown, Yokohama. The entrance of this restaurant is illuminated with the upside-down character for *fuku* (good luck), a popular good luck charm in China.

Peking Duck Restaurant. Chinatown, Yokohama. This shop with an eye-catching sign sells whole Peking ducks.

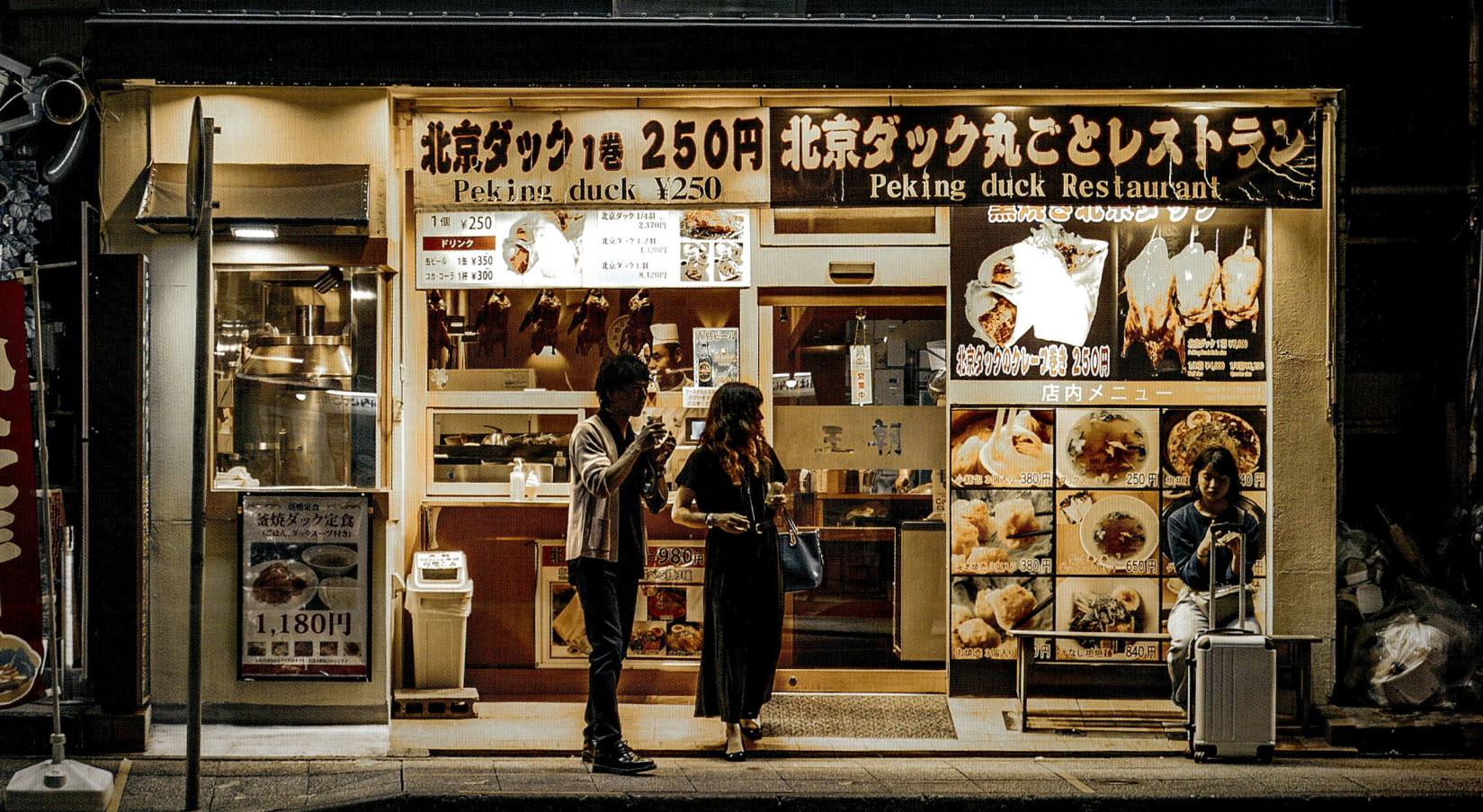

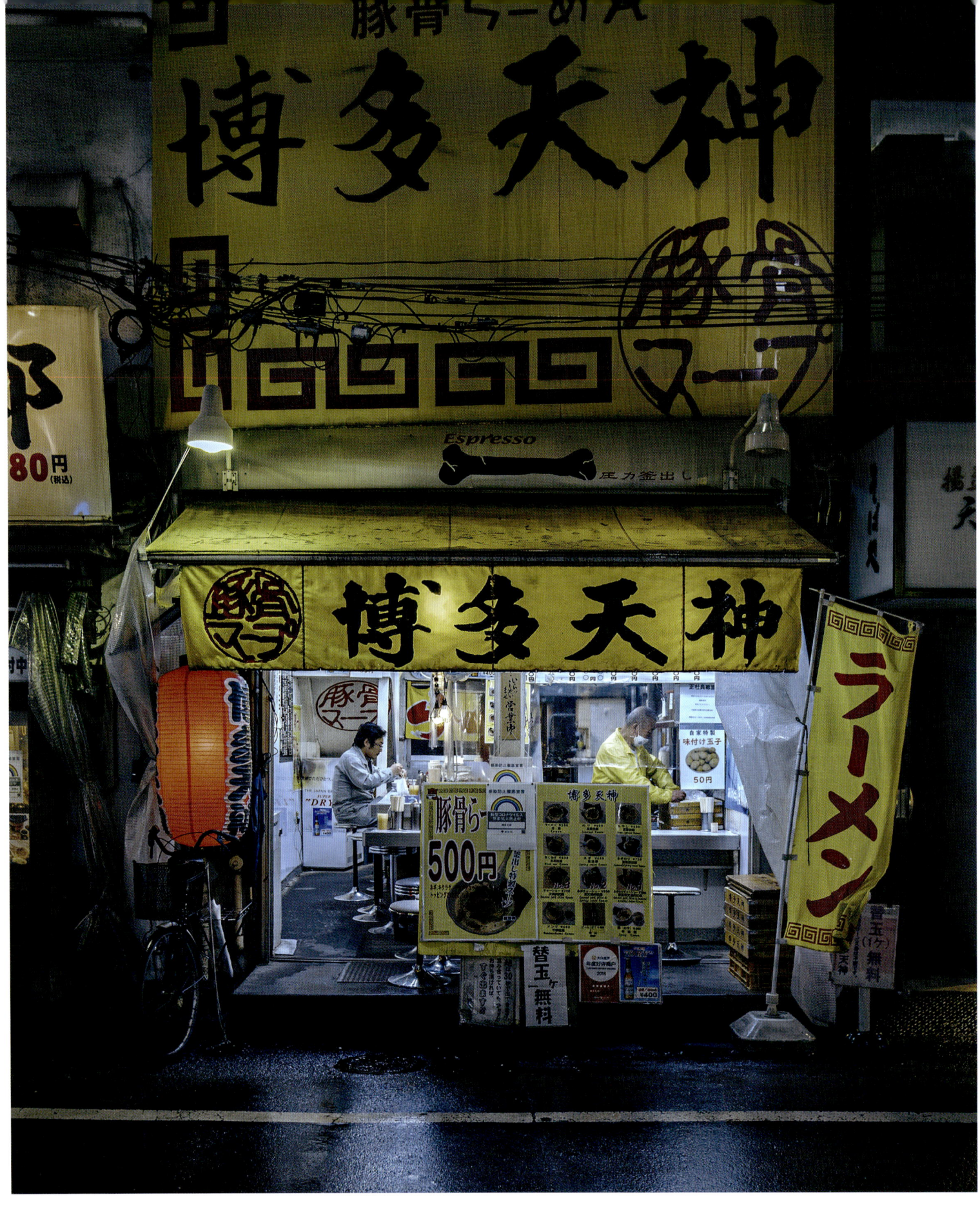

Tonkotsu Ramen Restaurant. Shinbashi, Tokyo.
I like this ramen restaurant because it has a
cool storefront. The impressive yellow sign is
illustrated with bold kanji characters.

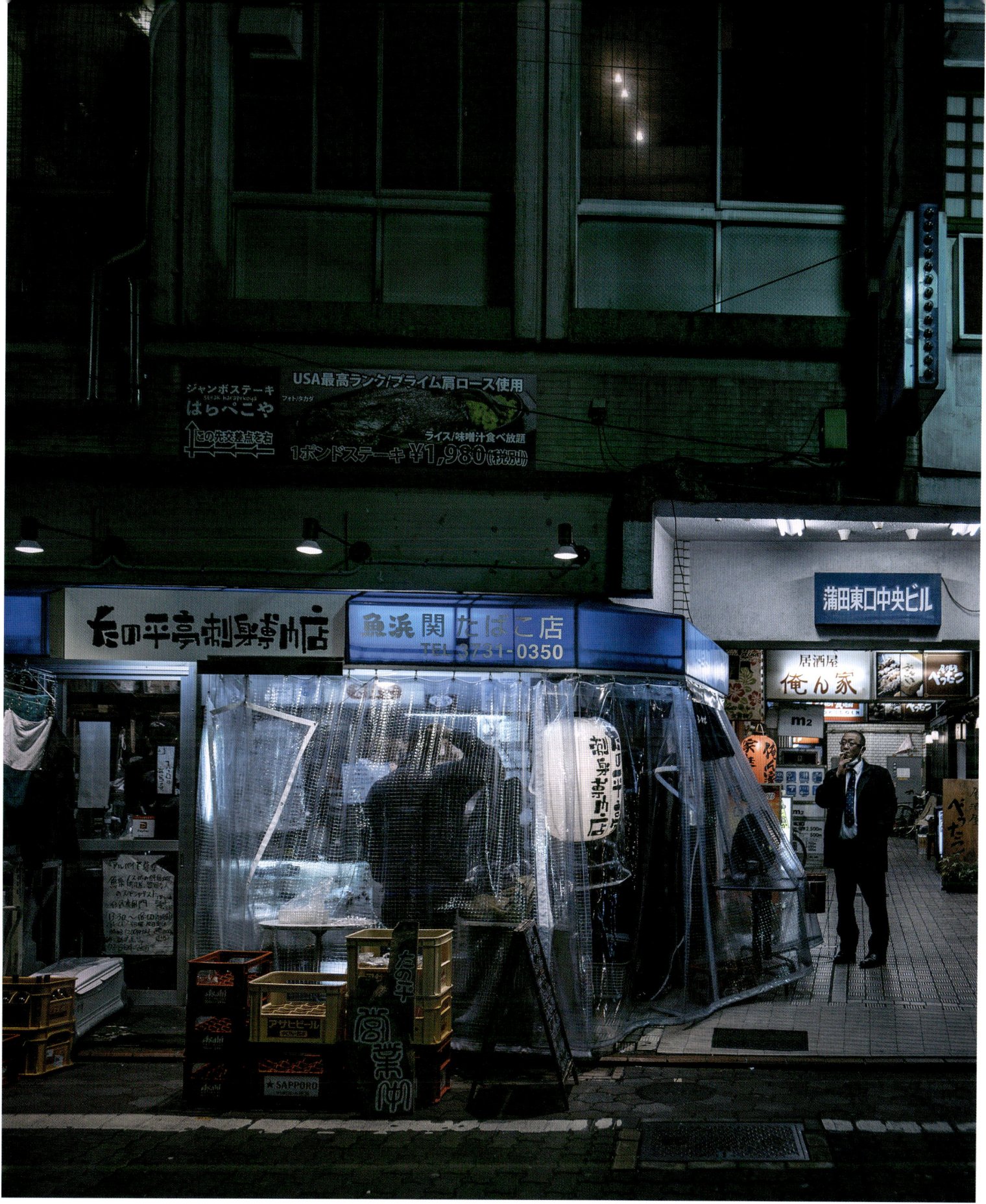

Tanoheitei Sashimi Specialty Restaurant.
Kamata, Tokyo. Though this is a standing bar,
it serves high-quality sashimi. It is rare to
find such a casual restaurant specializing in
sashimi in Japan.

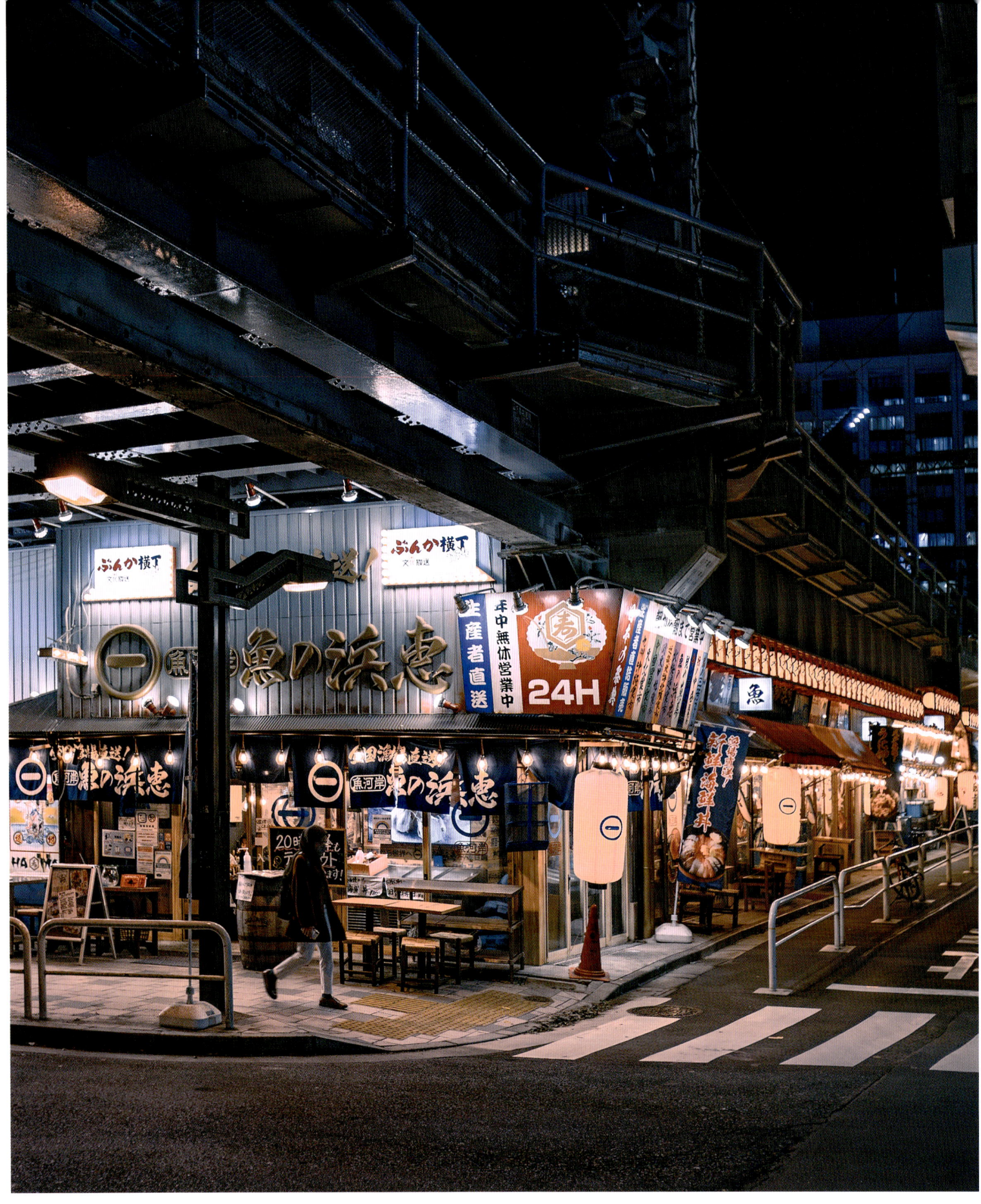

Sanchoku Yokocho. Yurakucho, Tokyo.
Eleven izakaya coexist under the train
tracks here. They serve a variety of dishes
and are open twenty-four hours a day.

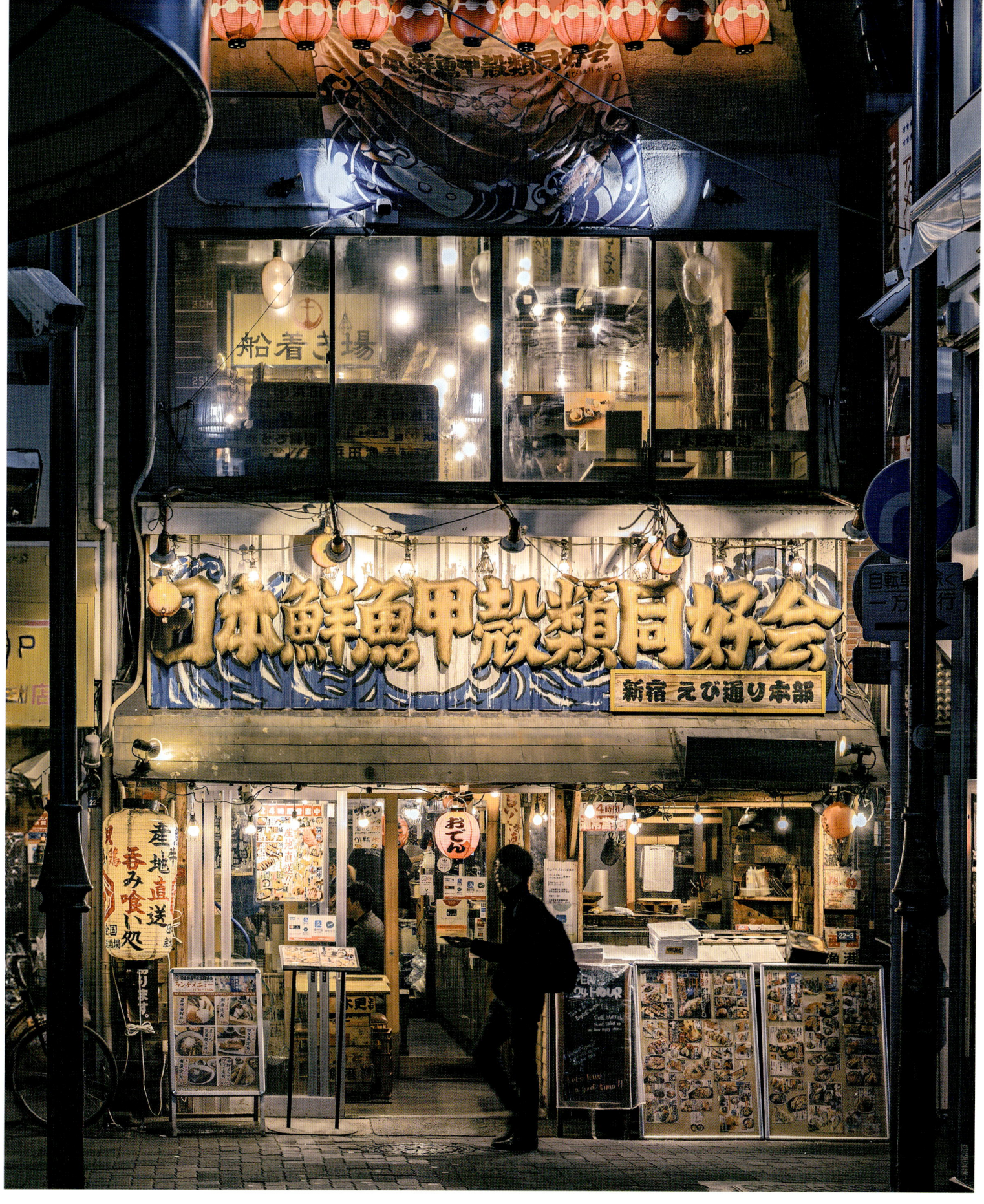

Seafood Restaurant. Shinjuku, Tokyo. Located at the end of the street commonly known as Ebi-dori, or Shrimp Street, is this izakaya that specializes in seafood.

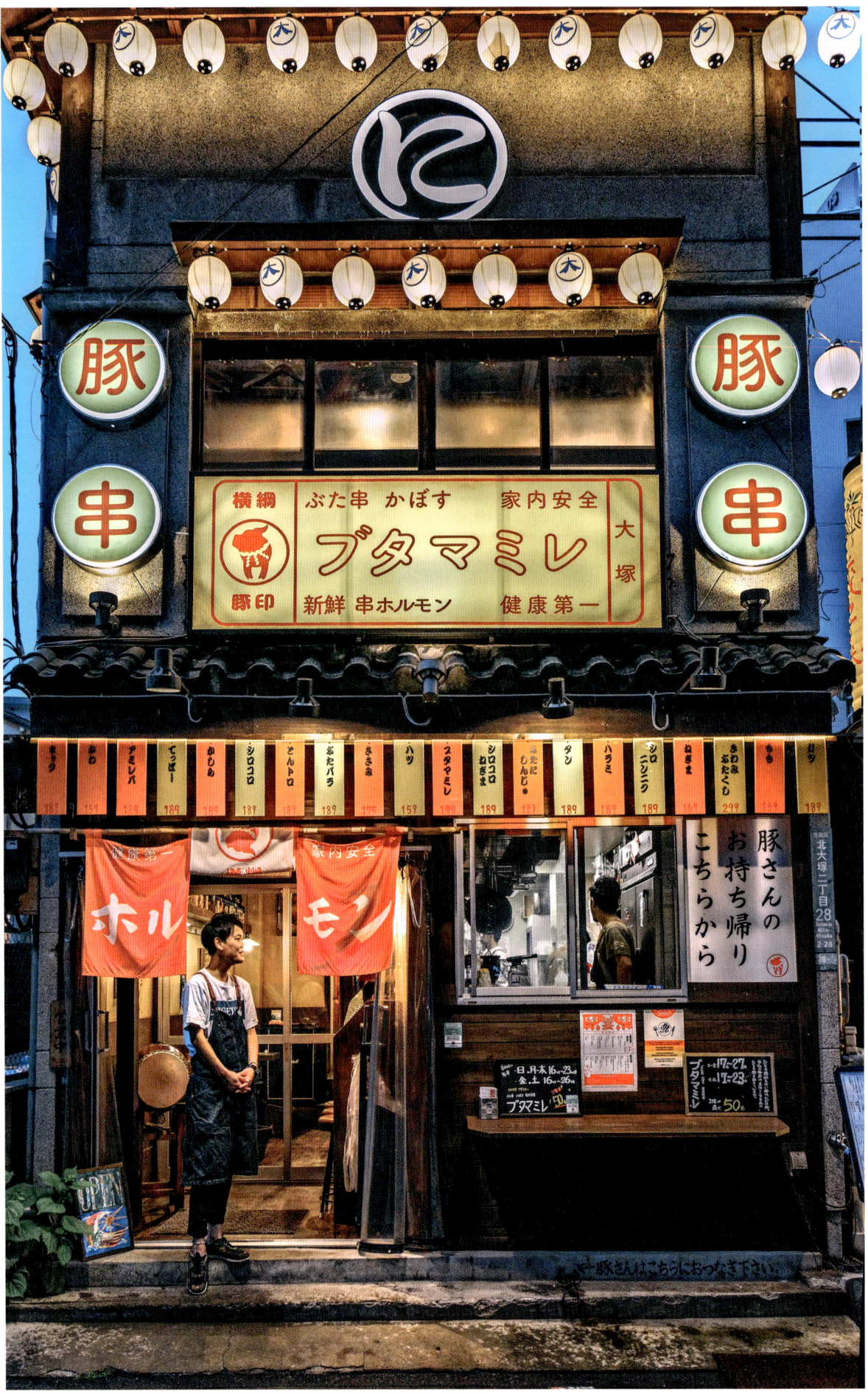

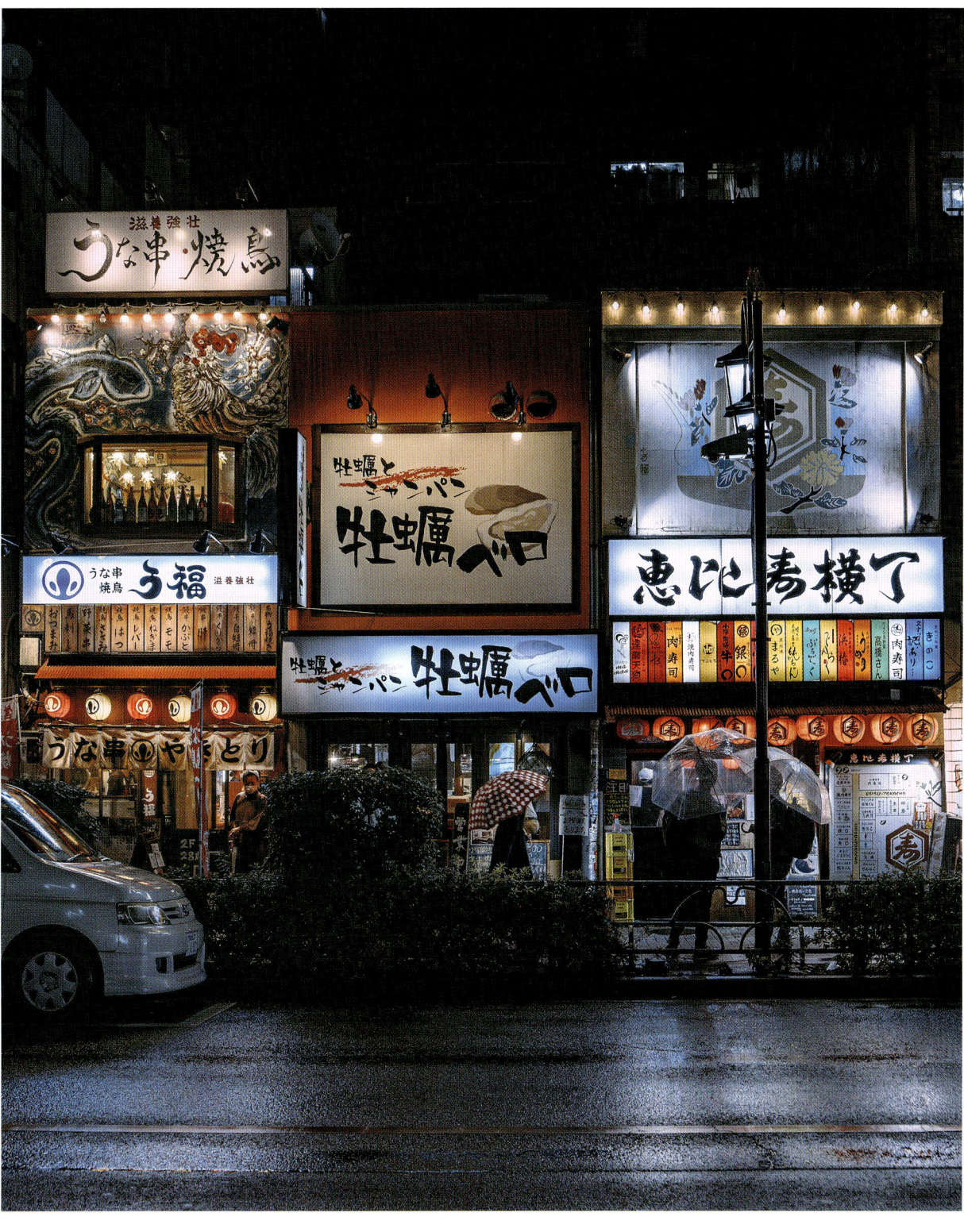

Skewered Pork Restaurant. Otsuka, Tokyo. Around Otsuka Station, there is a group of izakaya called Otsuka Noren-gai, where you can enjoy a variety of tastes.

Rainy Ebisu Yokocho. Ebisu, Tokyo. Ebisu Yokocho, a shopping center that was abandoned for many years, has now been renovated and houses many izakaya.

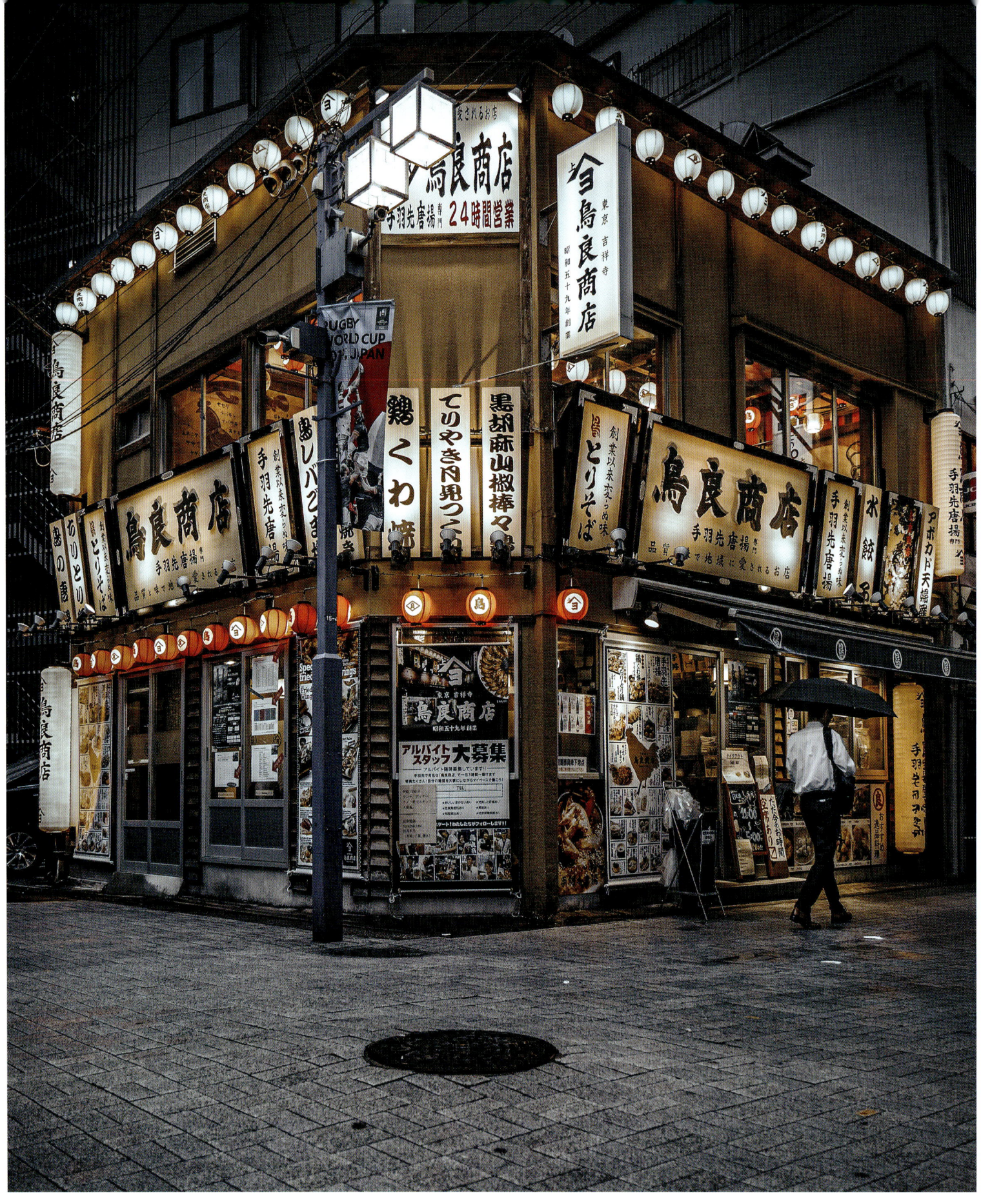

Chicken Restaurant. Kanda, Tokyo. The menu of this restaurant established in 1984 has all kinds of chicken dishes, which are written on the signs on the front of the restaurant.

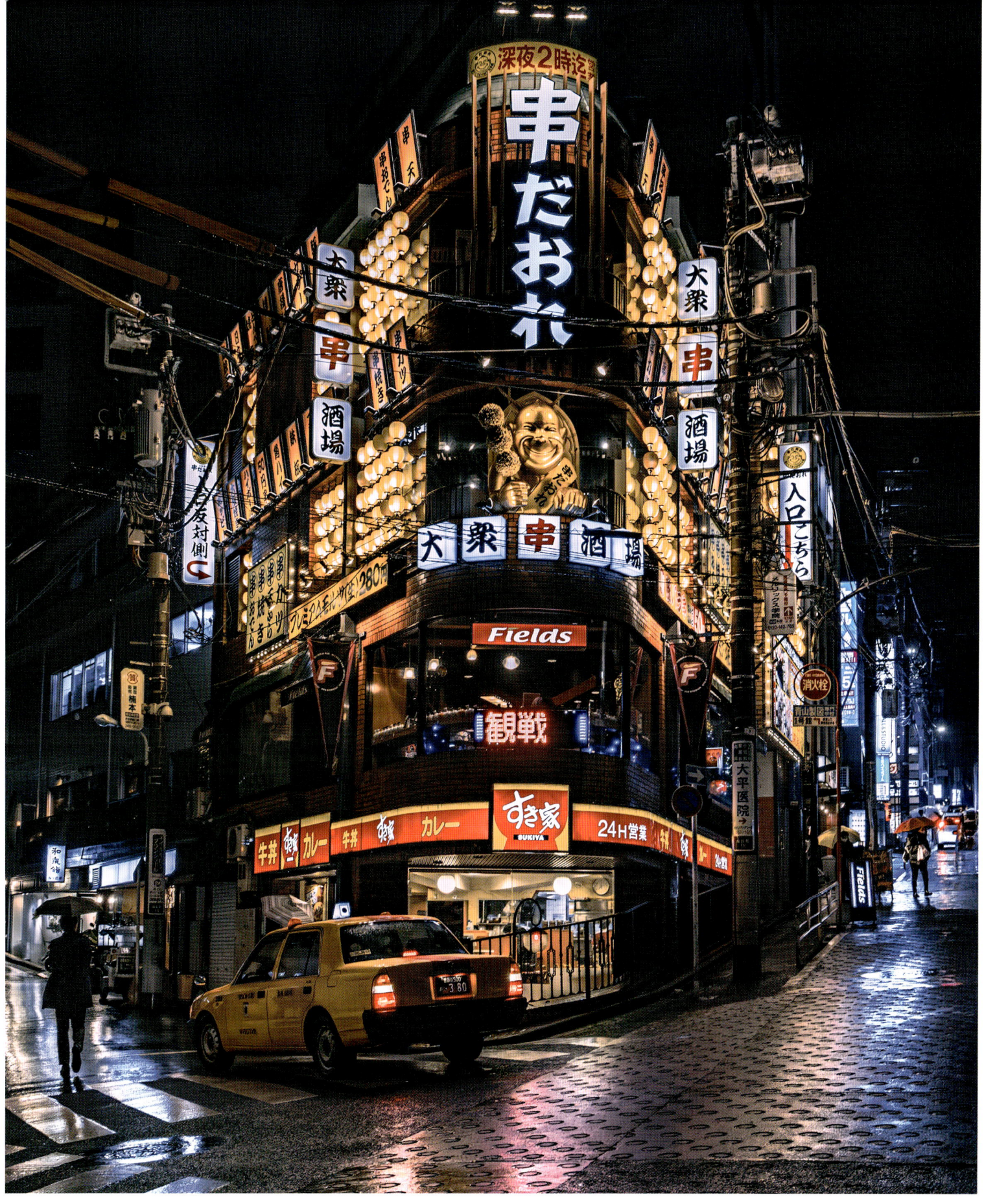

Izakaya at Y-Intersection. Shibuya, Tokyo. This izakaya, located a short distance from Shibuya Station, already has a great design, but on a rainy night, it makes for an even better photo.

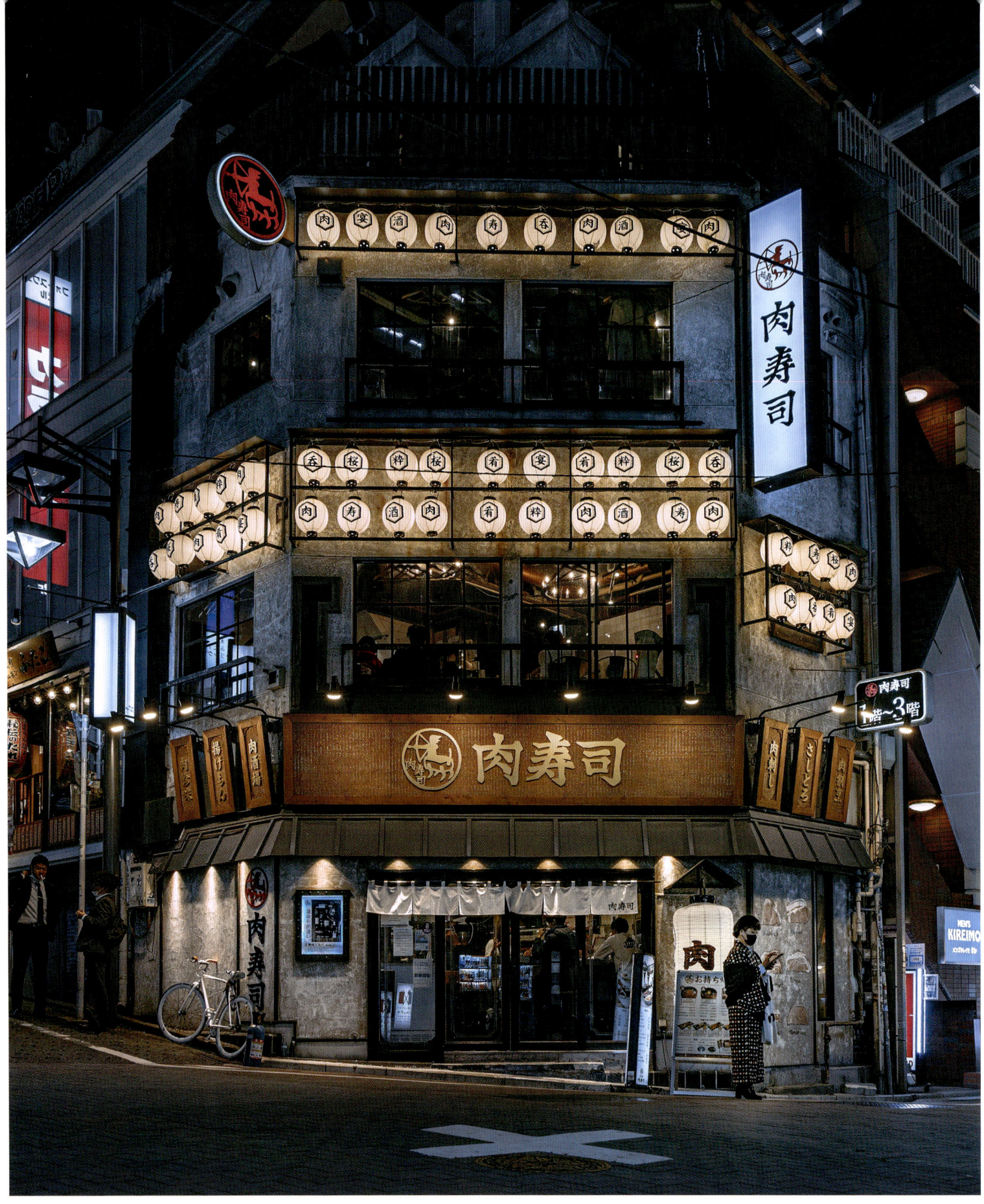

Meat Sushi Restaurant. Shibuya, Tokyo. Japanese sushi is generally a raw fish dish, but this restaurant offers raw meat sushi instead.

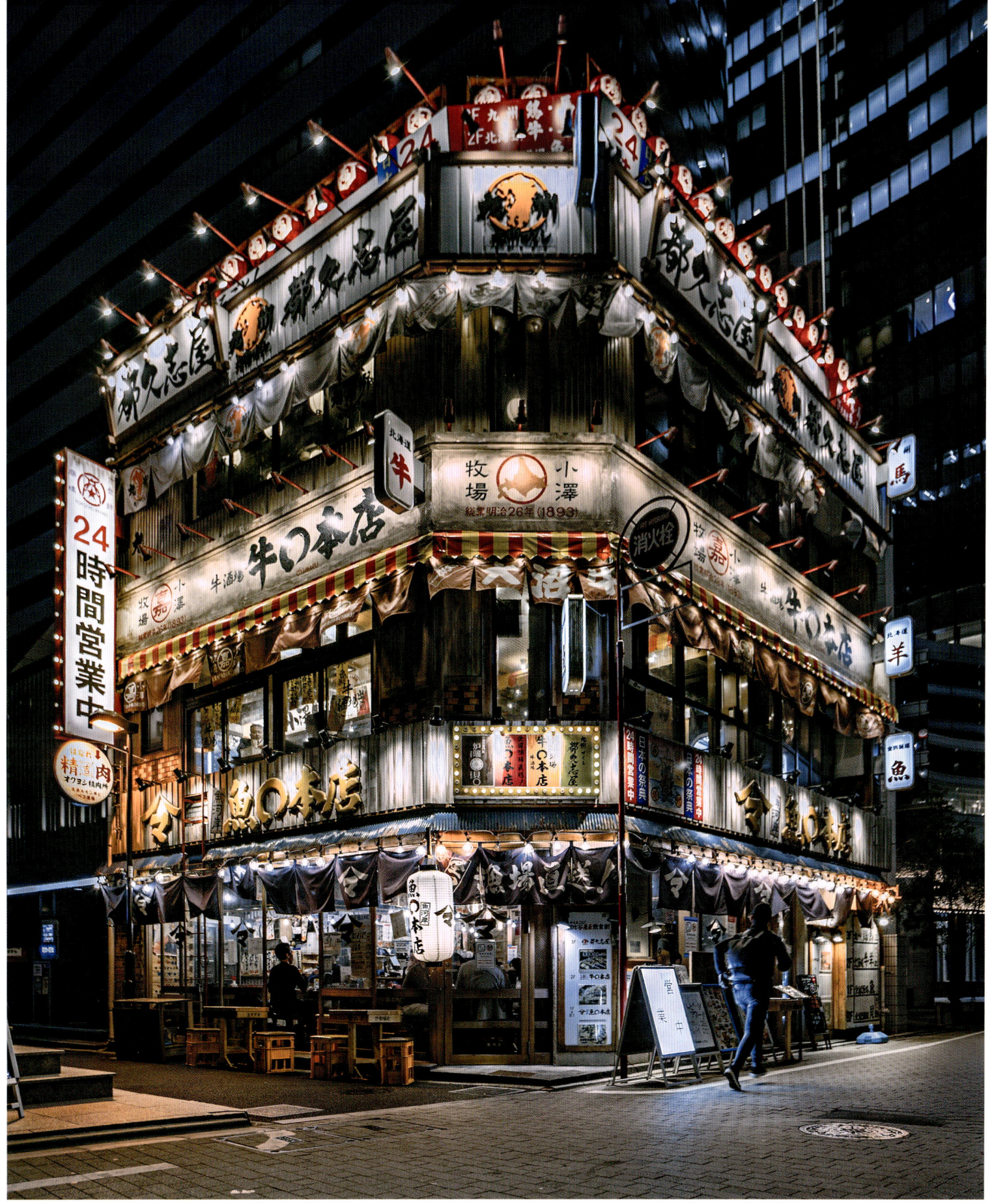

Glittering Storefront. Yurakucho, Tokyo.
This is a classic angle of this restaurant. The bluish-white light of the high-rise building behind it contrasts with the warmth of the retro storefront.

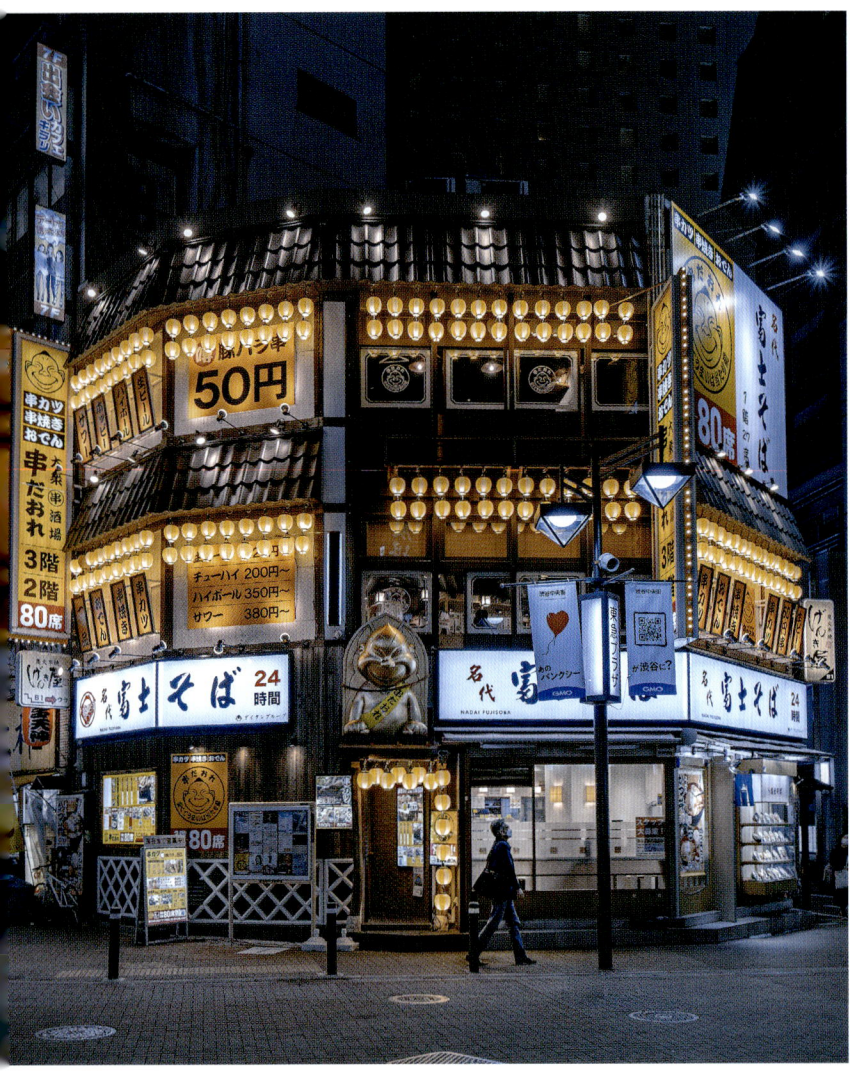

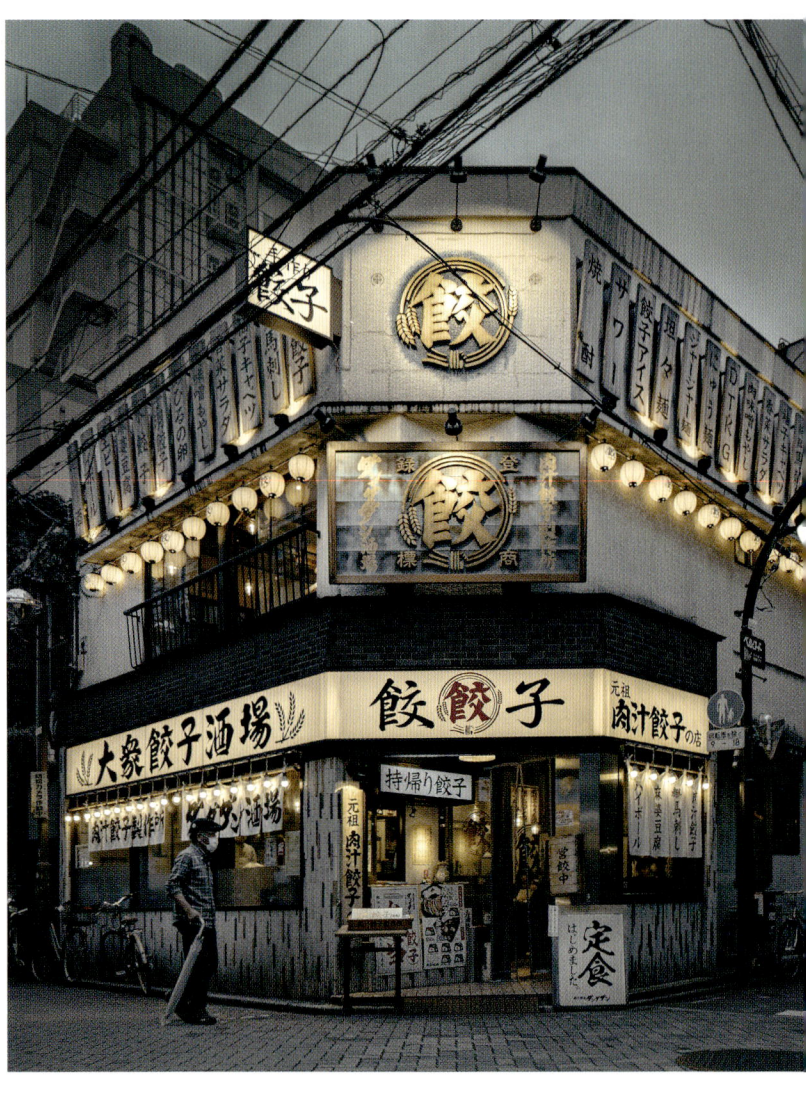

Lively Restaurant. Shibuya, Tokyo. Decorated with many lanterns, this restaurant has a comical statue in the center called Billiken-san, the god of good fortune.

Dandadan, a Popular Dumpling Bar. Kichijoji, Tokyo. I like to photograph corner stores from an angle. This restaurant is impressive with its corner entrance and many signs.

Gyoza Restaurant. Akabane, Tokyo. This is a popular *gyoza* (dumplings) restaurant filled with many signs and lanterns with kanji and hiragana characters. I took this photo with a superwide-angle lens because the alley is quite narrow.

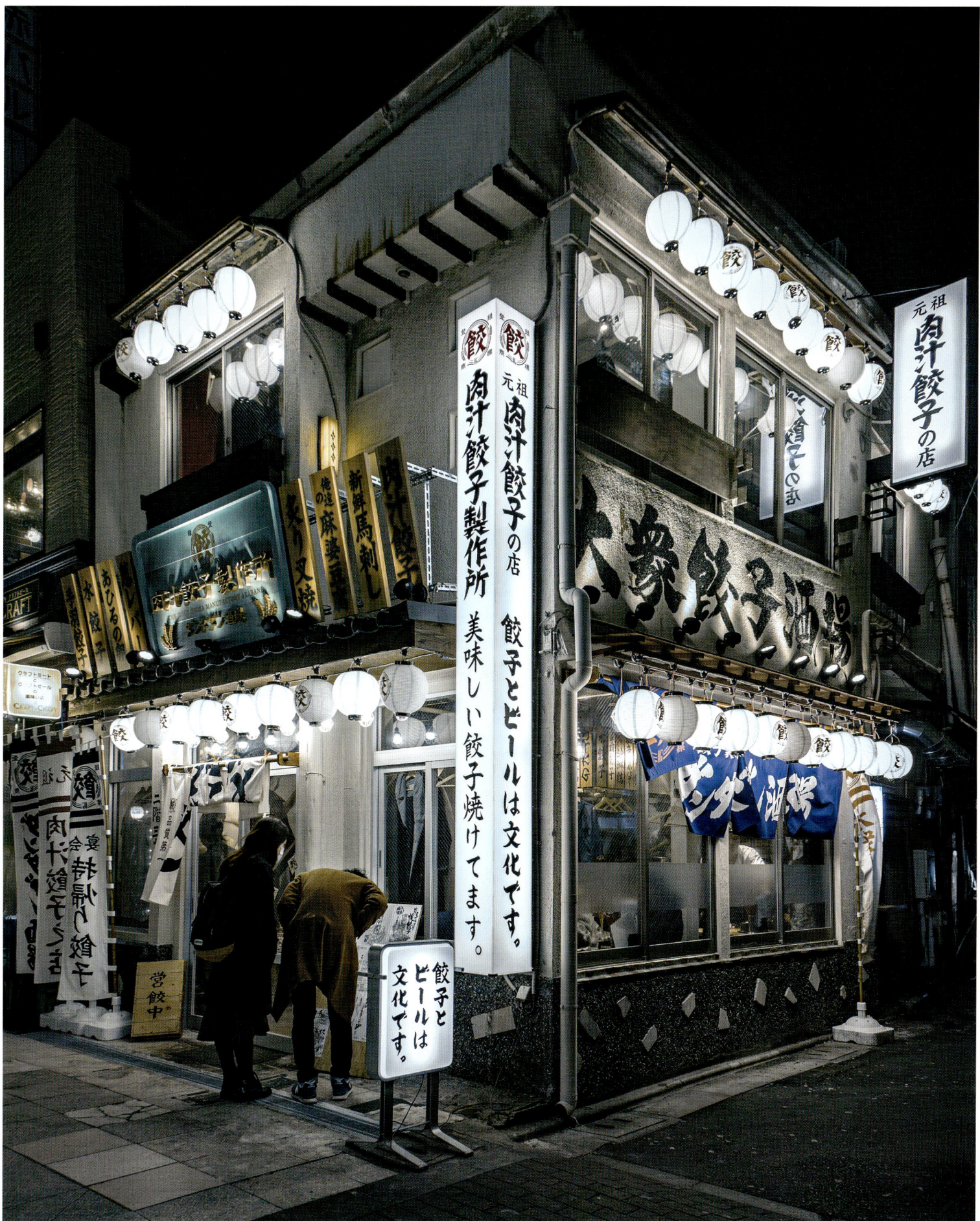

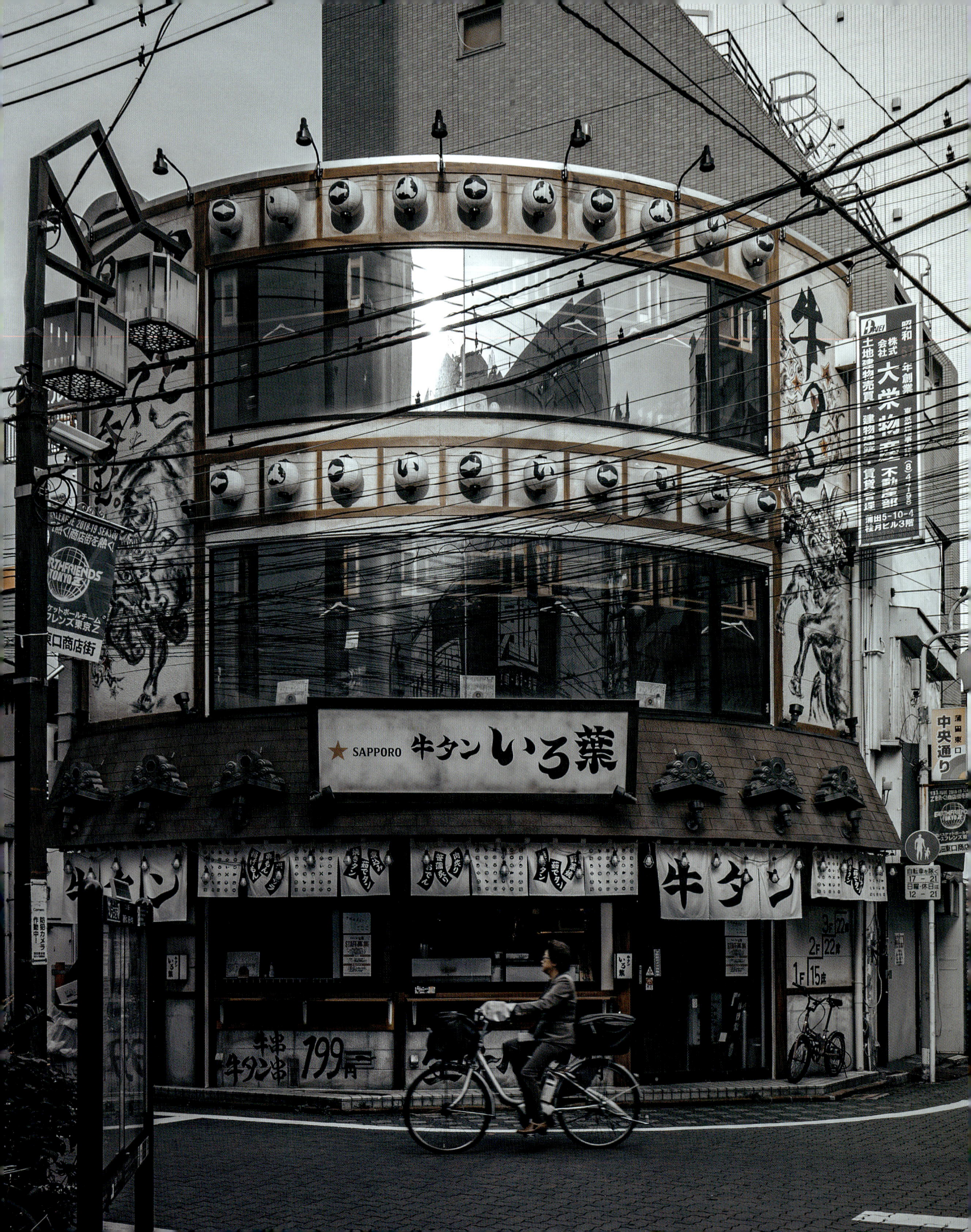

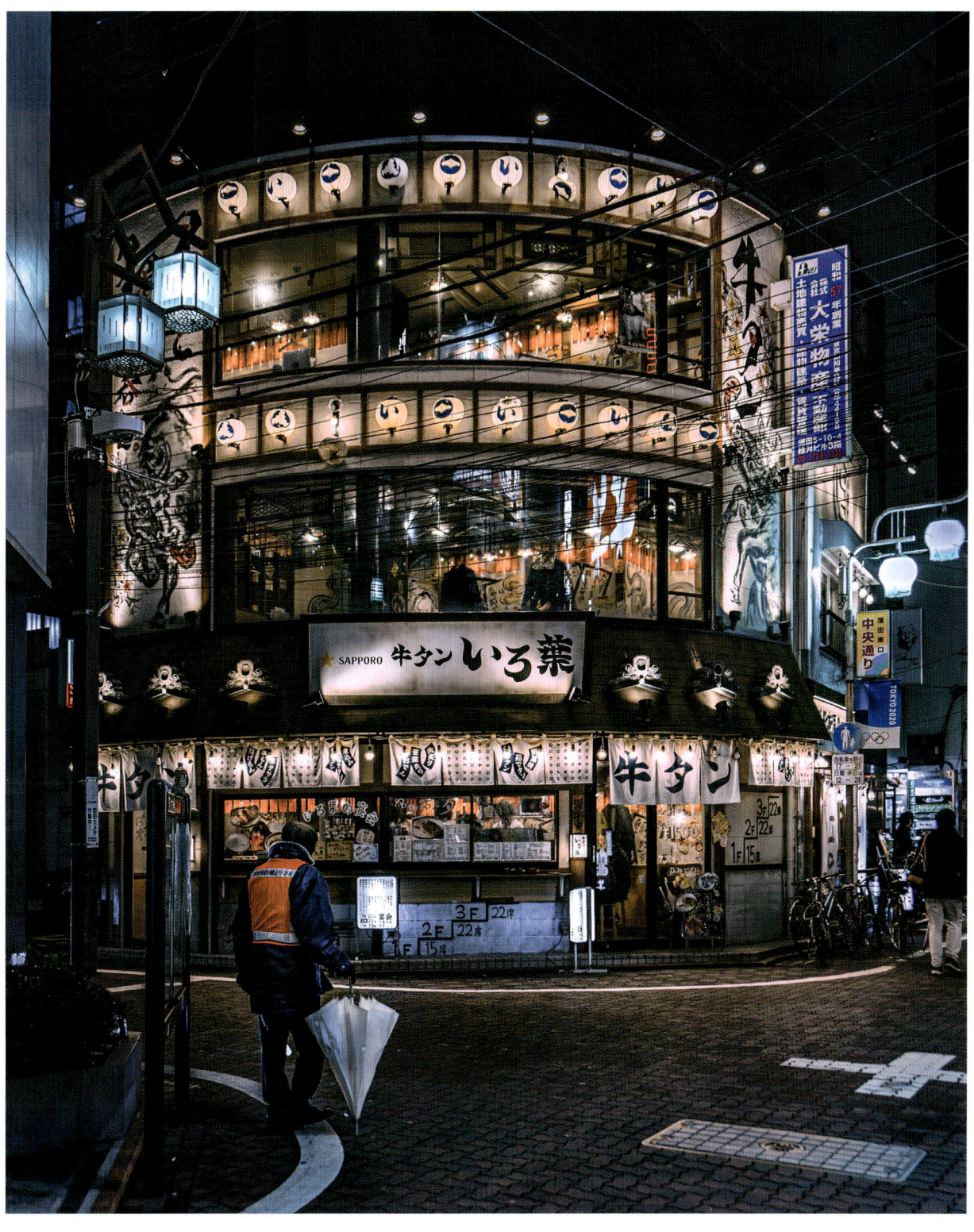

A Casual Moment 1. Kamata, Tokyo. This beef tongue restaurant has a different feeling during the day before it opens at night.

A Casual Moment 2. Kamata, Tokyo. The restaurant is now transformed into a flashy place at night.

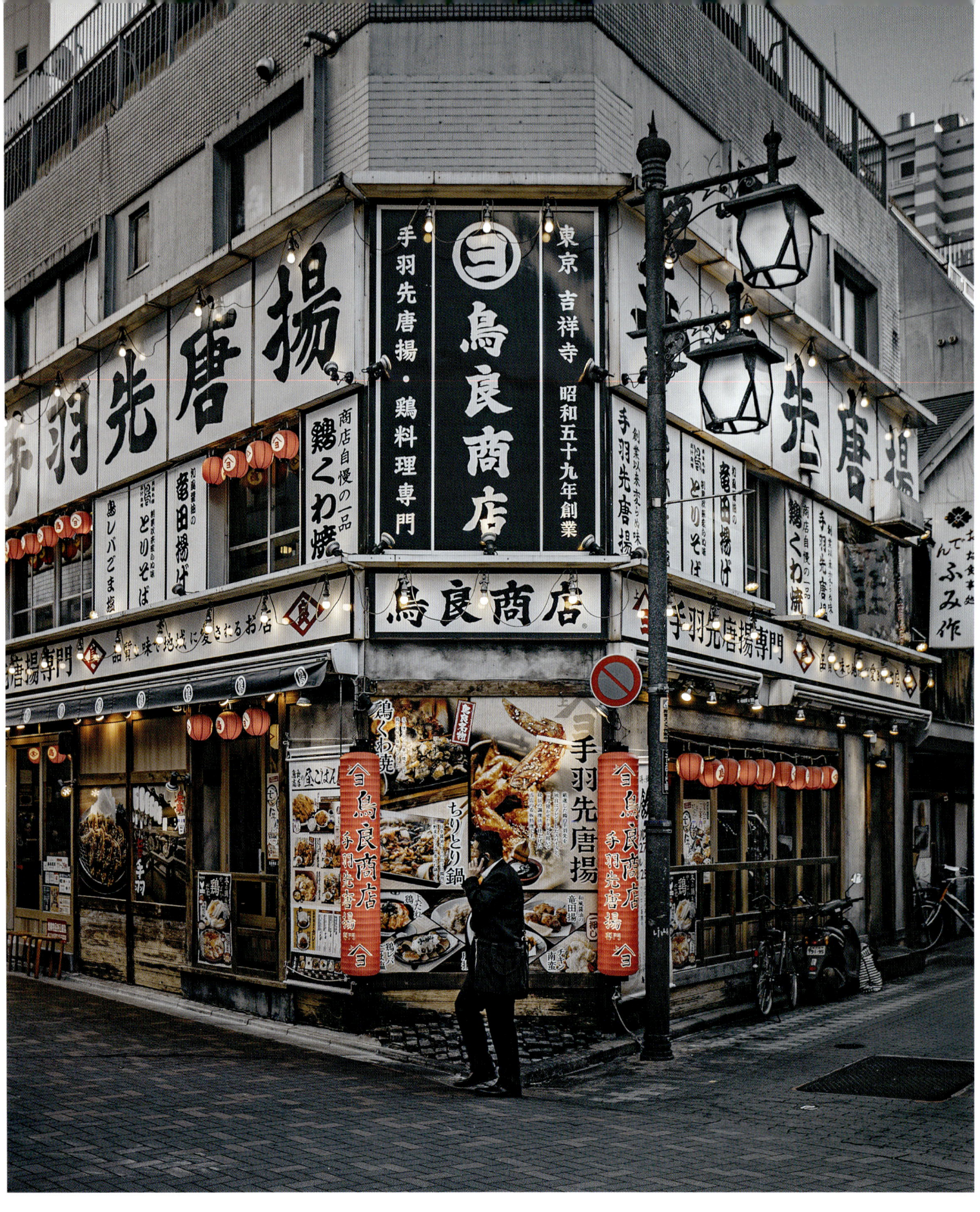

Chicken Menu. Ueno, Tokyo. This entire restaurant is covered with signs in kanji and hiragana with the names of the dishes served at the restaurant.

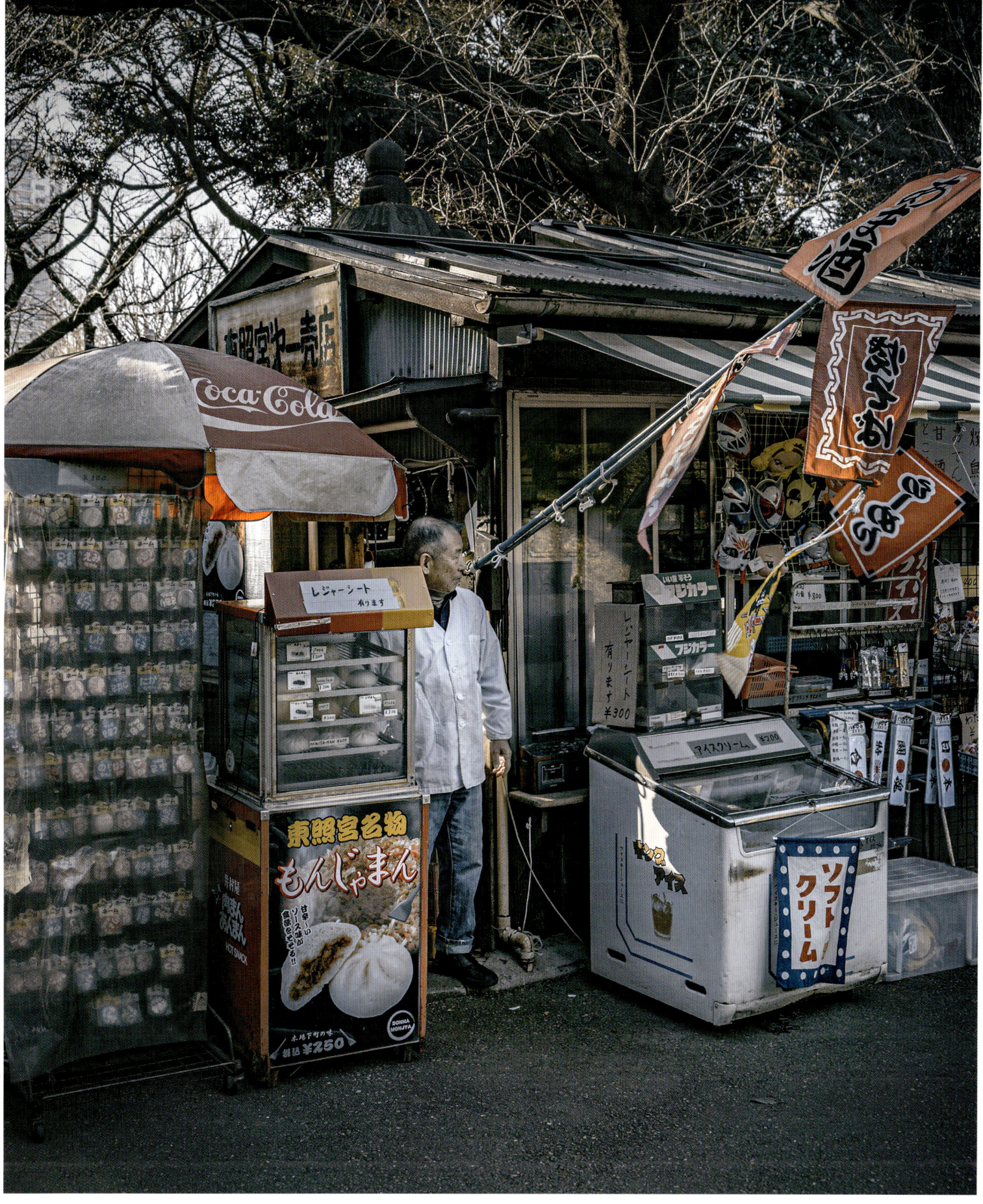

Toshogu Shrine Daiichi Shop. Ueno, Tokyo.
This store that is over seventy years old is
located next to the Ueno Toshogu Shrine.
Inside the store is a cafeteria where visitors
can enjoy a meal in a relaxed environment.

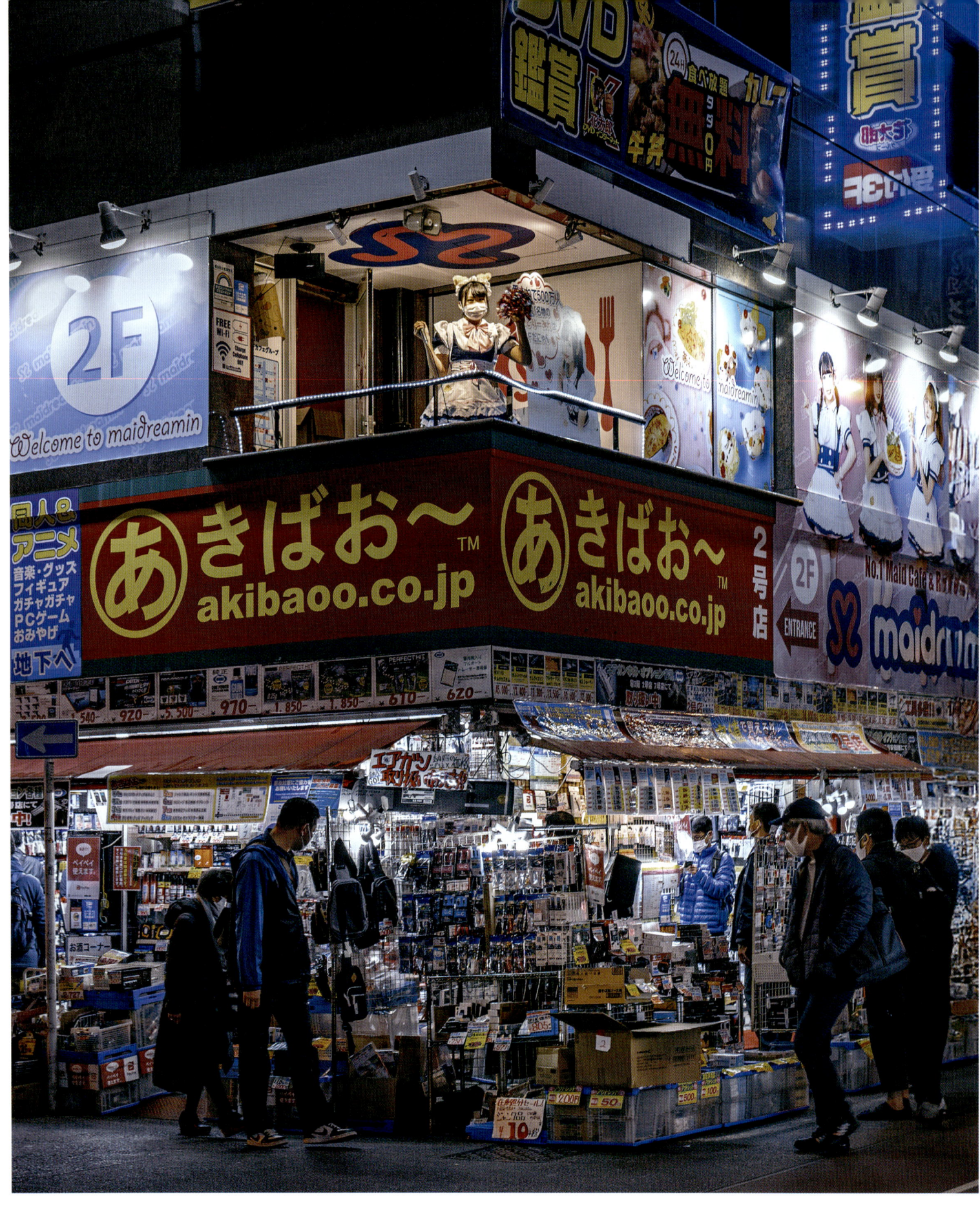

Maid Café. Akihabara, Tokyo. The maid
waved and smiled at me from the terrace
of the café above an electronics store.

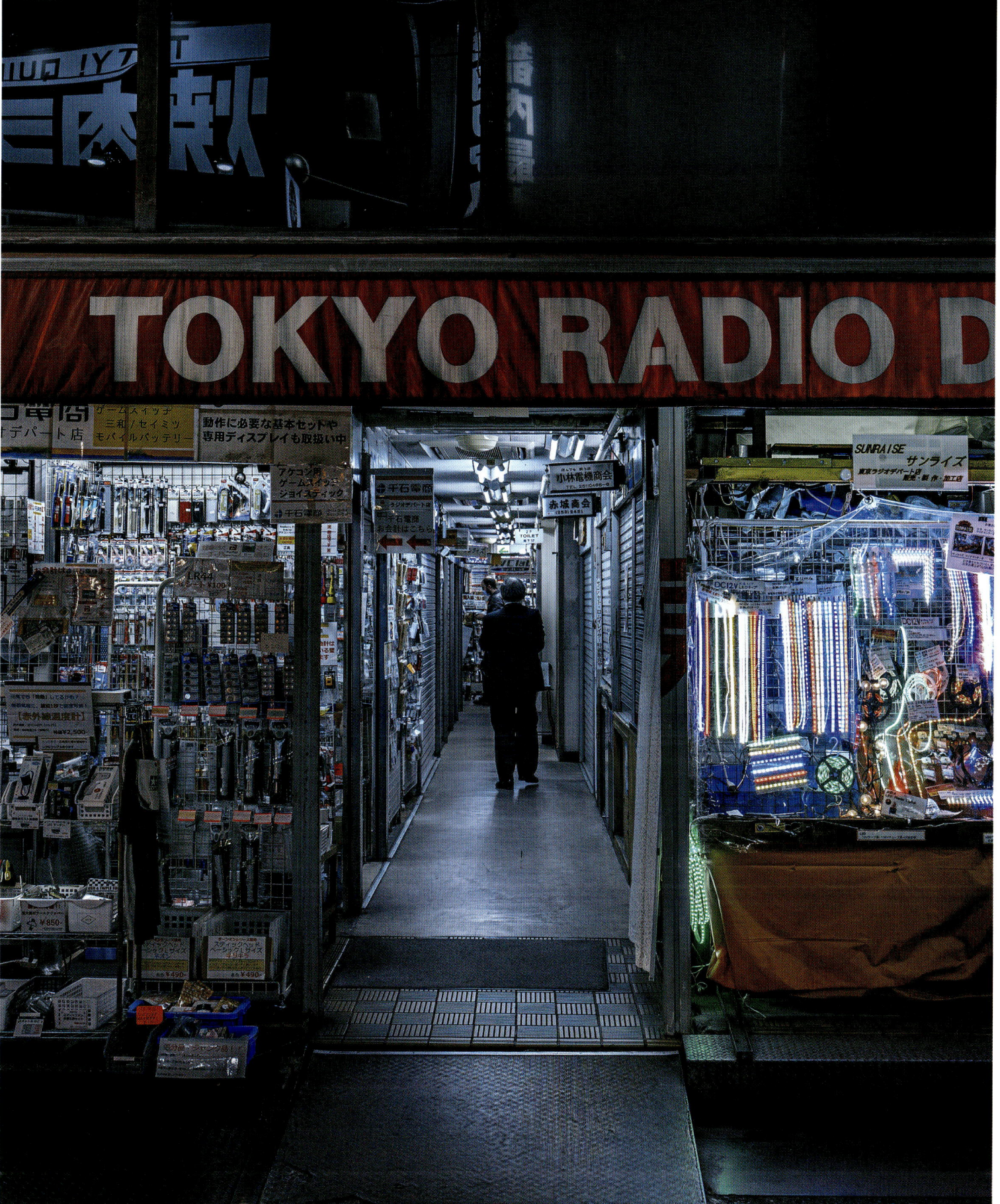

Cyber Store. Akihabara, Tokyo. I'm not sure what is sold at this electronics store with bright lights.

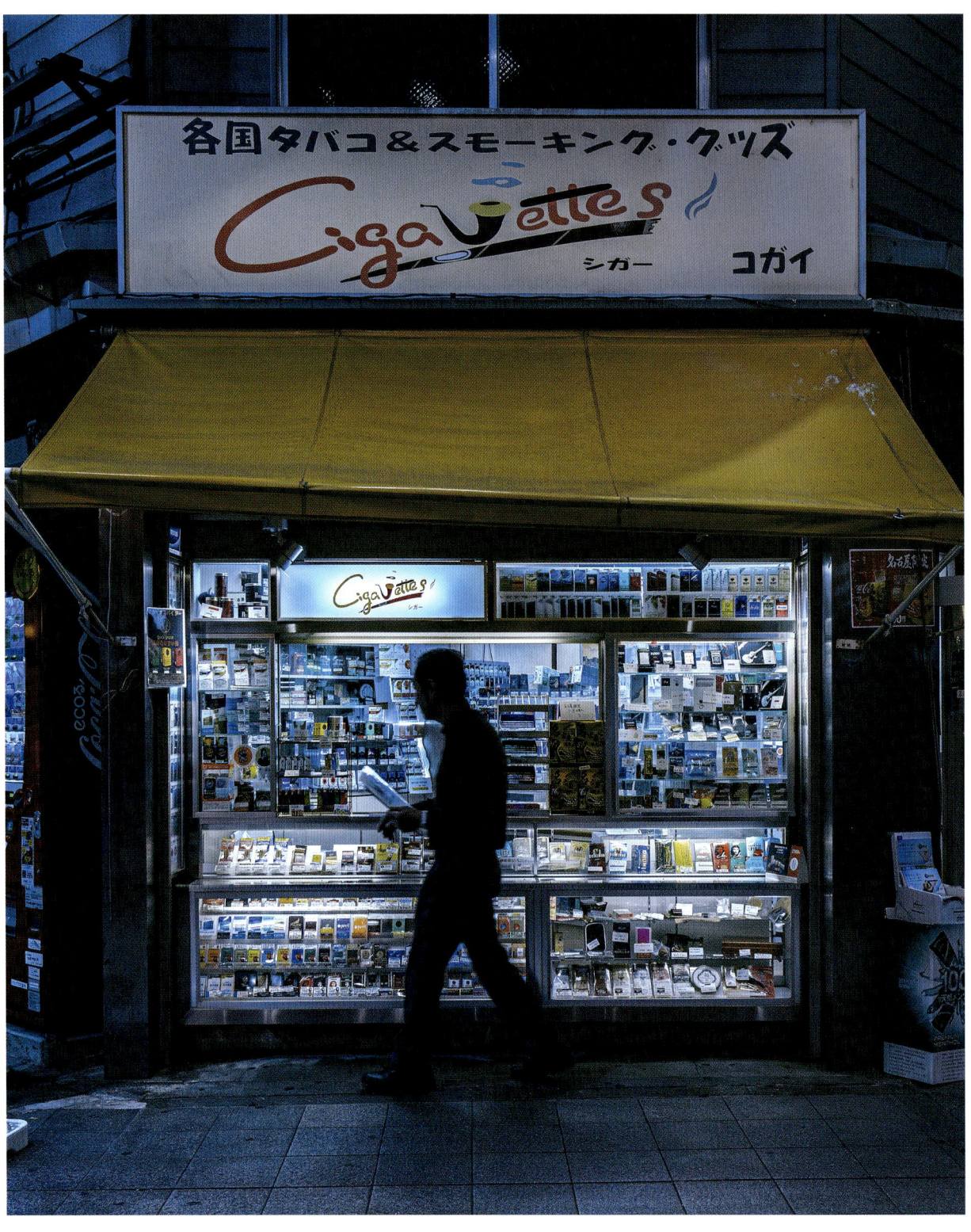

各国タバコ＆スモーキング・グッズ

Cigarettes

シガー　　コガイ

Small Tobacco Shop. Nagoya. This
small cigarette store located under
the arcade of Osu Shintenchi Street
seems to have closed.

Game Store. Akihabara, Tokyo. This
vibrant store is located below the
train tracks.

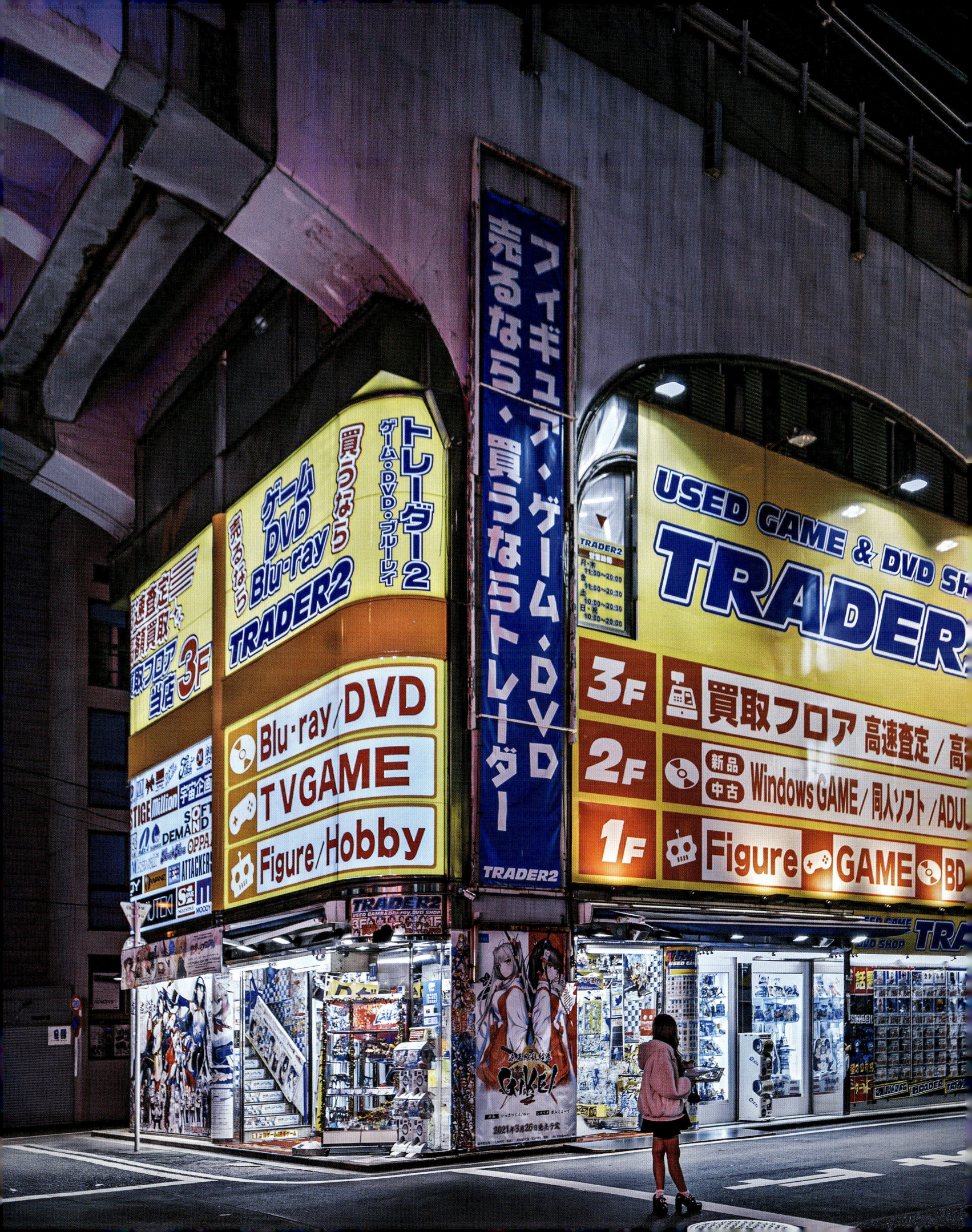

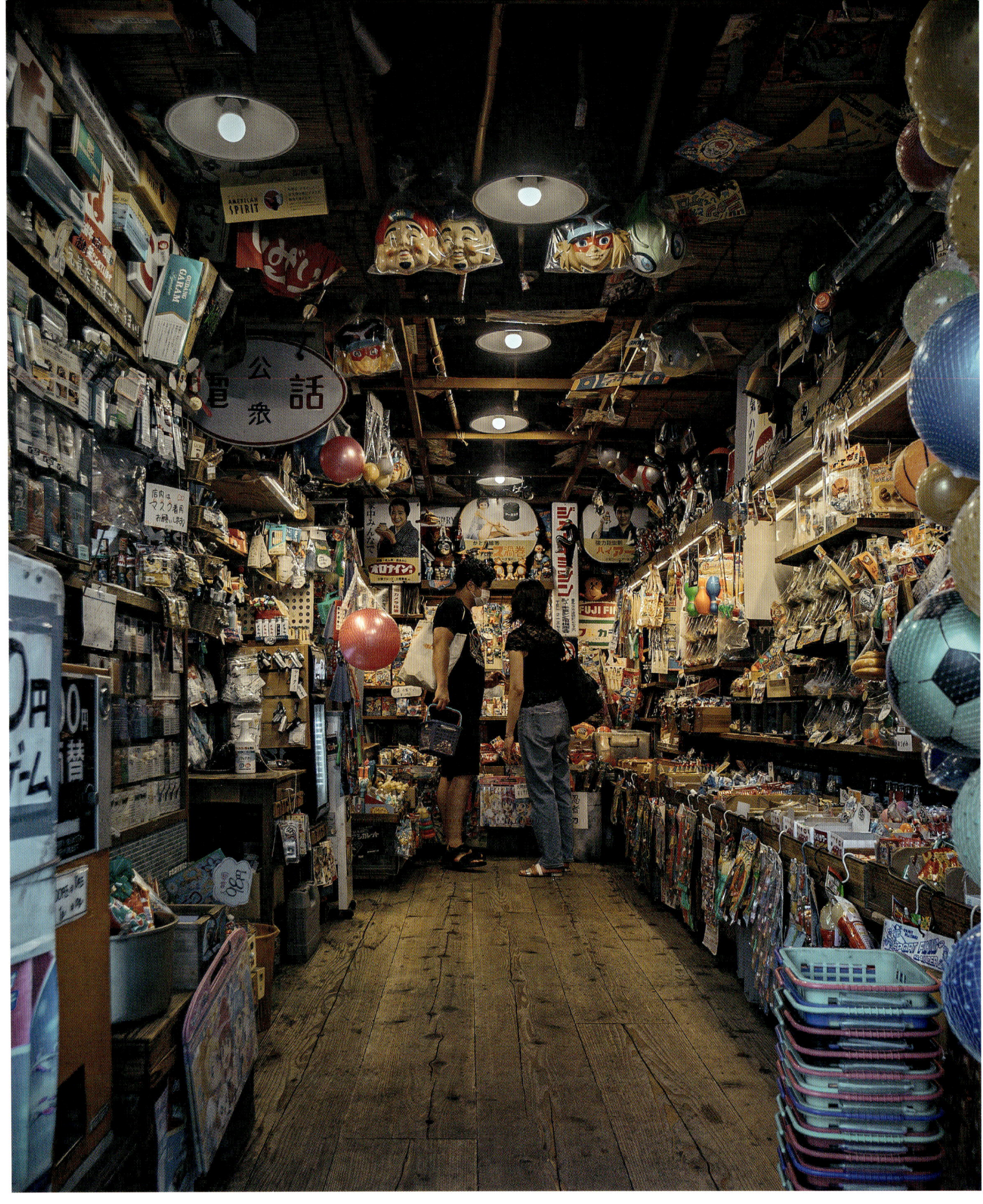

Candy Store. Nakano, Tokyo. Tucked away in a residential area, old-fashioned candy stores like this one have all but disappeared.

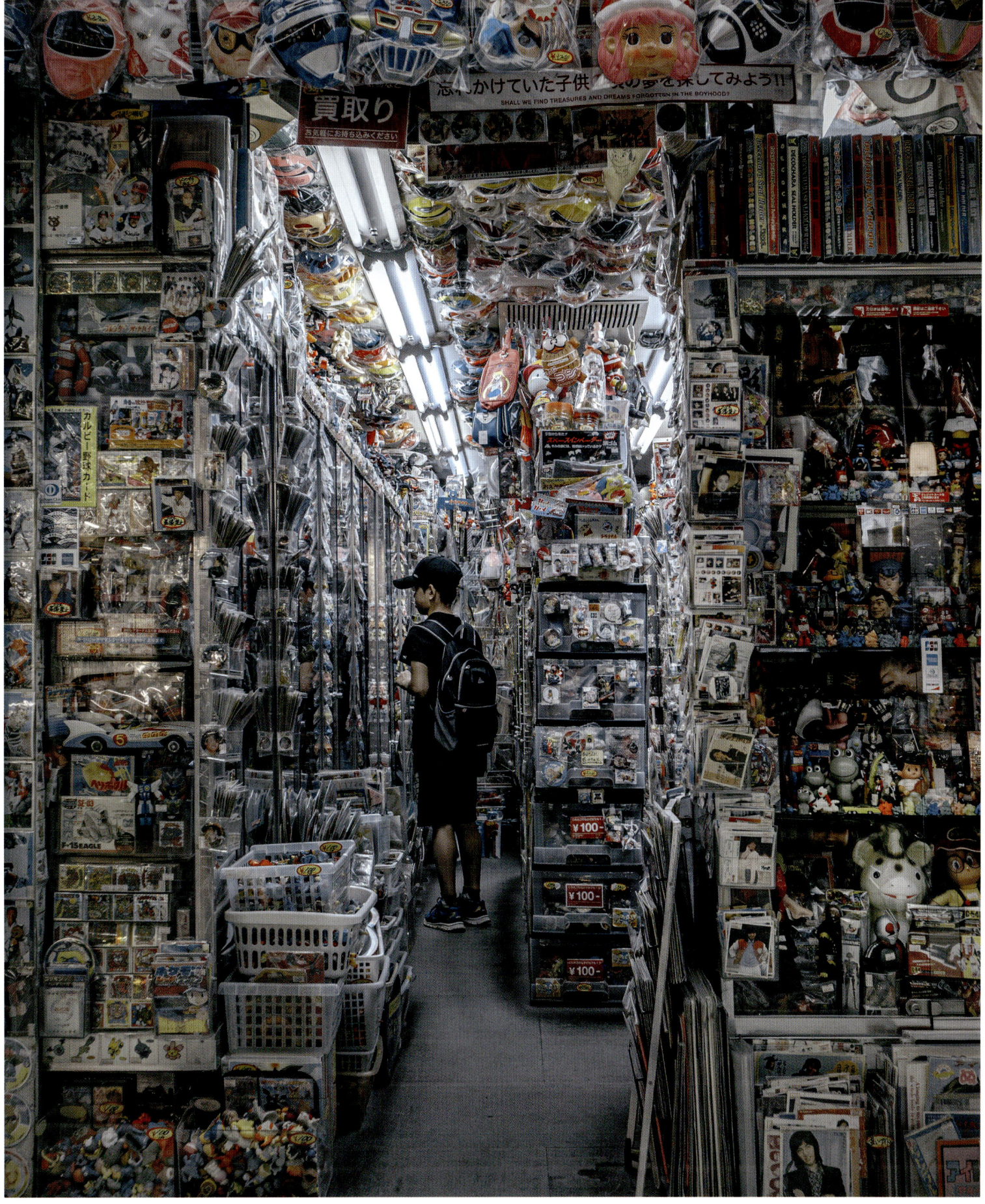

Retro Toy Store. Nakano, Tokyo. This toy store has been in business since I was a child, probably since the 1960s. The store is now popular with adults looking for expensive retro toys.

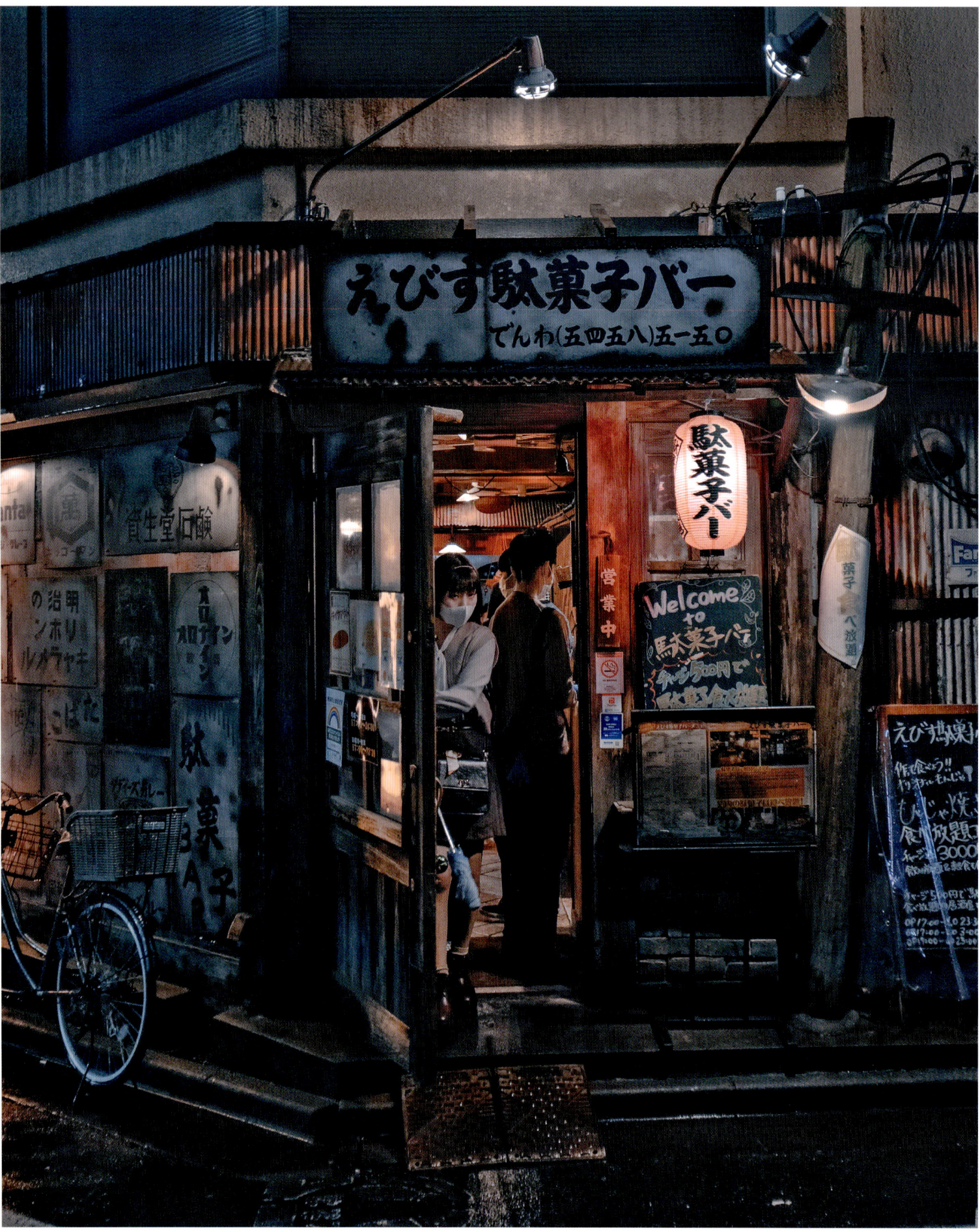

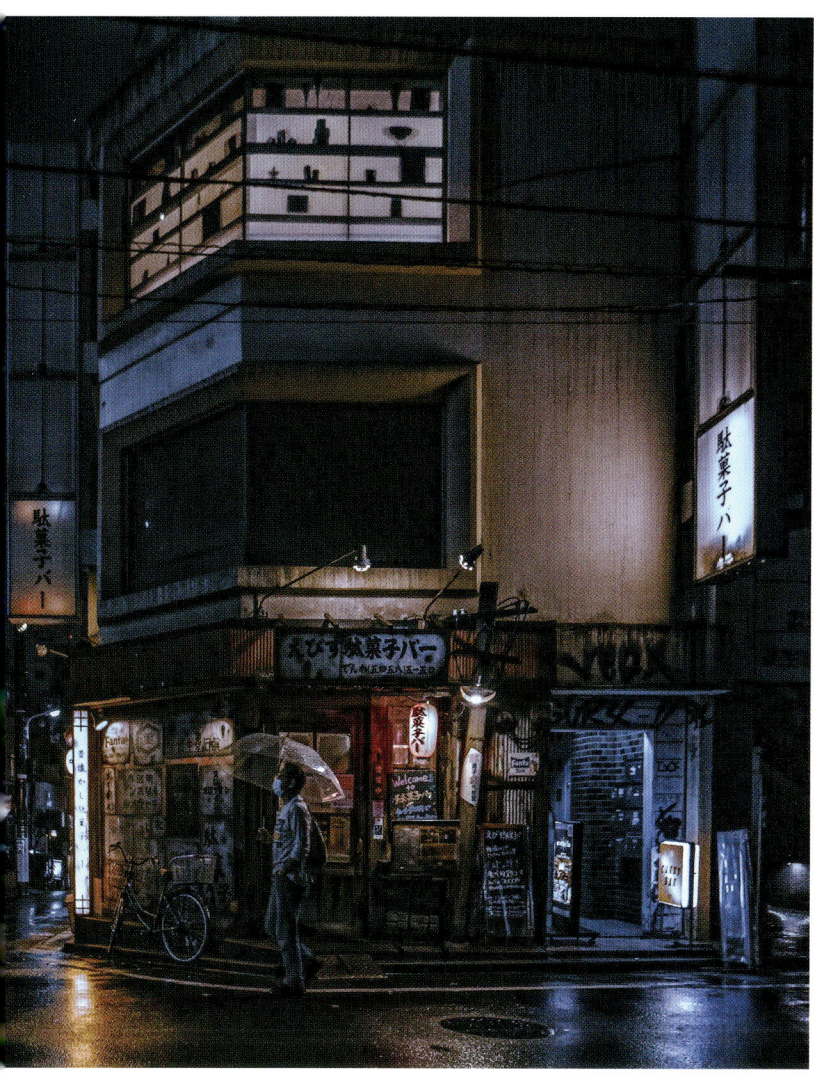

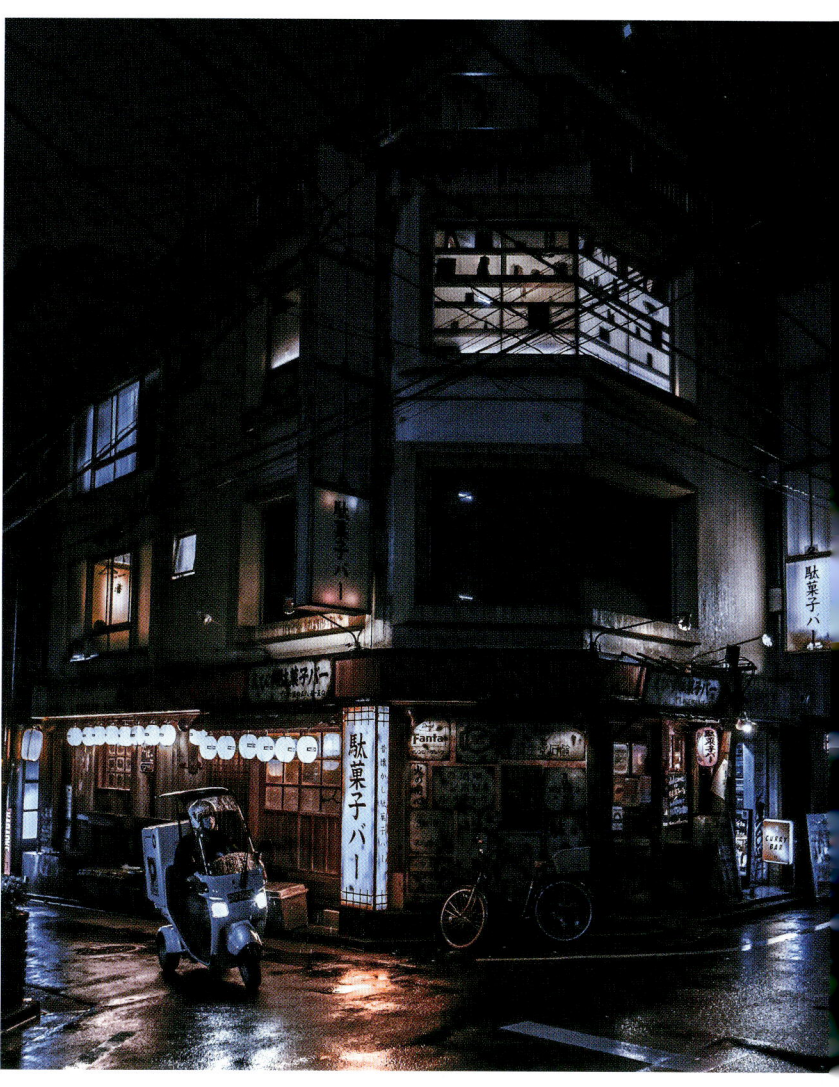

Storefront in the Rain 1. Ebisu, Tokyo. When I was a child, there were candy stores like this one near schools and parks where you could have fun spending a little pocket money.

Storefront in the Rain 2. Ebisu, Tokyo. Here is a view of the entire building that houses the candy store.

Storefront in the Rain 3. Ebisu, Tokyo. Here is the side view of the candy store.

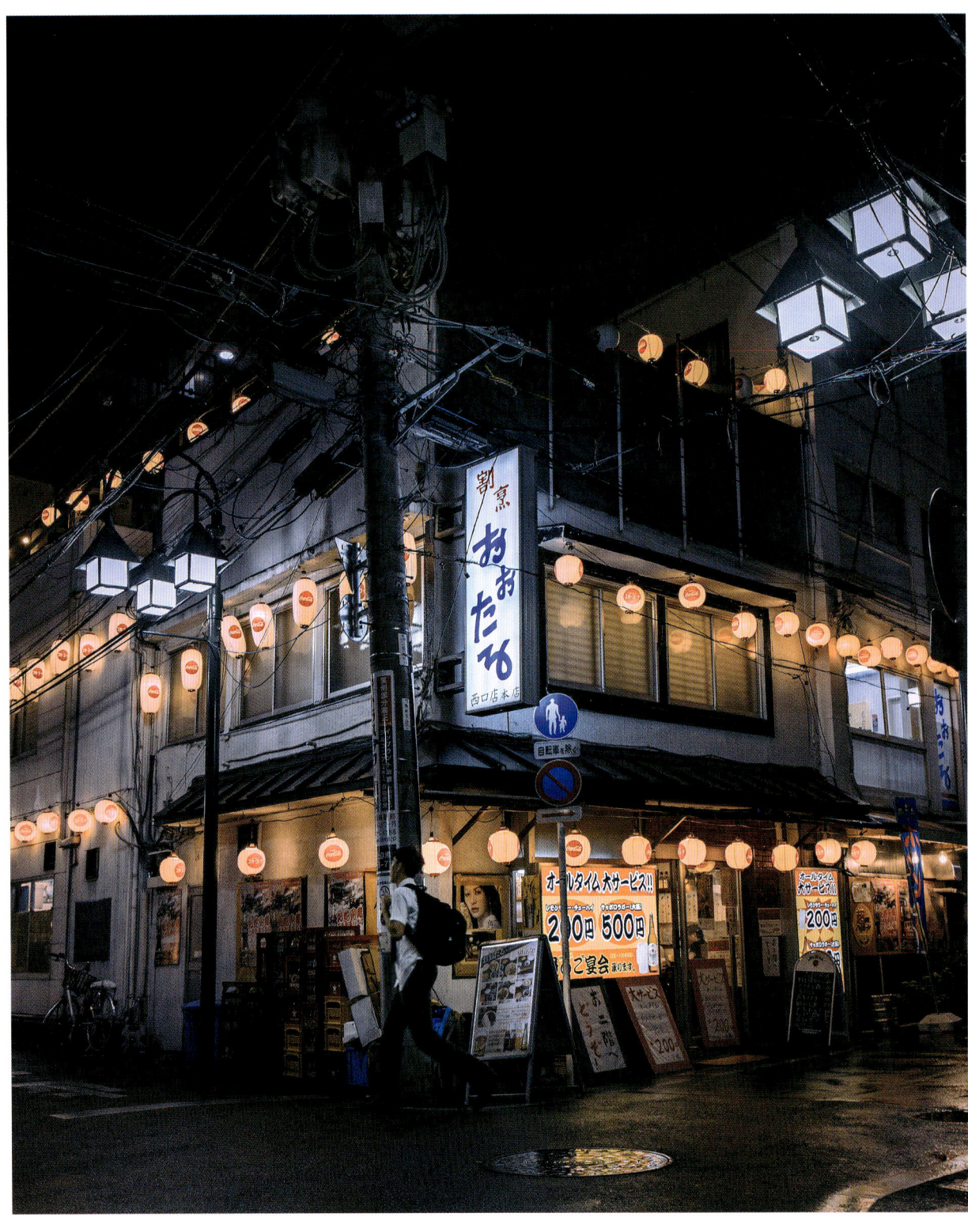

Orange Lanterns. Nakameguro, Tokyo. This popular izakaya is located on the road along the railroad tracks, just a short walk from Nakameguro Station. The orange lanterns give off a nice light.

Izakaya with Tattered Lantern. Nerima, Tokyo. This restaurant has a smoking area on the corner. Though the large overhead lantern is damaged, it lends the storefront its charm.

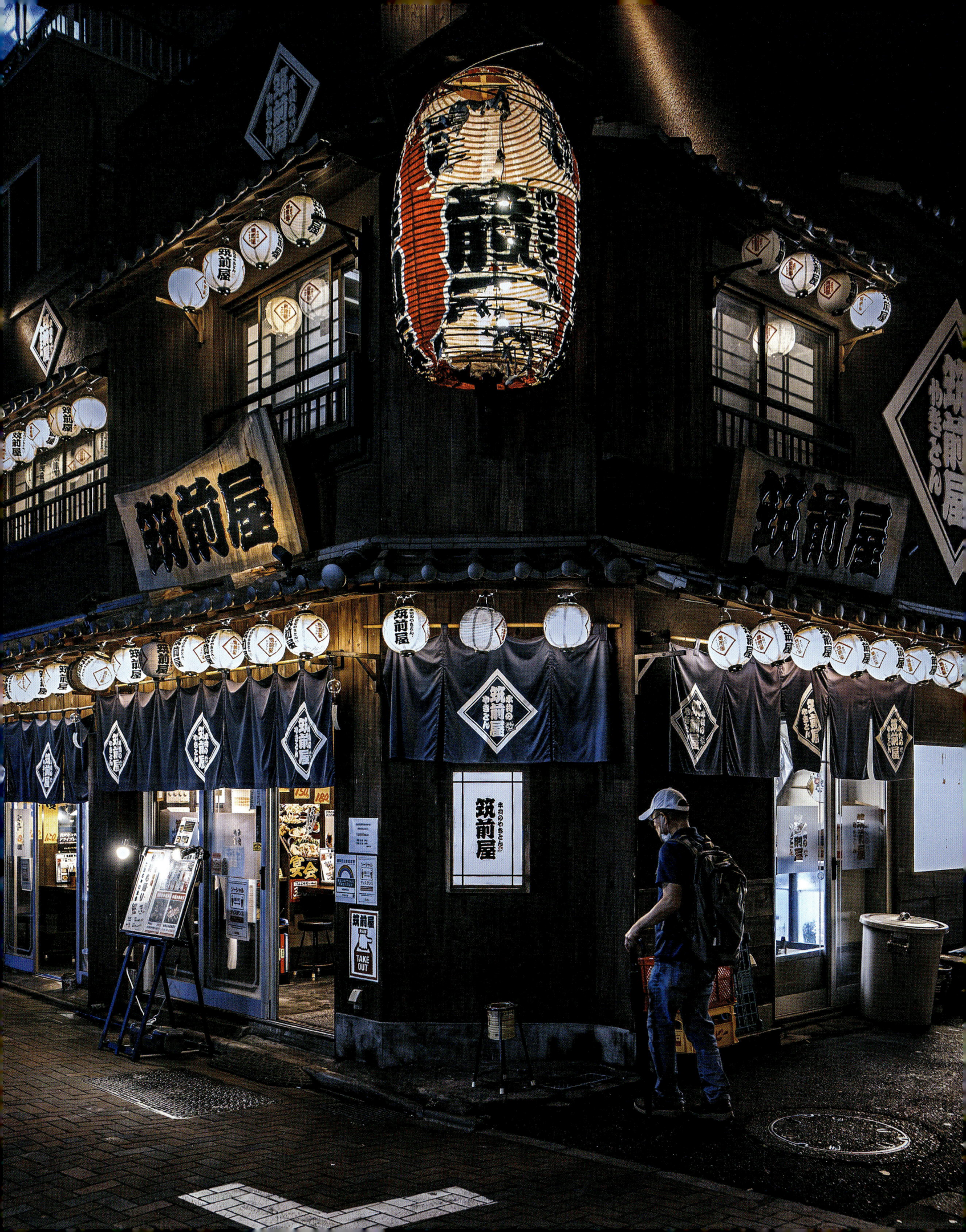

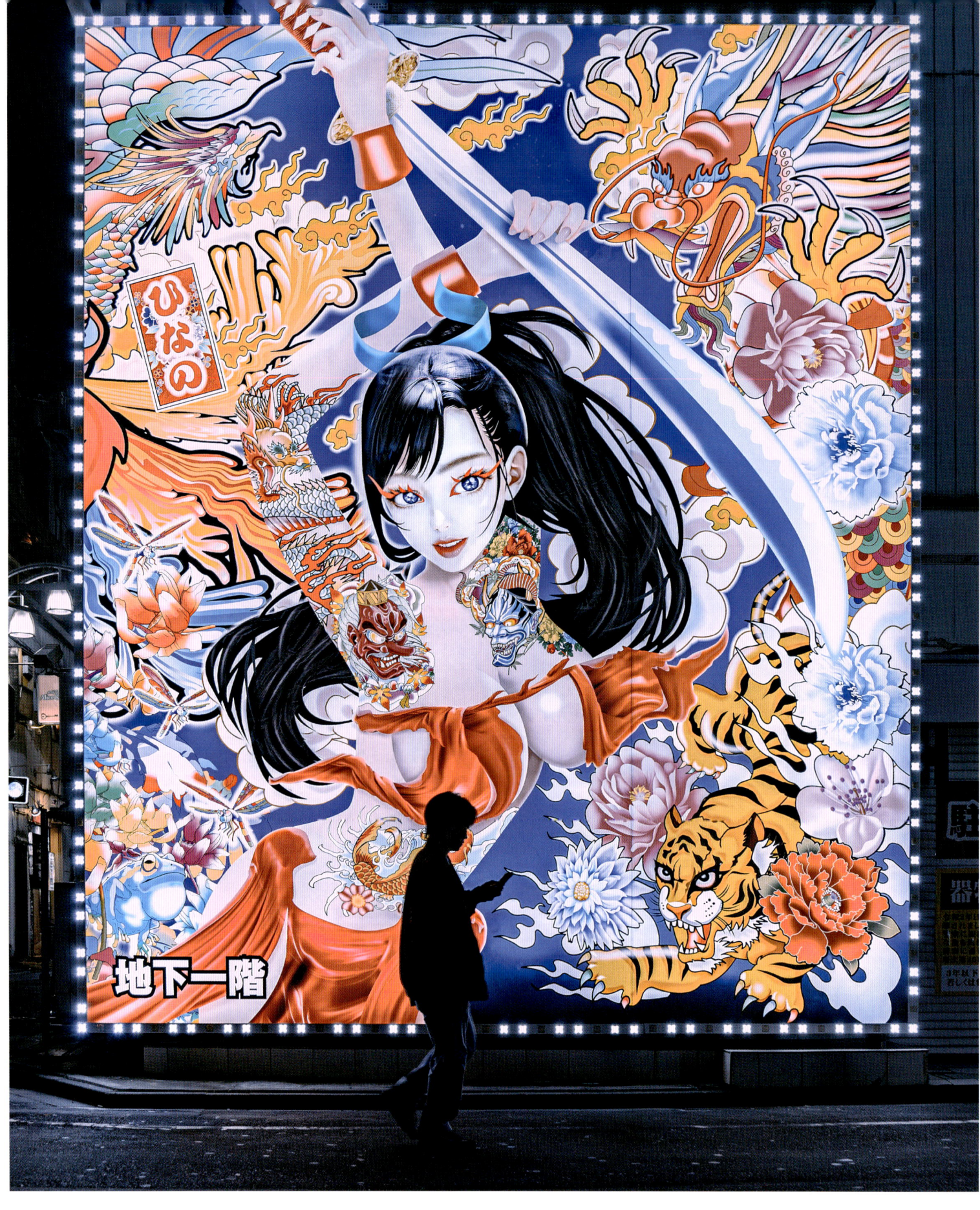

Girls Bar. Shinjuku, Tokyo. The contrast between the flashy signage with a tattoo motif and the silhouette is interesting.

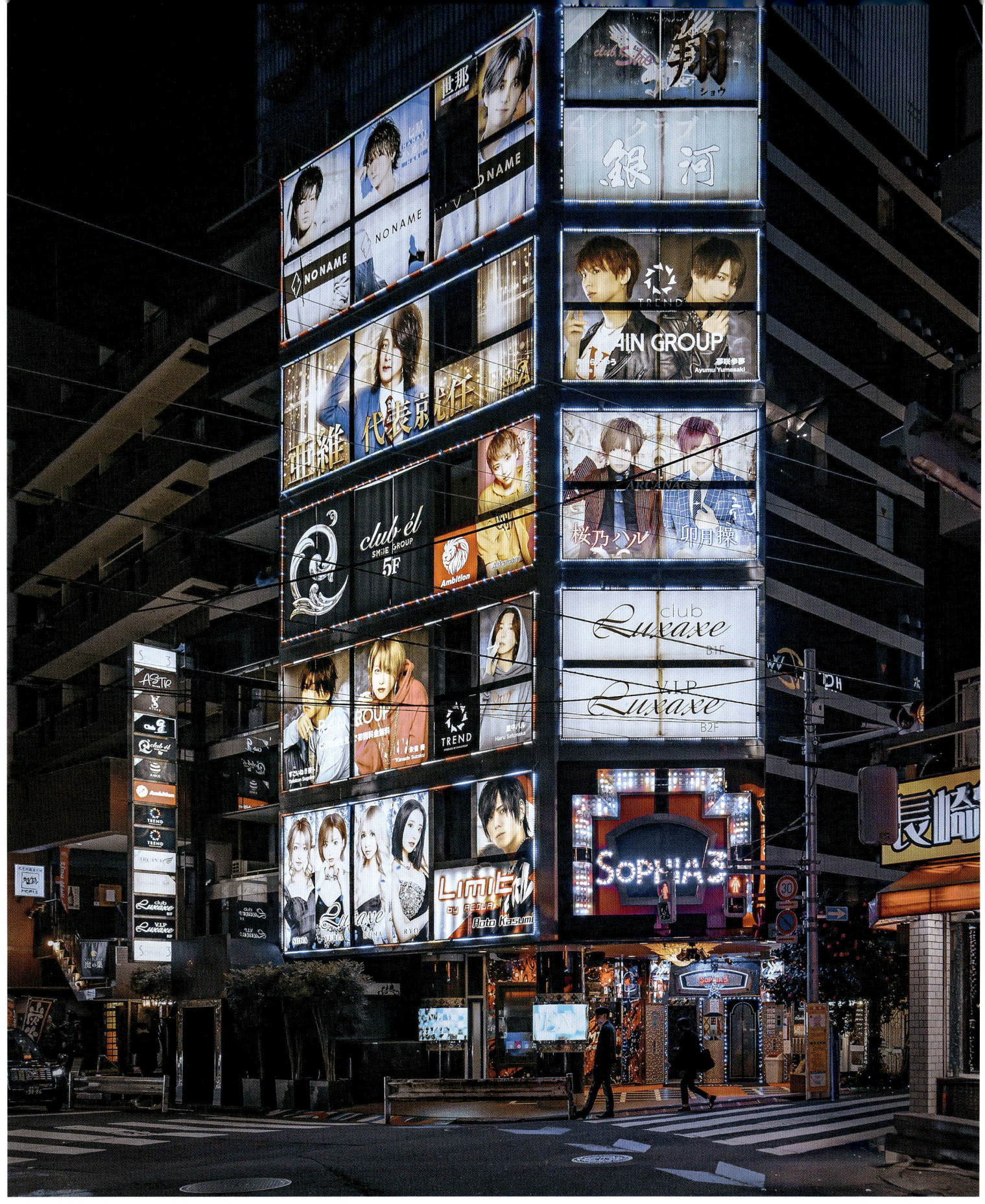

Host Club District. Shinjuku, Tokyo. Have you ever heard of a host club? It is one of the few businesses in Japan where women pay for entertainment from men.

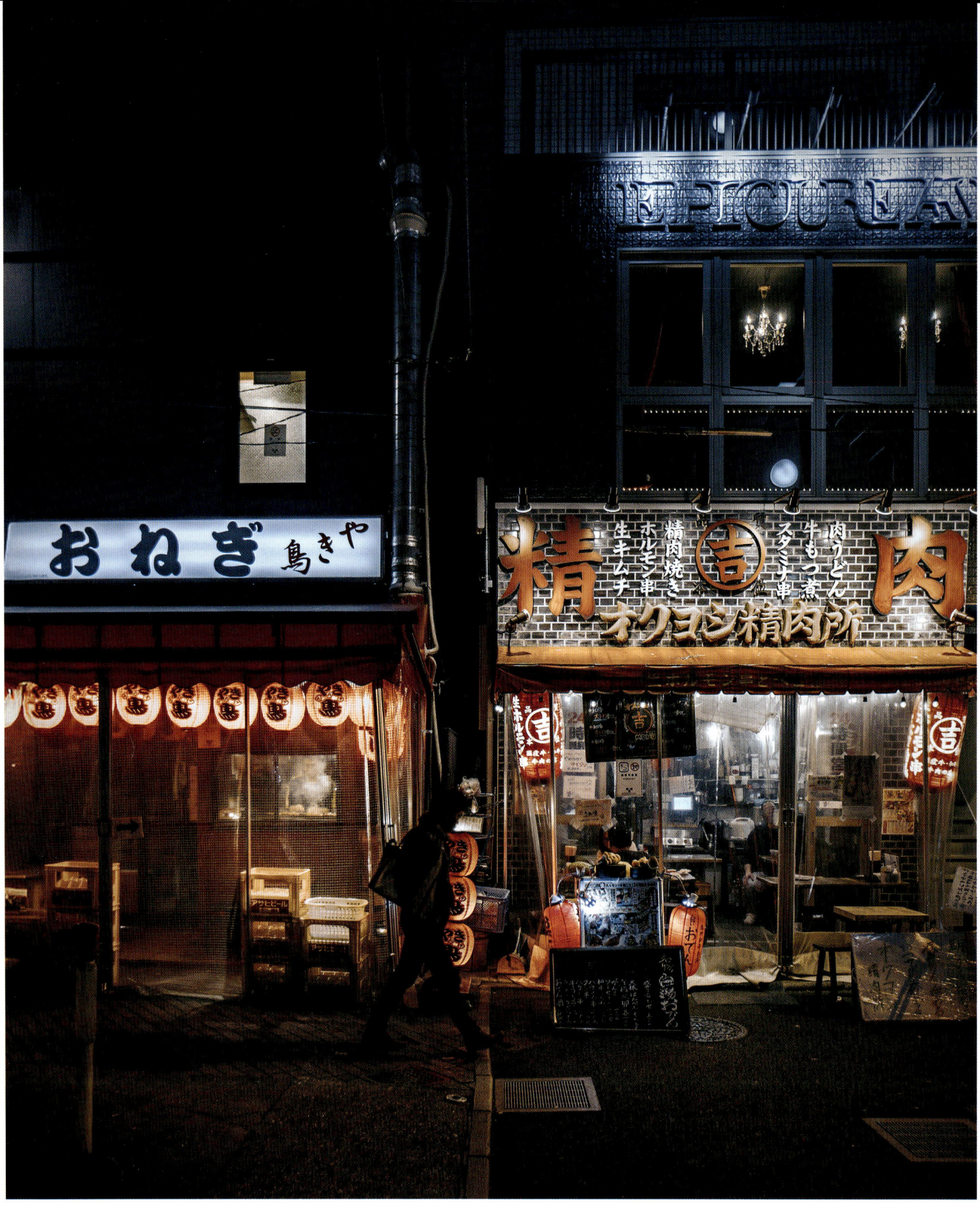

Warm and Cold. Yurakucho, Tokyo. This photo emphasizes the contrast between the warm lantern light on the ground floor and the bluish-white light on the second floor.

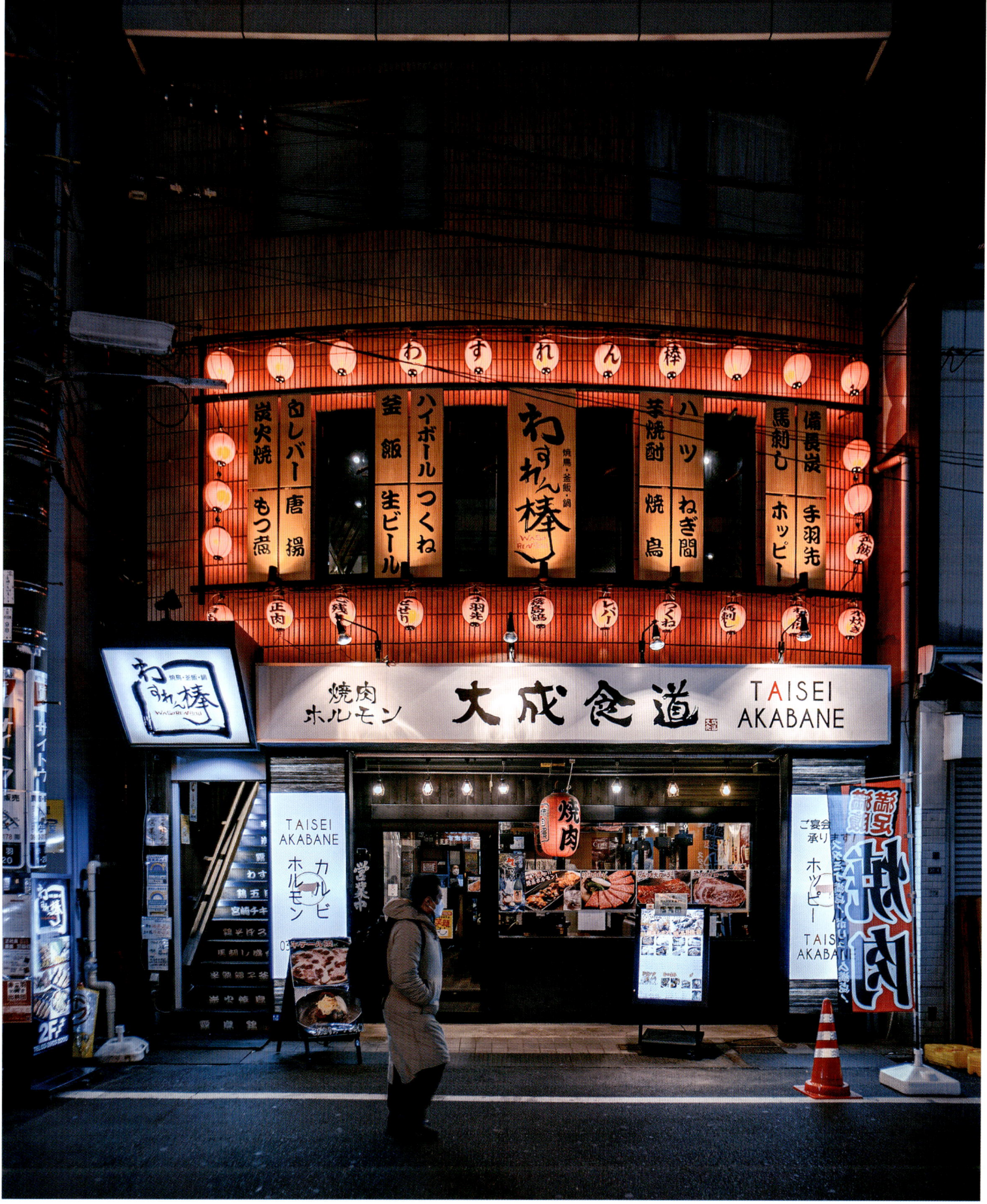

Yakiniku Restaurant. Akabane, Tokyo. I find the contrast between the warm light of the red lanterns and the cool light of the blue fluorescents interesting.

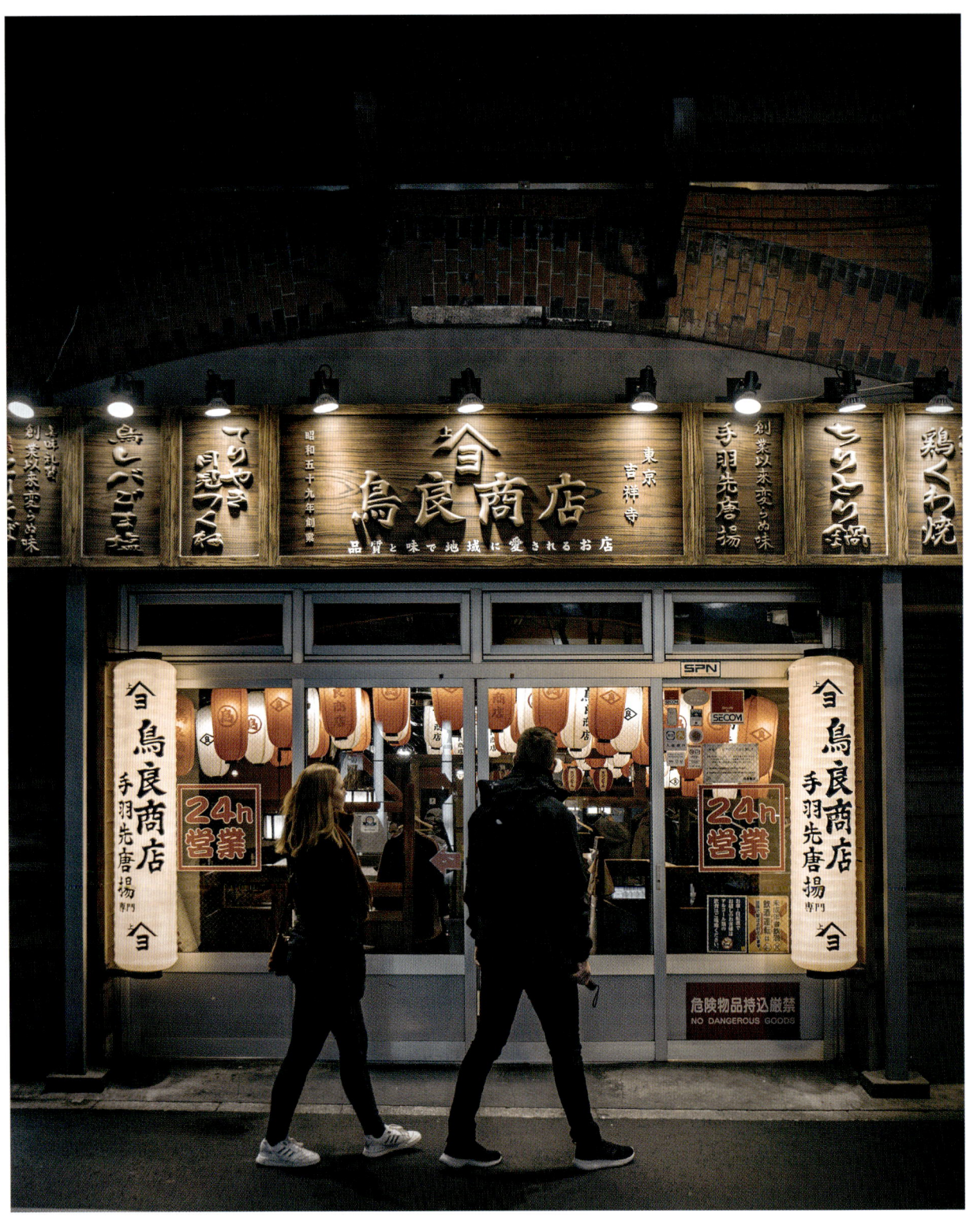

Chicken Restaurant Under the Tracks.
Yurakucho, Tokyo. This restaurant's interior is charmingly filled with lanterns.

Reikyo Taiwanese Restaurant. Shibuya, Tokyo. Established in 1955, this famous Taiwanese restaurant has a look that is different from other restaurants in Shibuya.

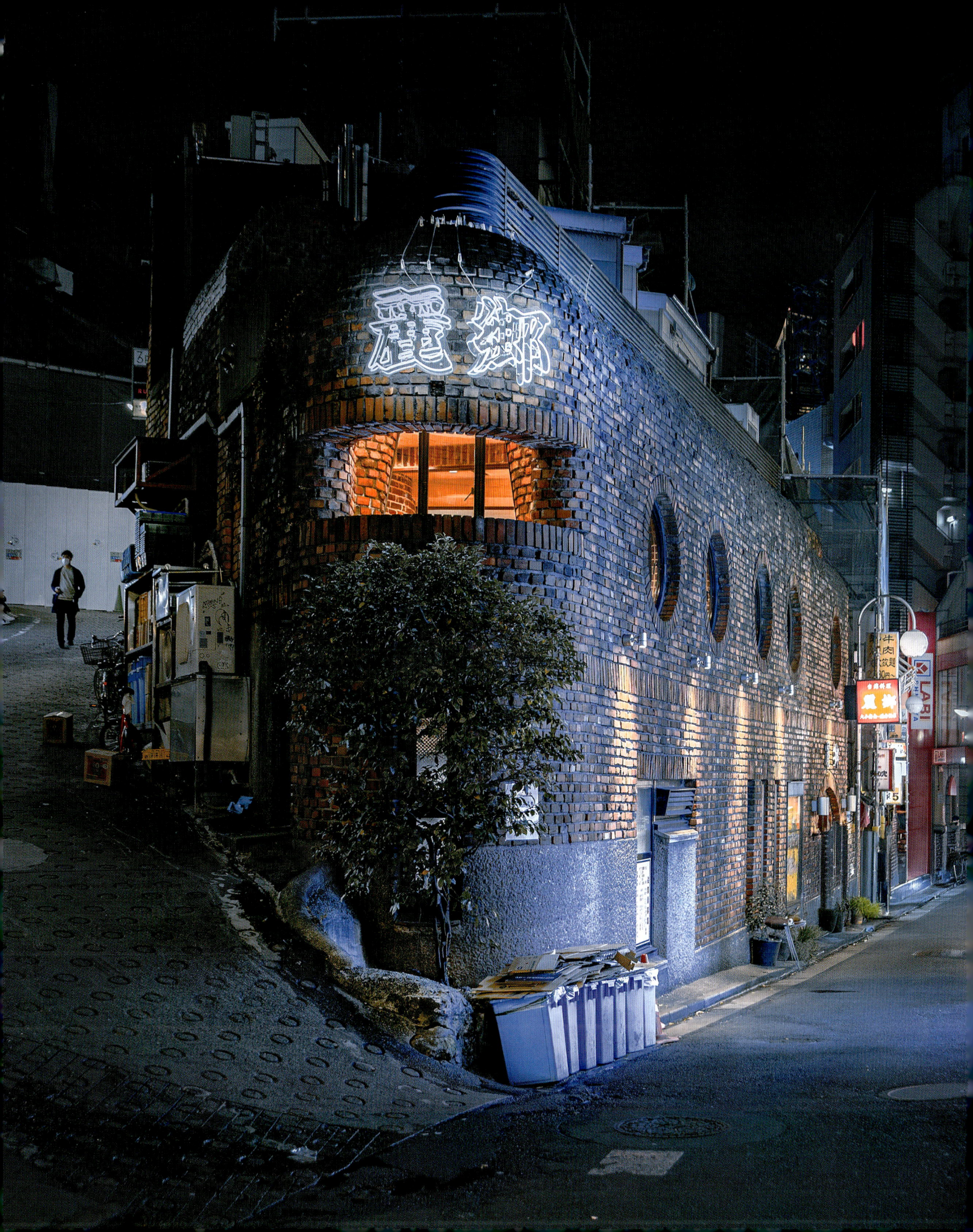

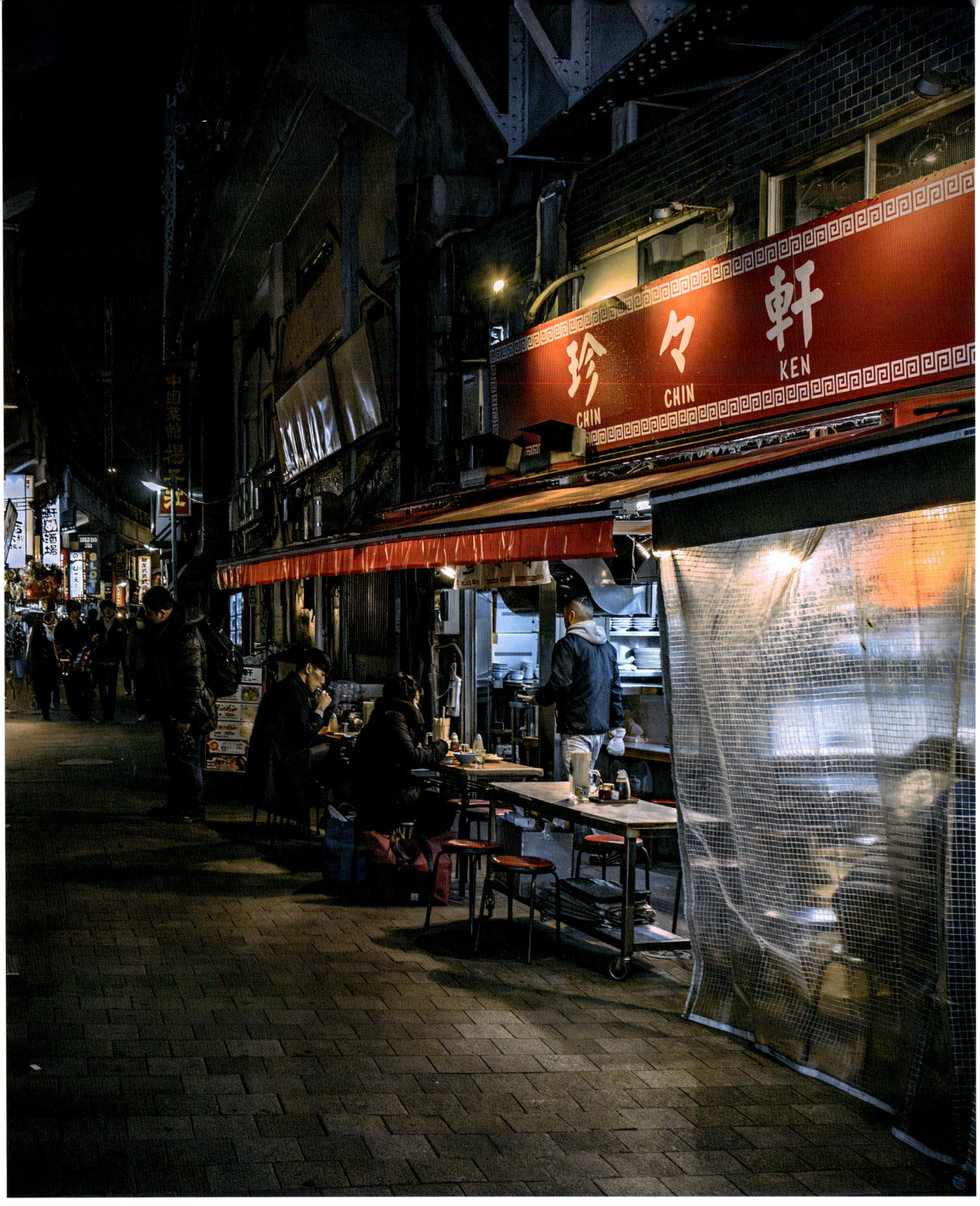

Popular Chinese Restaurant. Ueno, Tokyo.
This Chinese restaurant under the railroad
tracks in the Ameya Yokocho shopping
district is known for its fried rice.

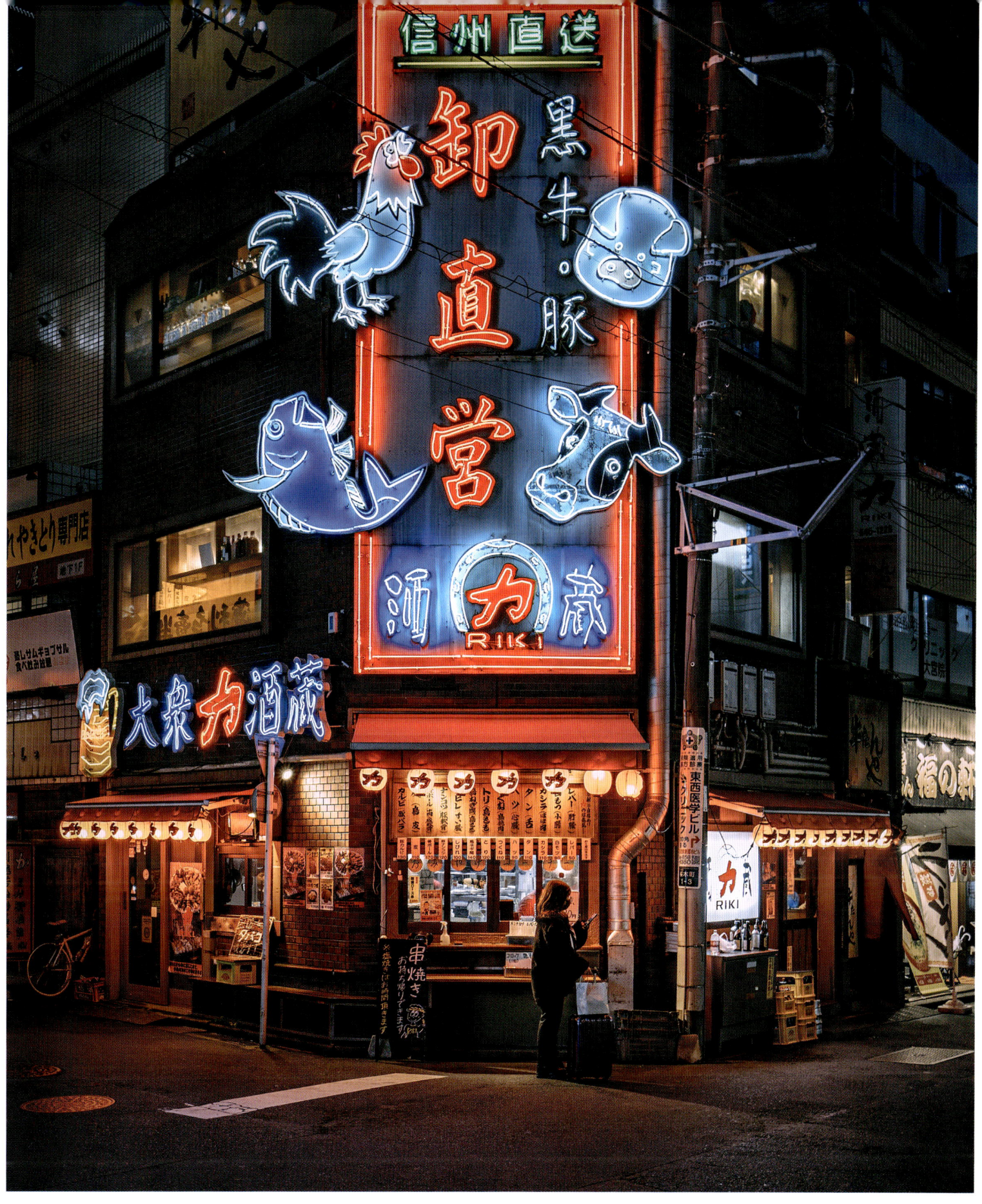

Sakagura Riki Izakaya. Omiya, Saitama.
Many people are attracted to this izakaya
near Omiya Station because of its flashy
neon signage.

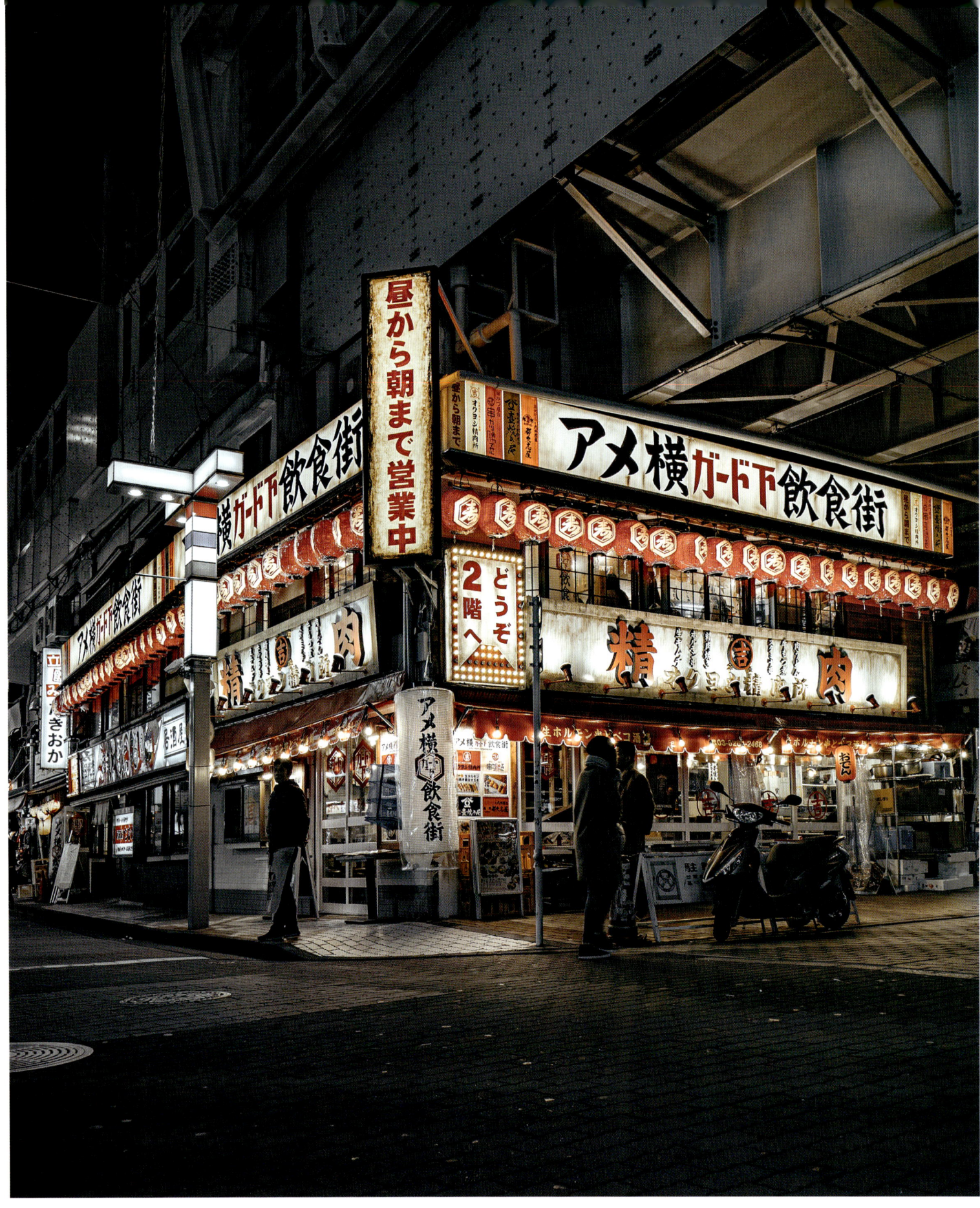

All-Day Izikaya. Ueno, Tokyo. This izakaya in the Ameya Yokocho shopping district is open from noon until the morning of the next day.

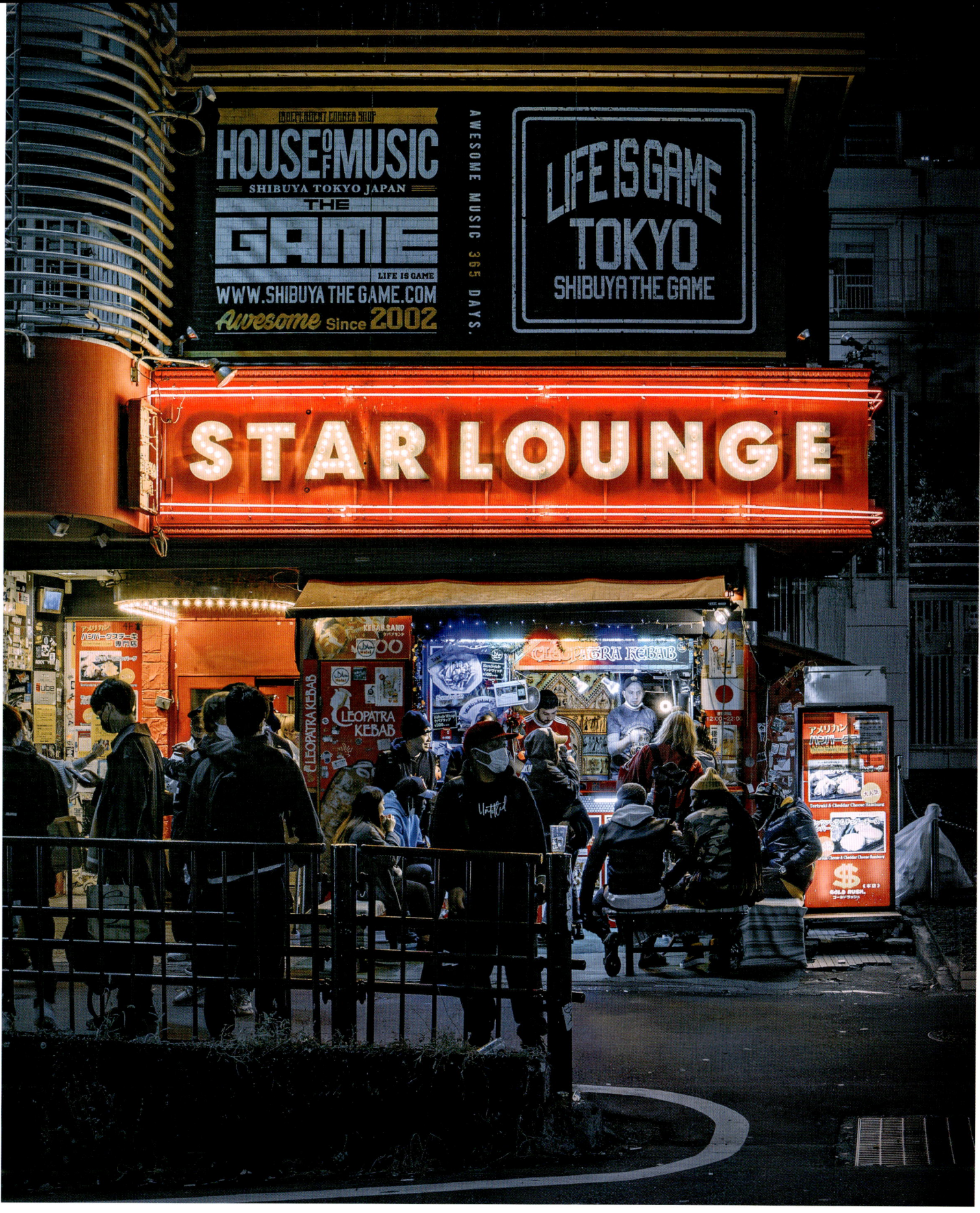

Kebab Restaurant. Shibuya, Tokyo. This restaurant in Shibuyu stands out with its Middle Eastern design.

Takoyaki Restaurant. Kanda, Tokyo. I like the composition of this photo with the person holding a red umbrella (whom I happened to meet) in front of the bold illustration of the octopus.

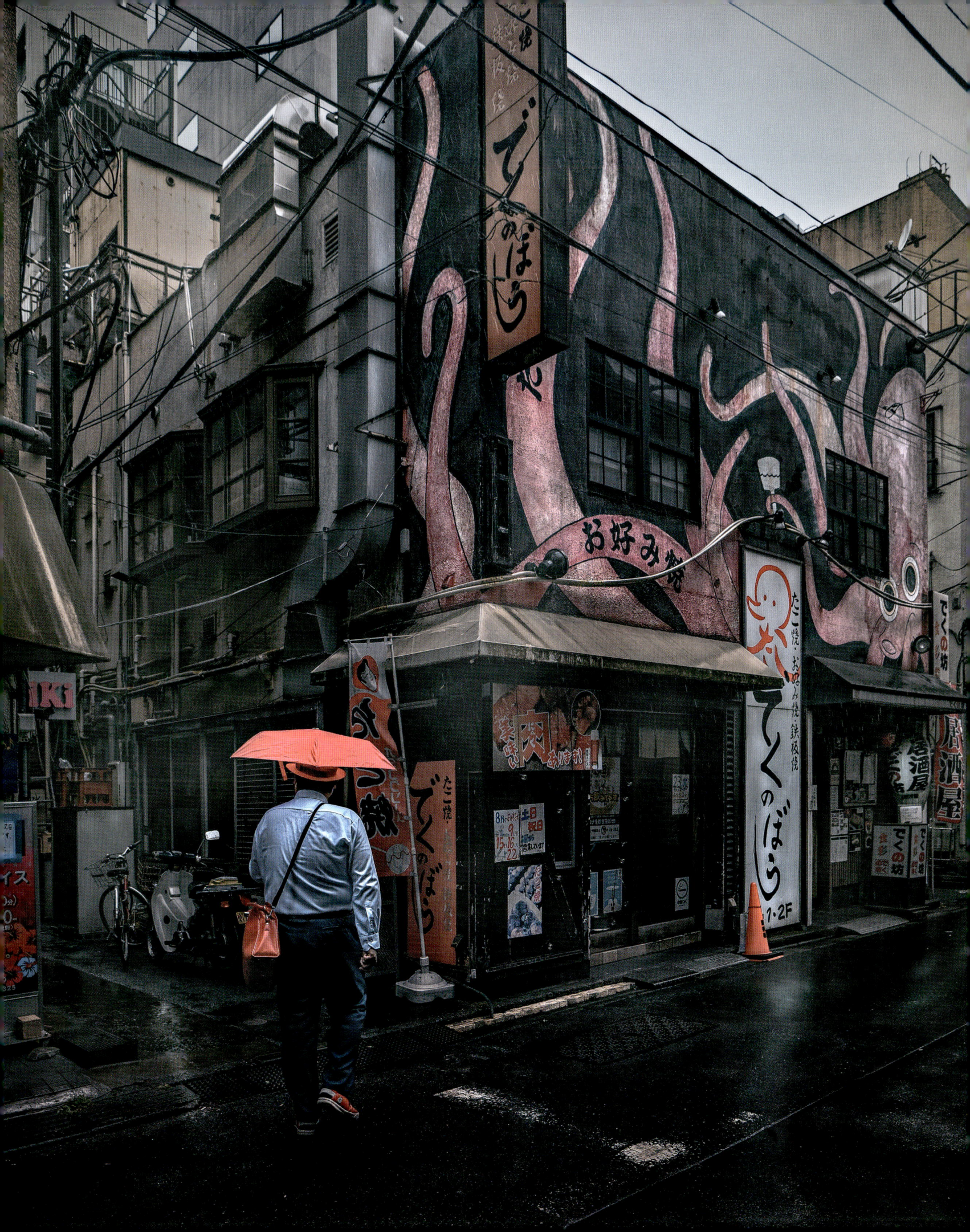

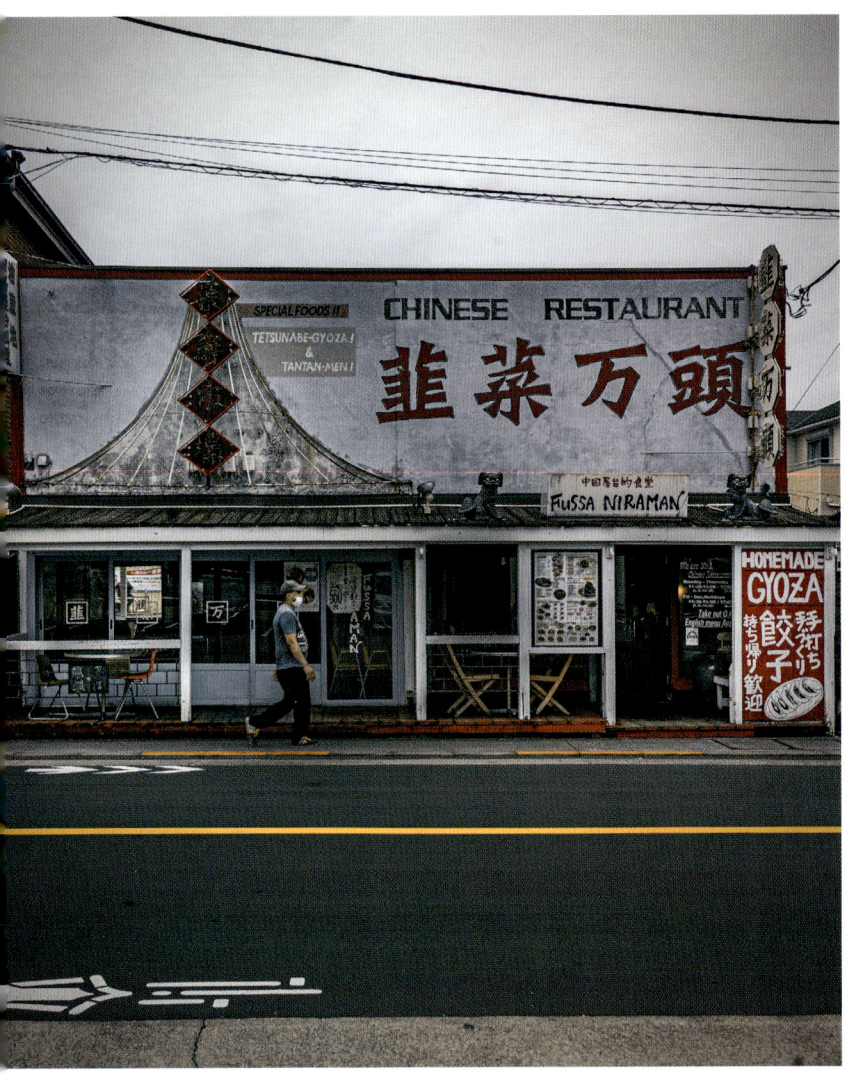

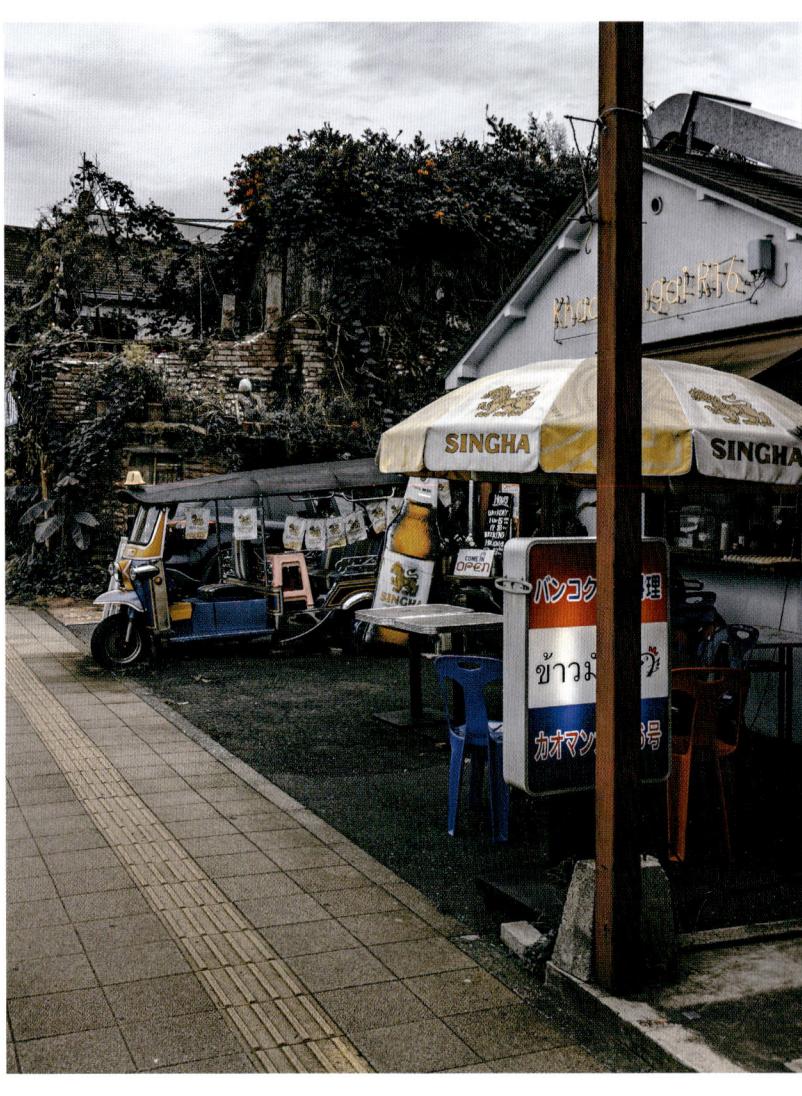

Chinese Restaurant. Fussa, Tokyo. The town of Fussa is home to the US Yokota Air Base, giving it a unique atmosphere with stores that cater to foreigners.

Khaomangai R16. Fussa, Tokyo. This Thai restaurant is located across the street from the Yokota Air Base.

April Flash. Fussa, Tokyo. This general store near the Yokota Air Base has an American military theme.

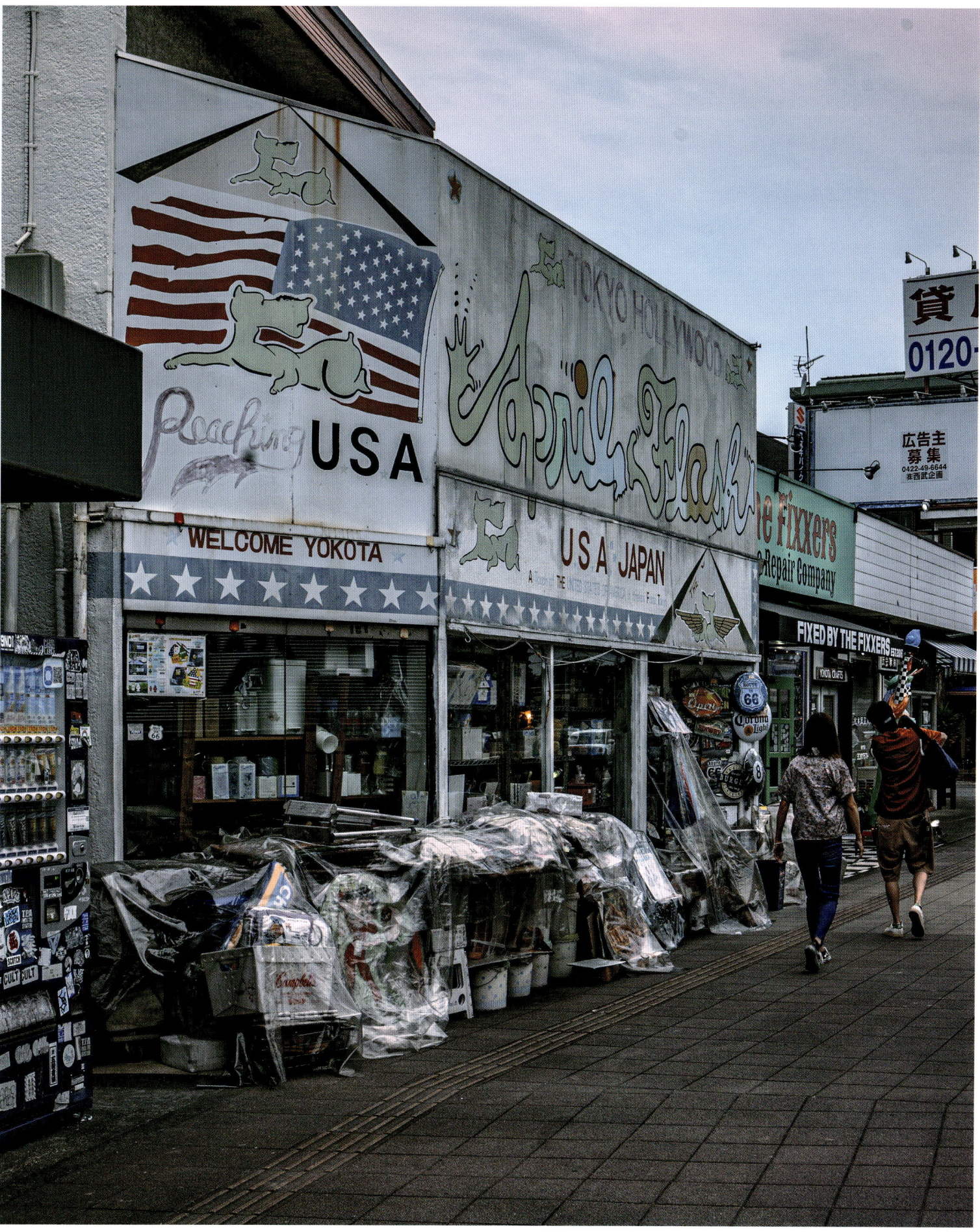

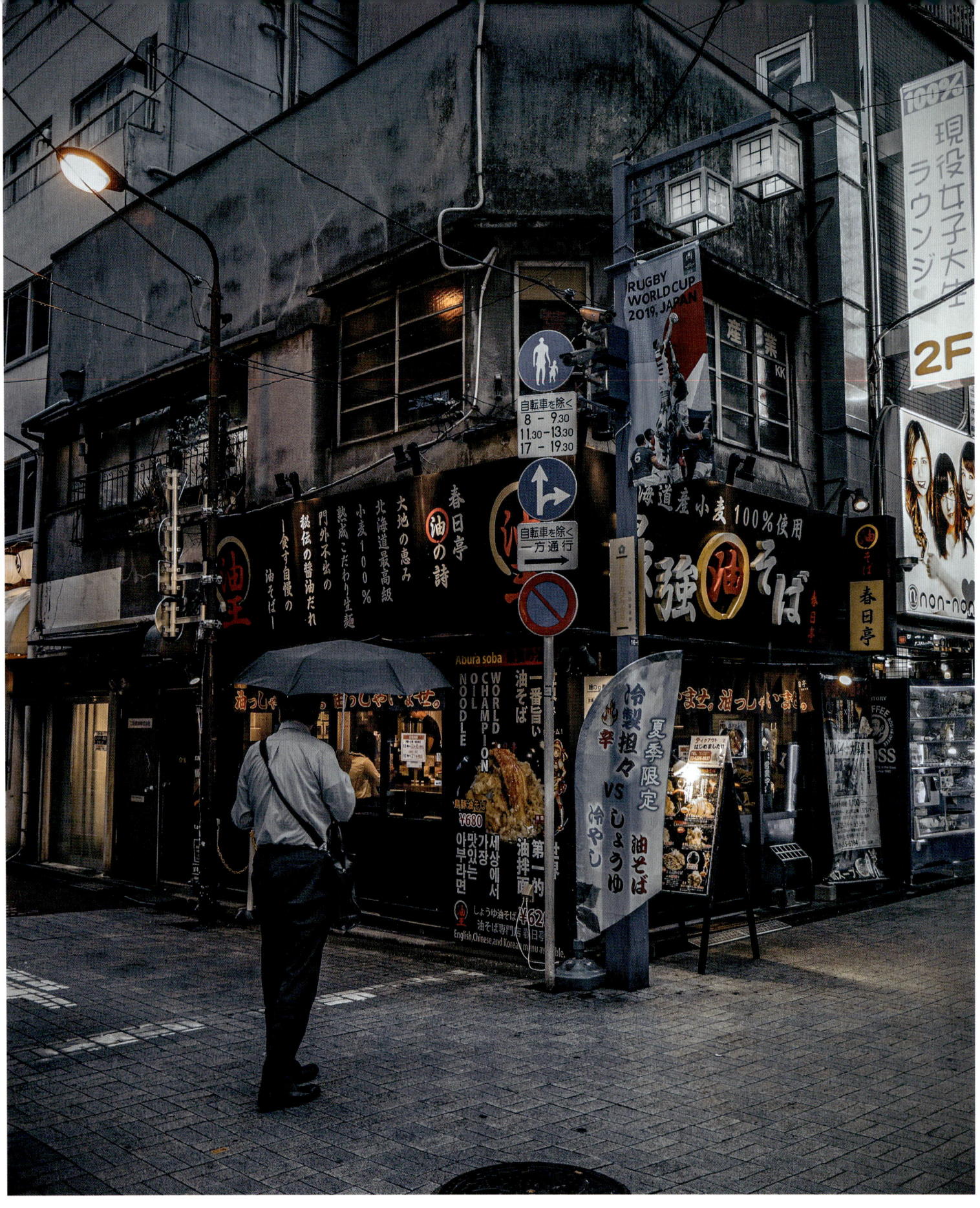

Ramen Restaurant. Kanda, Tokyo. This *abura soba* (ramen without broth) shop has an interesting black sign.

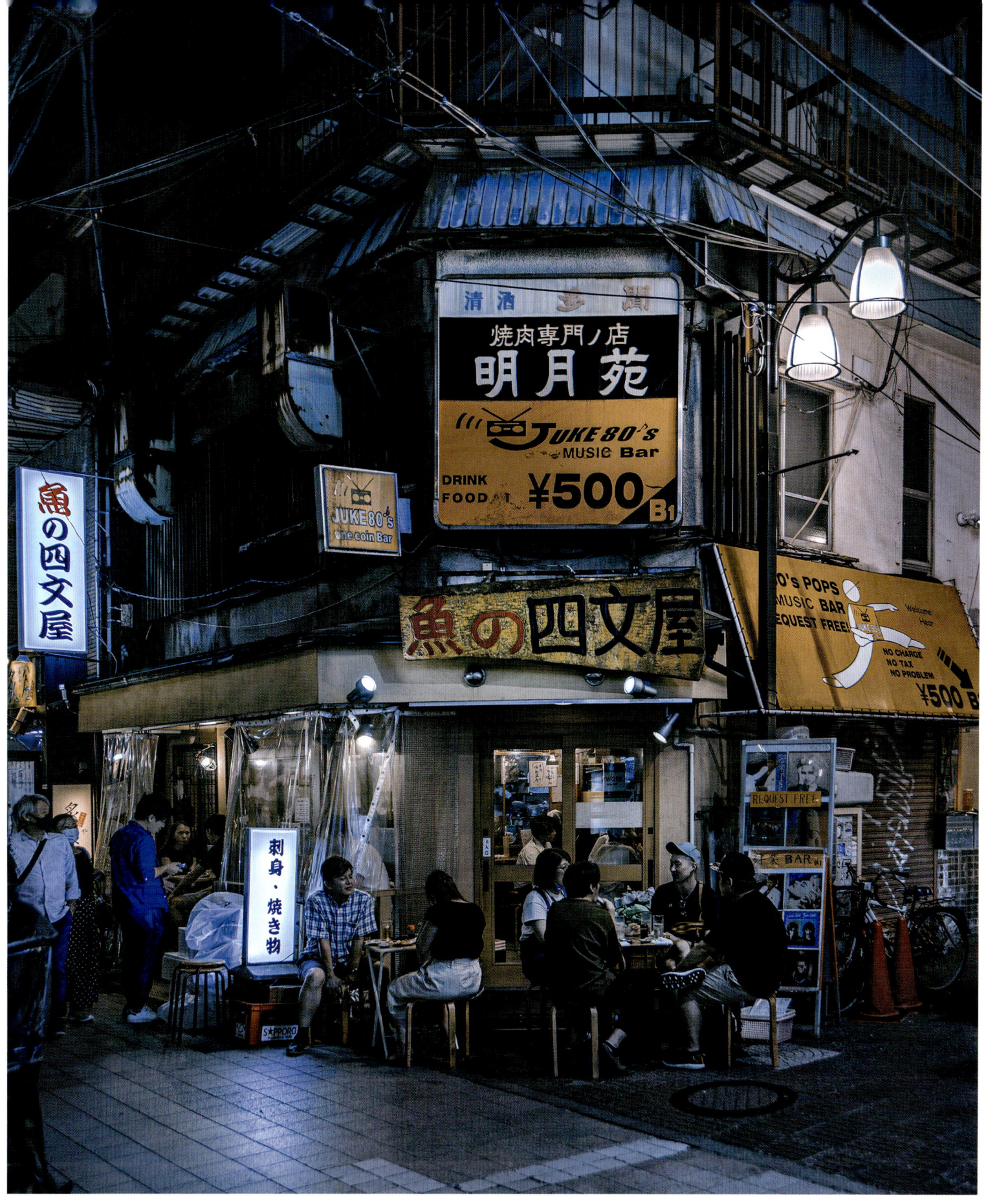

Corner Store. Nakano, Tokyo. Located on the corner of a narrow alley, this izakaya has lots of charm, with two exhaust ducts extending from the second floor, an old blue roof, and an oddly shaped sign.

Kushikatsu Tanaka. Shinbashi, Tokyo. This restaurant serves deep-fried meat, fish, and vegetables on skewers. The red and yellow lanterns and the bluish-white light from the fluorescent lamps nicely reflect on the wet road.

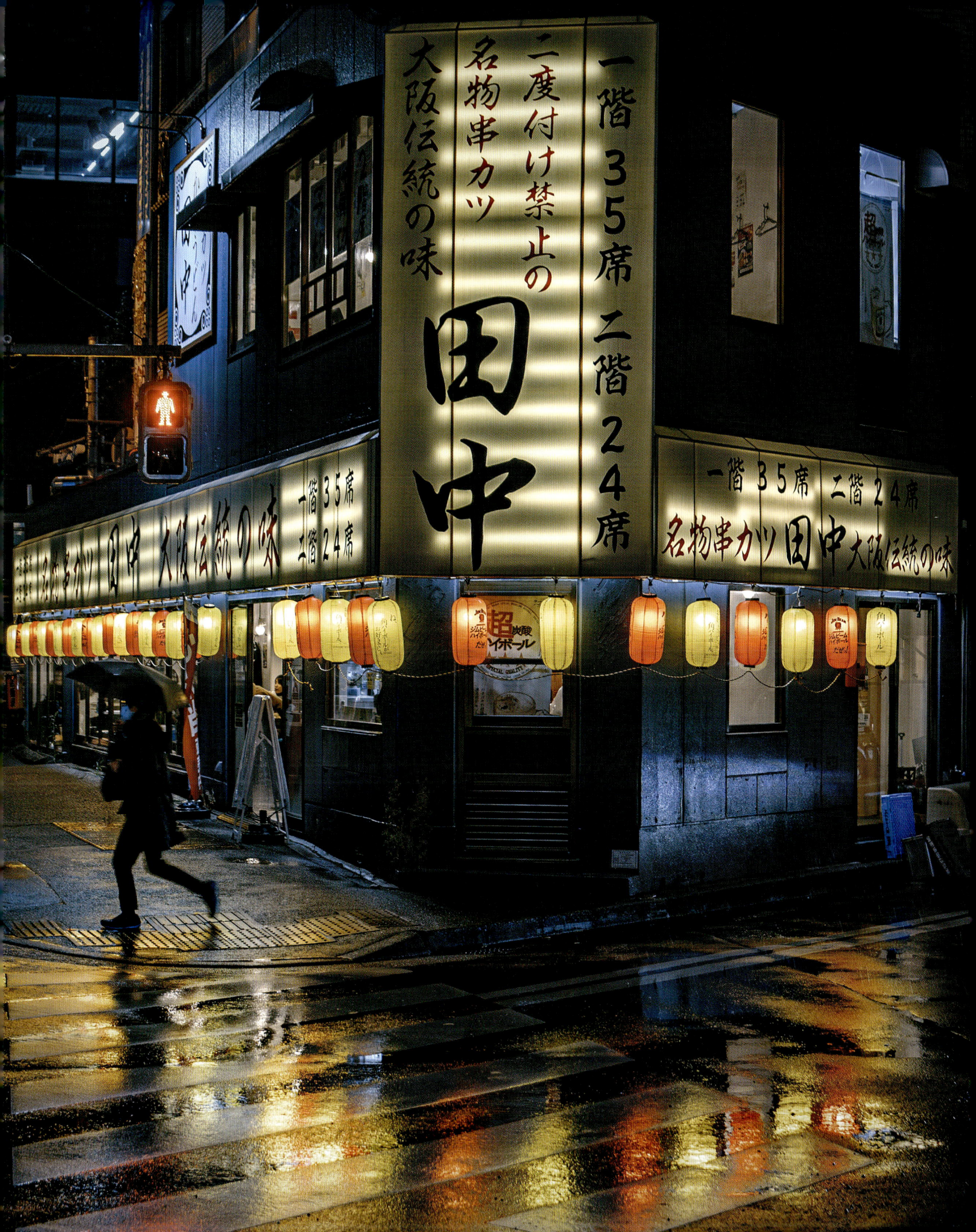

ACKNOWLEDGMENTS

First, I would like to express my sincere thanks to Erin Canning, editorial director at The Quarto Group. From the time she contacted me in July 2025 until the publication, she patiently dealt with my poor English and everything else faithfully. What made me happiest was that she appreciated my art. Thank you very much.

I would also like to thank publisher Rage Kindelsperger and creative director Laura Drew, along with the entire team at Epic Ink.

And to those of you who have picked up a copy of this photo book, thank you very much. I will be happy if you enjoy it, even for a moment.

Hiroki Harada is a Tokyo-based photographer who has been working in the field of street photography since 2018. He has contributed his Tokyo street photography to several international art galleries as well as to twenty thousand convenience stores throughout Japan.

In 2023, he was selected as one of the one hundred most exciting photo artists of the year by the art publication *Photographize*, and his photo *Izakya in Shibuya* was published in their book *100 Best Selected Volume 04*.

In the near future, Hiroki is planning an overseas expedition to expand his street photography in other Asian countries.

First published in 2025 by Epic Ink,
an imprint of The Quarto Group,
142 West 36th Street, 4th Floor,
New York, NY 10018, USA
(212) 779-4972 www.Quarto.com

EEA Representation, WTS Tax d.o.o.,
Žanova ulica 3, 4000 Kranj, Slovenia.
www.wts-tax.si

Epic Ink titles are also available at discount
for retail, wholesale, promotional and bulk
purchase. For details, contact the Special Sales
Manager by email at specialsales@quarto.com
or by mail at The Quarto Group, Attn: Special
Sales Manager, 100 Cummings Center Suite,
265D, Beverly, MA 01915, USA.

10 9 8 7 6 5 4 3 2 1

ISBN: 978-0-7603-9867-8

Digital edition published in 2025
eISBN: 978-0-7603-9868-5

Publisher: Rage Kindelsperger
Creative Director: Laura Drew
Managing Editor: Cara Donaldson
Editorial Director: Erin Canning
Cover Design: Laura Drew
Interior Design: Brooke Johnson

Printed in Huizhou, Guangdong, China TT072025